Diggin' Up Bones

Obituaries of Deerfield, Fairview, and Miscellaneous Kearny County Cemeteries, Kearny County, Kansas

Betty Barnes

HERITAGE BOOKS
2008

HERITAGE BOOKS
AN IMPRINT OF HERITAGE BOOKS, INC.

Books, CDs, and more—Worldwide

For our listing of thousands of titles see our website
at
www.HeritageBooks.com

Published 2008 by
HERITAGE BOOKS, INC.
Publishing Division
100 Railroad Ave. #104
Westminster, Maryland 21157

Copyright ©1997 Betty Barnes

Other books by the author:

Diggin' Up Bones, Book IV: Obituaries of Kendall, Lydia German Lutheran, Lydia Lutheran, Lydia Methodist, and Shockey Cemeteries -Located in Grant, Hamilton and Wichita County, Kansas
Diggin' Up Bones, Part I and II: Obituaries of Lakin and Hartland Cemeteries, Kearny County, Kansas

International Standard Book Numbers
Paperbound: 978-0-7884-0790-1
Clothbound: 978-0-7884-7040-0

Diggin' Up Bones
[Deerfield, Fairview, and Miscellaneous Kearny Co. Cemeteries]

Table of Contents

Deerfield Cemetery
by
Hazel Steenis Shriver

N

Potter's Field

EAST GATE

Section 3

Section 2

Section 4

Section 1

14	39	40	65
15	38	41	64
16	37	42	63
17	36	43	62
18	35	44	61
19	34	45	60
20	33	46	59

21	32	47	58
22	31	48	57
23	30	49	56
24	29	50	55
25	28	51	54
26	27	52	53

66	91	92	117	118
67	90	93	116	119
68	89	94	115	120
69	88	95	114	121
70	87	96	113	122
71	86	97	112	123
72	85	98	111	124

73	84	99	110	125
74	83	100	109	126
75	82	101	108	127
76	81	102	107	128
77	80	103	106	129
78	79	104	105	130

" DIGGIN UP BONES "

DEERFIELD CEMETERY

On June 28, 1892, W. P. Loucks and Amy M. Loucks, his wife, deeded to Lakin Township, five acres of land in NE/c SE/4 Section 2, Township 24S, Range 35W, to be used as a cemetery. At this time all of this area was part of Lakin Township, later it was divided and became Deerfield Township, and eventually became known as Cemetery District No. 3. In 1902 it was fenced with a neat barbwire fence. The first grave was of an unknown man who was killed by railroad cars in front of the depot in 1901.

The cemetery is divided into 117 blocks. Each block contains four lots, with the exception of blocks 105 through 117, which contains only two lots. Each lot has room for five burials, with the exception of blocks 105 through 117 which have places for only three burials per lot. Blocks 1 through 13 were included in the road on the north side of the cemetery. There are 28 burials in the "potters field" which lies along the west fence. 17 of these are Russian Germans, brought in by the U.S. Sugar and Land Company and died during the flu epidemic during 1918-19. They have no name markers, just a cement post at the head of each grave.

It is my understanding the old cemetery records were lost. Hazel Shriver, Barbara and Harold Jones are responsible for the good records they now have.

I have found a few that the dates on the tombstones do not agree with information I have found. I have noted dates of these stones by ts. and the tombstone dates.

1

DEERFIELD CEMETERY

ACOSTA, RAMON - (Lt. 4, Blk. 99, Sec. 1) (Nash Mortuary records) His parents were Anastacio and Juana (Hernandez) Acosta, both born in old Mexico. Ramon born Dec. 17, 1911, at Hutchinson, Ks. Died May 17, 1927, of TB. A brother, Domingo, lived in Garden City, and worked for Fanslers.

AGUILERA, FRANK M. - (Lt. 2, Blk. 110, Sec. 1) Frank Munzo Aguilera, 19, of Deerfield was killed Tuesday night, September 16, 1953, when his car plunged into an irrigation ditch just north of Holcomb.
Aguilera's 1946 Ford was found submerged in an irrigation ditch about three miles west of Holcomb. His body was in the front seat of the car.
The car, which apparently was traveling at a high rate of speed, missed a bridge, traveled 71 feet across the ditch and careened into the water, landing on its top.
Emanuel Schiffelbein, of Holcomb, discovered the tragedy shortly before eight o'clock Wednesday morning, when he saw the car's wheels in the water. He called a truck and men from the Northern Natural Gas station and they were able to right the car. The men found Aguilera's body sprawled in the front seat.
Trooper Jim Thornton and Undersheriff Dean Emberton said it is not known whether the boy was killed by the impact or whether he drowned. A doctor said Aguilera had been dead for some time before he was found. The boy was wearing a waterproof watch and it was still running.
Cause of the accident is unknown, but Thornton said indications are Aguilera went to sleep at the wheel. He had spent most of the evening in Garden City attending the fiesta.
Frank Aguilera was born March 9, 1934, in Deerfield, a son of Mr. and Mrs. Merced Aguilera, and attended the Deerfield schools.
He is survived by his parents and a sister, Doris, of the home; three brothers, Jessie Aguilera, of Garden City, A. M. Rodriguez, of Chattanooga, Tennessee, and John Rodriguez of Hutchinson. Another sister, Mrs. Leonard Alcarez, lives in Garden City.
He was a member of St. Mary's Catholic Church.

ALLEN, JAMES MILTON - (Lt. 4, Blk. 49, Sec. 2) James Milton, born 1860, died 1918. Wife, Jennie B., born in 1860, died in 1940. Daughter was Nora Pearl (Allen) Wilcox who died May 10, 1910.

DEERFIELD CEMETERY

(The Advocate, Feb. 7, 1919)   Rev. Allen, who resided at Deerfield several years ago but who was living on a claim south of Garden City, died of influenza and was buried at Deerfield, Saturday.   It is reported that a number of his family are still sick.

(The Garden City Telegram, January 31, 1919)   James Milton Allen was born Oct. 16, 1855, and died Dec. 7th 1918, being 63 years, 1 month and 18 days of age.   He was born near Monroe, Green County, Wisc.   His father died when he was only 5 years of age, and in 1863 he moved with his mother to Warren County, Iowa, and in 1874 they again moved to Smith County, Kans.   He was married to his now bereaved wife, Jennie B. Bloomer, on August 25th, 1878.   He united with the M.E Church at an early age and the greater part of his life was spent in the uplifting of humanity.   He was actively engaged in the gospel ministry for about 15 years.   From 1906 to 1914 he lived near Deerfield, Kans., and for the last five years he has been living on a farm 12 miles south of Garden City.

Three older brothers are still living; they are Rev. E. W. Allen of Topeka, Kans., Rev. W. R. Allen of Portland, Ore., and J. F. Allen of Vinton, Iowa.   He is also survived by eight children.

Funeral services were conducted in the M.E. Church at Deerfield by Rev. S. M. Van Cleve, Saturday, Jan. 25, 1919, and the remains were laid to rest in the Deerfield Cemetery.

ALLEN, JENNIE B. - (Lt. 4, Blk. 49, Sec. 2)   Jennie died Dec. 17, 1940, at 80 yrs of age.

She was born April 11, 1860, and died of chronic myocarditis and chronic interstitial nephritis.

ALMARAZ, CRISTOBAL ADAM - (Lt. 1, Blk. 109, Sec. 1)   10 day old son of Rafael and Sonia (Gloria) Almaraz, died June 22, 1986.

ALMARAZ, SONIA - (Lt. 1, Blk 109, Sec. 1)   Evening service for Sonia M. Almaraz, 38, was held at Garnand Funeral Home, with the Rev. Randy Caddell officiating. Funeral Mass was held at St. Mary Catholic Church, with the Rev. Pascal Klein officiating.   Burial at Deerfield Cemetery.

Mrs. Almaraz died July 13, 1995, at HCA Wesley Medical Center, Wichita.

The daughter of Jose and Josephine Sanchez Gloria, she was born Sept. 12, 1956, at Leveland, Texas. The family moved to Deerfield in 1967. She graduated from Deerfield High School in 1975 and attended Garden City Community College.

Mrs. Almaraz was a member of St. Mary Catholic Church and the American GI Forum. Her hobbies were her family, listening to music and reading.

On July 28, 1974, she married Rafael Almaraz at Garden City. They moved to Garden City where they lived until moving to Holcomb in 1977. He survives.

Other survivors are a son, Rafael S. Almaraz Jr., of the home; two daughters, America Almaraz, of the home, and Yesenia Casas, Garden City; her parents, Garden City; two brothers, Dario Gloria, Great Bend, and Joey Gloria, Wichita; two sisters, Omega Rangel, Wichita, and Suelema Cedillo, Texas; and a grandson. She was preceded in death by a son, Cristobal, and a brother..

ANDERSON, BOBBY - (Lt 3, Block 45, Sec. 3) Funeral for Bobby J. Anderson, 24, 2206 N. 6th, Garden City, was held at the First Church of God, the Rev. William O. Bath officiating. Burial at the Deerfield Cemetery.

He died Monday, July 28, 1986, at St. Catherine Hospital, following a long illness. Born Aug. 14, 1961, at Eads, Colo., he attended Garden City schools and lived in Garden City most of his life.

A painter's helper for I. R. Martinez, he enjoyed building models and playing the guitar.

Surviving are his mother, Edith Anderson, of the home; 10 brothers, William, Sumner, Wash., Jimmie, Alamorgordo, N.M., Ronald, Wiggins, Colo., David, Ludowici, Ga., Tommy, Fort Leonard Wood, Mo., Kenneth, Lakin, Richard, Holcomb, Jerry, George, and Gordon, of the home, and a sister, Susan Graves, Lakin.

ANDERSON, HERMAN E. - (Lt. 3, Block 45, Sec. 3) Herman (Ed) Anderson, 55, 2206 N. 6th, Garden City, died January 26, 1974, at St. Catherine Hospital following a long illness.

Born Nov. 24, 1918, at Grainola, Okla., he moved to Garden City with his parents when he was 11. He married Mary Edith Smith, Jan. 27, 1938, at Garden City.

Mr. Anderson worked for the Co-Op Feed Lot at Deerfield and later at Reed and Reed Dirt Contractors, until ill health forced his retirement.

DEERFIELD CEMETERY

He was a member of Trinity Wesleyan Church and a Navy
veteran of World War II.
   Survivors include the widow, of the home; 11 sons:
William Edward, Roseville, Calif., Jimmie Clifford and
Tommy Ray, both U. S. Army, Germany, Ronald Dean,
Wiggins, Colo., Ivan David, Garden City, Kenneth Leon,
Garden City, Richard Warren, Jerry Lee, George Breit,
Bobby Joe, and Gordon Eugene, all of the home; a
daughter, Susan Marie Graves, Rt. 1, Garden City; his
mother, Mrs. Ida Anderson, Webb City, Okla.; two
brothers, Charles Thomas, Sperry, Okla., and Clifford
Eugene, Lench, Okla.; four sisters, Wanda LaVerne Smith,
Garden City, Mary Jane Philips, Newkirk, Okla., Doris
Christine Carlisle, Grainola, Okla., and Delora
Earnestine Reaser, Webb City, Okla.; and 16
grandchildren.
   Funeral was held at Trinity Wesleyan Church, the Rev.
Kenneth Stone officiating. Burial in Deerfield Cemetery.

ANDERSON, JOSEPH JOHN - (Lt. 2, Blk. 78, Sec. 1)
Funeral service for Joseph John Anderson, 74, who died
Saturday, July 3, 1976, at St. Catherine Hospital in
Garden City, was held Wednesday afternoon at the Church
of the Nazarene in Garden City with the Rev. Leland
Watkins officiating. Burial was in the Deerfield
Cemetery. He was the father of Mrs. Mary Skipton,
Deerfield, and the brother of Mrs. Sophie Claar,
Deerfield.
   Born September 25, 1901, at Shawnee, Okla., he married
Ruth Rigdon, Oct. 5, 1949, at Dentonville, Ark. He had
lived in Deerfield thirty years where he was engaged in
farming, moving to Garden City in 1970.
   In addition to the widow, he is survived by five sons:
Frank Anderson, Notrees, Tex., Eugene Rigdon, Ogden,
Utah, Warren Rigdon, Mesa, Ariz., Charles Anderson,
Garden City and James Anderson, Mattituck, N.Y.; eight
daughters: Mrs. Laura Slattery, Chillicothe, Mo., Mrs.
Georgia Carter, Memphis, Tenn., Mrs. Estella McGinn,
Garden City, Mrs. Mary Katherine Skipton, Deerfield, Mrs.
Mary Sue Stanfield, Conoga Park, Calif., Mrs. Reva Welch,
Moorefield, Neb., Mrs. Judith VanVacter, Kansas City,
Mo., and Mrs. Frances Skipton, Garden City; a sister,
Mrs. Sophie Claar, Deerfield; 46 grandchildren and 16
great grandchildren.

DEERFIELD CEMETERY

ANDERSON, MABEL - (Lt. 1, Blk. 57, Sec. 2) Born Mabel Faldtz, Nov. 12, 1877, New York City, NY. Died June 1, 1946. Married Albert Anderson, Jan. 1, 1940.
(The Lakin Independent, Deerfield News, June 7, 1946) Friends extend deep sympathy to Mrs. George Buell in the loss of her sister, Mrs. Mabel Anderson, who passed away Sunday at Garden City.

ANDERSON, SYBIL - (Lt. 2, Blk. 78, Sec. 1) Sybil Leginia Jones was born at Sylvia, Kansas, Jan. 4, 1901, and passed away at a Hutchinson hospital, July 3, 1944. She was the daughter of Frank and Laura Jones. She moved with the family to Deerfield, Kansas, in 1918, and continued to make this her home. July 11, 1926, she was married to Jos. Anderson by Rev. John Q. Turner, pastor of the Deerfield Methodist Church. To this union 6 children were born; 3 boys and 3 girls. For many years she was a member of the Methodist Church at Deerfield. Among her activities in earlier years she organized the Jr. Epworth League. She was a loving daughter and a devoted wife and mother.
She leaves to mourn her loss, the bereaved companion; the 6 children, Frank, Charles, James, Laura, Mary and Judith; the mother, Mrs. Laura Jones of Hutchinson; 4 brothers, Ray Jones of Parsons, Frank Jones of Hutchinson, John Jones of Dodge City and Howard Jones of Ulysses; and a host of friends and relatives.

ANDERSON, TAMMI M. - (Lt. 1, Blk. 42, Sec. 3) (The Lakin Independent, March 22, 1990) Funeral for Tammi M. Anderson, 16, was held Wednesday, March 14, at 2 p.m. at St. Anthony Catholic Church in Lakin. Rev. Dave H. Kraus officiating. Burial in Deerfield Cemetery.
She died March 11, 1990, from injuries suffered in an automobile accident.
Born November 17, 1973, at Garden City, she was the daughter of Kenneth and Judy Anderson, Lakin. Survivors are a sister, Diana; grandparents, Mr. and Mrs. Melvin Fry Sr. and Edith Anderson, Garden City; great grandparents, Mr. and Mrs. Dale Fry and Mr. and Mrs. Al Dreiling, Garden City. Also several aunts, uncles and cousins.
Tammi was a sophomore at Lakin High School and had lived at Lakin since 1980, moving from Garden City. She worked at Geubelle Day Care Center and at High Plains Retirement Village as an activities aide. She was a

6

DEERFIELD CEMETERY

registered Girl Scout. She enjoyed art, geometry, and working on cars.

ARIAS, TIBURCIA - (Lt. 4, Blk. 100, Sec. 1) Died June 5, 1973. Mother of Grace Martinez Villenueva. Rosary for Mrs. Piburcia Arias, 82, Deerfield, was held in the Davis Funeral Home in Lakin. Mrs. Arias died in the Kearny County Hospital at Lakin. Funeral was held at Christ The King Catholic Church in Deerfield, Rev. F. C. Lauvick officiating. Burial in the Deerfield Cemetery. Mrs. Arias was born in Cb Lerdo Durango, Mexico, Aug. 10, 1890. She was a longtime resident of Deerfield. Survivors include a daughter, Mrs. Manuela Villaneuva, Deerfield; a son, Jose E. Lopez, Bayard, Neb.; 33 grandchildren and 51 great grandchildren.

ARNOLD, RHONDA LEE - (Lt. 3, Blk. 42, Sec. 3) Rhonda Lea Arnold, 4, daughter of Mr. and Mrs. Rex Arnold, 109 Mendenhall, died of cancer Friday evening, March 17, 1978, at Children's Hospital, Denver, Colo.
She also had suffered a heart condition since birth.
Born May 22, 1974, in Garden City, she participated in Head Start, and was a member of Trinity Lutheran Church.
Other survivors include a brother, Kevin, and sister, Patricia, both of the home; grandparents, Mr. and Mrs. Marvin Winter, 1912 "C", Mr. and Mrs. Emory Arnold, El Dorado; and great grandparents, Mr. and Mrs. Nial Hodges, Shidler, Okla., Mr. and Mrs. Sam Beisel, Herrington.
Garnand Funeral Home in charge of arrangements.

ARTMAN, ELIZA - (Lt. 3, Blk. 47, Sec. 2) 1859-1937. Died Feb. 2 or 4, 1937, at the age of 74 at St. Catherine's Hospital, Garden City of cirrohosis of liver, chronic myocarditis. C. A. Wiley was the undertaker.

ARTMAN, HAZEL - (Lt. 3, Blk. 47, Sec. 2) 1900-1911. Died Sept. 21, 1911, at Garden City at the age of 10 years of age. She died of typhoid fever. Bryant Garnand Funeral Home in charge of arrangements.

ARTMAN, JAMES M. - (Lt. 3, Blk. 47, Sec. 2) 1854-1930 (Lakin Investigator, June 3, 1909) J. M. Artman, who lives 12 miles NW of Deerfield was in Deerfield on Decoration Day.

7

Died in Sherlock Twp., Finney County, Aug. 7, 1930, at the age of 76. He committed suicide. He was married. Services were conducted by Wiley.

ARTMAN, MATT - (Lt. 3, Blk. 47, Sec. 2) (The Kearny County Advocate, January 7, 1909) Matt Artman, who was born in Allen County, Kansas, on August 21, 1889, died at his fathers home, Mr. and Mrs. J. M. and Eliza Artman, north and east of Deerfield on Dec. 31, 1908, after a brief illness.

Funeral services were conducted at the home on Jan. 1, by the pastor of the Lakin and Deerfield Methodist Church, Rev. I. W. Chambers, at which time a large concourse of friends and neighbors were present to show their last tribute of respect and love. He leaves to mourn his loss a father and mother, two brothers and five sisters, and other friends.

ARTMAN, ROY - (Lt. 2, Blk. 58, Sec. 2) (The Garden City Telegram, March 16, 1957) Roy Ortman, 69, a longtime resident of Garden City, died this morning while enroute to St. Catherine Hospital. A heart attack was given as probable cause of death.

Mr. Ortman was born in Lowground, Mo., July 16, 1887. In 1906 he moved to Finney County with his parents, Mr. and Mrs. James M. Ortman from Iola.

He was a member of the Christian Church here.

Surviving are one daughter, Mrs. Irvin Bowlly, Columbus, Ind.; two sisters, Mrs. Roy Hall, Lamar, Co., and Mrs. Fred Meyer of Garden City; one brother, Lott Ortman, Roseburg, Oregon, and two grandchildren.

(The Garden City Telegram March 18, 1957) Funeral services for Roy Artman, 69, who died Saturday were held March 19, at Phillips Chapel at 2 p.m. with the Rev. James Otis Pearce officiating.

Mr. Artman a longtime resident of this community, died while enroute to St. Catherine Hospital. A heart attack was given for the probable cause of death.

His name was inadvertently spelled Ortman in Saturday's Telegram.

DEERFIELD CEMETERY

BABCOCK, BABY - (Lt. 1, Blk. 51, Sec. 2)

BABCOCK, ELEANOR - (Lt. 1, Blk. 51, Sec. 2) 1888-1918
Born Eleanor Pelnar, wife of David Babcock. Died Oct.
17, 1918, in Finney County.

BARGAS, VINCENTE - Died April 9, 1946, at Kearny County
Hospital of pyloric stenosis, age 3 days. Buried at
Deerfield, April 10, 1946.
Born April 6, 1946, to Mr. and Mrs. Ciprano Bargas of
Deerfield.

BARNES, IDA ADALINE - (Lt. 1, Blk. 30, Sec. 2) (The Lakin
Independent, Jan. 7, 1921) Ida Adaline Bradford,
daughter of Corbin B. and Nancy Woodward Bradford, was
born in Clarkburg, West Virginia, December 21st, 1855,
departed this life December 31st, 1920, aged 65 yrs and
10 days. She was united in marriage to George Wesley
Barnes, September 16th, 1880. To this union was born six
children, Mrs. Elna Morgan, Cairo, West Virginia; George
C. of Clarksburg, West Virginia; Wm. C. of Grafton, West
Virginia; Annie, who died in childhood; Mrs. Pearl
Hawkins and Nellie West both of Deerfield, Kansas. She
was converted and joined the Baptist Church at the age of
13 and transferred to the M.E. Church after her marriage
and ever lived a Christian life and was fully prepared to
go home to her Master. She was a devoted wife and
mother. She leaves to mourn her departure the husband
and five children, her father, C. B. Bradford,
Clarksburg, West Virginia, two brothers, J. F. Bradford
of Clarksburg, West Virginia and D. H. Bradford of
Parkerburg, West Virginia and seven grandchildren,
besides a host of other relatives and friends. The
funeral was held at the M.E. Church by her Pastor, E. L.
Nicholson, Sunday, January 2nd at 11 a.m. and the body
tenderly laid to rest in the Deerfield Cemetery to await
the Resurection Morn.

BARRON, ABRAHM - (Lt. 2, Blk. 32, Sec. 2) Funeral
service for Abrahm Barron was held Dec. 29, at Christ the
King Mission in Deerfield, Fr. F. C. Laudick officiating.
Rosary was held the evening before at the Davis Funeral
Home in Lakin. Burial was in Deerfield Cemetery.
Abrahm Barron was born March 16, 1882, in Monterrey,
Mexico, and died at St. Catherine Hospital in Garden

9

DEERFIELD CEMETERY

City, Dec. 26, 1966, at the age of 84 years, 9 months and 10 days. Mr. Barron had been in the hospital two weeks. He came to the United States in 1920 and moved to Kearny County in 1930. At the time of his death he was living in Deerfield but since his retirement he spent much time visiting his daughter in Garden City and his son in Lakin. His wife died in 1929. He was a member of the Catholic Church in Deerfield. When his health permitted, nothing pleased him more than keeping the grounds around the church neat and clean. He is survived by his daughter, Mrs. Marcelina DeLaRosa, Garden City, and a son, Fortunato Barron, Lakin, and eight grandchildren.

BARRON, MARY LOUISE - (Sec. 1)

BARRON, PILAR - (Lt. 2, Blk. 32, Sec. 2) 1887-1929

BAUGH, ALVA E. - (The Kearny County Advocate, Dec. 31, 1908) (County Death Records, Lakin Twp.) We regret to learn of the sudden death of the three months old child of Mr. and Mrs. Thomas E. Baugh, at Deerfield, last Sunday, Dec. 27, 1908, the little one succumbing to an attack of congestion of the lungs. The child was born Sept. 12, and lived but 3 months and 15 days. He was laid to rest Tuesday by his stricken parents, with words of consolation by Rev. A. W. Yale, who conducted services at the M. E. Church.

BAUGH, GEORGE MILLER - (Lakin Investigator, July 19, 1907) George Miller Baugh, infant son of Thomas and Nannie Baugh, was born July 8, 1907, and died July 11, of congestion of the lungs. The little one came to only blossom and die as a flower, but while his life was of short duration, they learned to love him and look to Him who doeth all things well.
Interment was in Deerfield Cemetery, Friday.

BAUGHMAN, ETHEL - (Lt. 3, Blk. 86, Sec. 4) Ethel Rue Ann Baughman, 76, Deerfield, died Dec. 20, 1983, at St. Catherine Hospital, Garden City. She had lived in Deerfield since 1930, when she moved here from Oklahoma. Born May 11, 1907, at Lemons, Mo., she married Oral Baughman, Dec. 3, 1927, at Newkirk, Okla. A homemaker, she had been residing at Garden Valley Retirement Village, Garden City.

Mrs. Baughman was a member of Deerfield Methodist Church and served as nursery supervisor for several years.

Survivors are her husband, Oral, of Garden Valley Retirement Village; a son, Glen Baughman, Oberlin; two daughters, Daisy Martin, 2605 N. Main, Garden City and Juanita Crotty, 712 E. Fulton, Garden City; two brothers, Mantford McDannald, Jerome, Idaho, and LeRoy McDannald, Broken Arrow, Okla.; four sisters, Edna Bates, Chandler, Okla., and Georgia Daugherty, Gainesville, Texas; six grandchildren and four great grandchildren. A sister preceded her in death.

Funeral was held at the Deerfield Methodist Church, the Revs. Nellie Holmes and Harry Walz officiating.

BAUGHMAN, ORAL - (Lt. 3, Blk. 86, Sec. 4) Oral Baughman, 82, Garden Valley Retirement Village, Garden City, died Sept. 11, 1987, at St. Catherine Hospital. Formerly of Deerfield, he was a retired farm laborer and oil field worker. Born Oct. 24, 1904, in Carrol County, Mo., he married Ethel Rue Ann McDannald, Dec. 3, 1927, at Newkirk, Okla.

They moved to Deerfield in October 1930, from Newkirk. She died Dec. 20, 1983. Since March 1981, he lived in Garden City.

Mr. Baughman attended the First United Methodist Church, Deerfield. He enjoyed yard work, music, children, working with horses, attending rodeos and playing cards. In his early adult life, he played banjo in a dance band.

Survivors are a son, Glen Baughman, Oberlin; two daughters, Daisy Martin and Juanita Crotty, both of Garden City; a sister, Fanny Bolinger, Superior, Neb.; six grandchildren; and five great grandchildren. He was preceded in death by three brothers and three sisters.

Funeral was held at the United Methodist Church, Deerfield, the Rev. Nellie Holmes officiating and the Rev. Harry Walz assisting. Burial at Deerfield Cemetery.

BECHTEL, ADELYNE FERN (BILL) - (Lt. 2, Blk. 83, Sec. 1) Adelyne Fern Bechtel, 86, Deerfield, died Wednesday, Aug. 29, 1984, at the Kearny County Hospital at Lakin. Born Dec. 10, 1897, in Cole Camp, Mo., she moved to a farm north of Deerfield with her parents in 1906. She married William Bechtel, Jan. 2, 1929, at Deerfield. She had

DEERFIELD CEMETERY

lived in Deerfield since then.   Her husband died Sept.
23, 1970.
    Mrs. Bechtel was a member of the United Methodist
Church here, the Order of Eastern Star and Golden Ages
Club, both at Lakin, Social Order of Beauceant at Garden
City, and the Deerfield Garden Club.
    Surviving are a sister, Rose Dickins, Deerfield, 11
nieces and 7 nephews.
    Funeral was held at the Deerfield Methodist Church, the
Rev. Nellie Holmes officiating.   Burial at Deerfield
Cemetery.

BECHTEL, SARA - (Lt. 2, Blk. 83, Sec. 1)   See William
Morris Bechtel. She was born Aug. 19, 1854, and died
April 14, 1942.

BECHTEL, W. E. - (Lt. 2, Blk. 83, Sec. 1)   W. E. (Bill)
Bechtel, 81, long time Deerfield resident, died Wednesday
evening, Sept. 23, 1970, at Lakin Manor Rest Home
following a short illness.
    He was born Sept 1, 1889, at Jerico Springs, Mo. He
moved to Deerfield in 1915, where he was employed by the
Garden City sugar company.   He married Adelyn Thelen,
Jan. 2, 1929, in Deerfield.
    Upon returning from Army duty, Mr. Bechtel homesteaded
south of Deerfield in the sandhills. He later owned and
operated a Ford dealership, and a service station and
garage in Deerfield, and owned and drove his own school
bus for 20 years. He has been retired for 20 years.
    He attended the Methodist Church in Deerfield, was a
member of the Lakin VFW, a charter member of the
Deerfield Masonic Lodge and past master, and a World War
I Army veteran.
    He is survived by the widow and one sister, Mrs. Myrtle
Tackett, Deerfield.
    Funeral services were held at the Deerfield Methodist
Church, the Rev. Charles Hadley officiating.   Burial in
the Deerfield Cemetery.

BECHTEL, WILLIAM MORRIS - (Lt. 2, Blk. 83, Sec. 1)
William Morris, son of John and Sarah Ann Bechtel, was
born Oct. 20, 1849, at Findley, Ohio, passed away April
16, 1942, at his home in Deerfield. He moved to Morgan
County, Mo., near the home of Sara Ann Fisher, who became
his bride.

12

Mrs. Bechtel was born Aug. 19, 1854, near Versaillles, Mo., and passed away two days before her husband, April 14, 1942. They were married Dec. 26, 1875. They celebrated, with their two children, their 66th wedding anniversary last Dec. 26.

To this union, four children were born: John, Albert, Myrtle and William. The two older children preceded their parents in death.

Mr. Bechtel, being a miller, had the privilege of living in many Missouri towns, while the family remained mostly in Stockton and Jericho Springs. After the daughter married they moved to Emporia, Kansas, where they lived for five years, moving from there to Deerfield, where they spent the rest of their lives.

They leave to mourn their going, the daughter, Mrs. Ben Tackett and family, and the son, Will Bechtel and wife, beside many nieces and nephews. Mrs. Bechtel leaves two brothers, John of Tulsa, Oklahoma, and Ed of Salem, Oregon.

They had been members of the Missionary Baptist Church for many years, remaining in this church to the very last.

BECKER, AUGUST — (Lt. 1, Blk. 54, Sec. 2) Ludwig August Conrad Becker was born March 23, 1878, at Cook County, Illinois, and died November 9, 1951, at a Garden City hospital.

As an infant he was received unto Holy Baptism. At the age of 14 years he renewed his baptismal vow by the rites of confirmation. He was a faithful member of the Deerfield Lutheran Church and attended services regularly as long as he was able to do so, and read the scriptures diligently.

At the age of 10 years he moved with his parents to Sylvan Grove, Kansas. In October of 1904 he came to Deerfield, Kansas, and took an interest in farming.

On April 25, 1905, he was united in marriage to Elisa Penner. To this union were born two children, the son, Edwin, preceded him in death.

He leaves to mourn his passing: his wife and daughter, Lillie; seven brothers: Wilhelm, John, Otto, Alvin, Herman, Adolph and Martin; also five sisters; Amelia, Sophie, Alvina, Dena, and Martha; and other relatives and friends.

Funeral services were held on Monday, November 12, 1951, with the pastor, Karl E. Kuebler of Scott City,

DEERFIELD CEMETERY

Kansas, officiating. Interment in the Deerfield Cemetery.

BECKER, EDWIN O. - (Lt. 1, Blk. 54, Sec. 2) Born July 8, 1909, died May 4, 1927. (The Kearny County Advocate, Deerfield News, May 13, 1927) Mr. and Mrs. August Becker of Trinidad, Colorado, are here at the home of her mother, Mrs. Jacobs. They arrived here last of the week, bringing the remains of their only son, Edward, who was laid to rest in the Deerfield Cemetery.

BECKER, ELIZA LINDA - (Lt. 2, Blk. 79, Sec. 1) Funeral services for Mrs. August Becker were held Friday afternoon at the Immanuel Lutheran Church, Deerfield, with the Rev. Henry Knoke, officiating. Interment was in the Deerfield Cemetery.
Special music was furnished by a quartet composed of Mrs. Gilbert Merz, Luella Ploeger, Mrs. Herndon Campbell and Rose Hafner. The accompanist was Mrs. Harold Purdy. The casket bearers were: Charles Marquardt, Henry Molz, Herman Huner, Emil Barben, Ralph Gropp and William Kueker. The Garnand funeral service was in charge.
Elisa Linda Becker was born at Newton, Kansas, June 22, 1886, and died on January 30, 1952, at her home in Deerfield.
She was received into God's Kingdom of Grace in infancy through baptism. At the age of 14 years she renewed her baptismal vows in confirmation. She remained a lifelong and faithful member of the Lutheran Church.
When she was eight years of age her family left Harvey County and settled on a farm near Lakin. On April 25, 1905, she was united in marriage to August Becker. They were blessed with two children, a son and a daughter. Her husband and son have preceded her in death.
She leaves to mourn her passing: her daughter, Lillie, of Dodge City; a sister, Mrs. August Kettler, of Deerfield; and many other relatives and friends.

BECKER, LILLIE M. - (Lt. 2, Blk. 79, Sec. 1) Lillie M. (Becky) Becker, 72, died March 23, 1979. Funeral for the long time area resident was held at the Trinity Lutheran Church, the Rev. Merlin Reith officiating.
Miss Becker was born Feb. 18, 1907, in Deerfield. She attended school in Trinidad, Colo., where she graduated from high school in 1928.

She returned to Southwest Kansas to begin nursing training at St. Catherine Hospital, where she graduated in 1931. She worked here as a registered nurse for Dr. V. A. Leopold for 35 years before retiring eight months ago.

Survivors include three cousins, the Rev. Earl Kettler, Silver Springs, Md., Victor Becker, Rt. 1, Mrs. Lloyd (Esther) McMichael, 513 N. 8th, Garden City, and an aunt, Mrs. Meta Kettler, 513 N. 8th., Garden City.

Miss Becker was preceded in death by a brother, Edwin, in 1927.

Burial was in Deerfield Cemetery.

BECKER, WALTER H. - (Lt. 2, Blk. 79, Sec. 1)   Walter H. Becker, 87, former Garden City resident, died Wednesday, March 5, 1980, at Ft. Lyons Veterans Hospital, Las Animas, Colo.

Born June 2, 1892, at Sylvan Grove, Mr. Becker was a career military man.

He had been at Ft. Lyons for 26 years and then had lived in Garden City for some time with his brother, Otto, and nephew, Victor, at 416 Magnolia.   Mr. Becker had returned to Ft. Lyons four years ago and had lived there since.

A World War I veteran, he was a member of the Lutheran Church.

Survivors include five children and his nephew.

Graveside service was held at the Deerfield Cemetery, the Rev. Merlin Reith officiating.

BECKETT, CORNEILUS LUCIAN - (Lt. 3, Blk. 56, Sec. 2) (Lakin Independent, Aug. 1, 1930, Friday's Telegram) This community was shocked and saddened yesterday afternooon by the sudden death of Neal Beckett, pioneer and retired farmer, who passed away at 4:30 o'clock yesterday afternoon at his home on North 6th Street in this city.

While Mr. Beckett had been in rather poor health, owing to a stroke suffered about nine months ago, of late he appeared to be much improved and had been quite jovial. Hence, his departure from this life came as a shock to relatives and friends.

The deceased was a pioneer in these parts, coming here in 1886 and locating on a claim near Deerfield.   About 15 years ago he moved his family to Garden City, where he has since lived.   Born at Camp Point, Illinois, in 1851, he was at the time of his death 79 years, 1 month, and 9 days old. Left to mourn his loss are his wife: a daughter, Mrs. Ola Beckett, Kansas City, Mo.; his sister, Mrs. Mary Nevin, Golden, Il.: and his brother, R. A. Beckett. Two sons have preceded him in death, Fred in 1921, and Harry in 1907.

Mr. Beckett was a devoted husband, a loving father, and a loyal church member. He was a good citizen and has a host of friends in this community who will regret his passing.

Funeral services were held Saturday afternoon at 2:30 o'clock at the Methodist Church in this city with Rev. R. C. Walker in charge. Burial in the Deerfield Cemetery.

BECKETT, HARRY - (Lt. 3, Blk. 56, Sec. 2) (The Kearny County Advocate, February 14, 1907) Tuesday was a black-letter day for Lakin, Ks., for without warning the lives of two of the brighest, brainiest, most exemplary young men in this region were snuffed out like mere tapers.

J. A. Phillips, a rising young civil engineer, who for six months past, has been Engineer in Charge of the United States Land & Sugar Company's corp of surveyors in locating a Mammoth Irrigating Reservoir northeast of this city, and his chief rodman, are no more. They were both drowned in the waters of the artificial lake whose existence they had by their skill created, and both today sleep the sleep that knows no waking.

Monday last the day for testing their work by turning the waters in the Lake. Everything was not in readiness for the test until late in the afternoon Monday, when the signal was given and the pent waters of the Amazon Canal were turned into the Lake. The Reservoir was so astonishingly large that the Amazon made little headway in trying to fill the immense cavity. After running all night and until 4 o'clock Tuesday afternoon a vast bunch of dampness congregated in the north end of the valley, probably 7 or 8 feet on a level. The banks of the Reservoir did their duty and held the water. Messrs. J. A. Phillips, Harry Beckett, and Fred Frost, in a spring wagon drawn by Frost's span of mules were out inspecting the work, and about 4 o'clock Tuesday evening, being tired by their arduous duties of inspecting the work, and finding no break, decided to turn in for the night. They were then on the far side of the lake, it being between them and Lakin, and unfortunately for all concerned,

concluded to cross a corner of the lake and save time.
H. E. Hedge, the Sugar Co.'s Local Manager, who was
following them, did not take the "short cut," but drove
several hundred yards further around the spur of the lake
and escaped. Frost concluded to follow the road that had
been graded before the reservoir was contemplated. The
water was icy cold, muddy, and the mules soon wandered
off the grade and got beyond their depth, and tangled in
the rut, then one mule got down. Had the boys stayed in
the spring wagon, they would have been safe. But they
became panic stricken and jumped into water 7 feet deep.
Mr. Hedge saw their predicament and went to their aid.
He reached Phillips a pole and entreated him to take hold
of it, but he was daft, refused to touch it, and went
down without touching it. He could not swim, nor could
Harry Beckett. Harry's body was recovered in two hours.
It was 11 p.m. when Phillips' was recovered. Frost
narrowly escaped, but one mule drowned.

In memory of one we loved. Harry Warren, youngest son
of Cornelius L. and Martha E. Beckett, was born Sept. 26,
1880, at Camp Point, Adams County, Il., and died Feb. 12,
1907, aged 26 years, 4 months, and 17 days.

How very true it is that in the midst of life we are in
death. How little did we think three weeks ago when dear
Harry was at home to attend the funeral of the one so
recently laid to rest in Deerfield Cemetery that he would
be called to leave us so soon. Our hearts are broken.
How sad is our home today! When we think of the cold,
freezing water that swept him under, our lives are almost
crushed.

No boy was ever more devoted to his home, parents, and
brother than was Harry, and while the stroke seems
unbearable to us, yet we are consoled by the thought that
"God alone is able to soothe the anguished Soul, and we
bow submissively, knowing that he will help us to bear
our great affliction." How his voice will be missed,
sinking through the house! How we will miss his
home-coming, to spend the Sabbath with father and mother.

Harry united with the church at the age of 14 years,
and was a cheerful giver, always ready to assist in
charitable purposes and ever ready to minister to the
wants of others. We leave it all in the hands of Him who
is the way, the truth, and the life.

BEDOLLOS, JO - Died 3/14/1914.

DEERFIELD CEMETERY

BEISEL, SAM - (S/2 Lt. 1, Blk. 41, Sec. 3) Died Dec. 30, 1983, husband of Laverne Smith. Born Feb. 28, 1910. He was a veteran of the U.S. Army in WW II. Funeral for Sam Beisel, 73, was Monday morning at the Smith Funeral Chapel, Sapulpa, Okla. Mr. Beisel died Friday at the St. Francis Hospital, Tulsa, Okla. A retired Briggs Stratton Co. employee, he was the stepfather of Irene Winter, Garden City.

BELL, ELIZABETH EMMA - (Lt. 1, Blk. 14, Sec. 3) Elizabeth Emma Bell, 89, died Thursday, Feb. 29, 1996, at her home in Garden City.
   Born Oct. 25, 1906, at Moundridge, to Daniel M. and Mary M. Krehbiel Vogt, she was a graduate from the Salt City Business College in Hutchinson. She worked with her husband on their farm in Kearny County for numerous years before becoming a cook with the Deerfield school system for 19 years.
   She was a member of the United Methodist Church, Hobby Club, EHU and Pitch Club, all of Deerfield.
   On June 1, 1929, she married Harold A. Bell at Moundridge. She was preceded in death by her husband, five brothers, three sisters, one grandson, and one great grandson.
   Survivors include: three daughters, Eleanor Moreland and Lora Tackett, both of Deerfield; and Lorena Berry, Garden City; nine grandchildren; 23 great grandchildren and six great great grandchildren.
   Funeral was at United Methodist Church, Deerfield, with the Rev. Don Koehn.

BELL, ETHEL - (Lt. 2, Blk. 50, Sec. 2) (Kearny County Advocate, Deerfield News, April 21, 1911) Miss Ethel McCown was born August 25, 1890, and died April 14, 1911, aged 20 years, seven months and 20 days. She was married to George Frederick Bell, June 2d, 1909. She united with the Church of Christ at Deerfield, August 25th, 1907, and lived a Christian life until the Great Father called her home. She was in poor health most of her short married life. Still she bore her suffering with Christian patience, and was never heard to complain. She leaves to mourn, the great sad loss, a kind husband and an infant son, father and mother, four brothers and five sisters besides her husband's people, and many kind friends and neighbors. But they mourn not as those who have no hope. While everything was done that a kind husband and kind

18

DEERFIELD CEMETERY

friends and neighbors could do, she had to go. May the good Lord bless her. Card of Thanks signed by G. F. Bell, Geo. A. McCown, Mrs. Geo. A. McCown, Jay M. Bell, Anna L. Bell.

BELL, HAROLD A. - (Lt. 1, Blk. 14, Sec. 3) Harold A. Bell, 72, died Wednesday, Jan. 10, 1979, at St. Catherine Hospital, Garden City, following a long illness. Born June 22, 1906, at Larned, he married Elizabeth Vogt on June 1, 1929, at Moundridge. He was a lifetime farmer. He lived here since moving from Burdette in 1948.
Mr. Bell was a member of the United Methodist Church, the Lyons Club and the Grange, all of Deerfield.
Survivors include his wife; three daughters, Mrs. Lorena Berry, Mrs. Lora Tackett, and Mrs. Eleanor Moreland; five brothers, Lester, McPherson, Lee, Oklahoma City, Okla., Ralph, Mulvane, Robert, Larned, and Clayton, Boulder, Colo.; four sisters, Gladys Monroe, Oklahoma City, Myrtle Tregelles, Winnemucca, Nev., Marjorie Volkland, Los Altos, Calif., and Clara Saxe, Santa Rosa, Calif; nine grandchildren and nine great grandchildren.
Funeral was held Saturday at the United Methodist Church, Deerfield, the Rev. Harry Walz officiating. Burial in Deerfield Cemetery.
Funeral service was changed from Saturday to Monday, at 3 p.m. at the United Methodist Church, Deerfield.

BELTRAN, RAYMOND - (Lt. 3, Blk. 110, Sec. 1) 1916-1938. Raymond Beltran, a native Mexican male, 21 years of age died Jan 3, 1938, 5 miles west and 1 mile north of Holcomb in Sherlock Twp, Finney County. He died of a fractured cervical vertebra, fractured ribs and a ruptured liver.
(The Garden City Telegram, Jan. 3, 1938) Raymond Beltran, 21, Mexican beet field worker, was found dead shortly before 8 o'clock this morning in a ditch along a country road 10 miles west of Garden City. Sheriff J. C. Standley and Undersheriff Tom Reed were investigating what Reed termed "peculiar circumstances" connected with the death.
Held in the county jail for investigation pending developments were Manuel Beltran, the dead youths brother and John Calderon, Manuel Beltran's brother-in-law.
Dr. H. C. Sartorius, county coroner, planned a post-mortem examination of the body this afternoon to

determine the cause of Beltran's death. A hurried examination this morning revealed a laceration at the back of Beltran's head and a severe bruise just above his right knee. Sartorius said Beltran may have died of a skull fracture. He said Beltran probably died about daybreak.

Reed said Beltran had been attending a party which lasted into the early morning hours at the home of Fred Martinez, 1 1/2 miles north of the place where the body was found. He said approximately 20 other Mexicans had been at the Martinez home during the night and that several of them had been drinking heavily.

Those attending the party at which the christening of a baby was being celebrated, told conflicting stories of events surrounding the death.

Sartorius expressed the opinion that the dead youth either was struck by some blunt object or had been struck by a motor car.

Jackson Morgan, field supervisor for the Garden City Company discovered the body and notified Sheriff Standley, shortly before 8 o'clock.

The dead youth lived with his mother and step father, Mr. and Mrs. Salvador Ramirez at a beet farm a half mile north of the place where the body was found.

BELTRAN, SARAH C. - (Lt. 2, Blk, 126, Sec. 1)   Mrs. Sarah C. Beltran, 69, 2603 N. Main, Garden City, died Saturday, June 9, 1979, at St. Catherine Hospital following a long illness.

Born on Sept. 15, 1909, in Wichita, she married Manuel R. Beltran on March 15, 1932, in Garden City. She came to Garden City from Wichita with her parents at an early age.

Mrs. Beltran was a member of the St. Mary Catholic Church, Altar Society and the H.D. Unit.

Survivors include her husband, of the home; six sons, Henry Monoz, LaJunta, Colo., Nick Beltran, Corona, Calif., Alfred Beltran, 1208 N. 9th, Paul Beltran, Lakin, Manuel Beltran Jr., Gardendale, and Joe Beltran, 1608 Taylor Plaza; four daughters, Tessie Monoz, Santa Ana, Calif., Mrs. Rita Herrera, 210 N. Taylor, Mrs. Esther Perez, 2505 C. and Mrs. Caverly Rojas, 2205 N. Main; five brothers, John Calderon, San Jose, Calif., Fred Martinez Jr., Rt. 1, Michael Martinez, 1613 York, Dave Martinez, R&R Trailer Court, and Danny Martinez, Midway City, Calif.; three sisters, Mrs. Carmen Hayward and Suzie

DEERFIELD CEMETERY

Reynoso, both of Santa Ana, Calif., and Mrs. Sally Cassillas, Costa Mesa, Calif.; 52 grandchildren and eight great grandchildren. She reared one of those grandchildren, Raymond Lee of the home. Rosary and Altar Society rosary were held Tuesday at the church. Funeral was Wednesday at the church, the Rev. James Schrader officiating. Burial in the Deerfield Cemetery. Several survivors were not included in funeral information published in Monday's Telegram. They were a daughter, Gerry Gomez, Liberal; five sisters, Angie Diaz, Socorro Diaz, Eva Diaz, Martha Diaz and Connie Diaz, all of Colorado; and two brothers, Daniel Diaz, Texas, and Earnie Diaz, Los Angeles.

BENDER, JOHN - (Lt. 2, Blk. 52, Sec. 2) 1883-1918. Died Dec. 29, 1918, age 35 yrs., 3 mos., 4 days, of lobar pneumonia influenza. Farmer, married, father Henry Bender, mother Sophia Oaks.
(The Kearny County Advocate, Dec. 31, 1918) The saddest incident resulting from the Flu was the death of John Bender, north of Deerfield. When undertaker Nash reached there Sunday there were four bad cases in the home and the father lifeless. Tuesday an effort was made to get a casket to the home and the trip was abandoned after a mile or two of the way covered.

BENDER, VIOLA - (Lt. 2, Blk. 52, Sec. 2) 1916-1917. Daughter of John Bender.

BENTRUP, BRIAN E. - (Lt. 3, Blk. 44, Sec. 3) Born Nov. 13, 1955, died Feb. 13, 1956, child of Eldor and Maryann (Hennick) Bentrup.
(Lakin Independent, February 17, 1956) Friends extend their heartfelt sympathy to Mr. and Mrs. Eldor Bentrup in the loss of their three month old son, Brian Edward, who passed away February 13, 1956, at the University Medical Center at Kansas City.

BENTRUP, CHARLES - (Lt. 2, Blk. 28, Sec. 2) Charles Bentrup born Oct. 20, 1878, Hainel, Ill., died June 8, 1956, Deerfield, Ks. First marriage to Louise (Schaaf) second marriage to Rose Neimers.
(Lakin Independent, June 15, 1956) Charles Bentrup was born in Worden, Ill., on October 20, 1878, and departed this life on June 8, 1956, at the age of 77 years.

21

He was brought to his Savior in infancy through the sacrament of Holy Baptism. He was confirmed in the Lutheran faith in early youth at Sylvan Grove, Kans. He was an active worker in his church and remained with this faith unto his end.

He came to Kearny County at the age of 27 and this was his home ever since.

On December 25, 1907, he was married to Louise Schaaf; she was taken in death 12 years later. On February 20, 1921, he was married to Rose Wiemers.

Mr. Bentrup actively participated in the life of his community and was well known as a successful farmer and rancher in Kearny County.

Surviving are his wife, Rose; five sons, Henry, Walter of Monroe, La., Carl, Paul and Eldor; one daughter Mrs. Ruth Purdy; and six grandchildren; two brothers, Rev. Herman Bentrup of Elk River, Minn., and Henry of Sylvan Grove; three sisters, Mrs. Albert Hilmer of Sylvan Grove, and Mrs. Will Dierker and Mrs. Will Graesch of Buhl, Ida. Two brothers preceded him in death.

BENTRUP, FREDERICK - (Lt. 2, Blk. 28, Sec. 2) (Nash-Davis Funeral Records) Baby of Chas Bentrup, stillborn, January 5, 1919.
Other records show Jan. 4.

BENTRUP, LOUISE - (Lt. 2, Blk. 28, Sec. 2) (Nash-Davis Funeral Records) Born Oct. 30, 1880, died Jan 15, 1919, age 38 yrs., 2 mos., 16 days. Father Dan Schaaf. Died of uterine hemorhage, contr. weak heart. Born in Seneca, Ks. Died 10 days after the birth of her fifth child (stillborn).

BENTRUP, MERCEDES J.- (N/2 Lt. 2, Blk. 19, Sec. 3) Funeral for Mercedes J. Bentrup, 81, was held Wednesday at the United Methodist Church of Deerfield, with the Rev. Warren Hett officiating. Burial at Deerfield Cemetery.

Mrs. Bentrup died Sunday, Sept. 1, 1996, at Kearny County Hospital, Lakin.

She was born March 25, 1915, at Gypsum, the daughter of Edgar E. and Emma E. Walker Schmitter.

She grew up in Gypsum and graduated from high school there. She graduated from Emporia State Teachers College with a degree in music education. In 1941 she moved to

DEERFIELD CEMETERY

Deerfield where she taught music and government for four
years at the high school.
   After teaching, she became a well-known piano teacher
for many years.   She was also the organist and choir
director at the United Methodist Church in Deerfield for
more than 40 years.   Her special interest was the success
of her former piano students in their activities.
   Mrs. Bentrup was a member of the United Methodist
Church, United Methodist Women, P.E.O., and was a former
member of Piano Teachers League of Garden City.
   She married Carl E. Bentrup on August 16, 1938, at
Gypsum. He survives.
   She is also survived by a sister, Claire Winkler,
Wichita. She was preceded in death by a brother, Russell
Schmitter.

BENTRUP, ROSE - (Lt. 2, Blk. 28, Sec. 2)   Funeral
services for Mrs. Rose Bentrup was held Monday afternoon
at the Immanuel Lutheran Church in Deerfield with the
Rev. Norman Heironimus officiating.   Burial was in
Deerfield Cemetery.
   Rose Wiemers Bentrup, 87, died December 17, 1976, at
Briar Hill Manor in Garden City. Born June 11, 1889, at
Prairietown, Ill.   She taught in both public and
parochial schools in Illinois for 11 years.
   She was married to Charles Bentrup in 1921 and they
came to live on a farm near Deerfield. He died in 1956.
Both were lifelong members of the Lutheran Church.
   She is survived by five sons, Henry, Garden City,
Walter, Monroe, La., Carl, Paul and Eldor, all of
Deerfield; a daughter, Mrs. Ruth Purdy, Deerfield; a
sister, Mrs. Mary Meyer, East St. Louis, Ill.; a brother,
Dr. Julius Wiemers, Marietta, Ohio, 11 grandchildren and
one great grandchild.

BERRY, CHARLEY M. - (Lt. 1, Blk. 40, Sec. 3)   Charley M.
Berry, 80, died Dec. 6, 1987, at his home in Deerfield.
   Funeral was held at Deerfield United Methodist Church,
the Rev. Nellie Holmes officiating. Burial at Deerfield
Cemetery.
   Born June 21, 1907, in Thomas County, he married Leora
Irene Martin, Nov. 4, 1929, at Goodland. She died Sept.
14, 1969, at Garden City. He married Bessie E. Tackett,
Jan. 20, 1979, at Deerfield.

23

Mr. Berry was a retired self employed carpenter and had been a Deerfield resident since 1941, moving from Garden City.
Survivors include his wife, of the home; three sons, Donald D. Berry, Garden City, W. Dale Berry, Cimarron and Dennis G. Berry, Westminster, Colo.; two stepsons, E. Stanley Tackett and Douglas Tackett, both of Deerfield; a stepdaughter, Myrtle Goetz, Kingman; three brothers, Elby Berry, Brighton, Colo., Bake Berry, Seattle, Wash., and Sherman Berry, Pensacola, Fla.; 12 grandchildren; eight step grandchildren; 16 great grandchildren; and four step great grandchildren. He was preceded in death by a son.

BERRY, CLEM - (Lt. 3, Blk. 60, Sec. 3) ts. 1881-1933 (The Kearny County Advocate, Feb. 10, 1933) The funeral of Mr. Berry was held at the M.E. Church in Deerfield, February 3. Mr. Berry for many years resided on a farm south of Deerfield but a few months ago moved near Syracuse where he passed away with pneumonia, February 1st. Quite a number of southside folks attended the funeral of C. C. Berry in Deerfield, Friday last. Sincere sympathy is extended to the bereaved family, who for several years were residents of southside.

BERRY, HAROLD DEAN - (Lt. 1, Blk. 40, Sec. 3) Harold Dean Berry, 26, died at his home Tuesday afternoon, March 9, 1971, after a short illness. He was born January 27, 1944, in Garden City and had been a life long Deerfield resident.
He attended Deerfield schools and was a member of the United Methodist Church in Deerfield.
He is survived by his father, Charley Berry, Deerfield, three brothers, Donald, Deerfield, Dale, Garden City, and Dennis, in the U.S. Navy, and grandparents, Mr. and Mrs. Earnest Martin, Garden City.
His mother, Mrs. Leora Berry, died September 14, 1969.

BERRY, LEORA - (Lt. 1, Blk. 40, Sec. 3) Funeral service for Mrs. Leora Berry was held at the United Methodist Church in Deerfield, Wednesday, Sept. 17, 1969, at 10 a.m., Rev. Charles Hadley officiated. Burial was in Deerfield Cemetery.
Leora Irene Martin, daughter of Ernest and Goldie Martin was born April 17, 1910, in Kinross, Iowa. She moved with her family to Kansas in 1916. She was married

to Charley Berry, Nov. 4, 1929. She had lived in Deerfield since 1940. She was a member of the United Methodist Church in Deerfield. She died in St. Catherine Hospital in Garden City, Sept. 14, after a three year illness. Surviving is the widower of Deerfield; her parents, Mr. and Mrs. Ernest Martin, Garden City; four sons, Dale, Garden City, Donald, Deerfield, Harold Dean, Deerfield, Dennis Gene, San Diego, Calif.; a brother, Ralph Martin, Garden City; four sisters, Mrs. Delores Moore and Mrs. Bonnie Jameson, both of Garden City, Mrs. Ilene George living in Louisiana, and Mrs. Neva Reigle, Newburg, Ore. and nine grandchildren.

BIEHN, BABY - (Lt. 4, Blk. 48, Sec. 2) (Nash-Davis Funeral Records) Funeral Dec. 13, 1917, father, Moses Biehn, Jr., mother, Adda Whitehead Biehn.

BIRD, NORMAN "BILL" SCOTT - (N/2 Lt. 4, Blk. 36, Sec. 3) Funeral for Norman "Bill" Scott Bird, 74, was held at 2 p.m. Friday at the United Methodist Church in Deerfield, with the Rev. Donald J. Koehn officiating. Burial at Deerfield Cemetery with graveside services conducted by Garden City Area Veterans Group.

Mr. Bird died Wednesday, April 10, 1996, at the Kearny County Hospital, Lakin.

He was born April 10, 1922, at Kingfisher, Okla., to Elwood D. and Edna Gladys Smiley Bird, and moved to Crowley, Colo., when he was one year old. He attended Crowley schools.

Mr. Bird was a life member of John J. Haskell Veterans of Foreign Wars Post No. 2279, Harry H. Renick American Legion Post No. 9, the Eagles Lodge, and was a charter member of Moose Lodge, all at Garden City, and had served 12 years on Deerfield City Council. He enjoyed bowling, dancing, playing cards and traveling.

A U.S. Navy veteran, he served on the USS Lapan in the South Pacific.

On Dec. 12, 1946, he married Patricia Fimple at Raton, N.M. In 1955 they moved to a farm northeast of Deerfield. A farmer/stockman, Mr. Bird had been a Pioneer Seed Co., dealer since 1959.

Survivors are his wife; two sons, Michael Bird and Philip Bird, both of Deerfield; a daughter, Connie Penick, Dodge City; a brother, Merle Bird, Garden City;

two sisters, Helen Strever, Layton, Utah, and Hazel
Pearson, Rolla, Mo.; seven grandchildren; and three great
grandchildren.
He was preceded in death by two brothers, Harold Bird
and Dale Bird, and two sisters, Margueraite Selders, and
Pauline Bird.

BISTERFELT, ELMER J. - (S/2 Lt. 4, Blk. 76, Sec. 1)
Elmer J. Bisterfelt, 80, died May 11, 1992, at Sublette.
He was born July 2, 1911, at Bison. A Liberal resident
since 1967, he was a farmer and mechanic for the
Deerfield School District. He was a member of the Grace
Lutheran Church, Liberal.
On March 1, 1936, he married Lydia Grauberger at
Deerfield. She died October 30, 1986.
Survivors include: two daughters, Dorothy Ann Amman,
Westminster, Colo., and Helen Jancie "Wayne" Long, Wylie,
Tx.; two brothers, Calvin and Leon Scheuerman, both of
Deerfield; three sisters, Eloris McAffee, Garden City,
Betty Johnson and Mable Abbie, both of Pasadena, Tx.;
five grandchildren; and three great grandchildren.
Funeral was held at the Grace Lutheran Church,
Deerfield, with the Rev. Paul I. Johnston presiding.
Burial in the Deerfield Cemetery.

BISTERFELT, LYDIA - (S/2 Lt. 4, Blk, 76, Sec. 1) Funeral
for former Deerfield resident Lydia Bisterfelt, 74,
Liberal, was held at the Grace Lutheran Church, Liberal,
the Rev. Richard Bode officiating. Graveside service was
held at Deerfield Cemetery. She died Thursday, Oct. 30,
1986, at St. Catherine Hospital, Garden City.
Born Feb. 21, 1912, at Deerfield, she married Elmer J.
Bisterfelt, March 1, 1936, at Deerfield.
A Liberal resident for 19 years, she moved there from
Deerfield. Mrs. Bistefelt worked for J. C. Penney before
retiring in 1977. She was a member of the Grace Lutheran
Church, Liberal.
Surviving are her husband, of the home; two daughters,
Dorothy Ann Amman, Denver, and Helen Janice Long,
Garland, Texas; two brothers, George Grauberger, Jr.,
Fort Collins, Colo., and Carl Grauberger, Deerfield; six
sisters, Marie Urich, Oakley, Elizabeth Boxberger,
WaKeeney, Mollie Hanneman, Garden City, Eva Hanneman,
Fort Collins, Anna Elliot, Deerfield, and Pauline
Winters, LaJunta, Colo.; five granchildren; and one great
grandchild.

26

DEERFIELD CEMETERY

BOMAN, JOSEPHINE ELIZABETH - (Lt. 3, Blk, 75, Sec. 1)
Josephine Elizabeth Boman, Deerfield, 86, died June 1,
1977, at Western Prairie Nursing Home in Ulysses. Born
Sept. 12, 1890, in Creston, Nebr., she had been a
Deerfield resident for 66 years.
   She was married to Glen E. Steward, March 1, 1910, at
Emporia. He died October 26, 1952. She was then married
to Samuel E. Boman, January 22, 1957, at Deerfield.
   She was a member of the United Methodist Church,
Deerfield, Order of Eastern Star #244, Deerfield Grange
#1925 and Green Thumb Garden Club, Deerfield.
   Survivors include the widower; son, Dennis R. Steward,
Jeanerette, La.; daughter, Mrs. Donald (Carol) Burden,
Lakin; foster son, Don A. Erwin, Garden City; three step
sons, Samuel R. Boman, Lincoln, Nebr., Arthur H. Boman,
Lamar, Colo., James R. Boman, Garden City; and a step
daughter, Mrs. Ardis M. Novotny, Thayer, Kans.; eight
grandchildren and six great grandchildren.
   Funeral service was held June 4 at 10:30 a.m. CDT at
United Methodist Church, Deerfield, Dr. Ruben Reyes
officiating. Burial in Deerfield Cemetery.

BONILLA, ALCADIO - (Lt. 1, Blk. 99, Sec. 1) Died Jan.
23, 1947, one of twins, eleven days old.
   Mr. and Mrs. Fortunato Bonilla of Deerfield are parents
of twin boys, born Jan. 12. They were named Benino and
Alcadia. They weighed 6 lbs, 4 oz, and 5 lbs.

BONILLA, BENINO   - (Lt. 1, Blk. 99, Sec. 1) Died Jan.
23, 1947, one of twins, eleven days old. See Alcadio
Bonilla.

BONILLA, FRANK - (Lt. 1, Blk. 99, Sec. 1) Mexican male,
died Feb. 6, 1938, at Deerfield, 9 days old.

BONNON, MRS. ABRAM - see Mexican

BOYD, JOY - (Lt. 3, Blk. 23, Sec. 2) Born in 1906, died
Sept. 10, 1925, at the age of 19 yrs., 2 mo., 7 days.
Daughter of George B. and Nancy Martin. Joy was the
mother of two boys, Jay and Gail Boyd.

BRABO, ANDREW - (Lt. 2, Blk. 125, Sec. 1) Died in April,
1938. Father Joe Brabo.

27

BRADFIELD, MYRTLE A. - (Lt. 4, Blk. 42, Sec. 3) Mrs.
Myrtle A. Bradfield, 66, died Friday, Dec. 26, 1969, at
her daughter's home in Colorado Springs, Colo., following
a five week illness. Born June 16, 1903, at Stafford,
she had been a resident of Finney County since 1929,
moving to Garden City from Greensburg. She attended the
Christian Church, Garden City.
    Survivors include daughters, Mrs. Norman Heinlen,
Colorado Springs, Colo., Mrs. Marlene Baier, Colwich;
sons, Henry, Cupertino, Calif., LeRoy, Millard, Neb.,
Ervil, Garden City; brothers, Leora Algrim, Montezuma,
Verna and Chester Algrim, Dodge City; 16 grandchildren;
and one great grandchild.
    Funeral was at the Phillips-White Funeral Home, Garden
City; Rev. Lester Myers. Burial at Deerfield Cemetery.

BRENGMAN, MARSHA ANN - (Lt. 1, Blk. 44, Sec. 3) Marsha
Ann, daughter of Leighton and Norma Jean Brengman, was
born Aug. 23, 1952, and departed this life Dec. 26, 1958,
at the age of six years, four months and three days.
    On Nov. 16, 1952, whe was received into God's Kingdom
of Grace through sacrament of Baptism at the Immanuel
Lutheran Church in Deerfield.
    In July of 1956 the family moved from the Lakin
community to their present home in Elkhart, Kans.
    Surviving her are her parents; one brother, Raymond;
the grandparents, Mr. and Mrs. E. L. Kleeman of Lakin and
Mr. and Mrs. Lawrence Brengman of Strasburg, Colo.; the
great grandparents, Mr. and Mrs. S. R. Harbaugh of
Halstead, Kans., and R. L. Edelen of Strasburg, Colo.
    A 6 year old former Lakin girl was killed Friday when
she was hit by a television aerial, which was being
installed at her home in Elkhart.
    Marsha Ann Brengman, daughter of Mr. and Mrs. Leighton
Brengman, died about 11 a.m. in the Morton County
hospital at Elkhart. Death came about a half hour after
she was struck on her head by the falling TV aerial.
    Funeral services were held Monday at 2 p.m. in the
Immanuel Lutheran Church at Deerfield with the Rev. Henry
Knoke officiating. Burial was in Deerfield Cemetery.

BROWNLEE, IRVING E. - (Lt. 4, Blk. 65, Sec. 3) Irving
Earl Brownlee, 82, died Dec. 12, 1982, at Hamilton County
Long Term Care Home, Syracuse, after a long illness.
Born June 11, 1900, at Zenith, he married Leota Anderson,
June 6, 1930, at Dodge City. She died Sept. 17, 1982.

He was a retired farmer and had been a Deerfield resident
since 1948.
He was a member of the Methodist Church and Gideon
Society, both of Deerfield.
Survivors: son, David, Syracuse; daughter, Eldena
Griswold, Wichita; brothers, Oscar, Lawrence, Clarence of
Zenith, Frank of Larned; sisters, Mary Wattles and Eva
McComb, both of Zenith, Theresa Brownlee, San Diego; nine
grandchildren; two great grandchildren.
Funeral was held at the church; the Rev. Harry Walz.
Burial at Deerfield Cemetery.

BROWNLEE, LEOTA ARNETA - (Lt. 4, Blk. 65, Sec. 3)
Funeral for Leota Arneta Brownlee, 76, was held at the
United Methodist Church, Deerfield, the Rev. Harry Walz
officiating.   Burial at Deerfield Cemetery.   Mrs.
Brownlee died Friday, Sept. 17, 1982, at Kearny County
Hospital, Lakin, after a short illness.
Born Dec. 3, 1905, at Wellington, she was married to
Irving Earl Brownlee, June 7, 1930, at Dodge City.   A
former school teacher, she had been a resident of
Deerfield since 1948, moving here from Burdette.
She was a member of United Methodist Church, Deerfield,
and a life member of Kansas Master Farmers and
Homemakers.
Survivors are her husband, of the home; a son, David,
Syracuse; a daughter, Mrs. Ray (Eldena) Griswold,
Wichita; two brothers, Hershel D. Anderson, Buffalo,
Okla., and Forrest H. Anderson, Oregon City, Ore.; a
sister, Elizabeth Wilson, Albuquerque, N.M.; nine
grandchildren, and two great grandsons.

BRUCE, BABY - (Lt. 3, Blk. 50, Sec. 2)   Infant daughter
of Claude and Mollie Bruce, died May 27, 1907.

BUELL, GEORGE - (Lt. 1, Blk. 58, Sec. 2)   George A.
Buell, 84, died Tuesday morning, May 19, 1964, in Briar
Hill Nursing Home, Garden City, after a long illness.
Born July 9, 1879, in Waubunsee Co, Ks., he had been a
long time resident of Deerfield and Garden City.   He
moved to Garden City in 1946, after having operated the
Deerfield Hotel several years.   He married Hattie A.
Faldtz, Nov. 26, 1905, in Deerfield.
Member: The Deerfield Methodist Church, Finney County
Historical Society.

Survivors: The widow, of the home in Garden City; brothers, Ray, Fullerton, Calif., Bert, Los Angeles, Charlie, Hinton, Okla., Harvey, Topeka; sisters, Mrs. Gertrude Aldridge, Sulphur, Okla., Mrs. Nellie Cook, Wellington, Tex., Mrs. Blanche Galloway, Oklahoma City, and Mrs. Grace Grose, Tipton, Okla. Funeral: 2 p.m. Friday, Deerfield Methodist Church; Rev. E. P. Rogers. Burial: Deerfield Cemetery.

BUELL, HATTIE - (Lt. 1, Blk. 58, Sec. 2) Funeral service for Mrs. Hattie Buell, 87, who died Thursday, March 14, 1968, at St. Catherine Hospital in Garden City after a long illness, was held at Garnand chapel, Saturday afternoon. Rev. C. M. Fogleman, Jr. officiated. Burial was in the Deerfield Cemetery.
Mrs. Buell was born June 2, 1880, in Cleveland, Ohio, and moved with her parents, Mr. and Mrs. William Franz Faldtz to Kearny County in the 1880's. She was married to George A. Buell, November 26, 1905, in Deerfield. She and her husband owned and operated the Buell Hotel in Deerfield, many years before moving to Garden City in 1946, where she lived until her death. Mr. Buell died, May 19, 1964. They were instrumental in the beginning of the Deerfield cemetery.
She was a member of the Methodist Church in Garden City and the Finney County Historical Society.
Survivors are a brother, Egnor Faldz, Los Angeles and a nephew, Leon Faldz, Wichita.

BURCH, JIMMY LEE - (Lt. 2, Blk. 102, Sec. 1) Premature baby of Mr. and Mrs. Donald M. Burch, died April 20, 1955.

BURCH, JOY IRENE - (Lt. 2, Blk. 102, Sec. 1) Joy Irene Burch, infant daughter of Mr. and Mrs. Donald M. Burch, Deerfield, died Monday, June 8, 1964, at St. Catherine's Hospital in Garden City, seven hours after birth.
Other survivors are brothers, Kenneth, Gary, Tom, Terry and Danny, all of the home; maternal grandparents, Mr. and Mrs. L. H. Hughes, Holly, Colo.; paternal grandparents, Mr. and Mrs. J. E. Burch, Larkspur, Colo.

BUTLER, CHARLES C. - (Lt. 4, Blk. 47, Sec. 2) (The Lakin Independent, Feb. 28, 1936) Charles Clinton Butler was born in Hancock County, Illinois, February 3, 1860, and

30

departed this life on Wednesday, February 19, at 1:30 a.m. at his home northwest of Deerfield. On February 2, 1882, he was married to Miss Nettie Tanner. In 1889 they moved to southeast Kansas and in 1908 to Kearny County, where they filed on a homestead nine miles north and three miles west of Deerfield. He has since resided on this farm.

He leaves his wife, Mrs. Nettie Butler; one sister, Mrs. Ara J. Welsh of Kansas City, Missouri; two sons, Guy V. and Giles S. Butler; and two grandchildren, Velma and Verle Butler. One sister, Mrs. Herring preceded him in death a year ago.

One of his many friends has written the following tribute to him:

"Neighbor Butler has not at any time let fall from his lips any word that would indicate that he is not in harmonious accord with the Divine Creator and Maker and that he always loved his neighbor as himself. Mr. Butler has always been a quiet, unassuming doer of the Golden Rule.

"During all these years he has commanded the respect of his entire acquaintance, and has deeply inculcated in the hearts of his children in his quiet, unassuming way, that commandment: 'Honor thy father and thy mother; that thy days may be long upon the land which the Lord thy God giveth thee.'

"During all these twenty-six years I have been associated with Mr. Butler, I heartily commend his home life as a criterion for every God-fearing family to follow."

Funeral services were held from the Deerfield Methodist Church on Friday, February 21, 2:00 p.m., with Rev. Glen W. Palmer conducting the service. The Garnand funeral directors were in charge. The text of the sermon given by Rev. Palmer was: "They shall mount up with wings as eagles," taken from Isaiah 40:31. Interment was made in the Deerfield Cemetery.

BUTLER, FERN - (Lt. 1, Blk. 47, Sec. 2) Funeral for Mrs. Fern Butler, 95, was held Tuesday at 10:30 a.m. at the Garnand Funeral Chapel, Garden City. The Rev. Nellie Holmes of Deerfield United Methodist Church officiated. Burial was in Deerfield Cemetery. She died Saturday, May 18, 1985, at High Plains Retirement Village, Lakin.

Born February 6, 1890, in Indianola, Iowa, she married Guy Butler, February 7, 1909, at Hepler, Kansas. He died

July 28, 1955. Mrs. Butler was a homemaker and had lived in Kearny County all her married life. Survivors include a son, Verle Butler, Garden City; a daughter, Mrs. Frank (Velma) Thomas, Lakin; a brother, Dwight Alexander, Geneseo; seven grandchildren and 10 great grandchildren. A daughter, Vera Butler, and five brothers preceded her in death.

BUTLER, GILES - (Lt. 4, Blk. 47, Sec. 2) Funeral for Giles Butler, 89, was held at 10 a.m., Wednesday at Garnand Funeral Chapel in Garden City. He died Saturday, Oct. 4, 1980, at St. Catherine Hospital, Garden City. He was a retired farmer.
Born June 1, 1891, in Illinois, he had been a resident of the Lakin area for 72 years. The family came from Helpler to Kearny County in 1908, where they homesteaded. Mr. Butler kept weather records for the government in his part of the county for 35 years. He moved into Lakin in 1963 and made his home there until he moved to Briar Hill Manor two and half years ago. He had never married.
A brother, Guy Butler, died July 28, 1955. Survivors include a nephew, Verle Butler, Garden City, and a niece, Mrs. Velma Thomas, Lakin.
Burial was in Deerfield Cemetery, Deerfield, the Rev. Cecil Swindle officiated.

BUTLER, GUY V. - (Lt. 1, Blk. 47, Sec. 2) Guy V. Butler was born in Stillwell, Ill., April 19, 1885, the son of Chas. Clinton and Nettie Butler. He died July 28, 1955, in the Kearny County Hospital at the age of 70 years, three months and nine days.
Guy came to Crawford County, Kansas, at the age of four. He homesteaded in Kearny County in 1908. At the age of 18 he united with the Christian Church at Hepler, Kansas.
He married Fern Alexander on February 7, 1909. To this union three children were born. One daughter died in infancy. He is survived by a son, Verle Butler of Deerfield, a daughter, Mrs. Frank Thomas of Lakin, his wife, Fern, a brother, Giles S. Butler of Lakin and four grandchildren.
Mr. Butler was a farmer and auctioneer and had been actively engaged in these pursuits until about six weeks ago when he was stricken.
Out of town relatives and friends who attended the funeral services included Mr. and Mrs. John Seibert, Mr.

32

and Mrs. Harry Seibert and Mr. and Mrs. Clyde Hoover, all of Macksville, William Barnhill, Cimarron, Carl Alexander, Salina, Dwight, Dale, Wes and Earl Alexander all of Geneseo, Ks.

BUTLER, NETTIE - (Lt. 4, Blk. 47, Sec. 2) Nettie, daughter of Hugh M. and Mary C. Tanner, was born near Stillwell, Ill., on Dec. 7, 1863. She was married to Charles Clinton Butler on Feb. 2, 1882. To this union two children were born, Guy and Giles.

She moved with her family to Crawford County, Kansas, in 1888, where she lived until 1908, when the family located in Kearny County, Kansas, on the farm on which she lived until her death, April 3, 1939, at the age of 75 years, 3 months and 27 days.

Her husband preceded her in death February 19, 1936.

Besides her two sons she leaves two grandchildren, Velma and Verle, a sister, Mrs. Electa Damerell of Macksville, Kansas, nieces and nephews, cousins and a host of friends.

In her girlhood she became a member of the Christian Church and has ever lived a very conscientious and sincere Christian life.

A wonderful mother, a loving wife and a good neighbor, she will be greatly missed by all who knew her.

Funeral services were held at the Methodist Church in Deerfield, April 5, at 2:00 p.m. Rev. O. Matthew, pastor, and Rev. C. V. Pierce of the Garden City Christian Church, conducted the service. Interment was made in Deerfield Cemetery.

BUTLER, VERA GWENDOLYN - (Lt. 1, Blk. 47, Sec. 2) Born March 3, 1911, died Sept. 5, 1912, daughter of Guy and Fern Butler.

DEERFIELD CEMETERY

CADENA, FRANCISCO - (Lt. 1, Blk. 110, Sec. 1) Died Jan. 6, 1928, age 34 yr., 9 mo., 4 da., son of Lebonio Cadena and Elisa Olgin Cadena, both born in Old Mexico. He was a day laborer and was married. Died of leakage of the heart.

CALDERON, JOHN SR. - (N/2 Lt 2, Blk. 127, Sec. 1) Former Garden City resident, John M. Calderon Sr., 73, died Nov. 15, 1984, at his home in San Jose, Calif., after a long illness with cancer. He was born June 12, 1911, at Salina.
Mr. Calderon was a meatcutter for 15 years for Farmland Industries here, retiring in 1977. Previously, he had worked 20 years at the Pueblo, Colo., Ordinance Depot. After retiring in 1977, he moved to San Jose.
Surviving are eight sons: John Jr., Lakin; Anthony, Red Bluff, Calif.; Alfred, Pueblo; Frank, Topeka; and J. R., Peter, Mike and Roger, all of San Jose; six daughters: Genevieve Calderon, Memphis, Texas; Josephine Calderon, Red Bluff, Calif.; Lillian Hernandez and Susie Herrera, both of Pueblo; and Rita and Stephanie Calderon, both of San Jose; four brothers: Fred Martinez, Jr., Rt. 1; Dave Martinez, R&R Trailer Park; Michael Martinez, 1613 York, Garden City, Kans.; and Danny Martinez, Midway City, Calif.; three sisters: Sally Cassillas, Costa Mesa, Calif.; and Carmen Hayward and Suzie Reynoso, both of Santa Ana, Calif.; 33 grandchildren and 18 great grandchildren.
Funeral was held at St. Mary Catholic Church, the Rev. Alan Hartway officiating. Burial at the Deerfield Cemetery.

CANNON, DOROTHY - (Lt. 3, Blk. 64, Sec. 3) Mrs. Dorothy Cannon, 95, 1706 N. 7th, Garden City, Kansas, a long time area resident, died Friday evening, July 18, 1969, at St. Catherine Hospital following a short illness.
Born July 24, 1873, near Elk Point, S.D., she was married Aug. 19, 1896, to Phillip Cannon at Clarence, Mo. He died in 1912.
She also was preceded in death by a son, Wilbur, and a daughter, Ruby Clutter.
Mrs. Cannon was a member of the Deerfield Methodist Church.
She moved to the Deerfield area in 1929 from Casper, Wyo., living on a farm in that community until moving to

DEERFIELD CEMETERY

Garden City in the spring of 1967. She had made her home with her sons, Harry and Paul Cannon, since that time. Survivors include three sons, Harry and Paul, Garden City and Lynn, Deerfield; a sister, Mrs. Annie Clark, Shelbyville, Mo.; five grandchildren and four great grandchildren. Funeral was held Monday at the Deerfield Methodist Church, the Rev. Charles Hadley, officiating. Burial in the Deerfield Cemetery.

CANNON, HARRY W. - (Lt. 3, Blk. 64, Sec. 3) Harry W. Cannon died November 4, 1995, at Garden Valley Retirement Village, Garden City. He was born April 4, 1906, at Clarence, Mo., the son of Phillip B. and Dorothy W. Wallace Cannon. He attended school in Clarence, Mo. In 1923, he moved to Wyoming to work in the oil fields. In 1927, Harry moved to Western Kansas where he was a farmer and stockman in the Deerfield area for 40 years. In 1967, he moved to Garden City where he spent the rest of his life.

He was a former member of the Garden City Kiwanis Club and the Optimists Club. He enjoyed bowling. Survivors include a brother, Lynn Cannon, Deerfield. Funeral was at 10:30 a.m. Tuesday at Garnand Funeral Home, Garden City, with the Rev. Donald J. Koehn, of the United Methodist Church of Deerfield, presiding. Burial was in the Deerfield Cemetery.

CANNON, PAUL - (Lt. 3, Blk. 64, Sec. 3) Paul Cannon, 82, died Monday, Dec. 22, 1980, at St. Catherine Hospital. He had been living at Garden Valley Retirement Village.

Born Jan. 5, 1898, in Clarence Mo., he worked for the city of Indianapolis, Ind., retiring when he was 65 years of age. He came to Garden City from Indiana in 1963.

He was a World War II Army veteran and a member of the Masonic Lodge of Greybull, Wyo.

He was preceded in death by his father in 1912, his mother in 1969, a brother, Wilburn, and a sister, Ruby Clutter.

Survivors are two brothers, Harry Cannon, Garden City, and Lynn Cannon, Deerfield.

Funeral was at 10 a.m. Friday, at Garnand Funeral Chapel, the Rev. Floyd E. Born, chaplain of Garden Valley Retirement Village officiating. Burial was in Deerfield Cemetery.

CANNON, WILBUR - (Lt. 3, Blk. 64, Sec. 3) Wilbur Cannon, 68, died Monday, September 23, 1968, at St. Catherine Hospital, Garden City. Born July 23, 1900, at Clarence, Mo., he was a farmer. He had lived in Deerfield for 36 years.
Survivors include his mother, Mrs. Dorothy Cannon, Garden City; brothers, Harry and Paul, both of Garden City, Lynn, Deerfield.
Funeral was held at the Deerfield Methodist Church; Rev. Charles Hadley. Burial was in Deerfield Cemetery.

CASWELL, MARY F. - (Lt. 2, Blk. 75, Sec. 1) (Kearny County Advocate, Jan. 10, 1913) Mrs. Caswell, mother of Mrs. S. H. Corbett, of Deerfield, died at the home of Mr. Corbett, Tuesday, Jan. 7. Born in 1839.
The funeral was held Wednesday at 1:30 p.m., Rev. McNiel, officiating. Mrs. Caswell has been a resident of this county about thirty years, coming here from Milwaukee. She is a sister of Henry Cleveland, who was among the first settlers of the county. Interment was made in the Deerfield Cemetery.

CERVAY, EMMA JEAN - (Lt. 4, Blk. 60, Sec. 3) Funeral for former Holcomb resident, Emma J. Cervay, 69, of Waukesha, Wis., was held at Gethsemane United Methodist Church in Pewaukee, Wis. Graveside service was held Tuesday at Deerfield Cemetery, with the Rev. Harry Walz officiating. Mrs. Cervay died Thursday, Feb. 1, 1996, at Waukesha Memorial Hospital.
She was born Sept. 12, 1926, at Holcomb, the daughter of Lester and Rhoda Smith Clampitt.
Mrs. Cervay had previously lived in St. Louis, moving there in 1944 from Holcomb. She was a member of Gethsemane United Methodist Church at Pewaukee, and Order of the Easter Star.
On April 24, 1954, she married Robert "Bob" Cervay at Evanston, Ill. He survives. She is also survived by a nephew, Conlee Clampitt, Sepulveda, Calif. She was preceded in death by three sisters and one brother..

CLAAR, FRANK LESTER - (Lt. 3, Blk. 76, Sec. 1) (Lakin Independent, Jan. 4, 1924) Frank Lester, son of Zarl and Emma Claar was born in Thomas County, Kansas, Nov. 7, 1885. He grew to manhood in Kansas and Iowa. On Dec. 28, 1905, he was married to Miss Blanche Row at Iowa

City, Iowa. To this union were born four children, Emma, Milton, Harry and Grace.

With the family he came to Finney County in 1911 and has since lived in Finney and Kearny counties. He has followed the trade of a plasterer for many years. Death came at the Rewerts Hospital at Garden City, Dec. 28, 1923.

Those left in sorrow are the wife and four children; two brothers, George of Topeka, and Leonard of Lakin; a sister, Mrs. Elsie Pickens of Jerome, Idaho; father and mother who live at Topeka; with other relatives and friends.

Funeral was in charge of Garnand Undertaking Company of Garden City. The service was conducted at Deerfield church by R. L. Wells. Burial was made at the Deerfield Cemetery, Dec. 29, 1923.

CLAAR, JAMES ZARL - (Lt. 3, Blk. 76, Sec. 1) Died April 25, 1939, age 20 days. Son of Harry Thomas and Mildred Beissel Claar.

CLAAR, MILDRED CATHRYN - (Lt. 3, Blk, 76, Sec. 1) Mildred Cathryn Beissel Claar, 76, died at her home in Lakin, Friday, February 14, 1992. Born, August 5, 1915, in Wichita County, Kansas, she was the daughter of Abraham Lincoln and Flora Ella Beissel. The family moved to Kearny County in 1916.

On November 14, 1934, she married Harry Thomas Claar at Syracuse, Kansas.

With the exception of four years when they were living in Hasty, Colorado, she spent her entire lifetime in Kearny County.

Mildred was a member of the Methodist Church. She and Hap were active in the Golden Agers and were avid travelers until her health recently began to limit their trips and activities.

She very much enjoyed her family, especially her grandchildren and was always interested in knowing about their activities.

She kept family genealogy records, keeping them current by adding each birth, marriage, or death as it would occur.

She also enjoyed writing letters and especially receiving letters from her family and friends. She rarely forgot a birthday or anniversary remembering each with a card and note.

DEERFIELD CEMETERY

She is survived by her husband, Harry; a son, Thomas of
Cimarron, Ks.; a daughter, Linda Randolph, Kansas City,
Mo.; six grandchildren: Tad Claar, Dodge City, Luke
Claar, Cimarron, Jeff Claar, Great Bend, Eric, Michael
and Holly Randolph, Kansas City, Mo.; and a great
granddaughter.
An infant son, James Zarl, a brother, Jesse Beissel,
and a sister, Fern Palmer, preceded her in death.
Funeral services were held Tuesday, February 18, 1992,
at the United Methodist Church, Lakin, with the Rev.
Nathan Morgan presiding. Burial was in the Deerfield
Cemetery.

CLAAR, SOPHIE ESTHER - (Lt. 2, Blk. 81, Sec. 1)
1908-1982 see Sophia Claar Lehman

CLAAR, ZARL MILTON - (Lt. 2, Blk. 81, Sec. 1) Zarl
Milton Claar was the victim of a tragic accident on a
county road north of Deerfield, Friday afternon, Sept. 6,
1963.
Milton was born Dec. 15, 1908, at Topeka, the son of
Ella and Frank Claar. He had lived and farmed near
Deerfield some 25 years. He came to Garden City about
1910 and lived in Finney County ten years before.
He was united in marriage to Sophia Esther Anderson on
April 10, 1930. To this union two sons were born:
Charles of Garden City and Ralph of Deerfield.
He was a member of the Methodist Church of Deerfield.
He is survived by his widow; two sons and their wives;
seven grandchildren; a brother, Harry of Lakin; two
sisters, Mrs. Frank Mathew, Monette, Mo., and Mrs. Walter
Bryant, Beaumont, Tex., and many other relatives and
friends.
A Deerfield farmer, was killed Friday about noon when
his pickup and a semi-trailer truck collided at a blind
intersection 4 1/2 miles north of Deerfield.
Driver of the semi-trailer was Floyd S. Organ, 46,
Perryton, Tex. He was taken to the Kearny County
Hospital for treatment of bruises and shock and released.
According to the highway patrol officer investigating
the crash with Kearny County sheriff's officers, the
intersection is obscured from all directions by a heavy
growth of tall weeds.
According to Trooper Ralph Peetzen the southbound
pickup plowed into the right rear side of the trailer,

38

with both vehicles being flung from the roadway into the ditch.
Funeral services were held Monday morning in the Deerfield Methodist Church with Rev. Robert Fleenor officiating. Burial was in Deerfield Cemetery.

CLOWER, ROBERT J. - (Lt. 4, Blk. 39, Sec. 3) Funeral services for Robert J. Clower, 39, Deerfield, were held at 2 p.m. Monday at the United Methodist Church, Deerfield, the Rev. Charles Hadley officiating. Burial was in the Deerfield Cemetery.
Mr. Clower died early Friday morning, April 16, 1971, as the result of a two vehicle accident near Deerfield.
Born Nov. 23, 1931, at Branson, Colo., he married Doris Elaine VanMatre, March 10, 1951, at Raton, N.M. He was shop foreman of the Garden City Co-op Feedlot and moved to Deerfield in 1964 from Lakin.
Survivors include the widow; two sons, Rodney and Andrew, of the home; three daughters, Judith, Janie and Doris, of the home; his mother, Mrs. Minnie Clower, Branson; one brother, John Clower of Pueblo, Colo.; three sisters, Mrs. Velma VanDerwater, Denver, Mrs. Dale Goodwin, LaJunta, Colo., and Mrs. James (Ida Mae) Shelden, Lakin.

CLYMER, CECIL - (Lt. 2, Blk. 38, Sec. 3) Funeral for Cecil Clymer, 62, was held at the United Methodist Church, Deerfield. The Rev. Donald J. Koehn officiating. Burial in Deerfield Cemetery.
Mr. Clymer died on Nov. 15, 1991, at his home in rural Deerfield.
He was born on April 16, 1929, at Butler, Okla. He grew up in Sweetwater, Okla., and attended schools there. On Sept. 5, 1951, he married Dolly Moore at Sayre, Okla. The couple moved to Sublette in 1957 and in 1959 to Garden City where Mr. Clymer worked for Fansler Tires and for the Garden City Co-op. He continued to work for the co-op when he moved to Deerfield in 1984. He was a charter member of the Road Riders Cycle Club, Garden City.
Survivors are his wife, of the home; seven daughters, Rosie Carter, Deerfield, Joyce Croft, Ingalls, and Theresa Orozco, Laura Porter, Cecile Gassett, Ovanda Partridge, and Glenda Clymer, all of Garden City; and 12 grandchildren.

He was preceded in death by his parents and two brothers, Clell and Glen, and one sister, Polly Lehewe.

COERBER, ALVIN L. — (N/2 Lt. 2, Blk. 34, Sec. 3) Funeral for Kearny County Commissioner, Alvin L. "Tuffy" Coerber was held at 2 p.m. Thursday at Immanuel Lutheran Church, Deerfield, the Rev. Robert Roberts officiating. Burial at Deerfield Cemetery. He died July 20, 1992, at the Kearny County Hospital, Lakin.

Born Jan. 1, 1919, at Lakin, he married Vivien Humphrey May 28, 1939, at Deerfield. Mr. Coerber was born in Lakin and moved to Allison, Colo., as a child. He moved to Alamosa, Colo., in 1923, where he lived until moving to Deerfield in 1928.

He was manager of the Santa Fe Motor Company, Deerfield, for many years. He was a former Deerfield city councilman and had served as a Kearny County Commissioner for 12 years and had filed for re-election.

While on the commission he helped in getting the High Plains Retirement Village built in Lakin, and was one of the main organizers to help build the Kearny County Community Center in Deerfield.

He was a member and elder of the Immanuel Lutheran Church, Deerfield, and was a charter member of the Deerfield Lions Club.

Survivors include his wife, of the home; a daughter, Carmen Knapp, Wichita; a brother, Milton Coerber, Lakin; three sisters, Luella Brack, Belle Vista, Ark., Ruth Kuhlman, Lakin, and Ione Shuck, Fort Worth; a granddaughter and a great grandson. He was preceded in death by two brothers and a sister.

Green-Schneider Funeral Home, Lakin, was in charge of arrangements.

COERBER, H. WALTER — (Lt. 4, Blk. 101, Sec. 1) H. Walter Coerber, 59, Deerfield, died unexpectedly Friday morning, October 15, 1976, at his home of an apparent heart attack.

Born July 4, 1917, at Lakin, Mr. Coerber was a lifetime resident of Kearny County. He was employed as custodian for Deerfield high school. He was married to Laura Adella Merz, May 19, 1940, at Deerfield.

Mr. Coerber was a member of Trinity Lutheran Church, Garden City.

Survivors include the widow; two daughters: Mrs. Everett (Karin) Glenn, Garden City and Mrs. Gary (Joyce)

DEERFIELD CEMETERY

Kraft, Deerfield; three brothers: Harold of Eugene, Ore.,
Alvin of Deerfield, and Milton of Lakin; three sisters:
Mrs. Luella Brack, Pomeroy, Iowa, Mrs. Ruth Kuhlman,
Lakin, and Mrs. Ione Shuck, Orleans, Nebr.; and seven
grandchildren. A daughter, Linda Leanne, and a sister,
Alice, preceded him in death.
Funeral was held at the Trinity Lutheran Church, Garden
City, Rev. Merlin Reith officiated. Burial was in
Deerfield Cemetery.

COERBER, LAURA A. - (Lt. 4, Blk. 101, Sec. 1) Funeral
for Laura Adella Coerber was held at 10 a.m. Friday at
Trinity Lutheran Church, Garden City, the Rev. Vernon
Oestmann officiating. Burial was in Deerfield Cemetery.
She died October 16, 1991, at her home. Born Laura
Adella Merz, August 2, 1918, at Deerfield, she married H.
Walter Coerber, May 19, 1940, at Deerfield. He died
October 15, 1976.
Mrs. Coerber was a homemaker, former Social
Rehabilitation Service homemaker and Deerfield High
School custodian. She had been a lifetime Deerfield
resident.
She was a member of the Trinity Lutheran Church, Garden
City, the Ladies Card Club, Deerfield, and the American
Diabetes Association.
Survivors include two daughters, Karin Glenn, Garden
City and Joyce Kraft, Deerfield; a brother, Melvin Merz,
Liberal; two sisters, Ida Kopper, Hutchinson, and Edna
Shertz, Duarte, Calif.; seven grandchildren and two great
grandchildren. She was preceded in death by a daughter
and three brothers.

COERBER, LINDA J. - (Lt. 2, Blk. 108, Sec. 1) Linda
Jeanne, four day old infant of Mr. and Mrs. Walter
Coerber of Deerfield, died Monday morning, Feb. 9, 1953,
at a Garden City hospital.
She is survived by her parents; two sisters, Karen K.
and Joyce Ann; and her grandparents, Mr. and Mrs. Herman
Coerber and Mr. and Mrs. J. W. Merz. Burial was in the
Deerfield Cemetery.

COLERON, FREDRICK - (Lt. 3, Blk. 27, Sec. 2) Born in 1936
and died May 29, 1936.

COLGIN, ROSALIND MARIE - (Lt. 1, Blk. 101, Sec. 1)
(Garden City Telegram, June 17, 1949) Funeral services

41

for Rosa Marie Colgin, infant daughter of Mr. and Mrs. Kenneth Dale Colgin, Deerfield, was held at the graveside in the Deerfield Cemetery, Saturday at 10 a.m. The infant was stillborn in a local hospital yesterday, June 16, 1949. Colgin is an engineer for the Deerfield Petroleum Co., Inc.

COMBS, MAMIE A. - (Lt. 2, Blk. 16, Sec. 3)   Funeral services for Mamie Anna Combs were held Saturday, September 9, at 10:30 a.m. at the United Methodist Church in Deerfield, with the Rev. Donald J. Koehn officiating. Burial in Deerfield Cemetery.

Mrs. Combs died September 5, 1995, at the Kearny County Hospital in Lakin. She was a homemaker and had lived in Deerfield since 1940.

Mamie was born December 27, 1906, at Argonia, Kansas, the daughter of Ashley Armstrong and Clara Adelia (Hartung) Cone. She lived in various places during her growing up years.

On March 15, 1926, she married Maurice R. Combs in Wellington, Kansas. They moved to Deerfield in 1940 from Argonia and had lived there since. Maurice died on August 22, 1987.

Mrs. Combs was a member of the United Methodist Church, the Hobby Club and the Grange, all of Deerfield. She enjoyed crocheting, knitting, and sewing.

Survivors include four sons: Leland Combs, Loran Combs, and Larry Combs, all of Deerfield, and Darrel Combs of Garden City; a daughter, Clara Wynne Grauberger, Deerfield; a brother, Walter Cone, Lakin; and 14 grandchildren; 14 great grandchildren; also many nieces and nephews.

Besides her husband, Maurice, she was preceded in death by her parents, a daughter, Phyllis Combs, a son, Milford Combs, sisters, Ruth Cone, Katherine Parr, and an identical twin sister, Masie Morris, a granddaughter, Jeannene Grauberger, and a grandson, Tyson Metcalf.

Garnand Funeral Home in Lakin was in charge of arrangements.

COMBS, MAURICE R. - (Lt. 2, Blk. 16, Sec. 3)   Maurice Rush Combs, son of Elza Miles and Annie Melinda Combs, was born June 23, 1905, at Mechanicsburg, Illinois, and passed away at his home in Deerfield, on August 22, 1987. He was 82 years of age.

DEERFIELD CEMETERY

Maurice was joined in marriage on March 15, 1926, to Mamie Anna Cone at Wellington, Kansas. Maurice was a farmer and stockman until his death. He came to Argonia, Kansas, as a small child, and farmed in that area until he came to Deerfield in 1936. He brought the rest of the family to Deerfield in 1940. He was a member of the Deerfield United Methodist Church, the Independent Order of Odd Fellows Lodge of Garden City, the Kearny County Saddle Club, the Senior Citizens club of Lakin, the Kearny County Historical Society of Lakin. He served as a 4-H leader for 15 years at Deerfield.

Maurice's special hobbies and interests were hunting and trapping. He also was very interested in wildlife, the outdoors, county fairs, antique farm equipment, and rodeos.

Survivors are his wife of the home; a daughter, Clara Wynne Grauberger of Deerfield; sons, Leland, Loran, Larry of Deerfield, and Darrel of Garden City; sisters, Belva Wheeler of Wellington, Kansas, Lela Wimp of Wichita, Kansas, Anna V. Hull of Garden City; a brother, Adrian of Enid, Oklahoma; fourteen grandchildren, and seven great grandchildren. A daughter, Phyllis and a son, Milford, and a granddaughter, Jeannene, preceded him in death.

Funeral services were held August 26, 1987, at the Deerfield United Methodist Church, the Rev. Nellie L. Holmes officiating. Burial in the Deerfield Cemetery

COMBS, MILFORD - (Lt. 2, Blk. 16, Sec. 3) Milford Gene Combs, son of Mr. and Mrs. Maurice Combs was born at Argonia, Kansas, September 25, 1926, and departed this life on June 1, 1948, at the age of 21 years, 8 months and 7 days, at San Bernardino, California.

He was baptized into the Baptist Church at Argonia, Kansas, at the age of 13 years.

At the age of 14 he moved with his parents to Deerfield, Kansas, where he lived with his parents until he enlisted in the Navy Reserve in the fall of '43. After attending radio school for seven months and one week he was sent to the Philippines where he served his country until November 1948, with the exception of a furlough home two years ago.

He was returned to the States in November of '48 and spent three months in the hospital at Oakland, California. After his release there he started home but went to an aviation school at Kingman, Arizona. That being what he wanted to do most, he enrolled and attended the school. He had completed his course and received his pilot's license and would have returned home in a few days, but wished to see a friend who was in a hospital near there. It was on his return trip that his plane crashed.

He leaves to mourn his departure, his father and mother, four brothers, Leland, Loran, Darrel and Larry, and one sister, Clara Wynne, all of the home, also two grandmothers, Mrs. E. M. Combs of Garden City and Mrs. Beuchaw of Oxford, Kansas, other relatives and a host of friends.

Funeral services were held at the Garnand Chapel in Garden City and burial was made in the Garden City cemetery. Later his remains were removed to Deerfield Cemetery in Sept. 1944.

COMBS, PHYLLIS ANNA - (Lt. 2, Blk. 16, Sec. 3) (The Lakin Independent, October 19, 1945) Phyllis Anna Combes, daughter of Mr. and Mrs. Maurice R. Combes, seven miles north and one mile east of Deerfield, was fatally injured in an automobile accident. She was taken to St. Catherine's Hospital in Garden City where she passed away Wednesday morning at ten o'clock.

She was born December 31, 1937, and died October 17, 1945.

Buried in Garden City cemetery and removed to Deerfield Cemetery, Sept. 1994.

COMBS, SANDRA - (Lt. 1, Blk. 15, Sec. 3) Sandra "Sandy" Combs, 42, died Dec. 25, 1984, at St. Catherine Hospital, Garden City, after a short illness. Born Sandra Miller, Sept. 16, 1942, at Colby, she married Darrel D. Combs, Jan. 22, 1961, at Deerfield. She was the co-owner and operator of Coyote Sports Center, Garden City, and had lived in Garden City since 1962.

She was a member of Sand and Sage Rifle and Pistol Shooting Club and was active in Bowling League, both of Garden City.

Survivors: husband, of the home; son, David, of the home; daughter, Bonnie, of the home; parents, Verle Sr. and Twila Miller, Hoxie; brothers, Verle Jr. and Donald, both of Dighton; sisters, Karol Havel, Imperial, Neb., and Barbara Colson, St. Francis.

Funeral was held Saturday at Deerfield Methodist Church, the Rev. Nellie Homes. Burial in Deerfield Cemetery.

DEERFIELD CEMETERY

CONE, RUTH MARIE - (Lt. 2, Blk. 16, Sec. 3) Ruth Marie
Cone died Friday, April 14, 1995, at High Plains
Retirement Village, Lakin. She was born August 22, 1899,
at Belle Plaine, Kansas, the daughter of Ashley Armstrong
and Clara Adelia Hartung Cone. She grew up in Argonia,
Kansas, and graduated from Argonia High School.
After high school she taught school for two years in
the Argonia area. While in Argonia she was also a
substitute mail carrier. She moved to Colorado Springs
in 1938 where she attended college for one year.
Ruth lived in Colorado Springs until the 1950s when she
moved to Denver. During the time she lived in Colorado
Springs and in Denver, Ruth worked as a governess in
various homes.
In August of 1984, Miss Cone moved to Lakin where she
had lived since.
She was a lifetime member of the Argonia Methodist
Church and a lifetime member of the Order of the Easter
Star of Argonia. Her hobbies included writing, reading
the Bible, and hiking.
She is survived by a brother, Walter Cone, Lakin, and a
sister, Mamie Combs, Lakin, also many nieces and nephews.
She was preceded in death by her parents and two
sisters, Katherine Parr and Maisie Morris.
Funeral service was held Tuesday at the United
Methodist Church, Deerfield, with the Rev. Donald J.
Koehn, officiating. Burial was in the Deerfield
Cemetery.

COPLEY, DAVID J. - (Lt. 1, Blk. 18, Sec. 3) Funeral for
David Copley was held at Garnand Funeral Home, Garden
City, Wendell Bradford officiating. Burial at Deerfield
Cemetery. He died Oct. 30, 1991, at his home.
Born Aug. 11, 1921, at Fullerton, Neb., he was a
farmer. He lived in various places throughout his life
and attended high school in Seibert, Colo. He moved to
Holcomb in 1971.
He was a member of the First Baptist Church, Deerfield.
Survivors include a son, Bill, Limon, Colo.; a
daughter, Donna Tucker, Colorado Springs; four sisters,
Betty Glunt, Jetmore, Laura Kemp, Seal Beach, Calif.,
Neoma Cowan, Montrose, Colo., and Esther Kapsch, Colorado
Springs; and four grandchildren. He was preceded in
death by two brothers and a sister.

DEERFIELD CEMETERY

CORBETT, BERT OMRO - (Lt. 2, Blk. 82, Sec. 1)   Bert O.
Corbett passed away Monday, Nov. 15, 1943, at St.
Catherine's Hospital in Garden City after a long illness.
He was a son of the late Sam Corbett, who came here in
the first settlement of the county. Bert Corbett made
his home near Deerfield and spent his whole life in that
community, living on a farm south of the river. Funeral
services were at the Deerfield Methodist Church.
Interment in Deerfield Cemetery.
   Death, this time not unexpected, came to our community
and Bert Omro Corbett answered to the summons. He was a
son of Samuel H. and Dolly E. Corbett, born in the
Deerfield community, December 3rd, 1884, and lived here
his entire life.
   On June 5, 1912, he was married to Ednah Lemern Thomas.
To this union one child was given. The wife passed away
in 1925, the 13th anniversary of their wedding day. On
December 16, 1927, he was married to Stella Mae Netzer.
To this union five children were given.
   In 1913, he with his first wife, united with the
Methodist Church in Deerfield.
   Bert had been in poor health for some years, with a
heart ailment, and although up and going most of the
time, was unable to live an active life. On November 15,
1943, he quietly slipped away from us at St. Catherine's
Hospital in Garden city, aged 58 years, 11 months, and 11
days. He leaves to cherish in memory, the wife, Mrs.
Stella Corbett; six children, Warren Omro of Lakin,
Samuel, Maxine, Billy, Fred and Gene, all of the home;
his mother, now of Colorado Springs; two brothers, Carl
of Deerfield and Jacob of Wichita; three sisters, Mrs.
Maud Kell, Deerfield, Mrs. Louise Smith, Elmodino,
California, and Ruth Melton, Colorado Springs; and many
friends who have known him all his life.

CORBETT, INFANT SONS - (Lt. 4, Blk. 57, Sec. 2) Infant
twin sons of Karl and Ola E. Corbett, July 13, 1914, May
15, 1915.

CORBETT, KARL STANLEY - (Lt. 4, Blk. 57, Sec. 2)
Funeral services for Karl Corbett, 68, of Deerfield was
held May 29, at 2 p.m. at the Methodist Church in
Deerfield.
   Mr. Corbett died at his home here of a heart attack
while using the telephone Monday night about 7:30
o'clock. He had been talking to Mrs. George Grauberger

46

on the telephone at about that time. He said goodbye and Mrs. Grauberger hung up the phone. He apparently suffered the heart attack before he could replace the receiver because he was found slumped under the telephone and the receiver was still off of the hook.

Mr. and Mrs. Ed Downing found him when they returned home about 10:30 that evening.

Mr. Corbett was born in Deerfield, April 18, 1886, and had lived in that community all of his life. For a number of years he operated a grocery store and general store in that city.

Survivors include a son, Harris B. Corbett of California; three sisters, Mrs. W. T. Kell of Deerfield, Mrs. Lou Smith of Orange, Calif., Mrs. Roy Milton of Colorado Springs; and two grandchildren, Clark and Claudette Corbett of Deerfield.

Karl Stanley Corbett, son of Samuel Harris and Dolly Casswell Corbett, was born on the Corbett ranch near Deerfield, Kans., April 18, 1886, and departed this life very suddenly on May 24, 1954, at the age of 68 years, one month and six days.

He was educated in the schools of Kearny County, and entered business in Deerfield, where he was in the grocery business for forty eight years.

He was united in marriage with Ola Ernestine Tuggle, Dec. 11, 1911. To this union four children were born, three of them died in infancy. His companion passed away Oct. 18, 1934.

He became a member of the Deerfield Methodist Church in 1911, and remained a member until the time of his death.

He leaves his son, Harris Corbett, of Yosecite National Park, Calif.; one granddaughter, Claudette Corbett, who is a member of the U.S. WAVES; one grandson, Clark Dean Corbett, of Deerfield; three sisters, Mrs. Maud Kell, Deerfield, Kans., Mrs. Louise Smith, El Modeno, Calif., and Mrs. Ruth Melton, Colorado Springs, Colo.; besides many nephews and nieces and a large number of friends.

CORBETT, OLA EARNESTINE — (Lt. 4, Blk. 57, Sec. 2) (The Kearny County Advocate, Oct. 26, 1934) Mrs. Ola Earnestine Corbett, daughter of Mr. and Mrs. Thomas B. Tuggle, was born at Lakin, Kansas, July 13, 1892, and passed to her reward from her home in Deerfield, Kansas, Thursday morning, October 18, 1934.

In the year 1900 she moved with her parents to Deerfield, where she has spent her life. Here she attended school, and here she made her home and raised her family.

On December 14th, 1911, she was united in marriage to Karl Corbett, of Deerfield. To this union seven children were born. Harris, who is with us today and six who died in infancy.

Mrs. Corbett was always active in the social life of the community, even after her health began to fail, she was of a cheery disposition, she never worried her friends or neighbors with her troubles, and wore a smile most of the time, and never carried a grudge against any one.

She was a member of the Methodist Church at Deerfield, was active in Sunday School and church work. Just a short time before her death, she expressed her wishes for other members of the family, and said she had peace with God and was ready to go.

She leaves to mourn her loss, a husband, Karl Corbett; her son, Harris, wife and baby; her parents, Mr. and Mrs. Thomas B. Tuggle; one sister, Mrs. Ida Wade; four brothers, Turney, Clem, Loyd and Curran and other relatives and a host of friends.

Funeral services were held at the Methodist Church in Deerfield, Sunday, October 21st, 1934, conducted by Rev. Markwell, and the remains laid to rest in the Deerfield Cemetery, for their last long sleep.

CORBETT, SAMUEL HARRISON - (Lt. 2, Blk. 75, Sec. 1) Samuel Harrison Corbett was born February 7, 1859, at Baltimore, Maryland, and was deceased February 20, 1931, at Colorado Springs, Colorado.

His father having died, his mother moved with the family when Samuel was 11 years old to Waynesboro, Pennsylvania, where they lived for 7 years. Then he moved to Lincoln County, Kansas, where he lived until 1879, when he moved to Graham County. In 1880 he started with a caravan to go to Silver Cliff, Colorado. However, when arriving at Fort Wallace, Kansas, he decided to remain and became a sheep herder. About one year later he joined himself with the XY Cattle Company, which soon after moved its ranch activities to the Arkansas River near Deerfield, Kansas. Since that time, 1881, Mr. Corbett has called Deerfield his home. However, in 1918 he took up his residence in Colorado Springs, Colorado, where he lived until his death.

DEERFIELD CEMETERY

Soon after taking his position as cowboy with the XY Cattle Company, the pioneers of Kearny County began to arrive and settle up the land. With them came Miss Dolly Caswell, who became his bride May 24, 1883. To this union were born six children, three boys and three girls, all of whom are still living.

Mr. Corbett was among the first settlers of Kearny County. He helped to develop this open prairie from a cattle range to a fine agricultural paradise. He has left a fine, wholesome influence upon this community.

He was a prominent citizen, a whole-souled and active Christian, a devoted husband and father, a man highly respected by all who knew him.

He was converted and united with the Methodist Church at Deerfield in January 1903. He was an active Christian the rest of his life.

He leaves to mourn his going his wife; his six children, Mrs. A. R. Melton, Colorado Springs, Colorado, Mrs. L. M. Smith, El Modena, California, Mrs. W. T. Kell, Bert Corbett, Karl Corbett, Jacob Corbett, all of Deerfield, Kansas; seven grandchildren; two brothers and one sister, John G. Corbett, Waynesboro, Pennsylvania, Mrs. Margaret Morison, Waynesboro, Pennsylvania, E. H. Corbett, Kansas City, Kansas; and a host of friends.

Funeral services were conducted at the Deerfield Methodist Church, with Rev. B. E. Willoughby in charge, assisted by the pastor, Rev. R. A. Corrie. Interment was made in the Deerfield Cemetery.

Mr. S. H. Corbett, father of Mrs. Maude Kell and the three Corbett boys, died at his home in Colorado Springs Friday. Funeral services and burial in Deerfield Monday afternoon. Mr. and Mrs. Corbett were early settlers here, and he will be missed here, because he spent much of his time in this vicinity. Mrs. S. H. Corbett, Mr. and Mrs. L. M. Smith and daughter, Virginia, of San Diego, California, and Mr. and Mrs. Ray Melton came in for the funeral.

CORBETT, STELLA MAE — (Lt. 2, Blk. 82, Sec. 1) Funeral service for Mrs. Stella Corbett was Friday, October 7, at the United Methodist Church in Deerfield with the Dr. Ruben Reyes officiating. Casket bearers were grandsons of Mrs. Corbett. Burial was in Deerfield Cemetery.

Stella May Netser, daughter of Daniel and Lillian Moffet Netser was born March 12, 1898, at North English, Iowa. She moved to Deerfield in 1925 and was married to

DEERFIELD CEMETERY

Bert Corbett, November 16, 1927, and moved to a farm south of Deerfield where she lived until her death. He died in 1943.

She had been in ill health several years and died at St. Catherine Hospital, October 5, 1977, at the age of 79 years, 6 months and 23 days.

She is survived by three sons, Sam of Deerfield, Fred of Garden City, and Gene of Iowa City, Iowa; two daughters, Mrs. Maxine Merz and Mrs. Betty Stephens both of Garden City; a sister, Mrs. Blanche Humphrey of Garden City; a brother, Boyde Netser of North English, Iowa; 14 grandchildren and two great grandchildren.

COUCH, HELEN MAUDE - (Lt. 4, Blk. 75, Sec. 1)   Born March 2, 1907, died Feb. 22, 1940.

(The Lakin Independent, March, 1940)   Mrs. Boyd Couch of Syracuse, passed away at the Donohue Memorial Hospital Thursday morning after an illness of about two years.

Before her marriage she was Helen McNellis, living north of Deerfield, and her many friends and acquaintances here are grieved to learn of her death. She is survived by her husband and an eight year old son who have the sympathy of the community in their bereavement.

Funeral services were held Friday afternoon at Syracuse and interment was made in the Deerfield Cemetery.

COY, CLELL C. - (Lt. 3, Blk. 57, Sec. 2)   Funeral services for Clell C. Coy were held, Wednesday afternoon, Nov. 5, at the United Methodist Church in Deerfield. Rev. Charles Hadley officiated.   Burial was in the Deerfield Cemetery.

Mr. Coy, 71, died at St. Catherine Hospital, Saturday afternoon, Nov. 1, 1969, after a short illness. He was born Jan. 11, 1898, in Gove County and moved to a farm north of Deerfield in 1925.   He moved there from Nickerson. He was married to Maggie L. Kersten at Valley Center in 1946. She died in 1964.

He was a member of the Deerfield United Methodist Church.

Survivors include a step-son, C. A. Kersten, Dobbs Ferry, N.Y.; two brothers, Frank L., Deerfield and Donald K., Dodge City; and two grandchildren. A sister, Hazel Coy Monroe, died in 1938.

DEERFIELD CEMETERY

COY, FRANK L. - (Lt. 3, Blk. 57, Sec. 2)   Frank L. Coy, 70, a longtime Kearny County farmer in the Deerfield community, died Sunday, July 26, 1970, at St. Catherine Hospital, Garden City, after suffering an apparent heart attack at the Lakin Gun Club.
Mr. Coy was on the line shooting in a registered match when he collapsed.
Born March 26, 1900, in Kansas, he had lived on a farm north of Deerfield since 1925.
He is survived by a brother, Donald K., Dodge City. Another brother, Clell, died in November of 1969.
Funeral services were held Wednesday morning at the Garnand Funeral Chapel in Garden City, with the Rev. Frank Garcia officiating.   Burial was in Deerfield Cemetery.

COY, MAGGIE LEOTA - (Lt. 3, Blk. 57, Sec. 2) Mrs. Maggie Leota Coy, Deerfield, died at her home, August 10, 1964, following a long illness. She was born March 19, 1895, at Sunnydale and had been a resident of Kearny County since 1907.
Mrs. Coy is a member of the Deerfield Methodist Church and Order of the Eastern Star No. 437.
She was married to C. C. Coy, Sept. 10, 1946, at Wichita.
Survivors include the widower; one son, Cecil A. Kerston, Akron, Ohio; three brothers, L. M. Smith, Orange, Calif., Ira Smith of Scott City and Orval Smith of Deerfield; and two grandchildren.
Funeral was held in the Deerfield Methodist Church with the Rev. Wesley Davis officiating.   Burial in the Deerfield Cemetery.   Phillips-White Funeral Home in charge of arrangements.

CRUZ, ALFONSO G. - (Lt. 3, Blk. 109, Sec. 1) Funeral for Alfonso G. Cruz, 86, was held at St. Mary Catholic Church, the Rev. Alan Hartway officiating.   Burial at Deerfield Cemetery.   He died Thursday, May 28, 1987, at Terrace Garden Care Center, where he had lived for the past year and a half.
Born Aug. 2, 1900, at Leon, Mexico, he married Shirley Ortega, March 14, 1943, at Deerfield.
Mr. Cruz came from Mexico in 1920.   He was a laborer, retiring in 1966.   He was a member of Christ the King Catholic Church, Deerfield.   His hobby was carpentry.

DEERFIELD CEMETERY

Survivors include his wife, Shirley, Deerfield, of the home; two sons, Angel, Deerfield, of the home, and Michael Cruz, 1309 A St., Garden City; three daughters, Veronica Garcia, 2610 Carriage Lane, Garden City, Alice Urteaga, Jr., 2109 Arapahoe, Garden City, and Maryann Nau, Spearville; 10 grandchildren; and one great granddaughter.

DEERFIELD CEMETERY

DEARMOND, ELMER ROY - (Lt. 1, Blk. 58, Sec. 2) (Funeral
Records) Died Nov. 10, 1918, age 33 yrs., 11 mos., 2
days, father, Edwin DeArmond, mother, Sara C. Prebble.
Died of pneumonia. Christian Minister from Garden City.
(The Kearny County Advocate, Nov. 15, 1918) Elmer R.
DeArmond, who has been a resident of Deerfield for the
past six years, suffered an attack of influenza, when
pneumonia was contracted, and he died at the home of his
father-in-law, Franz Faldtz, Sunday last, aged
thirty-three years. He had been married only one short
week, and his wife has the heart felt sympathy of the
entire community in her deep affliction.
(The Kearny County Advocate, Nov. 22, 1918) Elmer Roy
De Armond was born December 8th, 1884, near Tyro, Kansas,
and died Novebmber 10th, 1918, at Deerfield, Kansas,
after a brief illness of pneumonia brought on by an
attack of influenza.
He grew to manhood near Caney, Kansas, and then went to
Independence, Kansas, and worked for a time. Later
living at Larned and Scott City before coming to
Deerfield where he has lived for a number of years. He
was a member of the I.O.O.F. Lodge at Independence,
Kansas.
At the age of nineteen years he united with the
Christian Church. He had received his call to report for
the army on November 14, but God in his Almighty wisdom
called him home before his time to report to the army.
He was loved and respected by all who knew him and by his
death the community loses one of its ablest and most
respected citizens and was always loyal to all who knew
him. He was married to Dollie Faldtz on November 2nd,
1918. He leaves to mourn his loss, his wife, mother,
father, two brothers, and three sisters. Two brothers
having passed away before him.

DOWNING, AMOS ROBERTSON - (Lt. 1, Blk. 48, Sec. 2) Born
Mar. 15, 1850, in Illinois, came to Kearny County 1885,
died Aug. 23, 1934.
(The Kearny County Advocate, Aug. 31, 1934) Amos
Robertson Downing died at the home of his
daughter-in-law, Mrs. O. J. Downing, in Deerfield,
Thursday, August 23, 1934. Mr. Downing had been bedfast
for the past fourteen years with paralysis. For many
years he was one of the leading farmers in the Amazon
ditch territory, where he settled with numerous others
from Crown Point, Illinois, in 1886. He leaves a wife;

53

two sons, W. E. Downing, of Deerfield and C. O. Downing, of Topeka; and a daughter, Mrs. Harrison McAfee, of Deerfield; and other relatives and friends to mourn his demise. Funeral services were held Sunday at the Methodist Church in Deerfield, conducted by Rev. Turner, after which the Masons took charge, and he was laid to rest for his last long sleep in the Deerfield Cemetery.

DOWNING, CLARENCE O. — (Lt. 1, Blk. 48, Sec. 2) Clarence Oliver Downing, 90, Garden City, died Monday, Sept. 13, 1965, at St. Catherine Hospital, Garden City, after a six month illness. He was born Dec. 17, 1874, at Golden, Ill., son of Amos R. and Mary M. (Oliver) Downing. Came to Kearny County in 1886 with his parents. He lived in Deerfield for 40 years. He had been a resident of Garden City for 30 years.

Retired, he formerly had been engaged in business and real estate. He was a member of the Methodist Church.

Survivors include four nephews, Oscar, Maurice and Madison, all of Deerfield, and Lucien of Garden City; three nieces, Mrs. Christabelle Maddux of Deerfield, Mrs. LeRoyce Grosjean, Scott City and Mrs. Luella Henning, Ottawa.

Funeral was held at the Deerfield Methodist Church with the Rev. Wesley Davis officiating. Burial was in the Deerfield Cemetery.

DOWNING, E. ALLENE — (Lt. 3, Blk. 19, Sec. 3) Memorial service for Allene Downing, Deerfield, was held at Deerfield United Methodist Church, the Rev. Nellie Holmes officiating. Private family committal service was at the Deerfield Cemetery. She died April 12, 1989, at Corondolet Manor, Kansas City, Mo.

Born Allene Bolin, May 30, 1909, at Maryville, Mo., she married Maurice Downing, May 19, 1940, at Deerfield. He died June 22, 1971.

Mrs. Downing was a school teacher for all eight grades in a rural school near Maryville, Mo., and for first and second grade at Deerfield from 1931 to 1947. She and her husband owned and managed the Santa Fe Motor Company. She had been a Deerfield resident since the fall of 1931, when she moved from Maryville.

She was a member of the Deerfield United Methodist Church, where she taught Sunday School classes and was the church pianist for several years. She was a charter member of Deerfield Woman's Society of Christian Service, and den mother for the Deerfield Cub Scouts. She was an active member of Chapter FF of PEO, Garden City, since 1953 and held offices including presidency. She became a member of the Beta chapter of Delta Kappa Gamma in 1946 and served on committees, holding several offices.

She graduated from Maryville High School in 1926 and attended Northwest Missouri State Teachers College, Kansas City Teacher's College and the University of Kansas.

Survivors include a son, Rhett, Deerfield; a sister, Helen Bolin, Kansas City; and two granddaughters. She was preceded in death by a brother.

DOWNING, EDGAR MAURICE - (Lt. 3, Blk. 19, Sec. 3)   E. Maurice Downing, 61, Deerfield, died Tuesday morning, June 22, 1971, in St. Catherine Hospital, Garden City, after a short illness.

A lifetime resident of Deerfield, Mr. Downing was owner of Santa Fe Motors, Deerfield. He was born, Dec. 2, 1909, in Deerfield, son of William Edgar and Flora May (Kell) Downing, and he married Emma Allene Bolin, May 19, 1940, in Deerfield.

He was a member of the Deerfield United Methodist Church and the Deerfield Lions Club, and many other civic organizations. He had served on the Deerfield city council. Mr. Downing and his Santa Fe Motors were ardent supporters of many community and county projects.

He is survived by the widow; a son, Rhett Alan, 2004 N. 6th, Garden City; brother, Lucien, 204 N. 7th, Garden City; two sisters, Mrs. C. W. Henning, Ottawa, and Mrs. Joe Gibson, Globe, Ariz.; and a grandson.

Funeral was held at the church with Rev. Charles Hadley officiating. Burial in the Deerfield Cemetery.

DOWNING, FLORA MAY - (Lt. 1, Blk. 48, Sec. 2) Flora May Kell was born May 10, 1881, at Pierce City, Mo., came to Kearny County with parents in 1884. Married William Edgar Downing. Died April 5, 1959, at Garden City, Ks.

Funeral services were held Tuesday afternoon at 2 p.m. at the Deerfield Methodist Church for Mrs. Flora May Downing, 77, of Garden City. Burial was in Deerfield Cemetery.

Mrs. Downing was a pioneer resident of the Deerfield area and was the mother of Maurice Downing, Deerfield businessman.

She had been ill for the past year and hospitalized since January 1.

Mrs. Downing was born May 10, 1881, and moved to Finney County in 1886, on a homestead north of Deerfield. She had lived in Garden City the past three years.

Survivors include the husband, William E., of the home; two sons, Lucien, Garden City, and Maurice, Deerfield; one daughter, Mrs. C. W. Henning, Ottawa; two brothers, A. S. Kell and Ed Kell, both of California; four sisters, Mrs. Cliff Witt, Hays, Mrs. J. W. Sower, Bayfield, Colo., Mrs. Carl Porter, Bartlesville, Okla., and Mrs. Frank Robinson, California; and six grandchildren.

DOWNING, MARY M. - (Lt. 1, Blk. 48, Sec. 2) Born May 15, 1850, in Kentucky and died Nov. 6, 1916, at Garden City, Ks., of accidental burns. Services were conducted by Garnand's. Daughter of William and Zerelda (McClarey) Oliver. Wife of Amos Robertson Downing, married Sept. 23, 1873.

(Lakin Independent, Nov. 10, 1916) E. E. Oliver, proprietor of Olivers Rest Room, Monday evening received the sad news that his sister, Mrs. A. R. Downing, who was so horribly burned about two weeks ago while building a fire in the kitchen stove, had died. The funeral was held Wednesday from her late home with interment at Deerfield.

DOWNING, MICHAEL E. - (Lt. 1, Blk. 61, Sec. 3) Citizens of Deerfield and this county were stunned late Saturday, January 5, 1952, to learn of the death of two of the community's popular young men in an automobile accident in California where the pair were vacationing.

Michael Eugene Downing, 20, was instantly killed and Raymond R. Douglas, was fatally injured Saturday when their car struck a sand truck loaded with 17 yards of sand. The crash occurred at a highway intersection about five miles from Brawley.

Mike was driving the car and was killed instantly. Ray was taken to a hospital in the California town where he died a few hours later. The driver of the truck, Frank F. Baker, of El Centro, California, was not injured.

Downing and Douglas were returning to Deerfield after an extended trip through the western part of the United States and Canada.

The trip has taken the two men to Nampa, Idaho, for the wedding of a friend, Norman Sowards. From there, they visited in Canada and then drove down the west coast to San Francisco where they visited Robert Novotny in Letterman General Hospital.

At Los Angeles, they visited Downing's uncle, Robert Meadows, and attended the Rose Parade and other events in that area during the New Year's holiday. They were returning home by way of Yuma, Arizona.

The time of the accident was not definitely set, but was believed to have occurred sometime before 5 p.m. central time.

Officers reported that Downing skidded 60 feet attempting to avoid hitting the truck, but was unsuccessful.

Douglas was the manager of the alfalfa dehydrating plant at Deerfield. He lived in Neodesha and his body is being returned there for burial.

Mike Downing was born September 6, 1931, at Deerfield. He was graduated from Deerfield High School in May of 1949 and since that time, he has been farming with his father about three miles northeast of Deerfield. He is survived by his mother and father, Mr. and Mrs. Oscar J. Downing, Deerfield; two sisters, Rebecca, who is attending nurse's training at Wesley Hospital in Wichita, and Mrs. Venita Beth Hickman of Dighton; his maternal grandmother, Mrs. Charles Meadows of Deerfield; his paternal grandmother, Mrs. Bruce Parker of Denver, Colorado; and several uncles, aunts, and cousins.

Funeral services were held Friday, Jan. 11, 1952, at 2:30 o'clock, at the Deerfield High School auditorium. Burial in the Deerfield Cemetery.

DOWNING, MURIEL - (Lt. 4, Blk. 55, Sec. 2) (The Kearny County Advocate, June 14, 1918) Lula Muriel, daughter of Oscar J. and Myrtle B. Downing, passed out of this life, May 31st, 1918. Aged eight years, nine months and nine days. Jesus said: "Suffer little children to come unto me", and little Muriel went, after only a few days severe illness, caused by Diphtheria. Born Aug. 22, 1910.
We said:
"Hence forward, we will only think of her,
As one too good for selfish tears to stir
A saint, who touched and blessed us and then passed on;
Our Angel, ever more, to bend and take
Our broken prayer to God, for loves dear sake."

DEERFIELD CEMETERY

DOWNING, OSCAR J. - (Lt. 4, Blk. 55, Sec. 2) (The Lakin Independent, Sept. 23, 1932) This county lost a pioneer settler and substantial citizen in the death of Oscar J. Downing of the Deerfield neighborhood. He had been in poor health for some time and recently was taken to Garden City, where he passed away Saturday, September 17th, 1932, at the home of his aunt, Miss Ada Oliver.

Funeral services were held in Deerfield, Monday afternoon in the Methodist Church. Rev. Nicholson of Turon assisted the pastor and gave the funeral discourse. Mr. Nicholson was a former pastor and a very close friend of the deceased. Interment was made in the Deerfield Cemetery, where the Masons conducted the burial service at the grave.

Mr. Downing was a valuable and esteemed citizen, a successful farmer, true to himself, his family, his neighbors, and his friends. He was active in public affairs, served as county commissioner, and could always be counted upon to support any measures for the betterment of the community.

Oscar Julian Downing was born at Camp Point, Illinois, January 20, 1877, died at Garden City, September 17, 1932, age 55 years, 7 months and 27 days.

He came to Deerfield, Kansas, with his father and mother and their family in 1886 and made his home in Deerfield since that time.

On September 19, 1900, he was married to Myrtle B. Tedford, who survives to mourn the loss of husband and companion. To this union five children were born: Christabelle Maddux of Holcomb, Kansas; Oscar J. Downing Jr., Madison T. Downing, and LeRoyce Downing, of Deerfield, Kansas. One little daughter, Lula Muriel, preceded her father in death, thirteen years ago. Two granddaughters and one grandson brought cheer and happiness into his home life. Of the close relatives left to mourn his passing are his aged father, A. R. Downing; two brothers, W. E. and C. O. Downing; one sister, Mrs. Harrison McAfee; four nephews, Lucien and Maurice Downing, Vern and Wayne McAfee; one niece, Mrs. Luella Downing Henning; and his aunt, Miss Ada Oliver of Garden City, Kansas

He was a faithful member of the Masonic order and the Order of the Eastern Star and was Master of the Deerfield lodge at the time of his death. In early manhood he was converted and joined the Methodist Church in his home

DEERFIELD CEMETERY

town and lived his Christian life in his quiet, unassuming way.

He was ready and willing to go, for life had been wearisome the past few months.

Rev. E. L. Nicholson, a personal friend and former pastor, and his own pastor and friend, Rev. Roy Corrie, conducted the funeral service. He was laid to rest in the Deerfield Cemetery, the services there conducted by his brothers of the Masonic order.

He will be sadly missed by his family and friends, but we will try to remember,
> "There is no death,
> What seems so is transition.
> This life of mortal breath
> Is but the suburb of the life Elysian,
> Whose portals we call death."

DOWNING, OSCAR J., JR. - (Lt. 1, Blk. 61, Sec. 3) Oscar J. Downing, 68, Deerfield, died Saturday, Jan. 19, 1974, at St. Catherine Hospital, Garden City, after a long illness.

Born March 21, 1905, at Deerfield, he married Ruth Ina Meadows, January 15, 1927, at Cimarron. He was a retired farmer and lifetime resident here.

Mr. Downing was a member of the Deerfield United Methodist Church, and Lions Club.

Survivors include the widow; two daughters, Mrs. Venita Hickman, Sublette, and Mrs. Rebecca Nugent, Paradise, Calif.; a brother, Madison, Lakin; two sisters, Mrs. Christabelle Maddux, Deerfield, and Mrs. Royce Grosjean, Scott City; seven grandchildren and one great grandchild. A son, Michael, preceded him in death in 1952.

Funeral was held at the Deerfield United Methodist Church, the Rev. Norman Heironimus officiating. Burial in Deerfield Cemetery.

DOWNING, RUTH M. - (Lt. 1, Blk. 61, Sec. 3) Memorial service for Ruth M. Downing was held at High Plains Retirement Village, Lakin, with the Rev. Donald Koehn officiating. Inurnment at Deerfield Cemetery. Mrs. Downing died Dec. 30, 1995, at the Kearny County Hospital in Lakin.

She was born Nov. 21, 1904, at Sharon Springs, the daughter of Charley and Edna Eugenie Burris Meadows.

A homemaker, she had been a Lakin resident since 1993, moving from Deerfield. She was a member of United

DEERFIELD CEMETERY

Methodist Church and United Methodist Women, both at Deerfield.

On Jan. 15, 1927, she married Oscar J. Downing Jr. at Cimarron. He died Jan. 19, 1974, at Garden City.

She was also preceded in death by a son, two brothers, two sisters and a great granddaughter.

Survivors are two daughters, Venita Beth Hickman, Kansas and Rebecca Muriel Nugent, California; seven grandchildren; 16 great grandchildren; and three great great grandchildren.

DOWNING, WILLIAM EDGAR - (Lt. 1, Blk. 48, Sec. 2) William Edgar Downing, 85, formerly of Deerfield and Garden City, died March 21, 1965, in Ottawa, following a lingering illness.

A retired farmer, Mr. Downing was born May 7, 1879, at Golden, Ill.

He moved to Kearny County from Golden in 1886 and to Garden City in 1952. In July 1964, he moved to Ottawa.

Mr. Downing was a member of the First Methodist Church of Deerfield and a past member of the Pioneer Grange.

On June 16, 1904, he married Flora May Kell at Deerfield. She preceded him in death on April 5, 1959. A brother and sister also preceded him in death.

Surviving are two sons, Lucien Downing of Garden City and Maurice Downing of Deerfield; two daughters, Mrs. Luella Henning, Ottawa, and Mrs. Marie Gibson, Globe, Ariz.; a brother, Clarence Downing of Garden City; seven grandchildren and five great grandchildren.

Funeral was held in Deerfield Methodist Church, the Rev. Wesley H. Davis and the Rev. E. P. Rogers officiating. Burial was in the Deerfield Cemetery.

DOYLE, CLARENCE - (Lt. 2, Blk. 80, Sec. 1) Clarence H. Doyle, 58 year old resident of the Windsor Hotel at Garden City, was found dead in his hotel room Saturday night, July 29, 1950. Death was apparently due to a sudden heart attack.

Doyle was born October 23, 1891, at Martinsville, Virginia. He came to Deerfield in 1913, where he started farming. In 1914 he married Pearl Towles. He farmed until 1921 when he went to work for Swift & Co. In 1929 he moved to Garden City and entered the implement business. He went to Syracuse in 1932 and set up his business there, continuing in operation until 1940.

DEERFIELD CEMETERY

Doyle spent six years as a civilian worker with a naval construction unit in Hawaii. For the past few years he has lived in Syracuse, Deerfield and Garden City. He was a member of the Methodist Church.

He is survived by his mother, Mrs. W. L. Mullins of Deerfield; one son, Clarence Jr., of Osborne; two daughters, Margaret Thompson of Indianapolis, Indiana, and Evelyn Lingo of Denver, Colorado; six brothers, James and Warner of Lakin, Robert of Pasadena, California, Raymond of Bristol, Colorado, Harry of Montevideo, Uruguay, S.A., and Russell of Buenos Aires, Argentina, S.A.; two sisters, Mrs. R. W. Pennekamp of Topeka and Mrs. W. S. Morrison of Abilene, Kansas; and one grandchild.

Funeral services were held at the Deerfield Methodist Church. The Rev. W. Hawes officiated at the service. Burial was in the Deerfield Cemetery.

DOYLE, THOMAS HERMAN - (Lt. 2, Blk. 80, Sec. 1) Thomas Hermond Doyle, son of Mrs. Ella Doyle Mullins, died June 8, 1947, after an extended illness. He was born July 20, 1898, in Martinsville, Virginia. He moved to Kansas with his mother, brothers and sisters, his father having passed away in 1910. He returned to Virginia a year later and remained in the Eastern states until 1940. The past six years he has been in business on the West coast.

He is survived by his mother, Mrs. Ella Mullins, and his step-father, W. L. Mullins; two daughters, Miss Vernon Doyle, Washington, D.C., and Mrs. Arthur Feil, Orange, Tex.; two sisters, Mrs. W. S. Morrison, Abilene, and Mrs. R. W. Pennekamp, Topeka; seven brothers, Warner H. Doyle and James H. Doyle, Lakin, Harry W. Doyle, Montevideo, Uruguay, Clarence H. Doyle, Honolulu, Hawaii, Raymond Doyle, Bristol, Colorado, Russell G. Doyle, Buenos Aires, Argentina, and Robert E. Doyle, San Francisco, California.

DOYLE, WARNER H. - (Lt. 2, Blk. 80, Sec. 1) Funeral services for Warner Howard Doyle, 76, were held at the Deerfield Methodist Church, the Rev. Bob Fleenor officiating. Mr. Doyle, a resident of Kearny County for 52 years, died Saturday, June 15, 1963, at a Topeka hospital following a long illness. He was a retired farmer.

He was born Sept. 14, 1887, in Martinsville, Va. He was a member of the Deerfield Methodist Church.

DEERFIELD CEMETERY

Surviving are his mother, Mrs. W. L. Mullins, Topeka; a
son, Howard, Fowler, Colo.; five brothers, Harry,
Phoenix, Ariz., J. H., Lakin, R. H., Bristol, Colo.,
Russell, Argentina, S.A., R. E., Los Angeles, Calif.; two
sisters, Mrs. Mary Pennekamp, Topeka, Mrs. Bess Jacobs,
Topeka; and three grandchildren.
Burial was in the Deerfield Cemetery.

DROVO, AMADA - (Lt. 2 in NW/c of cemetery) Oct. 1909.

DUNAVANT, J. K. - (S/2 Lt. 1, Blk. 18, Sec. 3) J. K.
Dunavant, 71, died Thursday, November 12, 1981, at Wesley
Medical Center, Wichita.
    Born December 21, 1909, at Vernon, Texas, Mr. Dunavant
married Vivian Bowers, December 15, 1934, at Clovis, NM.
    He had lived in Finney County for 47 years before
moving to Deerfield six years ago. He was employed at
Western Alfalfa.
    Survivors include his wife, of the home; a daughter,
Mrs. Garold (Linda) Farr, Lakin; a brother, Henry
Dunavant, Orange, Calif.; three sisters, Mrs. Ruby Boren,
Corpus Christi, Texas, Mrs. Lillie Tinney, Odessa, Texas,
and Mrs. Edna Reed, Fort Worth, Texas; and three
grandchildren.
    Funeral was held at Garnand Funeral Chapel in Garden
City, the Rev. Calvin Hartman of the First United
Methodist Church officiating. Burial was in Deerfield
Cemetery.

DUNCAN, HURLEY M. - (Lt. 1, Blk. 43, Sec. 3) Hurley
Marshall Duncan, son of John and Lura Duncan was born
near Brownell, Kansas, March 8, 1907, and departed this
life at St. Catherine Hospital, Garden City, Kansas, Nov.
9, 1966, at the age of 59 years, 8 months, 1 day. He had
been in ill health the last ten years. His mother
preceeded him in death Oct. 4, 1966.
    Mr. Duncan grew to manhood in the Ransom community and
attended Ransom High School.
    August 4, 1932, he was united in marriage with Miss
Lorene Ummel of Arnold, Kansas. They moved to the
Deerfield community in 1937. He was Canal Superintendent
for the Great Eastern, in that capacity he became a
congenial friend to all who knew him. He was a
considerate and sympathetic husband and father.
    He united with the Deerfield Methodist Church in 1941.

DEERFIELD CEMETERY

He is survived by his widow, Lorene; his three daughters and their husbands, Mrs. Ralph Claar, (Twila), Deerfield, Kansas, Mrs. Joe Pilla (Joyce), Gary, Indiana and Mrs. Richard Irwin (Elaine), Loveland, Colorado; ten grandchildren; two brothers, Carl of Arkansas, Lawrence of Washington; five sisters, Mrs. Nellie Petty, Sharon Springs, Kansas, Mrs. Fern Sonnenberg of Ransom, Kansas, Mrs. Stella Stieben, Mrs. Ola and Mrs. Lola Stierman of Denver; many relatives and friends.

DUNCAN, LORENE - (Lt. 1, Blk. 43, Sec. 3) Funeral for Lorene Duncan, 82, Deerfield, was held Friday, March 24, at the United Methodist Church in Deerfield. The Rev. Nellie L. Holmes officiating. Burial at Deerfield Cemetery. She died March 21, 1989, at St. Catherine Hospital, Garden City, after a long illness.

Born June 8, 1906, at Arnold, Kansas, she married Hurley Duncan, August 4, 1932, at Ness City, Kansas. He died November 9, 1966.

She was a member of the Deerfield United Methodist Church.

Survivors include three daughters: Twila Claar of Deerfield, Joyce Pilla of Portage, Indiana and Elaine Irwin of Loveland, Colorado; twelve grandchildren and twelve great grandchildren.

DYER, DENZEL C. - (Lt. 3, Blk. 67, Sec. 4) Funeral for Denzel C. Dyer, 65, was held at the Deerfield United Methodist Church, the Rev. Nellie Holmes officiating. Burial at Deerfield Cemetery.

He died Monday, January 5, 1987, at the Kearny County Hospital, Lakin.

Born May 15, 1921, at Beaver City, Neb., to Charles and Louise Dyer, he married Ann Heaton, January 19, 1946, at Colby.

Mr. Dyer was well known in Southwest Kansas, traveling the area for many years as a welder and farm repairman. He had been a Deerfield resident since 1954 and was a member of the Christian Church, Atwood. He was a veteran of World War II and a member of VFW Post 2279, Garden City.

Surviving are his wife, of the home; three sons, Michael Frank, Claremore, Okla., and William Denzel and Charles Clyde, both of Deerfield; and five grandchildren.

ECK, ANDREW J. - (Pottersfield) One of 2 children of
Jacob P. and Nettie Eck. Andrew was born July 31, 1908,
and died June 30, 1909.

ECK, LAVENA - (Pottersfield) One of 2 children of Jacob
P. and Nettie Eck. Lavena was born March 23, 1910, and
died Sept. 1910.

ELLIOTT, DASHA LAREE - (Lt. 2, Blk. 101, Sec. 1) Dasha
Laree Elliott, infant daughter of former Deerfield
residents, Mr. and Mrs. Richard Elliott, died Sunday,
November 12, 1978, shortly after birth at Memorial
Hospital, Shattuck, Okla.
   Survivors include her parents, Woodward; a brother,
Jeremy; and sisters, Jody and Shawn, all of the home;
grandparents, Mr. and Mrs. Carl F. Lorenzen, Olathe,
Colo., and Mr. and Mrs. Melvin Elliott, Deerfield; and a
great grandmother, Mrs. Clara Lorenzen, Coeur d'Alene,
Idaho.
   Funeral was at 2 p.m., Thursday, November 16, at the
Garnand Funeral Chapel, Garden City, the Rev. Frank
Crotts officiating. Burial in Deerfield Cemetery.

ELLIOTT, LELAND "LEE" - (N/2 Lt. 2, Blk. 42, Sec. 3)
Leland "Lee" Elliott, died July 14, 1995, at the Kearny
County Hospital, Lakin. He was born July 30, 1914, at
Menno Community in Kearny County to Carrie Coghill and
Lawrence Elliott.
   A lifetime resident of Kearny County, he was a retired
farmer. He attended Kearny County schools and married
Anna Grauberger on June 9, 1936, in Syracuse. In 1943
they moved to a farm north of Deerfield.
   In 1975, they moved to Deerfield where they have lived
since. Mr. Elliott was preceded in death by his parents,
five brothers and three sisters. He enjoyed hunting,
trap shooting, traveling and music.
   He was a member of Immanuel Lutheran Church, Lakin, the
Lakin Gun Club; a past board member of the Pioneer
Telephone Company for 26 years; and a past board member
of the Kearny County Hospital for 14 years.
   Survivors include his wife of the home and many nieces
and nephews.
   Funeral service was at Immanuel Lutheran Church in
Lakin with Pastor Vernon E. Oestmann presiding. Garnand
Funeral Home, Lakin, was in charge of arrangements.

ELLIOTT, THOMAS MELVIN - (Lt. 2, Blk. 100, Sec. 1)
Funeral for Thomas Melvin Elliott, 77, Deerfield was
Tuesday, April 27, at Garnand Funeral Chapel, Garden
City, with Frank Garcia officiating. Burial was in
Deerfield Cemetery.
   Mr. Elliott died, Saturday, April 24, 1982, at Briar
Hill Manor in Garden City. A rancher, he was also an
employee of Kansas-Nebraska Gas Co., retiring in 1969.
   Born September 17, 1904, in Peoria, Okla., he came with
his parents to homestead in Kearny County in 1910. He
married Doris Hetherington, February 13, 1930, in Lamar,
Colo.
   He was associated with Jehovah's Witnesses.
   Survivors are his wife, of the home; two sons, Neil
Elliott, Deerfield and Richard Elliott, Tyler, Texas; a
daughter, Dixie Marta, Grand Junction, Colo.; two
brothers, Henry Elliott, Montrose, Colo., and Leland
Elliott, Deerfield; a sister, Bertha Weldon, Dallas,
Texas; several grandchildren and great grandchildren.

ENOCHS, LOUISE - (N/2 Lt. 4, Blk, 19, Sec. 3) Louise
Enochs, 80, former Kearny County resident, died September
22, 1988, at Prather Methodist Convalescent Home,
Alameda, Calif.
   Born Louise Miller on Sept. 4, 1908, near Lakin she
married Joe Enochs. He died in February 1988. A retired
clerk at a clothing store, Mrs. Enochs had been a
resident of Seattle for the past 30 years. She was a
member of the Eagles Auxiliary, Seattle.
   Survivors are two daughters, Doris Zubeck, Deerfield,
and Juanita Petersen, Oakland, Calif.; two brothers, Ted
Miller, Garden City and Albert Miller, Wrens, Ga.; six
grandchildren and five great grandchildren.
   Funeral was held Saturday at the United Methodist
Church, Deerfield, with the Rev. Nellie Holmes
officiating. Burial was in Deerfield Cemetery.

EPPERS, BERTHA - (Lt. 3, Blk. 49, Sec. 2) (Lakin
Investigator, Sept. 3, 1909, Deerfield News) Mr. and
Mrs. Fred Eppers buried their infant child, on Monday.
   (Kearny County Vital Records) Bertha M. Eppers born
Feb. 15, 1908, in East Hibbard Township and died April 3,
1908.
   (Kearny County Advocate, Jan. 6, 1910) The Eppers
loaded a car the latter part of last week for Neosho Co.,
their former home.

DEERFIELD CEMETERY

EPPS, NEVA ONITA - (Unknown, probably Lt. 4, Blk. 56, Sec. 2) Neva Onita Epps was born Sept 26, 1920, at Holcomb, Sherlock Township, in Finney County to Luther Hubert and Ethel Mary Shindler Epps. She died Sept 28, 1920.

ERWIN, CORA - (Lt. 4, Blk. 74, Sec. 1) Cora Steenis Erwin was born June 11, 1902, at Creston, Platte County, Nebraska to Dennis and Katie Steenis. She moved with her family to Hartford, Lyons County, Kansas, in 1906, and moved to Deerfield, Kearny County, Kansas, in 1911. She died April 6, 1928, at Rewert's Hospital, Garden City, Kansas.
She died of septicemia. Wiley was the undertaker.
(The Lakin Independent, April 13, 1928) Cora Maye Steenis was born at Creston, Nebraska, June 11, 1902. Died at Garden City, April 6, 1928. Age 25 years, 9 months and 26 days.
She came to Kansas with her parents at the age of 3 years. She came with the family to Deerfield in 1911, which was her home except for a few months of happy married life spent at Garden City.
She graduated from the Deerfield High School in the class of 1920. After attending the Teachers' College at Emporia she devoted her time to teaching school.
She was married to Ralph Erwin, September 2, 1926. To this union one son was born.
She leaves to mourn: her husband and infant son, Don Alton, 5 months old; her parents, Mr. and Mrs. D. A. Steenis; three brothers, J. J. Steenis and R. J. Steenis of Deerfield, and H. H. Steenis of Hartford, Kansas; one sister, Mrs. Glenn Steward of Deerfield; six nieces and one nephew; other relatives and a host of friends.
The funeral was conducted by B. E. Willoughby from the M. E. Church at Deerfield, Sunday afternoon, April 8, and interment was made in Deerfield Cemetery.

ESCAMILLA, NATHEN LEIGH - (S/2 Lt. 2, Blk. 127, Sec. 1) dod 3/12/93.

ESKELUND, CHARLIE - (Lt. 1, Blk. 24, Sec. 4) Rosary for Charlie Eskelund, 71, a lifetime area resident, was held at 7 p.m. Friday, Nov. 1, at Garnand Funeral Home. Funeral Mass was at 12:30 p.m. Saturday, Nov. 2, at St. Mary Catholic Church. Burial at Deerfield Cemetery, with

DEERFIELD CEMETERY

military graveside rites conducted by Garden City Area Veterans. Mr. Eskelund, of 1831 Koster, Garden City, died Tuesday, Oct. 29, 1996, at St. Catherine Hospital.

He was born Dec. 28, 1924, at Holcomb, the son of Foster and Gladys Reigle Eskelund. He attended Deerfield High School, graduating in 1942. After serving in the U.S. Navy during World War II, he returned to Deerfield and farmed north of there.

Mr. Eskelund was a member of St. Mary Catholic Church, American Legion Harry H. Renick Post #9, fourth degree Knights of Columbus #2795, High Plains Bassmasters and various other organizations. He enjoyed fishing, camping, traveling and country music.

On Feb. 10, 1959, he married Jeanne Patterson at Garden City. She survives. He is also survived by two daughters, Charlotte Elliott, Garden City, and Pamela Lang, Liberty, Mo.; a brother, Dick Eskelund, Deerfield; a sister, Ardis Cole, Deerfield; eight grandchildren; six great grandchildren; three nieces; and one nephew.

ESKELUND, ESTHER L. - (Lt. 1, Blk. 66, Sec. 4) Funeral services for Esther L. Eskelund, 86, was held at the United Methodist Church, Deerfield, the Rev. Donald Koehn officiating. Burial at Deerfield Cemetery. Greene-Schneider Funeral Home, Lakin was in charge of arrangements. She died June 14, 1990, at St. Catherine Hospital, Garden City.

Born Esther L. Elliott, October 22, 1903, at Preston, she married Foster Eskelund, May 22, 1943, at Hugoton. He died October 27, 1980.

Mrs. Eskelund was a retired teacher and had been a longtime Deerfield resident.

Survivors include two sons, Charles, Garden City, and Dick, Deerfield; a daughter, Ardis Cole, Garland, Ark.; six grandchildren; and seven great grandchildren.

ESKELUND, FOSTER - (Lt. 1, Blk. 66, Sec. 4) Foster Peterson Eskelund, 87, of Deerfield, died Monday, October 27, 1980, at St. Catherine Hospital, Garden City, of an apparent heart attack. A lifetime resident of Kearny County, he was a retired farmer and stockman.

Born Aug. 11, 1893, in a dugout at his parents homestead 20 miles north of Deerfield, he married Gladys G. Reigle at Holcomb, May 2, 1923. She died Feb. 22,

1933. He married Esther E. Potts, May 22, 1943, in Hugoton.

Mr. Eskelund attended Deerfield United Methodist Church, was a 4-H Club organizer and leader and a member of the Moose Lodge. He held a teacher's certificate and Washburn scholarship. He served 22 years on the East Hibbard Township board and 34 years on the Harmony Hill School board. He was a charter member and former president of Kearny County Historical Society and had devoted much of his time to record history of the area.

Survivors include his wife, Esther, of the home; two sons, Charles E. Eskelund, Garden City, and Dick Eskelund, Deerfield; daughter, Mrs. Tom (Ardis) Cole, Garland, Ark.; six grandchildren, and ten great grandchildren.

Funeral was Wednesday at 10:30 a.m. at Deerfield Methodist Church, the Rev. Harry Walz officiating. Burial in the Deerfield Cemetery.

ESKELUND, JEANNE M. - (Lt. 1, Blk. 24, Sec. 4) Rosary for Jeanne M. Eskelund, 75, of 1831 Koster, Garden City, was held at 7 p.m. Friday at Garnand Funeral Home. Funeral Mass was at 10 a.m. Saturday at St. Mary Catholic Church, with the Rev. Pascal Klein officiating. Private family burial will take place later.

Mrs. Eskleund, a longtime Garden City resident, died Wednesday, Jan. 15, 1997, at St. Catherine Hospital.

Born Nov. 2, 1921, at Garnett, to Charlie Henry and Minnie Marguerite Kriftewirth Patterson, she moved with her family to Ordway, Colo., in 1936. She attended schools in both Garnett and Ordway, graduating from Ordway High School in 1939. The family moved to Garden City in 1939.

Mrs. Eskelund was a bookkeeper for Kemper Electric for 11 years. She retired in 1962.

She was a member of St. Mary Catholic Church, and a former member of Daughters of Isabella and the women's division of the Garden City Chamber of Commerce. She enjoyed fishing, citizens band radios and guiding truck drivers on her CB, sewing, and watching squirrels in her yard.

She married Charlie Eskelund on Feb. 10, 1959, at Garden City. He died Oct. 29, 1996.

Survivors are two daughters, Charlotte Elliott, Garden City, and Pamela Lang, Liberty, Mo.; three brothers, John Patterson, Garden City, Robert Patterson, Cleveland,

Okla., and David Patterson, Russell; two sisters, Vera
Bullock, Ulysses, and Mary Patterson, Montrose, Colo.;
eight grandchildren; and six great grandchildren.
Her body was donated for medical research.

ESKELUND, MARJORIE - (Lt. 1, Blk. 91, Sec. 4) Marjorie
Eskelund, 51, died of cancer, Saturday, September 15,
1984, at St. Catherine Hospital, Garden City.
Born September 3, 1932, at Hays, she moved from there
to Lakin in 1934. She married Dick Eskelund, September
19, 1954, at Lakin and was a homemaker.
Mrs. Eskelund was a member of the Deerfield United
Methodist Church, United Methodist Women, We Care Group
of the church and served as church financial secretary.
She also was a member of Kearny County Historical Society
and Eagles Auxiliary.
Survivors are her husband, Dick, Deerfield; a son, Joe
Eskelund, Deerfield; a daughter, Debbie Berry, Garden
City; her mother, Helen Kysar, Lakin; a brother, Kenneth
Kysar, Lakin; two sisters, Dorothy Jenks, Lakin, and
Florence Boyd, Hurst, Texas; and two grandchildren. Her
father preceded her in death.
Funeral was held Monday at the Deerfield United
Methodist Church, the Rev. Nellie Holmes officiating.
Burial was at Deerfield Cemetery.

ESTRADO, PETRA R. - (Lt. 4, Blk. 100, Sec. 1) Born in
1857 and died in 1924.

EYMAN, ELMER ROY - (Lt. 4, Blk. 32, Sec. 2) Elmer Roy
Eyman, 77, Deerfield, died Monday evening, April 24,
1972, at Lakin Manor. He had been in ill health for
several years.
Born March 29, 1895, in Deerfield, he grew up in Lakin.
After World War I he returned to Deerfield and married
Harriet Knight on Aug. 23, 1922, at Gridley.
Eyman was a retired mail carrier. During World War I
he served in the U.S. Army Medical Corps. He was a
member of the Deerfield United Methodist Church and the
Emerald Masonic Lodge, Order of the Eastern Star, and the
American Legion, all in Lakin.
Survivors include the widow, Harriet, of the home; a
son, Don, Shawnee Mission; a daughter, Kathleen Ernst,
Bartlesville, Okla.; and five grandchildren.

DEERFIELD CEMETERY

Funeral services were held in the Deerfield United Methodist Church, the Rev. Charles Hadley officiating. Burial in the Deerfield Cemetery.

EYMAN, SARAH - (Lt. 4, Blk. 32, Sec. 2) (Kearny County Advocate, Aug. 2, 1912 and July 26, 1912)   Grandma Eyman, mother of the Eyman boys of this county, died at Deerfield last Thursday, July 25th, at the advanced age of 89 years, 10 months, six days. The funeral was held from the home of Jas. Eyman on Saturday, conducted by Rev. Robinson and remains interred in the Deerfield Cemetery. Mrs. Eyman has been visiting her sons, George and James, for quite a long time and has been in poor health for the last year.

Sarah Taylor and George Eyman were married December 3, 1846, and to this union were born six children, as follows: Elijah, James T., Daniel, Susan Jane, Augusta C. and Isaac George.

Three members of this family have now crossed to the great beyond, the first being Susan Jane Eyman, who passed away April 24, 1858; next was the husband and father, George Eyman, who died May 17, 1863; and the last to go is Sarah Eyman, the wife and mother.

She was born in Randolph County, Ill., September 19, 1822. She moved to St. Clair County, Ill., with her parents, when only five years old. She moved to Adams County, Illinois, in 1854. Her husband enlisted in the civil war and died in the service of his country in 1863. She moved to Kansas in 1886, and since that time she has been living alternately with her children in Kansas and Illinois, spending the last year with her son, James, in Deerfield. Several months ago she fell and fractured her hip, from which she never recovered. During the weary months she was confined to her bed, she suffered a great deal, yet she bore it all with Christian fortitude, only praying that she might be relieved and taken home to the better world when it was her Father's good pleasure and after much suffering she heard the summons and being perfectly prepared she ascended to be with her Lord, leaving behind her the evidence of a good citizen, a noble and affectionate mother, and the sweet fragrance of a noble Christian life. May her noble example inspire all to exemplify like traits of character and Christian fidelity. Sister Eyman was converted and united with the Baptist church early in life.

FALDTZ, ANNA - (Lt. 1, Blk. 57, Sec. 2) (The Lakin Independent, Jan. 20, 1916) Mrs. Anna Charlotte Faldtz died Monday, at the family home 5 miles east of Lakin at the ripe old age of 70 years, 8 months and 21 days. She was born at Skara, Sweden. She is survived by the husband and six children. The funeral was held at the house with interment in the Deerfield Cemetery. J. J. Nash had charge of the funeral arrangements. (Funeral Record) Faldtz, Mrs. F. died Jan 17, 1916, married, housewife, died of Brights disease, 68 years old. Born April 5, 1845.

FALDTZ, FRANS WILLIAM - (Lt. 1, Blk. 57, Sec. 2) (The Kearny County Advocate, Sept. 10, 1920) Frans William Faldtz was born in Gothenborg, Sweden, May 15, 1850, and died September 5, 1920. At the age of seventeen years he left Sweden and came to America. He lived in New York City and Cleveland, Ohio, for a number of years. Later he came to Kansas in the spring of 1885 and located on the same farm on which he was living at the time of his death, being one of the pioneer settlers of this locality.

He was married to Anna C. Jacobson in 1876, who preceded him in death, January 17, 1916. To this union were born six children, four daughters and two sons, all of whom are living. All being present but one son who lives in California.

He was confirmed in the Swedish Lutheran Church at the age of fifteen years. His serious illness lasted over a period of six weeks although his health has been failing for several months. He was very patient all through his sickness. He was conscientious in all his dealings and was a kind and loving father to the end.

Funeral services were held at the home, conducted by Rev. Nicholson and interment was made in the Deerfield Cemetery.

FALDTZ, LILLIE IDA - (Lt. 1, Blk. 57, Sec. 2) Born Feb. 16, 1882, at Cleveland, Ohio, daughter of Frans and Anna Faldtz, died April 21, 1964, at Garden City, Kansas.

(The Lakin Independent, Deerfield News, April 30, 1964) Friends extend their heartfelt sympathy to Mrs. Geo. Buell of Garden City in the loss of her sister, Miss Lillie Faldtz, of Garden City, who passed away last Tuesday. Mrs. Buell and Miss Faldtz grew up in this

DEERFIELD CEMETERY

community. Mr. and Mrs. Buell were residents of
Deerfield many years.
Lillie Faldtz, 81, retired practical nurse, died April
21, 1964, at her home following a lengthy illness. Born
Feb. 16, 1883, at Cleveland, Ohio, she moved with her
family to a farm west of Deerfield in 1885. She lived
the rest of her life in this area.
She was a member of the Community Church.
Survivors: sisters, Mrs. Hattie Buell, Garden City;
Mrs. Dollie Hall, Los Angeles, Calif.; brother, Egner
Faldtz, Los Angeles, Calif.
Funeral was at 2 p.m., Friday, Community Church; Rev.
Malcolm Bertram. Burial in Deerfield Cemetery.

FLORER, BERNECE V. - (Lt. 2, Blk. 41, Sec. 3) Funeral
for Bernece Viola Florer, 81, Westminster, Colorado, was
Tuesday, January 28, 1992, at Deerfield Methodist Church,
the Rev. Donald J. Koehn officiating. Burial was at the
Deerfield Cemetery.
She died January 24, 1992, at Westminster. Born
Bernece Watson, November 11, 1910, at Leroy, she married
William Florer, May 29, 1939, at Garden City. He died
July 31, 1989.
Mrs. Florer taught school for 31 years. She grew up in
Haven and graduated from Haven High School in 1928. She
attended Pittsburg State Teachers College. After
college, she taught school in Spearville, Holcomb, and
Deerfield, where she taught for 14 years. She moved to
Lakin where she lived for two years before moving to
Westminster in 1989.
She was a member of the Deerfield United Methodist
Church, a life member of the Kansas National Education
Association, and American Association of Retired Persons.
Survivors include a son, Steve Florer, York, Nebr.; a
daughter, Sue Berry, Westminster; and three
grandchildren. She was preceded in death by three
sisters and two brothers.

FLORER, HUBER D. - (Lt. 2, Blk. 41, Sec. 3) Born June 10,
1912, died July 2, 1987.

FLORER, WILLIAM D. - (Lt. 2, Blk. 41, Sec. 3) William
Florer, age 89, died November 14, 1973, and was cremated
at Fort Myers, Florida. He was the father of William F.
Florer. Born in 1884.

FLORER, WILLIAM F. - (Lt. 2, Blk. 41, Sec. 3) Funeral
service for William F. Florer was held at Deerfield
United Methodist Church, the Rev. Donald J. Koehn
officiating. Burial in Deerfield Cemetery. He died July
30, 1989, at the Kearny County Hospital, Lakin.
    Born December 20, 1909, at Holcomb, he married Bernece
Watson, May 29, 1939, at Garden City. He was a retired
district electrician for Wheatland Electric.
    A Deerfield resident since 1958, Mr. and Mrs. Florer
moved to a High Plains Retirement Village apartment a few
years ago.
    He was a member of Deerfield United Methodist Church,
lifetime member of the Veterans of Foreign Wars, Garden
City, and was a World War II U.S. Navy veteran.
    Survivors: wife, Bernece, of the home; a son, W.
Steve, York, Nebraska; a daughter, Virginia Sue Berry,
Westminster, Colorado; and three grandchildren.
    Garnand Funeral Home was in charge.

FRANCIS, WELBERNE RAY - (Lt. 1, Blk. 39, Sec. 3)
Welberne Ray Francis, 57, died Wednesday, March 28, 1973,
at his home after a heart attack. Born April 27, 1915,
at Celina, Tex., he married Delena Ogle, June 25, 1945,
at Pennington, N.M. He was a well tender for Colorado
Interstate Gas Co. and lived here since 1960.
    He was a veteran of World War II, serving with the U.S.
Army Air Force.
    Survivors include the widow; sons: William, Denver,
Colo., Ricky, Lamar, Colo., Donnie, Biloxi, Miss., Martin
and Tommie, of the home; daughter: Mackie, of the home.
    Funeral was held at the United Methodist Church,
Deerfield; Rev. Charles Hadley. Burial in Deerfield
Cemetery. Phillips-White Funeral Home in charge of
arrangements.

FREDERICK, BABY - (Lt. , Blk. 45, Sec. 3) Died in May
1954. Buried on 22nd.

FULTON, ESTER OLIVE - (Lt. 1, Blk. 70, Sec. 4) Funeral
for Ester Olive Fulton was held at Deerfield United
Methodist Church, the Rev. Donald J. Koehn officiating.
Burial was in Deerfield Cemetery. She died November 30,
1990, at Terrace Garden Care Center, Garden City.
    Born Ester Olive Meadows, March 13, 1903, in Wallace
County, she married Frederick Fulton, May 2, 1924, at
Garden City. He died May 9, 1972.

DEERFIELD CEMETERY

Mrs. Fulton was a retired country school teacher and had been a Deerfield resident since 1921, moving from Hanston.

She was a member of the Deerfield United Methodist Church, sang in the choir, was a Sunday school teacher, and held many offices in the United Methodist Women.

Survivors include a son, James S., Hays; two daughters, Mary Lois Smith, Liberal, and Faith Landon, Deerfield; a sister, Ruth M. Downing, Overbrook; 14 grandchildren; and 22 great grandchildren. She was preceded in death by a son, a daughter, two brothers, and a sister.

Price and Sons Funeral Home was in charge of arrangements.

FULTON, FREDERICK P. - (Lt. 1, Blk. 70, Sec. 4)
Frederick P. Fulton, 70, Deerfield, died May 9, 1972, at St. Catherine Hospital, Garden City, after a long illness. He was a retired farmer and had been a Kearny County resident since 1923.

Born Oct. 27, 1901, in Pawnee County, he married Ester Olive Meadows, May 2, 1924, at Garden City. He attended the Methodist Church.

Survivors include the widow; two sons, Robert, Deerfield, and James, Springfield, Mo.; three daughters, Mrs. Mary Lois Smith, Liberal, Mrs. Jean Sutton, Aurora, Colo, and Mrs. Faith Landon, Deerfield; a brother, James Fulton, Antonito, Colo.; a sister, Mrs. Ida Bauer, California; and 14 grandchildren.

Funeral was at the Deerfield United Methodist Church, the Rev. Charles Hadley officiating. Burial in Deerfield Cemetery. Phillips-White Funeral Home in charge of arrangements.

FULTON, ROBERT FREDERICK - (Lt. 4, Blk. 70, Sec. 4)
Robert Frederick Fulton, 46, died February 13, 1975, at St. Catherine Hospital, Garden City, of cancer.

Born July 4, 1928, at Garden City, he married Viola Jean Meairs, Aug. 22, 1950, at Sublette. He was a lifetime resident of the Deerfield community where he was engaged in farming.

Mr. Fulton was a member of the Deerfield United Methodist Church, the Elks Lodge at Garden City, and the Aircraft Owners and Pilots Assn.

Survivors include the widow of the home; his mother, Ester Fulton, Deerfield; two sisters, Mary Lois Smith, Liberal, and Faith Landon, Deerfield; and a brother, Jim,

74

Springfield, Mo. His father and a sister, Esther Jean Sutton, preceded him in death.

Funeral services at Deerfield Lutheran Church, the Rev. Dr. Ruben Reyes officiating. Burial in Deerfield Cemetery. Phillips-White Funeral Home in charge.

DEERFIELD CEMETERY

GARCIA, DELORES M. "LOLITA" - (Lt. 2, Blk. 45, Sec. 3)
(The Lakin Independent, April 14, 1994) A longtime
Deerfield resident, Delores M. "Lolita" Garcia, 81, died
Tuesday, April 5, 1994, at her home in Deerfield.
She was born July 3, 1912, at Tepatitlan, Jalisco,
Mexico, the daughter of Alfredo and Isabel Torres Soto.
A Deerfield resident since 1934, moving from Mexico, she
was a homemaker and farmer.
Mrs. Garcia attended Christ the King Catholic Church,
Deerfield. She enjoyed flower gardening, embroidery,
sewing and music.
On October 18, 1980, she married Atilano Garcia at
Clayton, N.M. He survives.
Other survivors are four stepsons, Juan Antonio Garcia,
Lakin, Mario Garcia and Hector Garcia, both of Deerfield,
and Marcos Antonio Garcia, Mexico; two stepdaughters,
Ofelia Reyes, Mexico and Maria Del Rosario Anguiano,
Deerfield; and 15 step grandchildren.
She was preceded in death by her parents and a brother,
Alfred Soto.
Spanish rosary was held at 7 p.m. last Thursday evening
at St. Anthony Catholic Church in Lakin. Funeral was at
10 a.m. Friday at the church with the Rev. Gilbert P.
Herrman officiating. Burial was in Deerfield Cemetery.
Garnand Funeral Home of Lakin was in charge of
arrangements.

GARCIA, JOSEPH LEE - (Lt. 3, Blk. 107, Sec. 1) Graveside
service for Joseph Lee Garcia, infant son of Juan Garcia
and Linda Collins, was held Tuesday at Deerfield
Cemetery, with the Rev. John Janas officiating.
Joseph died after his birth Friday, Aug. 16, 1996, at
St. Catherine Hospital.
He is survived by his mother, Linda Collins, Garden
City; his father, Juan Garcia, Greeley, Colo.; two
brothers, Juan Garcia, Jr. and Jesus Garcia, both of the
home; a twin brother, Fransisco Garcia, of the home; a
sister, Adriana Collins, of the home; his grandparents,
Dickey and Diane Collins, Deerfield, Jesus and Gloria
Garcia, Garden City; and his great grandparents, Gordon
and Faye Baty, Lakin, Richard and Eulalia Mendez, Great
Bend.

GARZA, ADELINO H. SR. - (Lt. 1, Blk. 128, Sec. 1)
Adelino Garza Sr., 47, died Feb. 16, 1991, at St.
Catherine Hospital, after a sudden illness.

He was born June 17, 1943, at Leonora, Texas. He was a farmer and had lived in Garden City since last June 1990, moving from Lubbock.
In July 1984, he began his common law marriage to Sara Aguero at Tulia, Texas. She survives.
Other survivors include two sons, Adelino Jr., Garden City, and Alvin, of the home; three daughters, Brenda Grimaldo, Beatrice Maldonado and Sandra Garza, all of Slaton, Texas; two brothers, Pedro "Pete", San Antonio, and Lorenze, California; five sisters, Adelina Rodriguez, Garden City, Josie Lee, Plainview, Texas, Frances Garza, Midland, Texas, and Dolores Garza and Petra Garza, both of Beaville, Texas; and 13 grandchildren.
Graveside service was held in the Deerfield Cemetery, Deerfield, with Pablo Pequeno officiating.

GASS, ANNA C. - (Lt. 2, Blk. 27, Sec. 2) Born Aug. 28, 1902, died Nov. 22, 1934, at Red Bluff, Texas, of suicide. Daughter of Robert Harris and Anna C. Koch Gass.

GASS, ANNA CAROLINE - (Lt. 2, Blk. 27, Sec. 2) Wife of Robert H. Gass, born August 20, 1869, at Peoria, Ill., and died Jan. 18, 1930. She died of pneumonia at Garden City, Kansas, at the age of 70. Garnand was the undertaker. She was the daughter of George and Mary Elizabeth (Reihm) Koch.

GASS, JOHN - (Lt. 2, Blk. 27, Sec. 2) Funeral for John Henry "Harry" Gass, longtime Deerfield and Lakin area resident, was held at High Plains Retirement Village in Lakin, with the Rev. Leroy Smoot officiating. Burial at the Deerfield Cemetery.
Mr. Gass, a farm laborer, died Dec. 18, 1994, at Kearny County Hospital, Lakin.
The son of Robert H. and Caroline Koch Gass, he was born Sept. 11, 1912, at Girard. The family moved to Friend when he was 2 years old, and had lived in the Deerfield and Lakin areas since 1929.
He was a farm laborer and had served in the U.S. Army during World War II.
He is survived by a brother, Albert Gass, Satanta, and eight nieces and nephews. He was preceded in death by his parents, five sisters and three brothers.
Garnand Funeral Home in charge of arrangements.

DEERFIELD CEMETERY

GASS, ROBERT HARRIS - (Lt. 2, Blk. 27, Sec. 2) Robert
Harris Gass was born Oct. 26, 1864, at Sunbury, Penn.,
and passed away, June 14, 1942, at Deerfield, Kansas. He
had reached the age of 77 years, 8 months and 18 days.
He was married to Anna Caroline Koch, August 16, 1891.
She preceded him in death, January 18, 1930.
To this union 10 children were born, 2 having preceded
him in death. Those remaining are, George Gass of
Hutchinson, Charles Gass, Mrs. Robt. McGinn of Deerfield,
Mrs. Randolph Hoglund of Alameda, California, Albert Gass
of Garden City and Harry of Deerfield. Beside these, he
leaves 6 grandchildren and many friends.
He united with the Deerfield Methodist Church in April
1930.

GESKIE, BABY - (Lt. 4, Blk. 102, Sec. 1) Baby of Irene
Dicken's sister who married Henry Geskie.

GILLOCK, ANDREW JACKSON - (Lt. 4, Blk. 29, Sec. 2)
Andrew Jackson Gillock was born in Harrison County,
Indiana, January 8th, 1841, and died at the home of his
son, Jos. D. Gillock, near Deerfield, Nov. 24th, 1926,
aged 85 years, 10 months, and 16 days.
He was united in marriage to Belinda Benham, January
12th, 1867, in Green County, Indiana. To this union
seven children were born; four boys and three girls. One
son and one daughter and the beloved wife passed on
before. The children remaining are Mrs. Flora Kersten,
of Iowa, Mrs. Lyda Burge of Oklahoma, Samuel, of
California, and Wm. and Jos. D. Gillock of Deerfield.
In 1876 he came to Kansas, moving in a wagon and
locating in Reno County, near Nickerson. In 1900 he
moved to western Kansas and settled in Kearny County near
Deerfield. In early life he was converted and united
with the Methodist Church. The family altar was
established in the home from the beginning.
The funeral was held in the Methodist Church at
Deerfield, Friday, Nov. 26, at 10:30 a.m. Rev. J. Q.
Turner in charge. The body was laid to rest in the
Deerfield Cemetery.
He leaves to mourn his loss the surviving children, the
grandchildren, and a host of friends.
    "Servant of God, well done
    Thy glorious warfare's past
    The battles fought, the victory won
    And thou art crowned at last."

DEERFIELD CEMETERY

GILLOCK, ANDREW MONROE - (Lt. 4, Blk. 108, Sec. 1) Andrew Monroe Gillock, 83, died Nov. 6, 1993, at Garden Valley Retirement Village, Garden City. He was born Dec. 19, 1909, at Deerfield, the son of Joel D. and Jane E. Kell Gillock.
Mr. Gillock was a farmer/stockman and had been a lifetime Deerfield resident.
He was a member of the First United Methodist Church, Deerfield, Lion's Club, served on Deerfield City Council, was a church trustee and School District #20 board member and Amazon Ditch board member. He helped organize the Deerfield Men's Brotherhood and served on the rural fire district and cemetery boards. He was a Kearny County commissioner and ASCS committee member.
He married Maude Goodman, August 9, 1934, at Presbyterian Manse in Lakin. She survives.
Other survivors include two sons, Gordon W. Gillock and Myron R. Gillock, both of Deerfield; two daughters, Mavis Ottaway Thomas, Dodge City, and Neva J. Quakenbush, Garden City; a sister, Eunice Irminger, Seattle, Wash.; eight grandchildren and five great grandchildren.
Funeral was held at First United Methodist Church, Deerfield, the Rev. Don Koehn officiating. Burial in Deerfield Cemetery. Price and Sons Funeral Home was in charge of arrangements.

GILLOCK, BELINDA - (Lt. 4, Blk. 29, Sec. 2) Belinda Benham was born in Green County, Indiana, April 9, 1846, and died at her home in Deerfield, Kansas, May 26, 1922, aged 76 years, 1 month, and 17 days.
She was married to A. J. Gillock, January 12, 1868. To this union seven children were born. One daughter died at the age of 25 and one son at the age of 22. Her husband, three sons, and two daughters, and their families are left to mourn their loss.
She was converted when 14 years old and united with the M.E. Church, and lived a faithful Christian life. Eagerly she set out upon the gladsome journey, for which she had spent so many years in making preparation.
She emigrated with her family from Indiana to Reno County in 1876, where she lived until the year 1900 when the family moved to Kearny County where they have since made their home.

GILLOCK, ESTHER LUELLA - (Lt. 1, Blk. 24, Sec. 2) Esther Luella was born to Mr. and Mrs. J. D. Gillock of

DEERFIELD CEMETERY

Deerfield, Kansas, on November 4, 1907, and died at St. Catherine's Hospital, Garden City, Kansas, April 3, 1938. The early part of her life was spent at Deerfield until 1924 when she went for two years with her parents to Florida. When the family decided to make a second trip to that state in 1927 Esther went to Garden City to live with the R. A. Beckett family. After three years there she took a position at Dodge City for two years. Following that time she lived with Mrs. Zimmerman of Garden city and spent her time in office work.

Esther was a devoted Christian and member of the Methodist church, having been converted and baptized in childhood. She remained always true to her faith which in turn established in her many sterling qualities of character. The business women's organization and church groups will miss her fellowship a great deal.

There are left to mourn her passing: her father and mother; brothers, Thomas and Monroe of Deerfield; sister, Mrs. J. F. Irminger of Kansas City, Missouri; besides close companions and an abundance of friends.

GILLOCK, JOEL DOWNEY — (Lt. 1, Blk. 24, Sec. 2)   Joe D. Gillock, 69, well known irrigation farmer, was found dead Saturday in bed at his home by a son.

Gillock lived alone on his farm and had been at his duties on the farm Friday. His death was discovered when the son went to his father's place to consult him about some work.

Joel Downey Gillock was born April 18, 1877, in Reno County, Kan., and died at his farm home in Kearny County, Kan., on May 4, 1946, at the age of 69 years, 16 days.

He grew to manhood on a farm north of Hutchinson, Kan. In the spring of 1900 he moved with his parents to Kearny County.

On February 22, 1905, he was united in marriage to Jane Elizabeth Kell. They established their home on the farm north of Deerfield where he was living at the time of his passing. To this union were born four children, William Thomas of Deerfield, Esther Luella who preceded her father in death, Andrew Monroe of Deerfield and Eunice Mae Coggins of Seattle, Wash.

In early life he was converted and united with the Methodist Church in which he was a sincere and active worker.

He leaves to mourn his passing: the three remaining children; his sister, Eliza Burge of Hopeton, Okla.; four grandchildren and a host of relatives and friends.

GILLOCK, JOHN WILLIAM - (Lt. 3, Blk. 77, Sec. 1) John William Gillock, 66, resident of this area for the past 45 years, died at his home three miles north of Deerfield early Feb. 1, 1945, of a heart attack.
Gillock was a long time member of the Methodist Church. Survivors include the widow, Queen Esther Gillock; a son, Porter C. Gillock, Deerfield; three daughters, Mrs. Alice Drennen, Winfield, Mrs. Ruth Grahm, Arkansas City, and Mrs. Mildred Turpen, Sacramento, Calif.; a brother, Joe D. Gillock, Deerfield; and a sister, Mrs. Eliza Burge, Hopeton, Okla.
Arrangements were made by Garnand Funeral Home.
John William, son of Mr. and Mrs. A. J. Gillock, was born Oct 21, 1878, near Nickerson, Reno County, Kansas.
In 1900, the family moved to Kearny County and secured land for a home north of Deerfield. Here he grew to manhood attending the local schools and secured additional training at Nickerson Normal School and Southwestern College.
On May 1, 1907, he was united in marriage to Queen Esther Babcock. To this union God gave three daughters: Mildred, now Mrs. Turpin of Sacramento, Calif.; Ruth, now Mrs. W. M. Grahm of Arkansas City, Kans.; and Alice, now Mrs. West Drennan of Winfield, Kans.; and a son, Porter of Deerfield.
He was a progressive farmer ever keeping abreast of new methods and movements in the field of agriculture. For some years he was a member of Patrons of Industry or the Grange and was recently the Chaplain of this movement for agricultural progress.
As a youth, he accepted Christ as his Savior and was a valued and useful member and officer in the Deerfield Methodist Church for many years. His pastors valued his counsel and knew the warm hospitality of his home. The education of his family was a passion of his life and within the family circle his kind and sunny disposition was a constant inspiration.
He was a neighbor and friend who exemplified the fullest and truest meaning of this term. His active and useful life closed suddenly amid urgent tasks and busy days when he answered the call of the Great Beyond and

entered the Master's nearer presence on Feb. 1, 1945, having lived among us for 66 years, 3 months and 10 days.

He leaves to cherish his memory the dear wife and companion of nearly 40 years; the son and three daughters, with their families; 5 grandchildren; a sister, Mrs. Burge, of Hopeton, Okla.; a brother, J. D. Gillock of Deerfield; several nieces and nephews and a host of friends.

A tender memorial service was held at the Deerfield Methodist Church on Feb. 4, by Rev. R. L. Wells, a long-time friend of the family. Interment was in the Deerfield Cemetery with Garnand Mortuary in charge.

GILLOCK, QUEEN E. - (Lt. 3, Blk. 77, Sec. 1) Mrs. Queen Gillock, 75, a former long time Deerfield resident, died February 16, 1964, at a hospital in Sacramento, Calif., following an illness of two months.

Funeral services were held at the Deerfield Methodist Church with the Rev. Robert Fleenor officiating. Burial in Deerfield Cemetery.

She was born July 21, 1888, at Lebanon, Jewell County, Kansas. Mrs. Gillock lived in Deerfield from 1907 until 1946 when she moved to California to live with a sister. She was married to J. W. (Will) Gillock on May 1, 1907, at Deerfield. He died in 1945.

Survivors include three daughters: Mrs. Wes (Alice) Drennan, Winfield, Mrs. McKinley (Ruth) Graham, Sacramento, Calif., Mrs. James (Mildred) Green, Tokyo, Japan; a son, Porter Gillock, Garden Grove, Calif.; a sister, Mrs. Achsah Clasby, Sacramento. Also four grandchildren and five great grandchildren.

GILLOCK, TRUMAN CARL - (Lt. 1, Blk. 24, Sec. 2) Truman Carl Gillock, son of Monroe and Maude Gillock, was born on Oct. 1, 1935, and departed this life at the age of 25 years, 10 months and 17 days, at their home north of Deerfield, on Aug. 17, 1961. He grew to manhood in the Deerfield community, attended the Deerfield school and the Methodist church, was engaged in farming with his father.

He is survived by his father, Monroe Gillock; his mother, Maude Gillock; two brothers, Gordon and Myron of the home; two sisters, Mrs. Gary Jones of Tyrone, Okla., and Neva Janelle of the home; one niece and one nephew, one grandfather.

DEERFIELD CEMETERY

Although handicapped in so many ways, Truman had many friends and he loved them all dearly. Their friendship was his main interest.

GLICK, GIDEON A. - (Lt. 4, Blk. 52, Sec. 2) Born in 1876 and died April 21, 1967.
G. A. Glick, 92, formerly of Deerfield, died in Wichita, April 21, 1967.
Graveside services were held at 2 p.m., Monday in the Deerfield Cemetery, the Rev. Esley Davis officiating. Mr. Glick moved from Deerfield to Wichita in the 1940s. His wife, Elizabeth, preceded him in death.
Nine children, mostly in the Wichita area, survive.

GLICK, MARGARET ELIZABETH - (Lt. 4, Blk. 52, Sec. 2) Margaret Elizabeth Stinson was born November 26, 1883, at Pawnee City, Nebraska, and departed this life February 20, 1942, at her home in Deerfield, Kansas, at the age of 58 years, 2 months, and 20 days.
As a young girl she moved with her parents to eastern Kansas. In 1898 she was converted and joined the Presbyterian Church. On moving to Deerfield, she transferred to the Methodist Church and remained a faithful member to the last.
On June 10, 1903, in Paola, Kansas, she was united in marriage to G. A. Glick and to this union nine children were born. She leaves to mourn her passing: her husband; her nine children, Mrs. C. E. Calvert, Emporia, Kan., H. R. Glick, Hoisington, Kan., Mrs. J. M Soward, Wichita, Kan., J. M. Glick, Grand Coulee, Wash., Mrs. Elcy Bassett, St. Louis, Mo., Ida Marie, Garden City, Mrs. Clark Blevins, Paris, Tex., and George and Betty of the home; also one sister, four brothers, nine grandchildren, and a host of other relatives and friends.
Funeral was in the Deerfield Methodist Church with the pastor, Rev. Woolard, in charge.

GLORIA, JOSUE ARRON - (Lt. 1, Blk. 109, Sec. 1) Graveside service for Josue Aaron Gloria were held November 9, 1972, at the Deerfield Cemetery at 10 o'clock CST. The baby, son of Mr. and Mrs. Jose P. Gloria of Deerfield, was stillborn at the Hamilton County hospital in Syracuse, November 8.
In addition to the parents the child is survived by three sisters, Omega, Sonia, Zulema; and two brothers, Dario and Joe, all of the home.

GOMEZ, ADRIAN MICHAEL - (Lt. 2, Blk. 107, Sec. 1) Adrian Michael Gomez, 4 year old son of Manuel and Rosa Elia Martinez Gomez of 2403 Lee, Garden City, died March 9, 1995, at St. Catherine Hospital. Adrian was born Nov. 27, 1990, at Greeley, Colo.
A member of St. Mary Catholic Church, he attended Russell Child Development Center. He enjoyed riding his bike, playing with his brother, and attending Garden City School of Gymnastics.
Survivors are his parents; a brother, Zachary, of the home; a sister, Cathy Rodriguez, of the home; his grandparents, Vicente Martinez, Deerfield, and Jose and Andrea Flores, Garden City; and his great grandparents, Manuel and Phyllis Garcia, Garden City. He was preceded in death by his grandmother, Juana Martinez.
Wake service, rosary and funeral at St. Mary Catholic Church, the Rev. Brian Hipp officiating. Burial at Deerfield Cemetery. Garnand Funeral Home in charge.

GRAUBERGER, BABY - (Lt. 3, Blk. 25, Sec. 2) Stillborn September 22, 1922, daughter of George and Mary Elizabeth Grauberger.

GRAUBERGER, CARL W. - (Lt. 1, Blk. 63, Sec. 3) Carl William Grauberger, lifetime Deerfield resident, died Dec. 23, 1995, at his home. He was born Aug. 19, 1919, at Deerfield, the son of George John and Mary Elizabeth Steinmetz Grauberger. He attended Deerfield and Lakin schools.
Mr. Grauberger served in the U.S. Army from 1942 to 1945 during World War II. He was a military policeman serving mostly in Europe. After the service, he returned to Deerfield.
He was a member of Deerfield United Methodist Church, Veterans of Foreign Wars, Lakin, and the Kearny County Historical Society. A farmer, he enjoyed hunting, trapping, farming and reading.
He married Clara Wynne Combs on Dec. 17, 1950, at Deerfield. She survives.
Other survivors are two sons, Les Grauberger, Wichita, and Ron Grauberger, Deerfield; four sisters, Molly Hanneman, Garden City, Eva Hanneman, Fort Collins, Colo., Anna Elliot, Deerfield, and Pauline Sturges, La Junta, Colo.; and four grandchildren.
He was preceded in death by a daughter, Jeannene Kay Grauberger, three brothers and five sisters.

84

DEERFIELD CEMETERY

Funeral was held at Deerfield United Methodist Church, with the Rev. Donald J. Koehn officiating. Burial at Deerfield Cemetery. Garnand Funeral Home in charge of arrangements.

GRAUBERGER, CAROL - (Lt. 4, Blk. 21, Sec. 2) Carol Marie, daughter of Henry Grauberger and his wife, Opal, nee McGee, was born at Deerfield, Kansas, on June 9, 1941, and departed from this life on April 20, 1942, at the tender age of ten months and eleven days.

Carol Marie was received into the covenant of God's grace on Sept. 7, 1941, through the Sacrament of Baptism and thus made a child of God.

Carol Marie had been sick with measles and chickenpox, but seemed to be recovering, but on Sunday she became suddenly ill, and though everything humanly possible was done for her, she, according to God's wise counsel and will, was delivered from all the ills and tribulations of this life on Monday afternoon.

Her early departure from this life is mourned by her deeply grieved parents, two brothers, Thomas Henry and Kenneth Carl, one sister, Martha Elaine, her grandparents, Mr. and Mrs. George Grauberger and Mrs. Verna McGee and Mr. Gernie McGee, and other relatives.

GRAUBERGER, GEORGE J. - (Lt. 3, Blk. 25, Sec. 2) George Grauberger, Sr., was killed instantly Saturday noon when the tractor he was riding overturned and crushed his head and chest. The accident occurred near his farm home three miles north of Deerfield.

Mr. Grauberger had unhooked the ditcher he was pulling from the tractor when the irrigation ditch he was following intersected another ditch at right angles. It is believed he lost control of the tractor when it plunged up the opposite bank of the intersecting ditch. The tractor reared up in front and overturned. His body was found by his wife.

George John Grauberger, Sr., the son of George and Katherine Grauberger, was born March 14, 1882, at Dittel, Russia, and departed this life on June 12, 1948, at Deerfield, Kansas, having reached the age of 66 years, 2 months and 29 days.

In early infancy he was received into the covenant of God through the Holy Sacrament of Baptism and later having been thoroughly instructed in the chief parts of Christian doctrine, he was received into formal

85

membership of the Lutheran Church by the rite of confirmation. He remained steadfast in the Lutheran faith and confession even unto death.

He grew to manhood in Russian, and on February 13, 1901, he was united in holy matrimony with Mary Elizabeth Steinmetz. This union was blessed with 13 children, an infant daughter and son preceeding him in death.

In 1906 he and his wife and 3 children sailed from their native land to the United States of America. At first they settled in the vicinity of Holcomb, Kansas. In 1908 the family moved to Deerfield, where he lived with his family until his departure, with the exception of one year when they made their home in Colorado.

Mr. Grauberger was a charter member and one of the organizers of Immanuel Lutheran Church of Deerfield. He was always interested and active in the work of the church and faithfully and ably served for many years in the office of Elder of this congregation. He spent his entire life in this country engaged in farming. He was always sincere and honest in all his dealings with his fellow men and neighbors. He was a good provider for his family and a devoted husband and father.

He leaves to mourn his departure his living wife, 8 daughters, 3 sons, 36 grandchildren, 2 great grandchildren, 8 sons-in-law, 2 daughters-in-law and a host of friends.

His only sister preceded him in death in 1913; and his brother on June 6, 1948.

Children that survive him are: Mrs. Marie Uhrich of Oakley, Kansas; Mrs. Elizabeth Boxberger, Wakeeney, Kansas; Mrs. Mollie Hannegman, Garden City, Kansas; Mrs. Katherine Ploeger, Deerfield; Mrs. Eva Hanneman, Deerfield; Mrs. Lydia Bisterfelt, Lakin; Mrs. Anna Elliott, Deerfield; Henry, George and Carl, Deerfield; and Mrs. Pauline Winter, Lakin.

Funeral services were held June 15, 1948, at the Deerfield Lutheran Church with Pastor Paul H.C. Stengel officiating. Interment was made in the Deerfield Cemetery.

"Father, I will that they also, whom thou hast given me, be with me where I am; that they may behold the glory which thou hast given me; for thou lovest me before the foundation of the world." John 17, 24.

GRAUBERGER, GEORGE J. JR. - (Lt. 2, Blk. 86, Sec. 4) George J. Grauberger, Jr. died September 24, 1991, at his home in Fort Collins, Colorado. He was born February 22, 1917, at Deerfield, the son of George John Sr. and Marie Elizabeth Steinmetz Grauberger. A Fort Collins, Colorado, resident, formerly of Deerfield, he was a retired farmer and rancher.

He was a member of the Lutheran Church and the Deerfield Co-op, both at Deerfield, the Veterans of Foreign Wars, Lakin, and the Garden City Co-op, Garden City.

On May 3, 1945, he married Claudine DeBelle at Deerfield. She survives.

Other survivors include: two sons, Rockne L., Denver, and Clark D. Corbett, Moran, Wyo.; a daughter, Crystal Claudette Wilcox, Canon City, Colo.; a brother, Carl, Deerfield; four sisters, Eva Hanneman, Fort Collins, Colo., Anna Elliott, Deerfield, Mollie Hanneman, Garden City, and Pauline Sturges, La Junta, Colo.; five grandchildren; and five great grandchildren.

Funeral service was at the United Methodist Church, Deerfield, with the Rev. Donald J. Koehn presiding. Burial in the Deerfield Cemetery. Garnand Funeral Home handled arrangements.

GRAUBERGER, HENRY - (Lt. 4, Blk. 21, Sec. 2) Henry Grauberger was born October 25, 1915, the son of George and Maria Grauberger, and departed this life December 23, 1959, in his 44th year.

Mr. Grauberger suffered a stroke Saturday afternoon and died early Wednesday morning.

He was baptized in his infancy, and was confirmed in the Lutheran faith on June 1, 1930.

On August 31, 1936, he was married to Opal McGee at Wichita. For most of his life he lived in the Deerfield community where he had farming interests.

Survivors include his widow, Opal; two sons, Thomas and Kenneth, both with the armed services in Germany; four daughters, Mrs. Elaine Westerbuhr, Peggy, Susan and Donna.

Also surviving are eight sisters, Mrs. Fred Uhrich, Oakley; Mrs. George Boxberger, WaKeeney; Mrs. John Hanneman, Garden City; Mrs. Clarence Ploeger, Deerfield; Mrs. Henry Hanneman, Ft. Collins, Colorado; Mrs. Elmer Bisterfelt, Lakin; Mrs. Leland Elliott, Deerfield; Mrs. Alden Winter, Woodland Park, Colorado; two brothers, George and Carl of Deerfield; and one grandchild.

GRAUBERGER, JEANENE KAYE — (Lt. 1, Blk. 63, Sec. 3)
Jeanene Kaye Grauberger, daughter of Mr. and Mrs. Carl W.
Grauberger, was born on Aug. 30, 1959.

Two weeks later her parents brought her to the Lord, as
she was received into Christ's Kingdom of Grace through
Baptism at the Immanuel Lutheran Church.

After several months illness she departed this life
Dec. 3, 1961, at the age of 2 years, 3 months and 3 days.

She leaves to mourn her passing, her parents; two
brothers, Leslie and Ronnie; her maternal grandparents,
Mr. and Mrs. Maurice Combs; and her great grandmother,
Mrs. Annie Combs of Garden City.

GRAUBERGER, MARY ELIZABETH — (Lt. 3, Blk. 25, Sec. 2)
Mary Elizabeth Steinmetz was born June 28, 1879, at
Dittel, Russia. Soon after her birth she was received
into the Covenant of God's Grace through the Holy
Sacrament of Baptism, and after she was instructed in the
chief part of Christian doctrine, she was received into
communicant membership in the Lutheran Church by the rite
of confirmation.

She grew to womanhood in Russia. On February 13, 1901,
she was united in holy matrimony with George Grauberger.
To this union were born 13 children.

She came to this country with her husband and three
children in 1906 and settled in Holcomb, Kansas. Two
years later they moved to Deerfield.

She lived near Deerfield until the death of her
husband, June 12, 1948, and has since made her home with
her children.

Mrs. Grauberger was a charter communicant member of the
Deerfield Lutheran Church.

She had been ill a number of years, death resulting
from a cerebral hemorrhage on Sunday, December 11, 1949,
at Oakley, at the home of her oldest daughter, Mrs. Fred
Urich.

She is preceded in death by her husband, a daughter and
a son. The children passed away in infancy.

She is survived by her sons: Henry, George and Carl
Grauberger, all of Deerfield; her daughters, Mrs. Marie
Urich of Oakley, Kansas, Mrs. Elizabeth Boxberger of
Wakeeney, Kansas, Mrs. Mollie Hanneman of Garden City,
Kansas, Mrs. Lydia Bisterfelt of Lakin, Kansas, and Mrs.
Katherine Ploeger, Mrs. Eva Hanneman, Mrs. Anna Elliott
and Mrs. Pauline Winter, all of Deerfield; also by 39

grandchildren and 3 great grandchildren and a host of friends.
She reached the age of 70 years, 5 months and 13 days.

GRAUBERGER, OPAL - (Lt. 4, Blk. 21, Sec. 2)   Mrs. Opal Grauberger, Garden City, died suddenly of an apparent heart attack December 23, 1977, in Commerce City, Colo., where she had gone to spend Christmas with her brother, Earl McGee, and family. Funeral service was held Tuesday, December 27, at the Immanuel Lutheran Church in Deerfield with the Reverend Merlin Reith, pastor of the Trinity Lutheran Church of Garden City, officiating. Burial was in Deerfield Cemetery.
Opal Rose, youngest daughter of Gernie M. and Verna Stewart McGee, was born December 6, 1918, in Garden City where she received her schooling. She was married to Henry Grauberger, August 31, 1936, in Wichita.   They lived in Deerfield until Mr. Grauberger's death December 23, 1959.
She was employed at the Kearny County Hospital as a nurses aid and held the same position at St. Catherine Hospital until she moved to Dodge City. She attended Dodge City Community Junior College where she received her Licensed Practical Nurse's degree. She returned to St. Catherine Hospital where she worked until a few months before her death when failing health caused her retirement.
She was a member of the Trinity Lutheran Church, Garden City, and the Sweet Adelines.
She was preceded in death by her husband, Henry, her mother and a daughter, Carol, who died in infancy.
She is survived by two sons, Thomas H. of Ulysses and Kenneth C. of Deerfield; four daughters, Mrs. Elaine Westerbuhr, St. Paul, Minn., Mrs. Peggy Orbach, Hackensack, New Jersey, Mrs. Susan Skipper, Ft. Hood, Tex., and Donna Grauberger, Garden City. Other survivors include her father, G. M. McGee, Houston, Texas; a brother, Earl McGee, Commerce City, Colo.; two sisters, Mrs. Leona Davis, Lakin and Mrs. Esther Hardwick, Wichita; two half brothers, Clarence McGee and Jack McGee, Houston, Texas, and a half sister, Mrs. Ruby Belton, Houston, Texas.

GREEN, DELILAH FERN - (S/2 Lt. 1, Blk. 34, Sec. 3) Lila Fern Green was born on March 29, 1903, in Grant City, Missouri, the eighth child of Edward L. Miller and Ella

DEERFIELD CEMETERY

Long Miller. Her family migrated to Western Kansas when Lila was quite small. She attended Lakin and Deerfield schools, graduating from Deerfield High School in 1923. After graduation Lila attended teachers college at Hays and Emporia and taught in rural schools around Ulysses for several years. After the death of her mother, she returned home and kept house for her father and brothers. Lila married Glen Green on July 5, 1931.

Lila and Glen lived in Lamar, Colorado, where Glen was working until her health required them to move to New Mexico in 1935. During the war period they lived in Arizona, then moved to Fort Worth, Texas, where they made their home for many years. In Fort Worth, Lila attended the Methodist Church and was involved in extensive church work until her health began to fail. Later she was confined to several hospitals for extensive stays. Finally, Lila was admitted to a nursing home in Wichita Falls, Texas, until her death on September 18, 1984.

Preceding her in death were her parents, three brothers and three sisters. She is survived by her husband, Glen of Fort Worth, Texas; two brothers, Ted Miller of Garden City and Albert Miller of Wrens, Georgia; and two sisters, Ruby Landon of Napa, California, and Louise Enoch of Seattle, Washington; and many nieces and nephews.

Funeral was held at the United Methodist Church, Deerfield, the Rev. Nellie Holmes. Burial at Deerfield. Davis Funeral Home in charge of local arrangements.

GREEN, GLENN A. - (S/2 Lt. 1, Blk. 34, Sec. 3) Glenn A. Green was born March 16, 1905, to Effie Katherine Pogue Miller and Christian Snider Green in Garden City, Kansas. He died January 8, 1991, at Hurst, Texas, after a short illness. He was preceded in death by his wife, one brother, and two sisters. He is survived by a brother, Dale R. Green, Messick, Michigan, plus many nieces and nephews. Also a faithful friend, Eva Knowles, Ft. Worth, Texas, survives.

He married Lila Miller Green, July 5, 1931. They had a long loving marriage of 53 years. Lila died September 8, 1984, after a long illness. Glenn took care of his wife during most of her lengthy illness. Even though they had no children they had a special love for children, especially Kimberly Miller, a great niece, of Springdale, Arkansas.

90

DEERFIELD CEMETERY

He was a successful conservative business man. Glenn was head mechanic for American Airlines for many years at Ft. Worth, Texas. He did a lot of traveling but lived most of his life in Ft. Worth area.

Glen was artistic working mostly with wood and metals. Most of his friends and relatives have some of his handmade items to treasure. This hobby kept him busy making or repairing for his home or gifts. He kept a lot of neighborhood bicycles in working order for his many little friends.

He was a hard worker. Glenn was in his 70's when he helped a nephew harvest. He kept physically fit by biking, putting lots of miles on his bicycle. Glenn tried to bike every day for several miles, weather and health permitting. His philosophy was "age is just a number" and he lived his age to the fullest!

Glenn was buried by his beloved wife in the Deerfield Cemetery. He had a special love for the small community of Deerfield where he often visited his wife's relatives. He said his wife's relatives were his family too and he continued to keep in touch often after his wife died. He was family oriented and when he could not drive to visit his loved ones he telephoned. He always had a large telephone bill but said he kept his relatives in touch with each other as well as himself.

Glenn will be missed by his many loved ones but his fond memories remain with us forever.

Funeral service was held Saturday afternoon at Greene-Schneider Funeral Chapel, Lakin, with the Rev. Don Koehn presiding.

GROF, KATIE - (Lt. 3, Blk. 84, Sec. 1) Died November 28, 1931, age 78 yrs, 8 mos., 13 days. She was a widow and died of chronic nephritis. Nash Funeral Home in charge of arrangements.

GROPP, AGNES H. - (Lt. 3, Blk. 61, Sec. 3) Mrs. Agnes Henrietta Gropp, 49, a long time resident of the Deerfield community, died at St. Catherine's Hospital in Garden City, Nov. 20, 1956. Death followed a lengthy illness and more than a three month stay in the hospital.

Mrs. Gropp had been a resident of Deerfield for the past 31 years. She was born in Dexter, Mo., March 23, 1907, the daughter of Theodore and Amelia Ploeger.

She was married to George Gropp in Kendall, Sept. 8, 1928. She was a member of the Deerfield Lutheran Church.

91

Surviving are the husband; her father, Theodore Ploeger, and two brothers, Clarence and Herbert Ploeger, all of Deerfield. Contribution to the Bethesda home in Wattertown, Wisc. instead of flowers have been requested by the family.

GROPP, GEORGE SAMUEL — (Lt. 3, Blk. 61, Sec. 3) George Samuel Gropp, a liftime resident of Kearny County, died on Aug. 28, 1992, at the Kearny County Hospital, Lakin.

He was born on Sept. 18, 1898, in north Kearny County. On Sept 18, 1928, he married Agnes Ploeger at Kendall. She died on Nov. 20, 1956.

Mr. Gropp was a retired farmer and dairyman. He was a member of Immanuel Lutheran Church at Deerfield and held a number of offices in the church. He was a former member of the Kearny County Southside Ditch Company.

Surviving are a brother, Arthur E. Gropp, Greenbelt, Md.; a sister, Emma Molz, Lakin; and nieces and nephews.

Funeral was held at Immanuel Lutheran Church, Deerfield, the Rev. Robert Roberts officiating. Burial at the Deerfield Cemetery. Greene-Schneider Funeral Home, Lakin, in charge.

GROPP, RICHARD MARTIN — (Lt. 3, Blk. 61, Sec. 3) Richard Martin Gropp, the son of John Samuel and Henrietta Anna Gropp, was born on Nov. 10, 1896, at Kendall and departed this life on Sept. 12, 1955, at the age of 58 years, 10 months and two days.

In infancy he was brought to his Savior through Holy Baptism. He was confirmed in 1909 at Zion Lutheran Church, Lydia, Kansas, by the Rev. Theodore Arndt. Later he took his membership with Immanuel Lutheran at Deerfield, and he remained faithful to his Savior and this church for the remainder of his life.

His earlier years were spent on the home farm north of Kendall. In 1938 he made his home in Lakin with his mother. For many years ill health caused him to restrict his work and lead a less active life than he desired. Gradually his condition grew worse until death last Monday brought release from all suffering and translated him into the Church Triumphant in heaven.

Richard Gropp was a veteran of World War I, serving in the medical corps; he served as a member of the board of county commissioners of Kearny County; and in many other ways he served his community.

DEERFIELD CEMETERY

The survivors are: two brothers, and two sisters, Myrtle (Mrs. Oscar J. Kurtz) of Nyssa, Ore., George Gropp and Emma (Mrs. Henry Molz) of Deerfield, and Arthur Gropp of Washington D.C.

One half brother and one half sister, Rudolph Gropp of Lakin and Elizabeth (Mrs. Richard Parnell) of Wellington, Kansas.

Casket bearers were Ernest Marquardt, Emil Barben, Lewis Lohman, Joe Eves, Jack Rice, and Edd Murray. Interment was made in the Deerfield Cemetery.

Funeral services for Richard Martin Gropp were held at the Immanuel Lutheran Church in Deerfield with the Rev. Henry Knoke in charge.

Mr. Gropp, 58, a lifelong resident of Kearny County died Monday at the Kearny County Hospital after an illness of several years. He had been hospitalized the past five weeks with cancer.

GROSS, ANGELA - (Lt. 2, Blk. 105, Sec. 1) Angela Rey Gross, one month, died Tuesday, Oct. 31, 1978, at St. Catherine Hospital. She was born Sept. 24, 1978, at Garden City.

Survivors include her parents, Mr. and Mrs. Steven F. Gross, 707 Moores, Garden City, Ks.; two brothers, Richard and Chris Gross, both of the home; four sisters, Barbara, Deborah, Janie and Patricia Gross, all of the home; grandparents, Mrs. Grace Gross, 803 Summit, and Mrs. and Mrs. Jack McHenry, Pratt.

Graveside service was held Thursday at Deerfield Cemetery, Mrs. Larry Pitcher officiating.

GROSS, HARRY ALLEN - (Lt. 2, Blk. 105, Sec. 1) Funeral services for Harry Allen Gross, 57, were held Jan. 14, 1967, at the Deerfield Methodist Church with the Rev. Wesley Davis officiating. Burial was in the Deerfield Cemetery.

Mr. Gross was a farmer at Deerfield. He was born Jan. 20, 1909, at Macedonia, Iowa, and had been a resident of Deerfield for six years moving there from Holcomb. He was a member of the Deerfield Methodist Church.

He married Grace Florence Chilton, Oct. 15, 1943, at Sharon Springs.

Surviving are the widow; one son, Steven, of the home; two daughters, Mrs. Garry Adams, Lakin, and Kathy, of the home; his mother, Mrs. Mary E. Gross of Crook, Colo.; four brothers, M. J. of Iliff, Colo., William and Doyle of Ft. Collins, Colo., and Lloyd of Crook; two sisters, Mrs. Ruth Homan, Eads, Colo., and Mrs. Lucille Riley, Crook; and one grandson.

GUERRERO, (Gerrero) JESUS G. - (Lt. 3, Blk. 99, Sec. 1) Died September 21, 1926. Born in 1901. 28 years old, married, died at Deerfield of tuberculosis. Bryant Garnand undertaker.

DEERFIELD CEMETERY

HALE, CLARA F. - (Lt. 1, Blk. 50, Sec. 2) Clara Florence Denlinger, daughter of John R. and Elizabeth Denlinger, was born February 27, 1876, near Dayton, Ohio, and passed away November 4, 1947, at her home in Deerfield, Kansas, at the age of 71 years, 8 months and 7 days.
The family moved to Hartland, Kansas, when Clara was quite young. She attended the schools and grew to womanhood in the Hartland community. She taught school in Kearny County. A part of her teaching career was in Deerfield.
May 5, 1901, she was united in marriage to John R. Hale. Except for two short periods, they lived in or in the vicinity of Deerfield. She joined the Methodist Church in 1912 and had been an active member until her death. For a number of years she was Primary Superintendent of the Sunday School. Clara loved to teach children. Through an annuity she had helped to make provision for the retired ministers of her church. She was also a member of the Order of the Eastern Star and the Deerfield Grange.
Her husband, four brothers and one sister preceded her in death. She leaves three nephews, Floyd Denlinger of Lawrence, Kansas, Walter Denlinger of Lemon Grove, California, Roy Denlinger of San Diego, California; two nieces, Mrs. Myrtle Lankard of Madison, New Jersey, Mrs. Ava Luton of Lakeside, California, and a host of friends.

HALE, JOHN R. - (Lt. 1, Blk. 50, Sec. 2) John R. Hale was born in the state of Indiana, November 17, 1873, and departed this life at Deerfield, Kansas, October 10, 1945.
He moved with his parents to Ford County, Kansas, in 1885, where he resided for a few years, coming from there to Deerfield, Kansas, where he resided until his death.
He was married to Clara F. Denlinger at Hartland, Kansas, on May 5, 1901.
Mr. Hale was a member of the Methodist Church at Deerfield, Deerfield Lodge #432 AF & AM, Deerfield Order of the Eastern Star, the Chapter and Commandery of Garden City, Kansas.
He knew the hardship, the joy, and the challenge of pioneer life on the plains of western Kansas. He served several terms as commissioner of Kearny County and one term as state representative of his district.

He leaves to mourn his departure: his wife, Clara F. Hale of Deerfield; two brothers, Julian W. Wells of Deerfield and Elbert W. Hale of Morley, Michigan; several nieces and nephews; and a host of friends. Funeral services were held from the Deerfield Methodist Church, with Masonic rites at the graveside. Interment was in the Deerfield Cemetery. The 1900 Census of Kearny County shows he was born in 1872.

HALL, DOLLIE - (Lt. 1, Blk. 58, Sec. 2) Born Apr. 22, 1886, and died Nov. 23, 1966. (The Lakin Independent, December 1, 1966) Friends in Deerfield and community extend their sympathy to Mrs. Hattie Buell of Garden City, long time resident of Deerfield in the loss of her sister, Mrs. Dollie Hall, formerly of this community, who passed away last week at Los Angeles, Calif.

HALL, HARVE - (Lt. 3, Blk. 48, Sec. 2) Born May 25, 1856, and died May 19, 1939. Harvey H. Hall was a widower. Died of chronic myocarditis in Terry Twp., Finney County, Kansas. C. A. Wiley was the undertaker.
(Garden City Telegram, May 19, 1939) Harvey F. Hall, 82, farmer who lived nine miles North of Holcomb, died May 19, 1939, of a heart ailment with which he had been afflicted for the past two months. He had lived at this farm since 1905.
Funeral services Monday afternoon at the Wiley Funeral Home with Rev. O. R. Powell officiating. Burial at Deerfield Cemetery.
Survivors include two sons, Edward of Fowler and Roy of Holcomb; two grandchildren, Mrs. V. V. Hunt of Kinsley and Harold Hall of Holcomb; two sisters and a brother in Iowa.

HALL, NANCIE ELIZABETH - (Lt. 3, Blk. 48, Sec. 2) ts. December 24, 1862-November 28, 1931. (The Garden City Telegram, Wednesday, Dec. 2, 1931) Nancy Elizabeth Harrold was born in Munsey, Ind., Dec. 24, 1861, the second child in a family of three. At the age of 14 she moved with her parents to Ringold County, Iowa, living on a farm. In 1877 she was married to Harvey Hall. To this union were born three children, Edward and Roy Hall of Holcomb, and Mabel who preceded her mother in death, twenty eight years ago.

DEERFIELD CEMETERY

They moved to western Kansas in 1905 residing in Finney County with the exception of three years near Canon City, Colo. They returned to Holcomb last February and she departed this life Saturday morning, Nov. 28, 1931.
She leaves to mourn her departure, her husband, two sons, two grandchildren, a brother, Wm. Harold, Canon City, Colo. and sister, Mrs. May Duncan of Nebraska, other relatives and many friends extend their sympathy to the bereaved ones.
She was a devoted wife and loving mother and all her friends recognized in her a kind and helful neighbor.
Funeral services were held from the Wiley Funeral Home, Nov. 30, at 2 p.m. Interment at Deerfield.

HAMILL, FERN J. - (Lt. 2, Blk. 68, Sec. 4) Fern J. Hamill died June 24, 1995, at St. Francis Regional Medical Center, Wichita. She was born May 18, 1933, at Oklahoma City, the daughter of Leroy and Alpha Sexton Wilson. She grew up in Oklahoma City and attended school there.
Fern lived various places throughout her life before moving to Garden City in the early 1960s.
She married Roy C. Hamill on January 14, 1972, at Garden City. They moved to Deerfield in 1981 and have lived there since. Fern enjoyed needle crafts such as crocheting.
Survivors include her husband, Roy C. Hamill of the home; a son, Kenneth W. Hopper, Monahans, Tx.; step-sons, Roy Hamill Jr., Garden City, William Michael Hamill, Turon, Okla.; daughters, Audrey S. Smith, Ferris, Tx., Donna R. Rust, Galveston, Tx., Lory Lopez, Garland, Tx., Kristi L. Hamill of the home; step-daughters, Debbie Hamill, Guymon, Okla., Marsha Hamill, Liberal, Brenda Amen, Lincoln, Nebr., Rhonda Penn, Rogersville, Mo.; her mother, Alpha Phillips, Oklahoma City; a brother, Pete Wilson, Oklahoma City; a sister, Mary Ellen Chodrich, Edmond, Okla.; 24 grandchildren and five great grandchildren.
She was preceded in death by her father, one brother, Fred Wilson, and one daughter, Jody.
Graveside services were held at the Deerfield Cemetery with the Rev. Donald J. Koehn of the United Methodist Church, Deerfield, presiding.

HAMILL, ZELLA IRENE - (Lt. 2, Blk. 68, Sec. 4) Mrs. Zella Irene Hamill, 54, Deerfield, died February 20,

1976, in the Kearny County Hospital, Lakin. She had been ill with cancer since October.

Born Nov. 4, 1921, in Fulton, S.D., she was married to Rex Hamill, Jan. 28, 1945, in Vancouver, Wash. They came to Garden City in 1955, and had lived there and in the Holcomb area until 1963, when they moved north of Deerfield.

Surviving are the widower, of the home; three sons, Larry, with the Army in Korea, Francis, Garden City, and Richard, Satanta; two daughters, Mrs. Pat Pickens, Deerfield and Linda Hamill, Emporia; a brother, Orville Cummings, Camas, Wash.; her father, Charlie Cummings, Billings, Mont.; and eight grandchildren.

Funeral arrangements by Garnand Funeral Home.

HANNEMAN, MARY K. - (Lt. 1, Blk. 52, Sec. 2) Mary Katherine Wienick was born June 24, 1874, in Galga, Russia. Married George Henry Riffel in 1894 in Russia. Second marriage to Mr. Hanneman. She died in Jan. 1957.

HARROLD, ELIZABETH - (Lt. 3, Blk. 48, Sec. 2) ts. January 3, 1908. Died Jan. 3, 1906.

HARSH, ANITA JEAN - (Lt. 4, Blk. 78, Sec. 1) Anita Jean Harsh, nine year old daughter of Mr. and Mrs. Virgil Harsh, Holcomb, was killed, Aug. 6, 1973, in a two car accident near Lakin.

Born May 11, 1964, at Garden City, she had lived in Holcomb all her life.

Survivors in addition to the parents include two brothers, Rodney, of the home, and Robert, Port Townsend, Wash.; a sister, Pamela Sue Morris, Garden City; her grandparents, Cecil Harsh, Lancaster, Calif., and Mr. and Mrs. E. M. Foreman, Holcomb.

HARSH, ORLAND - (Lt. 4, Blk. 54, Sec. 2) Born May 23, 1918, and died Nov. 20, 1918.

HARSH, ROBERT W. - (Lt. 1, Blk. 79, Sec. 1) Robert Wayne Harsh, 27, of Port Townsend, Wash., and formerly of Holcomb, died Sept. 3, 1975, in a car accident seven miles west of Port Angels, Wash.

Born June 1, 1948, in Garden City, he grew up in Holcomb and attended the Holcomb schools. He served two years in the Army and was stationed in Germany where he finished his high school work. A construction worker, he had moved to Washington in May.

He was a member of the United Presbyterian Church, Holcomb.

Survivors include the widow, Marcy; a daughter, Riqui Renae of California; his mother, Mrs. Betty Harsh, Garden City; a brother, Rodney; a sister, Mrs. Pamela Sue Morris; and grandparents, Mr. and Mrs. E. M. Foreman. His father and a sister, Anita Jean, preceded him in death, both in 1973.

The body was returned here for the funeral and burial in Deerfield Cemetery. Garnand Funeral Home in charge of arrangements.

HARSH, VERA LUCRETIA - (Lt. 4, Blk. 54, Sec. 2) (Funeral Record) Died Feb. 11, 1922, age 2 yrs., 3 mos., 3 days. Father Cecil Harsh, mother Dora Russell. Died of pneumonia.

(The Lakin Independent, Feb. 17, 1922) Vera Lucretia, little daughter of Mr. and Mrs. Cecil Harsh, died at their home, Saturday evening, after a short illness. The funeral was conducted by Rev. Nicholson at the M. E. Church, Sunday, and the little body was laid to rest in the Deerfield Cemetery. The parents, sisters and brother have the sympathy of their many friends in their bereavement.

HARSH, VIRGIL S. - (Lt. 1, Blk. 79, Sec. 1) Virgil S. Harsh, 45, Holcomb, died Nov. 1, 1973, after a long illness.

Born Oct. 10, 1928, at Deerfield, he was reared there and spent most of his life farming in the Holcomb area. He had been forced to retire because of ill health. He was married to Betty Stebens, July 12, 1947, at Tonopah, Nev.

Mr. Harsh was a lifetime member of the VFW, a Navy veteran of World War II, and attended the Presbyterian Church.

Survivors include the widow; two sons, Robert, Deerfield, and Rodney, of the home; a daughter, Mrs. Pamela Sue Morris; three brothers, Orville, Lucine, and Russell, all Oxnard, Calif.; two sisters, Mrs. Lee Jenkins, Mojave, Calif., and Mrs. Ed Miller, Las Vegas, Nev.; and one granddaughter. A daughter, Anita, and a grandson, Brian, preceded him in death in August. His father, Cecil, preceeded him in death last month.

DEERFIELD CEMETERY

HARTMAN, CHRIS - (Lt. 3, Blk. 59, Sec. 3) (The Kearny County Advocate, Dec. 10, 1920) Chris Hartman one of the early settlers of Deerfield passed away Dec. 2nd, age 70 years. He was born in Germany and came to this country with his parents when quite young. He has been in poor health and his demise was no surprise. The remains were laid to rest in the Deerfield Cemetery.

HAUNSCHILD, INFANT - (Lt. 3, Blk. 81, Sec. 1) Stillborn April 4, 1948. Father W. A. Haunschild, Deerfield. Buried April 9. Garnand Funeral Home in charge.

HEINLEN, LEO - (Lt. 4, Blk. 42, Sec. 3) Robert Leo Heinlen, 64, died at St. Catherine Hospital, Saturday, Jan. 19, 1963.
Born July 20, 1898, Schuyler County, Mo. Lived here 40 years.
Survivors: son, Leonard E., Colorado Springs,; daughter, Mrs. Lois Spencer, Montana; step brothers, Arthur, Vancouver, Wash., Cloyd, Grand Junction, Colo.; sisters, Mrs. Grace Babcock, Yuampa, Colo., Mrs. Edith Russell, Garden City; and five grandchildren.

HEINLEN, LEONARD - (Lt. 4, Blk. 42, Sec. 3) Graveside service for Leonard E. Heinlen, 57, Colorado Springs, Colo., was held at 10 a.m., Saturday at Deerfield Cemetery, the Rev. Austin Herrman officiating. A former Deerfield resident, Mr. Heinlen died Dec. 20, 1980, in Colorado Springs.
He was born Nov. 30, 1923, in Deerfield.
Survivors are his wife, Norma Jean, of the home; three sons, Ronnie, James R., and Michael, all of Colorado Springs, and one grandchild.

HENDRICKS, ELFRIDA M. - (Lt. 2, Blk. 26, Sec. 2) (The Lakin Independent, Oct. 3, 1941) Mrs. Freda Hendricks of Liberal was killed Sunday when a freight train crashed into the car in which she was riding in Hooker, Oklahoma. Seven persons were in an automobile which stalled on the Rock Island tracks and all were killed.
State Highway Patrolman Curtis Busby said he could not determine who was driving the car, but he believed the mist obscured the vision of the driver and that he did not see the crossing nor the approaching train.

100

DEERFIELD CEMETERY

Mrs. Hendricks is a daughter of Mr. and Mrs. H. W. Meyer of Deerfield. She grew to womanhood in Pioneer community and was graduated from Lakin high school. Funeral services held Thursday afternoon at 2:30 o'clock in the Lutheran Church at Deerfield. (The Lakin Independent, Oct. 10, 1941) Elfrieda Margaretha Hendricks was born June 13, 1908, at Lakin, Kansas, and departed this life Sunday evening, September 28, at Hooker, Oklahoma, at the age of 33 years, 3 months, and 15 days. She was the oldest daughter of Mr. H. W. Meyer and his wife, Mary nee Slacik. She was baptized July 26, 1908, in the name of the Triune God and confirmed her baptismal vow on June 3, 1923, after having been duly instructed in the chief parts of Christian doctrine.

Oct. 5, 1932, she entered holy matrimony with Mr. Harlan Hendricks. One son, Wendell Harland, was born to this union.

The deceased was a faithful member of the Lutheran Church here at Deerfield until she transferred her membership to the Lutheran Church at Liberal, Kansas, where she was a member at the time of her death. Mrs. Hendricks was employed as chief clerk in the welfare office in Liberal for the last seven years.

This last Sunday evening, September 28, Mrs. Hendricks, in company of a group of her friends, met a sudden, tragic death at Hooker, Oklahoma. "Lord, teach us to number our days, that we may apply our hearts unto wisdom."

The death of the deceased is mourned by her son, Wendell; her parents, Mr. and Mrs. H. W. Meyer; her sister, Mrs. Glen McCue, and family; Harland Hendricks; and other relatives and friends.

> Who knows how near my end may be?
> Time speeds away, and death come on;
> How swiftly, ah! how suddenly,
> May death be here, and life be gone!
> My God, for Jesus' sake I pray
> Thy peace may bless my dying day.

Funeral services were conducted from the Lutheran Church at Deerfield on October 2, with Rev. Walter J. F. Lebien in charge. Interment was made in the Deerfield Cemetery.

HERNANDEZ, GONZALO, JR. - (S/2 Lt. 2, Blk. 127, Sec. 1) Rosary and funeral for Gonzalo Hernandez, Jr., 52,

Deerfield, was held at St. Anthony's Catholic Church, Lakin, the Rev. Richard Kolega officiating. Burial at Deerfield Cemetery. He died March 5, 1986, at the Kearny County Hospital, Lakin.

Born Oct. 9, 1933, at Eola, Texas, he married Mary Grace at Menard, Texas. Mr. Hernandez was self employed as a sheep shearer and had been a Deerfield resident for four years, moving from Menard, Texas.

He was a member of the Sacred Heart Catholic Church, Menard.

Surviving are his wife of Menard; a son, David Lee, and a daughter, Lataine Gomez, both of Menard; three brothers, Santos, Menard, and Johnny and Edward, both of Deerfield; two sisters, Rosa Ramon, Menard, and Amelia Urteaga, Deerfield.

HERNANDEZ, LIBRADO - (Lt. 1, Blk. 100, Sec. 1) Librado Hernandez, 68, died at the Bob Wilson Memorial Hospital, Ulysses, Dec. 2, 1968, following a short illness.

Born in Atachio, Mexico, October 13, 1901, Mr. Hernandez came to the United States in 1924. He was a Kearny County resident since that time working on the railroad and in the beet fields. He had lived at the Pioneer Rest Home in Lakin the past 10 years. He had been blind since 1950.

Funeral service was held at Christ the King Catholic Church in Deerfield with Rev. F. C. Laudick, C.P.P.S. officiating. Burial was in Deerfield Cemetery.

HERNANDEZ, MARTIN - (Lt. 1, Blk. 128, Sec. 1) Graveside service for Martin Salazar-Hernandez, infant son of Martin Hernandez Jr., and Juanita Salazar, was held at Deerfield Cemetery, the Rev. Frank Jordan officiating.

He was stillborn June 17, 1991, at St. Catherine Hospital. He was baptized in the Christian faith.

Survivors include his father, Martin Hernandez, Jr., Garden City; his mother, Juanita Salazar, Deerfield; his grandparents, Dale and Mary Salazar, Deerfield, and Martin Hernandez Sr., Mexico; and his great grandparents, Salvador and Juanita DeHerrera, and John and Cindy Salazar, all of Pueblo, Colo., and Macaria Hernandez and Trinidad Rodriguez, both of Mexico.

HERNANDEZ, VALENTIN, JR - (Lt. 3, Blk. 107, Sec. 1) Son of Valentin and Lupe Hernandez, died in September 1936. Born in 1933.

DEERFIELD CEMETERY

HERR, MABEL - (Lt. 2, Blk. 23, Sec. 2)   Mable Herr,
daughter of Mr. and Mrs. George Martin, was born June 9,
1888, in Keokuk County, Ia. She was the second child of
a family of 11 children. She departed from this life on
August 13, 1959, at the Kearny County Hospital.
She was married to William H. Herr on December 18,
1907, at the home of her parents at Kinross, Iowa. They
celebrated their 50th anniversary just two years ago.
They made their home near Kinross, Iowa, for 12 years
before coming to Kansas. They came to Kansas in 1919,
landing at Deerfield on November 13. They lived in the
home just south of town until February 28, 1952, when
they moved to their present home, which had been fixed
just like they wanted it for retirement.
She joined the Christian Church in her early life and
then became a member of Deerfield Methodist and served it
faithfully through the approximately 40 years they have
lived here.
She was a very active member of her community, serving
it through such organizations as the Eastern Star,
Grange, Garden club and many other committies and special
projects.
Surviving are her widower, of the home; two brothers,
Ernest Martin of Garden City and Harley Martin of
McMinniville, Ore.; two sisters, Mrs. Leta Netser of
North English, Ia., and Mrs. Ethel Stullken of Lakin;
many nieces and nephews and a host of relatives and
friends.
Mable, as she was known to each of us, was always where
there was need, arriving first and leaving last. Her
favorite place was in the kitchen. She shared the joy of
having everyone enjoy the pleasure of a good meal. The
crowd was never too large or too small for her to see
that food was on the table and ready for each and
everyone to help themselves.
There isn't a home in the community that has not been
touched by her hand. She always went right ahead and did
those things that needed doing without fearing the
criticism that sometimes comes to one that is ready to go
ahead with a task. Each task received its due because it
was never beneath her dignity or above her
accomplishments.
Her mind was easily spoken, exactly to the point.
Everyone knew the directness, but never felt the offense.

103

DEERFIELD CEMETERY

Unhampered by race or creed her seemingly endless energy and joy in helping those about her will be missed by all.
Her Christian way of life has been an inspiration to each of us because of her pleasant devotion as a friend and neighbor.

HERR, WILLIAM HENRY - (Lt. 2, Blk. 23, Sec. 2) Born March 31, 1883, in Kinross, Iowa, and died Nov. 8, 1963, at Cedaredge, Colo., where he had been making his home for the past two years. He married Mabel Martin, December 18, 1908. They moved to Deerfield shortly after their marriage. Mrs. Herr died in 1959.
Survivors include two sisters, Mrs. Eva McDowell, Kinross, and Mrs. Carrie Eittermiller, Wellman, Iowa.
Funeral services were held Tuesday at the Deerfield Methodist Church with the Rev. Robert Fleenor officiating. Burial in the Deerfield Cemetery.

HERRERA, ANISETO - (Lt. 4, Blk. 110, Sec. 1) September 19, 1933. Juan Herrera, a 6 month old Mexican male, died at Sherlock, Texas, of enteritis diarrhea. J. J. Nash Funeral Home in charge of arrangements.

HERRING, ARMETTA ELLA - (Lt. 4, Blk. 47, Sec. 2) ts. 1854-1935. Armetta Ella, daughter of Norman R. and Aphia W. Butler, was born in Hancock County, Illinois, October 18, 1853, and died in Deerfield, Kansas, March 24, 1935, being 81 years, 5 months, and 6 days of age.
She was married to Sanford Herring, September 25, 1873, and the couple located near LaBelle, Missouri, that fall. In 1876 they moved to Adair County, Missouri, and from thence to Hancock County, Illinois, in 1881. They returned to Missouri in 1882 and lived near Kirksville until 1902. During this time Mrs. Herring was converted under the preaching of Simpson Ely at Kirksville. She joined the Christian Church and has lived a consistent member.
In 1902 they moved to Nebraska, near Trumbull, where they remained one year. They then returned to Hancock County, Illinois, where the husband died September 21, 1903.
In 1905 Mrs. Herring moved to Kansas, where she made her home with her brother, C. C. Butler. In 1913 she returned to Hancock County where she lived until 1921.

Then she moved to Deerfield, Kansas, where she has since resided.

She leaves one sister, Mrs. Ara J. Welch of Kansas City, Missouri, and one brother, C. D. Butler of Lakin, Kansas; two nephews, Guy V. and Giles S. Butler of Lakin, Kansas; one niece, Florannah Welch of Kansas City, Missouri; one uncle, Hez Butler of Stronghurst, Illinois; a number of other relatives; and a host of friends.

Funeral services were held in the Methodist Church at Deerfield, Kansas, 2:30 Wednesday, March 27, Rev. Rains of Garden City was in charge, and Rev. Glen W. Palmer of Deerfield assisted.

HETZER, GEORGE B. - (Lt. 4, Blk. 22, Sec. 2) George B. Hetzer was born July 12, 1870, near Cairo, Illinois. He departed this life at 7:30 o'clock, October 24, 1937, at Fort Lupton, Colorado, having attained the age of 67 years, 3 months, and 12 days. His passing came after a brief illness, and at the end he simply fell asleep.

His family moved to Kansas when he was six years of age and he spent his young manhood in Linn and Crawford Counties. In 1905 he moved to Kearny County and has lived in or near Deerfield most of the time since. Four months ago he moved to Colorado in an attempt to regain failing health.

On April 27, 1913, he was united in marriage to Mary E. Thompson at Brownell, Kansas. To this union five children were born. Three of these, two daughters and a son, died in infancy.

Mr. Hetzer was active in community work. He was a member of the Methodist Church, the Masonic lodge, the Grange, and the Eastern Star. He served considerable time in clerical work and for a time as county commissioner.

He was known as a man of integrity and character. He stood for the right in his community. In his passing we have lost a useful and active citizen.

He leaves to mourn his passing: his wife, Mrs. Mary Hetzer; two sons, Bill and Bob; a brother, John Hetzer of Fort Scott, Kansas; and a host of relatives and friends.

Funeral services were conducted from the Deerfield Methodist Church, October 28, 3:30 o'clock, with Rev. Glen W. Palmer in charge. Interment was made in the Deerfield Cemetery. The Masonic ritual was employed at the grave. Relatives present for the services were: Mr.

DEERFIELD CEMETERY

and Mrs. William R. Thompson, Great Bend, and Miss Florence Thompson, Brownell.

HETZER, MARY - (Lt. 4, Blk. 22, Sec. 2) Mary Ellen Thompson, daughter of Alfred C. and Susan K. Thompson, was born at Brownell, Kansas, Jan. 17, 1884, and departed this life April 27, 1955, at the age of 71 years, three months and eight days.
She was united in marriage with George B. Hetzer, April 27, 1913. To this union five children were born, three of whom passed away in infancy.
She gave her heart to the Lord early in life and united with the Baptist Church in Brownell, Kans. She later transferred her membership to the Deerfield Methodist Church. Mrs. Hetzer always took a great deal of pleasure in the work of her church. She was also a member of the Eastern Star.
Her companion passed away October 24, 1937.
She is survived by her two sons, William A. Hetzer of Hugoton, Kans. and Robert C. Hetzer of Haswell, Colo.; two grandsons and two granddaughters; one sister, Miss Florence Thompson, of Larned, Kans.; and many friends.
She had been the Telegram's Deerfield correspondent for many years. According to friends Mrs. Hetzer was in good health and complained only of an occasional illness. She was found dead by a lady delivering her milk.

HETZER, ROBERT CARNS - (Lt. 1, Blk. 31, Sec. 2) Bob Hetzer, 42, son-in-law of Mr. and Mrs. Victor Haflich, died April 30, 1965, of a heart attack in Pueblo, Colo.
Mrs. Hetzer is the former Jane Haflich. Other survivors include four daughters of the home in Haswell, Colo.; and a brother, Bill Hetzer, Lancaster, Calif. His parents, Mr. and Mrs. George Hetzer, preceded him in death.
He was born April 25, 1923, at Deerfield. Funeral services were at Haswell, Colo., with burial in the Deerfield Cemetery. He was a veteran of World War II.

HICKMAN, CLARENCE W. - (Lt. 2, Blk. 70, Sec. 4) Clarence W. Hickman, 69, former school administrator at Deerfield and Sublette, died December 12, 1995, at his home in Topeka.
He was born November 8, 1926, at Larned, the son of Minor and Maude Hawley Hickman.

Mr. Hickman had been a school administrator for 39 years in public schools at Deerfield, Sublette and Overbrook. Mr. Hickman started teaching at Deerfield Grade School in 1954 and became principal when the new grade school was completed in 1957.

He married Venita Beth Downing on June 27, 1948. She survives.

Other survivors are a daughter, Rebecca Jo Hickman, Topeka; a son, Randall D. Hickman, Leavenworth; two brothers, Howard Hickman, Columbus, Ohio, and John Hickman, Tucson, Ariz.; seven grandchildren and three great grandchildren.

He was preceded in death by a sister, Margaret Kirkland, and a brother, Raymond Hickman.

Cremation was planned, with a memorial service and inurnment at Deerfield Cemetery. Penwell-Gabel Funeral Home in Topeka was in charge of arrangements.

HICKMAN, JESSICA DOWNING - (Lt. 2, Blk. 70, Sec. 4) Jessica Downing Hickman, infant daughter of Mr. and Mrs. Randall D. Hickman, Sublette, died April 26, 1975, at Denver Children's Hospital, Denver, Colo.

She was born Saturday morning at St. Catherine Hospital, Garden City, and flown to Denver.

Survivors include the parents; a brother, Christopher, of the home; paternal grandparents, Mr. and Mrs. Clarence Hickman, Sublette; maternal grandparents, Mr. and Mrs. Fred Tyler, Sublette; paternal great grandmother, Mrs. Ruth Downing, Deerfield; maternal great grandparents, Mr. and Mrs. Kenneth Menzie, Sublette, and Mr. and Mrs. Ernest Tyler, Copeland; and maternal great great grandmother, Mrs. Luella Menzie, Montezuma.

Graveside services at the Deerfield Cemetery, Deerfield, the Rev. Norman Heironimus officiating. Phillips-White Funeral Home in charge.

HORTON, NICK LEE - (Lt. 2, Blk. 89, Sec. 4) Vesper service for Nick Lee Horton, 14, was held at 7 p.m. Thursday, Nov. 28, 1996, at Christ the King Catholic Church, Deerfield. Funeral Mass was at 2 p.m. Friday, Nov. 29, at the church, with the Rev. John Waters as celebrant. Burial at Deerfield Cemetery.

The son of Jim and Laurel Mages Horton of Deerfield, Nick died Wednesday, Nov. 27, 1996, at his home.

DEERFIELD CEMETERY

He was born July 12, 1982, at Garden City, and was a lifetime Deerfield area resident. An eighth grader at Deerfield, he had attended schools at Holcomb and Deerfield. He was a member of Christ the King Catholic Church.

Survivors are his parents, a brother, T. J. Horton, and a sister, Stephanie Horton, all of the home; his grandparents, Dick and LaRue Horton, Deerfield, and Angie Mages, Spearville; and his great grandparents, Eva Frack, Cimarron, Helen Horton, Sparks, Nev., and Velma Horton, Dodge City.

Garnand Funeral Home in charge of arrangements.

HUMPHREY, CHARLES "DOC" - (Lt. 2, Blk. 34, Sec. 3) Born in 1892 and died October 10, 1969, wife, Blanche E.

(Lakin Independent, Deerfield News, Oct. 16, 1969) Deerfield and community extend to Mrs. Alvin Coerber and family their heartfelt sympathy in the loss of her father, C. A. Humphreys of Garden City, who passed away Friday after a long illness and to her mother, her brother and family, her sisters and families and all other bereaved relatives.

HUNER, HERMAN COURT - (Lt. 3, Blk. 79, Sec. 1) Born in 1888 and died May 20, 1953, wife, Martha A.

Funeral services for Herman C. Huner, 65, was held Friday, May 22, 1953, at 3:00 p.m. in the Immanuel Lutheran Church at Deerfield. The Rev. Henry Knoke was in charge. Burial in Deerfield Cemetery.

Mr. Huner died Wednesday, May 20, 1953, in the Kearny County Hospital following several months illness.

Although in poor health for the past two years, Mr. Huner was a cheerful, hard worker and made many friends in the Deerfield and Lakin communities.

Prior to his last illness he was custodian at the Kearny County Hospital.

HUNER, MARTHA A. - (Lt. 3, Blk. 79, Sec. 1) (The Garden City Telegram, May 4, 1957) Funeral services for Martha Anna Huner, 63, was held Tuesday at 2 p.m. (MST) in the Deerfield Immanuel Lutheran Church with the Rev. Henry Knoke officiating.

Mrs. Huner, a resident of the Lakin community for the past nine years died Saturday, May 4, 1957, in Kearny County Hospital following a short stay.

DEERFIELD CEMETERY

She was born at Napoleon, Ohio, December 30, 1893. Her husband died in May 1953. Survivors are one son, Martin Huner, Durango, Colo.; three daughters, Mrs. Ella Love of Camden, Mo., Mrs. Valita Dunsworth of Bloomfield, N.M., Mrs. Maxine Campbell of Deerfield; one sister, Mrs. Anna Ehlers of Michigan and six grandchildren. Burial in Deerfield Cemetery.

HUNT, NANCY A. - (Lt. 1, Blk. 83, Sec. 1) Nancy A. Ousley was born on March the twelfth, eighteen hundred thirty nine, in Harrisonville, Mo. She departed this life on June the first, nineteen hundred twentyfive, being eighty six years, two months and nineteen days of age.
She was united in the Holy bonds of matrimony to Samuel L. Hunt on May the third, eighteen fiftyfive. To this union were given twelve children, five of whom lived to be grown, the others preceded her in infancy and childhood to the home beyond the veil.
Three of the children died in later years. Leonard in eighteen ninety-eight, Anna Josephine in nineteen five, and Thomas Jesse Lee on May twenty-seventh, nineteen eighteen. Her husband preceded her in eighteen eight-nine.
She found Jesus precious as her Savior at the age of fourteen at which time she united with the Baptist Church and continued a member of the same through life.
She leaves to mourn her loss, two sons, Richard J. Hunt, of Deerfield, Kansas, Samuel M. of Parco, Wyo.; twenty-three grandchildren; twelve great grandchildren and four great great grandchildren; together with a host of friends.
Truly we can say "She hath done what she could" here, and now she has gone to be a light in the world above.
It was indeed a comfort to those left behind, to hear her say as she died "I am ready to go."
The funeral services were conducted in the Deerfield M. E. Church by the pastor, Rev. Robert L. Foster, on the afternoon of June the third and the body lain away in the Deerfield Cemetery to await the call of Him whose voice will awaken those who sleep in Him.

HUNT, THOMAS JUNIOR - (Lt. 1, Blk. 83, Sec. 1) (The Lakin Independent, Feb. 27, 1925) Thomas Junior Hunt, the eight year old son of Richard and Lena Hunt, was born

November the 10th, 1916, in Demoins, New Mexico. He moved with his parents to Deerfield, Kansas, in May 1924, where he entered school, where he was in the second grade of the course of study. And, although his time was short in the school, he made many warm friends in whose memory he will linger a long while.

He was taken ill with flu while in school and went home and, as was his nature, bravely fought for life. Not withstanding, and friends did all in their power to restore him to health and vigor, after several days of suffering, it seemed to please Him who had given him his life in this world to call him to the Celestial City where suffering and illness never come. And on the 19th day of February he stepped on board the old ship of Zion and went to be with Him whose blood atoned for his salvation.

Thomas Junior leaves to mourn his loss his father, mother, three sisters, three brothers, two grandmothers, one grandfather, seven uncles, five aunts, and a host of friends.

The funeral service was conducted at the Methodist Episcopal Church in Deerfield by the pastor of the church, Rev. Robert L. Foster, and the body lain to rest in the Deerfield Cemetery to await the great resurrection morning when all those who sleep in Christ shall come forth to life eternal.

DEERFIELD CEMETERY

JACOBS, RALPH - (Kearny County Advocate, Sept. 1, 1911) Ralph Jacobs, the two and a half year old, son of Casper Jacobs, who lives on the Nichols farm, just east of Deerfield, died Saturday, Aug. 26, 1911, and the funeral was held from the Catholic Church in this city, Sunday p.m. The little fellow met death in a most painful manner. He was at the table Friday noon and the parents poured out a cup of tea which was left in reach of the little boy who grasped it and took a swallow before they could stop him, and it burned him so that he died just twenty-four hours later. Medical help was called but nothing could save the child.

JACOBSON, LENUS - (Lt. 4, Blk. 58, Sec. 2) (Funeral Record) Born in Sweden in 1859, died May 8, 1933, age 73 yrs. 5 mos., of pneumonia.

(The Kearny County Advocate, May 26, 1933) Lenus Jacobson was born in Skara, Sweden, November 25, 1859, and passed away May 9, 1933, after a short illness. The cause of his death was pneumonia. When quite a young man he came to the United States, visiting at the home of his sister, who then lived in Cleveland, Ohio. In the year of 1883, he went west to Colorado where he was engaged in prospecting, mining and other activities. In the year of 1905 he returned to Deerfield for a visit of some weeks, then again in the year of 1927 he came back to Deerfield to live, making his home with his niece, Mrs. George Buell and Mr. Buell. He was quite active in the late years, he liked to help with the chores around the house, he enjoyed the home life very much. He was quiet and retiring in his disposition. He leaves to mourn his passing several nieces and nephews.

Mr. Jacobson's parents were Lutheran folks and he was confirmed in this church when just a lad. While Mr. Jacobson was never active in the church here, everyone who knew him as a good, kind considerate citizen.

He will be missed, not only by his relatives, but by those who passed by the Buell Hotel.

JAMES, EDWARD CADFYN - (Lt. 2, Blk. 51, Sec. 2) Born April 23, 1910, and died November 1, 1911, of poliomyelitis. He was the son of John and Elizabeth Davies James.

JAMES, ELIZABETH - (Lt. 2, Blk. 51, Sec. 2) On August 8, 1872, a daughter was born to Mr. and Mrs. Edward

111

DEERFIELD CEMETERY

Davies at their home in Montgomeryshire, Wales, who was called Elizabeth.

On Nov. 18, 1897, she became the bride of Mr. John James. To this union God gave 2 sons, William E. of Deerfield and Edward C. who preceded the parents in death in 1911; six daughters, Prudence, now Mrs. Orlie White of Lakin; Rosamond, now Mrs. J. M. Eves of Lakin; Blanche, now Mrs. Clarence Owings, of Syracuse; May of Topeka; Ruth of the home; and Alice, now Mrs. Thomas Roberts of San Francisco, California.

The family immigrated to America in March 1898, and settled in New York, then lived 10 years at Pontiac, Ill., moving to Deerfield, Kansas, in 1910. They saw the wide spreading prairie and cattle ranches transformed into homes surrounded by great fields of wheat and maize. The knew the hardships that attend the rearing of a large family as pioneers in western Kansas, coming in the second wave of immigration that sought homes where buffalo and antelope had long held domain.

Mrs. James was reared in the Wesleyan Methodist Church in her homeland and when her children began to answer the call to accept Christ, she reconsecrated her life to the Savior during the pastorate of Rev. R. L. Wells and has since been identified with the work of the Deerfield Methodist Church.

Ill health has been a burden for many months but the blessed fellowship with her Savior and loving care of her family has sustained her. She closed her eyes to earth's scenes on June 9, 1945, having reached the age of 72 years, 10 months, and 1 day.

Her memory will be cherished by the husband and companion of nearly 48 years, the one son, six daughters with their families, eleven grandchildren, a cousin at Utica, New York, a brother-in-law and two nieces, along with many warm friends.

Memorial services were held at Deerfield Methodist Church on June 11, by Rev. R. L. Wells, a long time friend of the family. Hymns of comfort were sung by a quartet consisting of Madison Downing, Oscar Downing, Wm. Burrows, H. N. VanDoren, and a solo by Miss Doris Murray. They were accompanied by Mrs. Maurice Downing at the piano.

The tired body was borne to its final rest in Deerfield Cemetery by the following neighbors: Paul Hagler, Lute Wagner, Walter Kraft, Geo. Buell, L. A. Maddux, and Ralph Miller.

JAMES, IRENE B. - (Lt. 4, Blk. 60, Sec. 3) Funeral services for Irene B. James, 78, was held at Deerfield United Methodist Church, the Rev. Nellie Holmes, Deerfield United Methodist Church minister, officiating. Burial in Deerfield Cemetery. She died April 24, 1988, at her home after a long illness.

Born Irene B. Clampitt, Oct. 28, 1909, at St. Louis, she married William E. James, May 8, 1930, at Garden City. He died July 1, 1964.

Mrs. James was a retired teacher, having taught grades 1 to 8 at the Eminence School District 5 in Finney County. She had been a resident of western Kansas since 1918, moving from Hamilton, Mo. She graduated from Holcomb High School and received her teachers certificate from Fort Hays State University.

She was a member of Deerfield United Methodist Church, past matron of Order of the Eastern Star, and was an active member of the Kearny and Finney county communities.

Survivors include a sister, Emma Jean Cervay, Waukesha, Wis.; a nephew, a great nephew and several great nieces. She was preceded in death by two brothers and two sisters.

JAMES, JOHN - (Lt. 2, Blk. 51, Sec. 2) Born March 19, 1875, at Llanerfyl, N. Wales, and died July 30, 1952, at Deerfield. Funeral services for John James, 77, of Deerfield was held Friday afternoon at 2:30 o'clock from the Methodist Church in Deerfield with the Rev. Denver Flowers officiating. Burial in the Deerfield Cemetery.

Mr. James died in a Garden City hospital, Wednesday, July 30, 1952, at noon.

Mr. James was a prominent Kearny County farmer and political leader. At the time of his death he was completing his fourth term on the board as county commissioner from the third district. He had served as a commissioner two terms during the '20's and then returned to that office in 1944. He had declined to run for another term although his many friends had urged him to do so.

In his many years of public service as a school board member, county commissioner and on numerous other community and county committees, he was known as a thoughtful and considerate individual who strove to do the best job he knew how. His knowledge of local needs gave him a rare insight into problems concerning the

DEERFIELD CEMETERY

county welfare. Although he was known to be very
conservative in his viewpoints concerning county finances
he was always ready and willing to help promote and
assist any worthwhile project for the good of the people.
Many of the county's worthwhile public works projects
were begun and completed during the past eight years
while Mrs. James served as commissioner. The new Kearny
County Hospital, the Veterans Memorial Building, county
unit system, which gave the county a modern highway
department, all were begun and completed while he held
office.

Mr. James was born and raised in Wales, British Isles.
During his youth he served as a cavalryman in the British
army. In November 1897, he married Elizabeth Davies in
Montgomeryshire, Wales. The young couple came to the
United States in March 1897, on a honeymoon trip and
intended to stay only a year.

John took a job in an iron foundry in Utica, New York,
and worked there for some time. Friends then persuaded
he and his young bride to come west to Illinois with them
and they settled near Pontiac, Illinois, where five of
their eight children were born.

In 1910 he and Mrs. James and family moved to Kansas
and settled near Deerfield where they remained the rest
of their lives. Mrs. James preceded him in death in June
1945.

Surviving are a son, Wm. E. James, of Garden City; six
daughters: Mrs. Orlie White and Mrs. Joseph M. Eves of
Lakin, Mrs. Clarence Owings, of Syracuse, Mrs. Ray
Cohorst of Marysville, Mrs. T. H. Roberts of San
Francisco and Miss Ruth James of the home. One son
preceded him in death. Also surviving are 15
grandchildren, two great grandchildren and three sisters
living in Wales and England.

JAMES, RUTH NAOMI - (Lt. 2, Blk. 51, Sec. 2) Ruth Naomi
James, daughter of John and Elizabeth (Davies) James was
born May 18, 1912, at her parents farm home six miles
north of Deerfield and departed this life September 27,
1993, age 81, at the Southwest Medical Center, Liberal,
Ks.

Ruth had "Brain Fever" (encephalitis) when she was six
weeks old. She attended Prairie View Grade School. She
enjoyed riding horses, feeding chickens, gathering eggs,
and feeding bucket calves as she grew up on the farm.

She lived at home with her parents until 1951, when her father passed away. Her father arranged for continued care for the rest of her life. She has been well taken care of for the past 42 years in rest homes. Her pastime was embroidering and playing cards. Her nieces, Shirley Henderson, Lakin, and Lois Creveling, Ulysses, have been her conservators in recent years.

Only one month ago she was diagnosed as having terminal cancer of the colon. Her surgery was August 26 at the Liberal Hospital.

Ruth was preceded in death by her parents, her brother, William, her sisters, Rosamond Eves and Blanche Owings.

She is survived by her sisters, Prudence White, Lakin; May Cohorst, Marysville; and Alice Roberts, San Francisco, Calif.; 13 nieces and nephews.

Funeral services were held September 29, at the United Methodist Church, Deerfield, with the Rev. Donald Koehn, officiating. Burial was in the Deerfield Cemetery.

JAMES, WILLIAM E. - (Lt. 4, Blk. 60, Sec. 3) W. E. (Bill) James, chairman of the board of Kearny County commissioners, died unexpectedly Wednesday morning about 8 o'clock at his home in Deerfield. Death was apparently due to a heart attack.

Funeral arrangements have not been completed pending notification of a sister, Mrs. Orlie White, who is on an European tour. Garnand Funeral home in Garden City is in charge of arrangements.

Mr. James was a prominent Deerfield farmer and had served two terms as county commissioner. He came to Kearny County in the 1900's with his parents, the late Mr. and Mrs. John James.

William E. James, son of John and Elizabeth James, was born on Feb. 6, 1904, at Chenoa, Ill. His death occurred on July 1, 1964, at the home in Deerfield. His parents and family moved to the Deerfield area in 1910 and he has made his home here ever since.

On May 8, 1930, he was united in marriage to Irene Clampitt of Garden City, Kans.

His life was spent in farming. He was also active in community affairs. He was a member of the Deerfield Methodist Church, the Lions Club, Masonic Lodge and Eastern Star.

DEERFIELD CEMETERY

At the time of his death he was in his second term as one of the county commissioners of Kearny County and was chairman of that group.
He is survived by his wife, Irene, of the home and six sisters: Mrs. Prudence White and Mrs. Rosamond Eves of Lakin; Mrs. Blanche Owings of Hill City, Kans.; Mrs. May Cohorst of Marysville, Kans.; Miss Ruth James of Garden City, Kans.; and Mrs. Alice Roberts of San Francisco, Calif.
Funeral services were held Sunday, July 5, with interment in the Deerfield Cemetery.

JARBOE, JAMES F. SR. - (Lt. 2, Blk. 90, Sec. 4)
Deerfield lost a longtime civic leader, former mayor, and businessman last week when James F. Jarboe, Sr. died, April 28, 1988, at the Kearny County Hospital in Lakin.
Mr. Jarboe had recently retired following a long career as an electrical technician. He had owned and operated Jarboe's Service and Sales in Deerfield. Jim installed and operated Deerfield's TV Cable System until he sold it last fall.
Born on February 13, 1926, in Ioka, Kansas, he married Louella Wise on April 18, 1948, in Sawyer. The Jarboes observed their 40th wedding anniversary on April 17, when about 50 members of their family and close friends attended a reception hosted by their children.
He was a member of the United Methodist Church, Deerfield, and the American Legion, Garden City. He served on the Beymer Park board of directors, was former regional vice president of the Kansas Electronics Association and was a scoutmaster for many years. He was a veteran of World War II.
Survivors are his wife, Louella, of the home; a son, James Jr., Lakin; two daughters, Marsha Koop, Grabill, Ind., and Michelle Jarboe, Topeka; three brothers, R. A., Claremore, Okla., Donald and Vernon, both of Topeka; a sister, Alice Carter, Ulysses; and five granchildren.
Preceding him in death was a son, David, and his parents, James Ray Jarboe and Charity Mae (Geer) Jarboe.
Funeral service was at 10 a.m. Monday at the United Methodist Church, Deerfield, with the Revs. Nellie Holmes and Byron Neufelt officiating. Burial in Deerfield Cemetery. Greene-Schneider Funeral Home was in charge of arrangements.

DEERFIELD CEMETERY

JONES, CLIFFORD W. - (Lt. 2, Blk. 22, Sec. 2) Son of Thomas Leslie and Hazel (Smith) Jones. Born Feb. 28, 1913, and died Nov. 28, 1937.
(The Kearny County Advocate, Dec. 3, 1937) Clifford W. Jones, 24, of Deerfield, employed as tool dresser at the Light N 1 gas test, 14 miles north of Hugoton, died while enroute to St. Catherine's Hospital following an accident at the well about 5 o'clock Sunday morning.

Jones and driller, Jack Mills, of Hugoton, were completing the test and were the only men working at the well at the time the accident occurred. The men were lowering cable into the well to bail out sand. Jones was standing on a platform near the reel, chopping markers off the cable with a hatchet, when his hand was caught in a pulley.

Driller Mills, seeing what had happened, rushed to the controls and reversed the cable in an attempt to save Jones' hand. When released, Jones fell into the reel, was thrown against the clutch mechanism on the opposite side of the reel from which he was standing and received three blows on the head, any one of which probably would have been fatal. He was taken to Hugoton and the physician there placed him in an ambulance and started for the hospital at Garden City but Jones died shortly before 8 o'clock on the way to the hospital.

Mr. Jones was employed by Joe Murphy, drilling contractor, who has been active in the southwest Kansas gas field. The Light N. 1 is being drilled for Panhandle Eastern and is located in section 3-32-38 in Stevens County. Murphy said Jones' death was the first resulting from an accident at any well he has drilled.

Jones has been living at Hugoton since he started work at the well November 6. He had been working for Murphy for several months but formerly operated a Texaco service station at Deerfield. His father is Leslie Jones, bulk dealer for Texaco at Deerfield.

In addition to his wife, son and parents, Mr. Jones is survived by two sisters, Mrs. Daryl Cox of Lakin and Miss Glenadine Jones of Deerfield.

The theft of his car late Saturday afternoon upset him and is believed to have been partly responsible for the accident. Mills said Jones had been worried by the loss of the car and expressed the opinion he may have been less cautious than usual as a result. The car was recovered at Johnson, Kansas, and a man whom the police said was Bob Smith was held in connection with the theft. The car had been badly damaged in a crash.

Funeral services were conducted at the Deerfield Methodist Church Tuesday afternoon at 2:30 o'clock, Rev. Palmer officiating.

(The Kearny County Advocate, Dec. 10, 1937) Clifford Warren Jones was born at Reading, Kansas, on February 28, 1913, and departed this life, November 28, 1937. He met his death accidentally while employed by an oil company at Hugoton.

When two years old he came with his parents to Deerfield. At five years of age they moved to Newton and returned to Deerfield eleven years ago. He attended school at Newton, Deerfield and Lakin. On January 15, 1934, he was united in marriage to Miss Mildred Spence of Lakin. Since his marriage he had lived at Deerfield, Lakin and Hugoton.

At eleven years of age he accepted Jesus Christ as his personal savior and united with the Methodist Church and since his marriage he and his wife renewed their vows. His friendly disposition and pleasing manner brought him a host of friends. He was well liked and highly spoken of by all who knew him. He was a loving son, husband and father.

He leaves his wife; his son, Clifford Warren Jr.; his parents, Mr. and Mrs. Leslie Jones of Deerfield; two sisters, Mrs. Daryl Cox of Lakin and Miss Glenadine Jones of Deerfield; one brother, J. T. Jones of Deerfield; a grandfather of Los Angeles, California; a number of other relatives and a host of friends.

Funeral services were conducted at the Deerfield Methodist Church, Tuesday, November 30, at 2:30 p.m. with Rev. Glenn W. Palmer in charge. Interment was made in the Deerfield Cemetery.

JONES, ESTER ELVARA — (Lt. 3, Blk. 83, Sec. 1) Ester Elvara Lawson was born March 14, 1881, near Iberia, in Miller Co., Missouri, and passed away at Lakin, Kansas, on October 2, 1942, at the Kearny County Hospital, at the age of 61 years, 6 months and 18 days.

On December 2, 1897, she was united in marriage to John F. Jones. In the earlier years of their married life, they lived in several different communities, since his contracting work took them from place to place. In September 1924, they moved to Deerfield, where they have since resided.

At the age of 11 years, she united with the Christian Church, later transferring her membership to the Nazarene Church at Sylvia, Kansas. Wishing to remain affiliated with the church, she joined the Deerfield Methodist Church, where she remained a devoted member, until the illness, which she so patiently bore, prevented her from attending.

Six children were born to this happy union, three preceding their mother in death, Cecil and Willard in infancy, Thomas Marion at 11 years of age. Those left to mourn her going are her husband; one daughter, Mrs. Mabel Lemen of Hutchinson, Kansas; two sons, Carl and Paul of Deerfield; 16 grandchildren; one half brother, W. W. Lawson of Ketchum, Oklahoma; and a host of friends.

JONES, GEORGE CARL - (Lt. 4, Blk. 83, Sec. 1) Funeral services for George Carl Jones, 51, was held at the Deerfield Methodist Church, Rev. Robert M. Fleenor officiating. Burial in Deerfield Cemetery.

Mr. Jones died August 13, 1963, at St. Catherine's Hospital in Garden City following a long illness.

He was born September 30, 1911, at Cedar City, Mo. He moved with his parents, John F. and Ester Lawson Jones to Kansas by covered wagon in 1914. The family lived in Sylvia and Hutchinson, Kansas, until 1924, when they moved to Deerfield. Carl was married to Josephine Steenis, October 8, 1929, at Garden City. For many years he operated the Chevrolet agency in Deerfield and had operated the Deerfield Recreation after that.

Carl was baptized when a boy in a Nazarene Camp meeting in Sylvia and later became a member of the Deerfield Methodist Church. He was also a member of the Deerfield Lions Club and the VFW.

Survivors include the widow of the home; sons, Keith, Lakin, Douglas, Garden City, Gary, Tyrone, Okla.; daughters, Mrs. Betty Young, Bend, Ore., Mrs. Carol Salvati, Taipei, Taiwan (Formosa); brother, Paul Deerfield; sister, Mrs. Mabel Lemen of Hutchinson and seven grandchildren.

JONES, GLEN DOUGLAS - (Lt. 4, Blk. 83, Sec. 1) Funeral for Doug Jones, 905 N. 5th, Garden City, was held at the First Christian Church, in Garden City, the Rev. Donald Carter officiating. Burial at Deerfield Cemetery.

He died November 18, 1989, at St. Catherine Hospital. Born January 17, 1934, at Lakin. He was the son of the late Carl and Josephine Jones of Deerfield and was raised in that community. He married Ida Marie, April 16, 1988, at Garden City.

Mr. Jones was the manager of the Co-op Country Corner for two years.

He was a member of the First Christian Church and graduated from Deerfield High School in 1952. His hobbies included fishing and cars.

Survivors include his wife, of the home; two sons, Todd, Colorado Springs, Colo., and Brett, Tucson, Ariz.; two brothers, Keith Jones, Lamar, Colo., and Gary Jones, Tyron, Okla.; two sisters, Betty Young, Bend, Ore., and Carol Salvati, San Diego, Calif.; and one grandson. He was preceded in death by his parents.

JONES, HAZEL - (Lt. 2, Blk. 22, Sec. 2) Mrs. Hazel S. Jones, 79, died February 8, 1973, at the Deaconess hospital in Billings, Mont., after a long illness. She was born, March 5, 1893, near Redding, Kansas. She was married to Lesley T. Jones, May 22, 1912, at Emporia. They came to Deerfield in 1915 where they lived until ill health forced her to go to Billings in September 1972, where she lived with her daughter, Mrs. Gaylord James. They lived in Lakin three years where Mr. Jones was employed at the Service Oil Co. He died in 1950.

She was a member of the Deerfield First United Methodist Church and was active in church and community affairs.

Survivors include daughters: Mrs. Vera Cox, Helena, Mont., Mrs. Glenadine James, Billings, Mont.; a son, J. T. Jones, Anaheim, Calif.; brothers: J. E. Smith, Hemet, Calif., J. B. Smith, Oakland, Calif., Glen H. Smith, Hawthorne, Calif.; sisters: Mrs. Harry Lane and Mrs. Ralph Manley, Modesto, Calif., Mrs. Kathryn Croxton, Hemet, Calif., Mrs. Harry Jones, Harveyville, Kans.; seven grandchildren and 13 great grandchildren.

Funeral was held at the church; Rev. Charles Hadley. Burial in Deerfield Cemetery. Davis Funeral Home in charge of arrangements.

JONES, JOHN FRANCIS - (Lt. 3, Blk. 83, Sec. 1) John Francis Jones was born on a farm near Dixon in Pulaski County, Missouri, on February 14, 1874, and departed this life at his home in Deerfield, Kansas, Sunday, April 22, 1945.

DEERFIELD CEMETERY

Mr. Jones grew to manhood in Pulaski County, and there was united in marriage to Esther Elvara Lawson on December 12, 1897. To this union six children were born, two of whom passed away in infancy, Cecil and Willard. Thomas Marion, another son, passed away at 11 years of age. His wife preceded him in death, October 22, 1942. About 1918 he moved to central Kansas and became a foreman for a road construction company which built one of the first hard surface roads in the state of Kansas. He had his headquarters at Hutchinson and Sylvia at this time.

Mr. Jones united with the Nazarene Church while residing at Sylvia, Kansas, and later transferred his membership to the Methodist Church at Deerfield, where he remained a faithful member until his death. He moved to Deerfield in 1924 and became engaged in the garage business, which he successfully carried on until he was stricken by a cerebral hemorrhage which brought about his death a short time later.

On October 22, 1943, Mr. Jones was married to Eula Barnhart of Meta, Missouri. At the time of his death he and Mrs. Jones were living in Deerfield. They had enjoyed life together and she and his other loved ones and many friends will mourn his passing.

The bereaved family includes his loving wife; one daughter, Mrs. Mabel Lemen of Hutchinson, Kansas; and two sons in the service of their country, Paul of the Army air base at Miami, Florida, and Carl in the southwest Pacific; also three sisters; one brother and 17 grandchildren.

John F. Jones, Chevrolet dealer, died Sunday noon at the Carl Jones home in Deerfield, following a cerebral hemorrhage Saturday evening when he fell on his way home from the garage. He never regained consciousness. He came to Deerfield over twenty years ago and was a very successful salesman until the war made it impossible to secure cars.

Funeral service was held Thursday afternoon at the Deerfield Methodist Church, of which he was a member.

JONES, PAUL RAYMOND - (Lt. 3, Blk. 101, Sec. 1) Paul R. Jones, 50, of Deerfield, was electrocuted accidentally Monday, November 21, 1966, while working at the Kansas Nebraska Compressor station west of Scott City.

121

Jones and a Scott City man, Gene Smith, were painting "vessels" at the station when a boom on their paint truck came in contact with a high voltage line.

A company spokesman said the accident occurred at 11:05 a.m. as the men attempted to move the truck and boom into position to begin painting.

Jones was apparently behind the truck on the ground attempting to move a paint pot out of the way when Smith, the boom operator, swung the boom around and it came in contact with a high voltage line.

The voltage arced through the truck, hitting Jones, who was touching the vehicle, killing him instantly. Burns were found on the paint pot and truck in addition to Jones body.

Smith was uninjured but was "visibly shaken" by the incident. Jones was foreman of the two man paint crew for Kansas-Nebraska.

Paul Raymond Jones was born Aug. 23, 1907, at Dixon, Mo., and married Zona Mae Ward, April 26, 1930, at Syracuse. He was manager of the paint crew for the Kansas-Nebraska Natural Gas Co. He had been a resident of Deerfield since moving there in 1924 from Sylvia.

He was a member of the Deerfield Methodist Church; served in the Air Corps in World War II; was a member of the American Legion, VFW, and Eagles Lodge.

Surviving are the widow; a sister, Mrs. Mabel Lemen, Hutchinson. One brother, Carl, preceded him in death.

Funeral was held in the Deerfield Methodist Church with the Rev. Wesley Davis officiating. Burial was in the Deerfield Cemetery.

JONES, TERRI LYNN — (Lt. 3, Blk. 43, Sec. 3) Terri Lynn Jones, infant daughter of Mr. and Mrs. Keith Jones of Lakin, died Tuesday evening, May 16, 1961, at the Kearny County Hospital in Lakin. She was born at Lakin on November 24, 1960.

Survivors include the parents; brother, Roger Keith, and sister, Cheryl, all of the home; the grandparents, Mr. and Mrs. Davis A. Williams, and Mr. and Mrs. Carl Jones of Deerfield; and a great grandmother, Mrs. Edith Steenis of Redmond, Ore.

Graveside services were held at 10 a.m. in the Deerfield Cemetery. Rev. Richard Holmes of the Lakin Presbyterian Church officiated.

JONES, THOMAS LESLIE - (Lt. 2, Blk. 22, Sec. 2) Thomas Lesley Jones, son of Lewis and Maria Jones, was born February 24, 1890, near Reading, Kansas, and departed this life July 5, 1950, at St. Catherine's Hospital, Garden City, at the age of 60 years, 4 months and 11 days. He was a member of the Deerfield Methodist Church.

He was united in marriage to Hazel Smith at Emporia, May 22, 1912. To this union four children were born, Clifford W., Vera, Glenadine and J. T.

He moved to Deerfield, Kansas, in January 1915. In 1917 he moved to Newton where he worked for the Santa Fe Railroad until 1919. Then he with his family moved back to Deerfield. They lived in Lakin for three years. It was while working for the Service Oil Co. in Lakin that he was severely burned in 1931. Since that time they have lived in Deerfield, Kansas.

In passing he leaves to mourn his going, his wife, Hazel; one son, J. T. of Deerfield; two daughters, Vera Cox and Glenadine James of Lakin; two sisters, Mrs. L. G. Wagner of Deerfield, and Mrs. Edith Van Sickle of Reading, Kansas; one brother, Charles Jones of Pierceville, Kansas; four grandchildren, Cliff W. Jones, Leslie Ann and Sheri James and Schuyler Dee Jones. His son, Clifford W., proceeded him in death, November 22, 1937.

He had a host of friends who will miss him with the relatives. He was a good father and kind husband.

A Brighter Home
Calm on the bosom of they God
    Fair spirit, rest thee now..
E"en while with ours thy footsteps trod
    His seal was on thy brow.
Dust to its narrow house beneath!
    Soul to its place on high!
They that have seen thy look in death
    No more may fear to die.
Lone are the paths and sad the bowers
    Whence thy dear smile is gone;
But Oh! A brighter home than ours,
    In Heaven is now thine own.

Funeral services were held at the Deerfield Methodist Church, Rev. Glenn Palmer of Ulysses officiating. Burial in the Deerfield Cemetery.

JONES, THOMAS MARION - (Lt. 3, Blk. 83, Sec. 1) (Funeral Record) Died January 12, 1929, of streptococsic pluresy, age 10 yrs., 5 mos., 10 days. Father Jno. F. Jones. (The Kearny County Advocate, Jan. 25, 1929) Thomas Marion Jones was born at Hutchinson, Kansas, August 2nd, 1918, and departed this life January 12, 1929. He spent the first two years of his life in Hutchinson; from there the family moved to Sylvia, Kansas, where they spent four years, then they returned to Hutchinson for fourteen months and moved to Deerfield, Kansas, where he has lived until the time of his death. He leaves his father and mother, Mr. and Mrs. J. F. Jones; two brothers, Paul Raymond, and George Carl, of Deerfield; and a sister, Mrs. S. E. Leman, of Springfield, Missouri, with her husband and three children; and also many friends to mourn his departure. Rev. J. H. Copley conducted the funeral service at the Methodist Church and interment in the Deerfield Cemetery.

JONES, ZONA MAE - (Lt. 3, Blk. 101, Sec. 1) Zona Mae Jones, 78, died March 1, 1986, at the High Plains Retirement Village, Lakin. Born Zona Mae Ward, July 28, 1907, at Latimer, Okla., she married Paul Jones, April 26, 1930, at Syracuse. He died in 1966. She was a resident of Deerfield for the past 55 years.
    She was a member of the United Methodist Church, Deerfield, and the United Methodist Women, Deerfield Book Club, and the Capsula Club. Survivors: nephews, Keith, Lamar, Colo., Douglas, Garden City, Gary, Tyrone, Okla.; nieces, Betty Lou Young, Bend, Ore., Carol Salvati, San Diego. Funeral was held Tuesday at the United Methodist Church, Deerfield, the Rev. Nellie Holmes. Burial in the Deerfield Cemetery. Greene-Schneider Funeral Home, Lakin, was in charge of arrangements.

DEERFIELD CEMETERY

KEENER, WILEY E. - (Lt. 4, Blk. 77, Sec. 1)   Wiley
Ellsworth Keener, passed away on December 31, 1945, at
the age of 51 years, 2 months, and 21 days. He had been
in ill health for several years and bronchial pneumonia
developed, causing his death. Funeral services were held
January 4, at the Lakin Methodist Church with Rev. A. C.
Ramsay in charge and interment was in Deerfield Cemetery
with graveside service by the American Legion.
    Mr. Keener was born at McCune, Kansas, and as a child
he lived with his aunt at Mineral, Kansas. He was
married to Mattie Maye Faucett in May 1922, at Lamar,
Missouri, and lived around Pittsburg, Kansas, until he
came to Kearny County in 1930. The past 15 years they
lived on a farm north of Lakin.
    He was a veteran of World War I, enlisting in May 1918,
in the 338th Machine Gun Battalion, and was a member of
Shepherd-Moore Post No. 208, American Legion. He became
a member of the Methodist Church at Walnut, Kansas, in
1927.
    Surviving are his wife, three step daughters, and one
stepson: Mrs. Bert Cox of Erie, Kansas; Mrs. Alva Stroud
of Chanute, Kansas; Mrs. Bob Hilton of Chichasha,
Oklahoma; and Marion Glaspy of Lakin; all of whom were
present at the funeral. There are also two brothers and
other relatives and friends who mourn his departure.

KEES, GEORGE JESS - (Lt. 2, Blk. 44, Sec. 3)   George J.
Kees, 62, died Sunday, Sept 3, 1972, at his home after a
short illness. Born Feb. 24, 1910, in Gate, Okla., he
married Lula Kees in 1960, at Oshkosh, Neb. She died in
1965. He was a retired truck driver and lived in Garden
City 40 years.
    Survivors include sisters, Mrs. Dorothy Romine, Garden
City; Mrs. Helen Truitt, Holcomb.
    Funeral was at the Garnand Funeral Home; Rev. Lester
Myers. Burial in Deerfield Cemetery.
    He served with the US Navy in WW II.

KEES, LULA B. - (Lt. 2, Blk. 44, Sec. 3)   Mrs. Lula B.
Kees, 51, died Sunday afternoon, Nov. 7, 1965, in Trinity
Hospital here, where she had been a patient, since Oct.
26, after an illness of about three months. Born March
7, 1914, at Adamana, Ariz., she had lived at Dodge City
two years, moving here from Garden City, where she lived
from 1945 to 1963. She was a waitress in Dodge City

DEERFIELD CEMETERY

before her illness. She married George J. Kees in 1945 at Oshkosh, Neb.

Survivors: The widower; daughters, Mrs. Jay D. Landon, Deerfield, Mrs. Jimmy Dixon, Sulphur Springs, Tex.; brother, Jack Lasater, Blythe, Calif.; sisters, Mrs. Marie Medlock, Globe, Ariz., Mrs. Leta McElhaney, Fresno, Calif.; five grandchildren.

KELL, HELEN MAUD - (Lt. 2, Blk. 75, Sec. 1) Funeral service for Mrs. Maud Kell was held at the United Methodist Church in Deerfield, August 29, at 10 o'clock, Rev. Charles Hadley officiated at the service. Burial was in Deerfield Cemetery.

Helen Maud Corbett, daughter of Samuel H. and Dolly Caswell Corbett, was born April 15, 1887, in Deerfield, Kansas. She attended the Deerfield schools and was married to William Thomas Kell, March 6, 1912. They lived in Deerfield most of their lives, returning there from Caldwell where they lived. She was a member of the Methodist Church, Order of Eastern Star and the Green Thumb Garden Club. She was active in the work of these various organizations until her health failed four years ago. She had been in the Kearny County Hospital several times and had been a resident of Lakin Manor Rest Home until a few days before her death when she was again taken to the hospital where she died Thursday, August 27, 1970, at the age of 83 years, 4 months and 12 days.

She was preceded in death by her parents and three brothers, Bert, Karl and Jacob Corbett.

She is survived by the widower of the home; two sisters, Mrs. Louise Smith, Orange, Calif. and Mrs. Ruth Melton of Colorado Springs, Colo.

KELL, WILLIAM THOMAS - (Lt. 2, Blk. 75, Sec. 1) Funeral service for William Thomas Kell was held in the United Methodist Church in Deerfield, April 23 at 10 a.m. Dr. Ruben Reyes officiated. Burial was in Deerfield Cemetery with Masonic rites by Emerald Lodge 289.

William Thomas Kell, son of James and Lucy Ann Brown Kell, was born June 25, 1883, in Illinois. He died April 21, 1975, at the Kearny County Hospital in Lakin after a long illness. He was a long time resident of Deerfield. He was engaged in farming and had owned and operated the Deerfield pool hall for many years. He was married to Maud Corbett, March 6, 1912. She died August 27, 1970. He had resided at Lakin Manor.

DEERFIELD CEMETERY

He was a member of the United Methodist Church, Deerfield and Masonic Lodge. He was a fifty year member and was recognized and presented his 50 year pin several years ago.
He is survived by his brother, Ed Kell, Chickasha, Okla., and several nephews and nieces.

KERR, CHARLES EDWIN - (Lt. 1, Blk. 45, Sec. 3)   Charles Edwin Kerr stillborn on April 21, 1936, son of John W. and Martha Kerr.

KERSTEN, FLORA BELL - (Lt. 4, Blk. 29, Sec. 2)   (Kearny County Advocate, March 18, 1927)   Flora Bell Gillock was born in Green County, Indiana, August 8th, 1873, and died in Harrison County, Iowa, March 16th, 1927, aged 53 years, 7 months and 8 days. She came with her parents, A. J. Gillock and wife to Reno County, Kansas, in 1876, where she grew to womanhood and taught school. In 1901 the family moved to Kearny County, settling north of Deerfield. On November 7th, 1905, she was united in marriage with W. A. Kersten, who died July 2nd, 1920. June 13th, 1922, she was married to Rev. A. Kersten. In the fall of 1924 they moved to Harrison County, Iowa.
She was converted, when a child, and united with the Methodist Church. Hers was a beautiful life of Christian faith and service. Her health had not been good for some time, but her death was unexpected and came as a shock.
Mrs. Kersten was highly esteemed and much loved by her friends. She was patient in suffering, thoughful of others and a loving wife and devoted mother.
She heard the Master's summons, "child, come home."
She leaves to mourn her loss, two daughters, Caroline, age 16 years, Myrtle, age 12 years; her husband, Rev. A. Kersten; three brothers, J. W. Gillock, of Deerfield, J. D. Gillock, of Moore Haven, Florida, Samuel Gillock, of Los Angeles, California; one sister, Mrs. P. C. Burge of Hopeton, Oklahoma; and a number of other relatives and friends.
The remains were brought to Deerfield. The funeral services were held in the Methodist Church at Deerfield, surrounded by friends who knew and loved her.
Rev. J. Q. Turner conducted the services, and the remains laid to rest in the Deerfield Cemetery.
          "Some day, when fades the golden sun
          Beneath the rosy tinted west,
          My blessed Lord will say, 'well done,'

127

DEERFIELD CEMETERY

And I shall enter into rest.
And I shall see Him face to face,
And tell the story saved by grace."

KERSTEN, KENNETH ROBERT - (Lt. 3, Blk. 57, Sec. 2)
(Funeral Records) died Aug. 19, 1918, age 2 yrs., 1 mo.
14 days. Father Carl Robert Kersten, mother Maggie Smith
Kersten, died of amacelic dysentery.

KERSTEN, WILLIAM AUGUST - (Lt. 4, Blk. 29, Sec. 2)
William August Kersten was born in Germany, November 25,
1866, and died at Garden City, Kansas, July 2, 1920, at
11 o'clock and 6 minutes a.m. When he was about four
years old his parents came to America and settled in
Eastern Kansas, where he grew to manhood. On November 20,
1895, he was married to Minnie M. Markillie, who died
October 10, 1898. Soon after her death he came to
western Kansas, where he was married to Flora B. Gillock,
November 7, 1905. When a boy he united with the
Evangelical Church but after coming to Western Kansas he
was a faithful attendant and supporter of the Methodist
Church. He lived a Christian life and was patient in all
his sufferings and was willing that the Lord's will
should be done. After his eyes began to grow dim to
earthly things he said that Jesus was leading him. He
was a kind and loving husband and father, and leaves his
wife and two little girls, Caroline, age 9 and Myrtle,
age 6, besides four sisters and two brothers to mourn
their loss. Funeral service were held at the Methodist
Church, July 4, at 11 a.m., and interment in the
Deerfield Cemetery.

KETTLER, ARMIN - (Lt. 4, Blk. 26, Sec. 2) Armin Edward
Kettler, 60, Deerfield, son of August and Meta Penner
Kettler, died Sunday, April 13, 1975, at St. Catherine
Hospital, Garden City, after a sudden illness.
    Born June 20, 1914, at Deerfield, he had been a farmer
and life time resident here. He was married to Fern
Tibbits, January 25, 1937, at Deerfield.(Lakin
Independent has marriage date at Jan. 24, 1937.)
    Mr. Kettler was a member of Immanuel Lutheran Church,
Deerfield, and the Kearny County Hospital Board.
    Survivors include the widow; a son, Grant, Cape
Hatteras, N.C.; a daughter, Mrs. Glenda Lewis, Deerfield;
his mother, Mrs. Meta Kettler, Deerfield; a brother, the

DEERFIELD CEMETERY

Rev. Earl Kettler, Hagerstown, Md.; a sister, Mrs. Esther McMichael, Canon City, Colo.; and four grandchildren. Funeral was held Wednesday at Immanuel Lutheran Church, Deerfield, with burial in Deerfield Cemetery. Davis Funeral Home was in charge of arrangements.

KETTLER, ARMIN, JR. - (Lt. 4, Blk. 26, Sec. 2) Armin Jr., infant son of Armin and Fern (Tibbits) Kettler, was born at Lakin, Kansas, in the early hours of the morning of October 6, 1938, and died about 30 minutes later. The Lord, in His wisdom took the child and spared it from enduring all the sorrows and tribulations of this life.
Those that mourn his early death are his parents, Mr. and Mrs. Armin Kettler; his grandparents, Mr. and Mrs. August Kettler and Mr. and Mrs. L. E. Tibbitts.
The tender body was laid to rest in the Deerfield Cemetery, services being in charge of the Rev. Walter J. F. Lebien, assisted by a quartet of girls: Ruth Coerber, Maxine Winter, Eileen Kraft, Nelly Jane Mathias.

KETTLER, ARNOLD CURTIS - (Lt. 1, Blk. 27, Sec. 2) Arnold Curtis Kettler, 54, died Sunday morning, August 19, 1973, at St. Catherine Hospital after suffering a heart attack at his home. Born Nov. 13, 1918, at Deerfield, he served as postmaster at Deerfield for the past 27 years. He married Violet Foos, January 10, 1951, at Great Bend.
He was a member of the Immanuel Lutheran Church, VFW, and a veteran of WW II.
He served in Africa and Europe during the war, and was a member of the Guard of Honor for President Roosevelt in North Africa.
Survivors include the widow of the home; a son, Wilmer Curtis; two daughters, Charlotte, and Vionetta, all of the home; mother, Meta Kettler, Deerfield; two brothers, Armin, Deerfield, Earl, Hagerstown, Md.; and a sister, Mrs. Esther McMichael, Canon City, Colo.
Funeral was held Wednesday morning at the Immanuel Lutheran Church, Rev. Norman Heironimus officiating. Burial was in Deerfield Cemetery.

KETTLER, AUGUST JOHN, JR. - (Lt. 1, Blk. 27, Sec. 2) August Kettler, Jr., 64, died Thursday afternoon, April 8, 1954, about 4 o'clock in the Kearny County Hospital following an illness of several weeks.

Mr. Kettler came to this county in 1911 from near Paola, Kansas, and has resided near Deerfield since that time.

Funeral arrangements are pending word from a son, Capt. Earl C. Kettler, who is a chaplain in the U.S. Army stationed at Yokohama, Japan.

The funeral service for August John Kettler, Jr., was conducted Tuesday afternoon at the Immanuel Lutheran Church at Deerfield with the Rev. Henry Knoke officiating and arrangements in the charge of the Garnand Chapel. Burial was at the Deerfield Cemetery.

The pallbearers were: Ernest Marquardt, Charles Marquardt, Henry Kleeman, Emil Barben, Henry Molz and William Kueker.

Music was furnished by a mixed octet and male quartet with the following taking part: Mrs. Calvin Scheuerman, Mrs. Donald Neff, Miss Agnes Kleeman, Miss Esther Molz, Donald Neff, Lewis Molz, Paul Bentrup, and George Grauberger. Mrs. Leon Scheuerman accompanied the singers.

August John Kettler, Jr., was born July 10, 1890, at Block, Kans., and departed this life Thursday afternoon, April 8, 1954, at the age of 63 years, 8 months and 29 days.

In his infancy he was received into Christ's Kingdom of Grace through the sacrament of Holy Baptism, and in 1904 he renewed his vows in confirmation in the Lutheran Church and remained a faithful member of his church until his death..

He served his church in various offices and was active in civic affairs in the community. He came to the Deerfield community in January 1911, coming from Sheridan Lake, Colo. He was a farmer until recently when he retired due to ill health.

He was united in holy wedlock with Meta Penner on August 20, 1913, at Deerfield. To this union were born four children.

He was preceded in death by his parents, one brother and four sisters.

He leaves to mourn his passing his wife, Meta Kettler; three sons, Armin E. Kettler and Arnold C. Kettler of Deerfield, and Chaplain Earl C. Kettler of the Army in Yokohama, Japan; one daughter, Mrs. Lloyd (Esther) McMichael of Peoria, Ill.; four sisters. Mrs. Gustav Schulz of San Antonio, Tex., Mrs. Herman Coerber of Deerfield, Mrs. Byron Hunter of Oakland, Calif., Mrs.

Olga Kuhlmann of Leoti, Kans.; one brother, Chris Kettler of Garden City; six grandchildren and other relatives and a host of friends.

KETTLER, CHRIS L. - (Lt. 4, Blk. 27, Sec. 2)   Son of Frederick Louis August and Gesche Kettler, born at Block, Ks., Oct. 21, 1886. World War I veteran. Came to Kearny County with his parents in 1910. Died August 14, 1956.
Funeral services were held Thursday morning for Chris L. Kettler, 69, who died Tuesday morning, August 14, 1956, in a Garden City nursing home. Services were at the Deerfield Lutheran Church with Rev. Henry Knoke in charge.
Mr. Kettler had been in poor health for several years and had been in the Garden City nursing home for the last four and a half years.
Mr. Kettler was born at Block, Kansas, on Oct. 21, 1886, and had lived in Kansas most of his life. Between 1921 and 1941 he resided in Colorado.
A veteran of World War I, Mr. Kettler served as a private with the 10th division, 69th infantry. He was a member of the Emanuel Lutheran Church at Deerfield and the American Legion.
Surviving are four sisters, Mrs. Helen Schultz, of San Antonio, Texas; Mrs. Emma Coerber of Deerfield; Mrs. Ida Hunter of San Bruno, Calif. and Mrs. Olga Kuhlman of Leoti.

KETTLER, ESTHER MAE - (Lt. 4, Blk. 26, Sec. 2)   Esther May, infant daughter of Armin, Sr. and Fern Tibbits Kettler, was born Wednesday evening, October 2, and died Thursday morning, October 3, 1940, living only about 12 hours. Although the parents felt much joy at first over the birth of their daughter, yet their joy was soon turned to deep sorrow, for the Lord willed it otherwise, taking their little one through an early death, sparing her all the sorrows and tribulations of this sinful life.
One infant brother, Armin Jr., preceded her in death. Her early passing is mourned by her deeply grieved parents; her grandparents, Mr. and Mrs. Aug. Kettler and Mr. and Mrs. L. E. Tibbitts; and other relatives.
The little body was interred in the Deerfield Cemetery, services being conducted by Rev. Walter J. F. Lebien, assisted by a quartet of girls, Ruth Coerber, Maxine Winter, Margaret Winter, and Eileen Kraft.

KETTLER, FERN ELLEN - (Lt. 4, Blk. 26, Sec. 2) Funeral service for Mrs. Fern Kettler, 58, was held Monday, December 4, at the Immanuel Lutheran Church with the Reverend Norman Heironimus officiating. Burial was in Deerfield Cemetery.

Fern Tibbitts, the daughter of Ledrew and Edna Iford Tibbetts, was born March 23, 1920, in Nashville, Kansas, and died November 30, 1978, at Garden City, Kansas, at the age of 58 years, eight months and seven days. She moved with her family to Deerfield where she attended grade and high school and lived until shortly before her death.

She was married to Armin Kettler, January 24, 1937. He preceded her in death, April 13, 1975. Also preceding her in death was a son and daughter, who died in infancy.

She was a member of the Immanuel Lutheran Church, Deerfield.

Survivors include a son, Grant Kettler, and a daughter, Mrs. Glenda Lewis, both of Deerfield; mother, Mrs. Edna Tibbitts, Sunnyvale, Calif.; brothers, Broyce Tibbitts, LaMesa, Calif., Wallace Tibbitts, Nice, Calif.; sisters, Mrs. Bernice Palmer, Nice, Calif., Mrs. Retha Phillips, San Jose, Calif.; and four grandchildren.

KETTLER, FREDERICK LOUIS AUGUST - (Lt. 4, Blk. 27, Sec. 2) Frederick Louis August Kettler, Sr., son of Louis Kettler and his wife, Rosina, nee Grosha, was born August 4, 1861, at Wheeling, West Virginia. Soon after birth he was received into God's covenant of grace through baptism, and May 25, 1877, at Paola, Kansas, he renewed his baptismal vow in the rite of confirmation.

On December 3, 1885, he was united in marriage with Gesche Tienken. To this union were born eleven children, three sons and eight daughters: Christ, William, August, Helen, Emma, Ida, Bertha, Clara, Dorothy, Olga, and Irene. Bertha and Clara, who died in infancy, and William in 1904, preceded their father in death.

In 1873 Mr. Kettler, with his parents, came from West Virginia and settled near Paola, Miami County, Kansas. Here he lived about 34 years, moving with his family to Sheridan Lake, Colorado, in 1907. After only three years he moved to Kearny County, near Deerfield, where he lived until the end of 1920, when he moved to Tiffany, Colorado.

Mr. Kettler comparatively enjoyed good health until Jan. 13, 1941, when he suffered a severe stroke, leaving

him helpless and bedfast for the last nine months of his
life. On Feb. 12, he was moved to Deerfield, where he
was cared for by his children. All was done for him that
was humanly possible.

Wherever Mr. Kettler lived, he was always a faithful
member of the Lutheran church and remained such unto his
end. He served the Church wherever and whenever he
could, being a member of the board of trustees of Trinity
Lutheran Church at Paola, an elder for a number of years
in the Deerfield Church, and an elder of Trinity Lutheran
Church at Tiffany, Colorado. Mr. Kettler, above all, was
a faithfdul Christian unto his end, placing his simple
faith and full confidence for his salvation upon the
Savior, Jesus Christ. He loved God's Word and frequently
partook of the Lord's Supper. Last Monday, as the pastor
visited him just a few hours before his death, and spoke
to him on the words of Jacob, "Lord, I have loved thy
salvation," he expressed that as his confession. Mr.
Kettler had no fear to face death, but rather welcomed
death and thus, after another light stroke, quietly fell
asleep Monday, Oct. 13, 1941, at the ripe age of 80
years, two months and nine days.

His passing is mourned by his sorrowing wife, eight
children: Christ Kettler, August Kettler and family of
Deerfield, Mrs. Helen Schulz and family of Boerne, Texas,
Mrs. Emma Coerber and family of Deerfield, Mrs. Ida
Keyser and husband of San Jose, California, Mrs. Dorothy
Winter and family of Deerfield, Mrs. Olga Kuhlmann and
family of Leoti, and Mrs. Irene Muir and children of
Durango, Colorado; 26 grandchildren and two great
grandchildren; other relatives and many friends.

Mr. Kettler's favorite hymn was:
        I'm but a stranger here,
            Heav'n is my home;
        Earth is a desert drear,
            Heav'n is my home;
        Danger and sorrow stand
            Round me on ev'ry hand;
        Heav'n is my fatherland,
            Heav'n is my home.

Funeral services were held on Friday, Oct. 17, at the
H. A. Coerber home with Pastor Walter J. F. Lebien in
charge, and in the Lutheran Church at Deerfield with
Pastor Walter Geihsler of Leoti in charge. A quartette,
composed of Carl Bentrup, Ruth Bentrup, Valeta Huner, and
Rev. Walter Lebien, accompanied by Minnie Coerber, sang

DEERFIELD CEMETERY

Mr. Kettler's favorite hymns at the services. Interment was made in the Deerfield Cemetery.

KETTLER, GESCHE A. - (Lt. 4, Blk. 27, Sec. 2) Mrs. Gesche A. Kettler passed away Wednesday morning at the home of her daughter, Mrs. H. A. Coerber, at Deerfield. Mr. and Mrs. August Kettler, Sr. returned from Colorado about five years ago and she had been living with her children since Mr. Kettler's death.

Gesche (Tinken) Kettler was born at Cole Camp, Missouri, on the 13th day of October in the year 1863. Soon after her birth she was received in God's Covenant of Grace through the Holy Sacrament of Baptism. Several years later she was thoroughly instructed in the chief parts of christian doctrine and renewed her baptismal vow in 1873 by the rite of confirmation, thus becoming a communicant member of the Lutheran Church.

On December 3, 1885, she was united in marriage with August Kettler at Paola, Kansas. To this union eleven children were born: three sons and eight daughters. Though she had made her home for a time in Sheridan Lake and Tiffany, Colorado, she spent the larger part of her life in Kansas, at Paola and for a number of years in Kearny County, particularly in the vicinity of Deerfield.

She is preceded in death by her husband, August Kettler Sr., one son, and three daughters. She is survived by two sons, Christ and August of Deerfield; five daughters, Mrs. Gustave Schulz of Divine, Texas, Mrs. Herman Coerber of Deerfield, Mrs. Orville Keyser, San Jose, California, Mrs. August Winter, Thayer, Kansas, Mrs. Herman Kuhlman of Lakin, Kansas; also by twenty-six grandchildren and ten great grandchildren; one sister, Mrs. Herman Wendte of Paola, Kansas; five sons-in-law; one daughter-in-law; and many other relatives and friends.

She fell asleep in Jesus on Wednesday morning, December 5, 1945, having reached the age of 82 years, 1 month, and 20 days.

Funeral services were held on Friday, December 7, 1945, at the Deerfield Lutheran Church with Pastor Paul H. C. Stengel in charge. Burial was made in the Deerfield Cemetery.

KETTLER, META - (Lt. 1, Blk. 27, Sec. 2) Meta Marie Kettler, 93, died Thursday, Jan. 26, 1984, at the St. Catherine Hospital, Garden City. A homemaker, she was a longtime resident of Deerfield.

134

Born Meta Marie Penner, Feb. 4, 1890, at Newton, she
came to Western Kansas with her parents at the age of
five. They lived south of the river near Deerfield. She
married August Kettler, Aug. 20, 1913, at Deerfield and
lived in Rocky Ford, Colo, for a short time before
returning to Deerfield. They moved to a farm west of
town in 1926, keeping their home in Deerfield. Mr.
Kettler died April 8, 1954.

Mrs. Kettler had lived in Garden City with her daughter
and son-in-law for the past five years, but she still had
her house in Deerfield and continued to call that home.

She was a member of Immmanuel Lutheran Church and
Women's Fellowship, both of Deerfield, and had served as
church organist for many years.

Survivors are a son, Pastor Earl C. Kettler, Silver
Springs, Md.; a daughter, Mrs. Lloyd (Esther) McMichael,
Garden City; eight grandchildren, and 10 great
grandchildren.

Funeral was held at the Immanuel Lutheran Church, the
Rev. Jerald Jeskewitz officiating. Burial at Deerfield
Cemetery. Garnand Funeral Home was in charge of
arrangements.

KEUNE, LEWIS H. - (Lt. 1, Blk. 56, Sec. 2) Baby born and
died 1911.

KIMBERLIN, ELISABETH HEATH - (Lt. 3, Blk. 55, Sec. 2)
Born in 1836, Indiana Territory near Germantown in what
is now Hamilton County, Indiana. Died 1915 at Holcomb,
Kansas.

KIMBERLIN, JAMES WESLEY - (Lt. 3, Blk. 55, Sec. 2) Born
1836, Indiana Territory near Germantown in what is now
Hamilton County, Indiana. Died May 8, 1914, Deerfield.
(Lakin Investigator, May 14, 1914) The funeral of Mrs.
Kincade's father who died Friday a.m., was held at the
Baptist Church, Sunday p.m. Buried Deerfield Cemetery.
A large crowd from Holcomb testified to the high esteem
in which he was held in his home community.

KISSELMANN, GEORGE JACOB - (Lt. 3, Blk. 105, Sec. 1)
(The Lakin Independent, May 9, 1941) Jake Kisselmann,
father of Mrs. Fred Schmidt, died Monday in Denver. The
funeral will be held from the Schmidt home in Lakin,
Friday afternoon and interment made in the Deerfield

DEERFIELD CEMETERY

Cemetery beside his wife who was buried there 35 years ago.
(The Lakin Independent, May 16, 1941) Rev. Jacob Kisselmann was born October 25, 1859. His parents were George Jacob Kisselmann and Elizabeth Grauberger Kisselmann. He was born in the village called Krimm, Russia. At the age of six months, his father died and he was brought up by his grandparents, Kisselmann's. He was confirmed in 1874 in Krimm in the Lutheran church. In 1881 he married Catharina Elizabeth Lindt. To this union ten children were born of whom six are living. In 1882 he became a minister in which he worked for 22 years. The family came to the United States November 22, 1906. His wife passed away the 22nd of August, 1909, at their home near Deerfield, Kansas. He then took up the work of a pastor and continued this work for 25 years. He passed away the 5th of May in Denver, Colorado, at the age of 81 years, 6 months, and 10 days. Those who mourn his passing are the children, Mrs. Mollie Kaufmann, Denver, Colorado, Mrs. Fred Schmidt, Lakin, Kansas, Alex Kisselmann, Scottsbluff, Nebraska, Jake Kisselmann and Carl Kisselmann of Denver, and Wm. Kisselmann of Neenah, Wisconsin.

KISSELMANN, KATHERINE E. - (Lt. 3, Blk. 105, Sec. 1) Born in 1862 and died August 22, 1909. (see obit of George Jacob Kisselmann)
(The Kearny County Advocate, Sept. 2, 1909) Mrs. Kisselman was buried last Thursday. She was the wife of Jacob Kisselman and was held in high esteem by the Russian German settlement.

KLEEMAN, ANNA - (Lt. 4, Blk. 25, Sec. 2) Anna Maria Martha Kleeman, daughter of Mr. and Mrs. Hoppert, was born on September 25, 1888, at Ebersdorf, Germany, and departed this life on April 6, 1935, at the age of 46 years, 6 months and 11 days. Our deceased sister came to America in 1912, landing at Sheboygan, Wisconsin, on February 16 of that year, where she lived till 1930. On April 8, 1930, she entered the estate of matrimony with Ernest Kleeman, Sr., and has lived near Lakin till her death.
The deceased was received into the communion of the Triune God by baptism in her early youth, and this covenant with God she renewed at the time of her confirmation. And as we hope and believe, she remained

DEERFIELD CEMETERY

true to her Savior until death. During a former illness,
she expressed her one wish as being that, when her hour
of death comes, she may be taken by her Savior into
eternal bliss and glory in heaven, and this wish, we
believe, has been fulfilled for her.

Although the deceased was not in the best of health,
her death was not expected, but God's thoughts are not
our thoughts, and God's ways are not our ways, for last
Saturday, while seated with her loved ones at the supper
table, God suddenly took her from this vale of tears to
Himself in heaven.

She leaves to mourn her departure her deeply grieved
husband; three stepchildren, Esther, Edwin, and Helena;
and other relatives and friends.

Funeral services were held in the Lutheran Church at
Deerfield on Friday, April 12, with Rev. Walter J. F.
Lebien in charge, and interment was made in the Deerfield
Cemetery. Those who served as pallbearers were George
Grauberger, Henry Scheuerman, Chas. Marquardt, George H.
Riffel, Chas. Hillman, and Henry Schroeder.

"Blessed are the dead that die in the Lord from
henceforth."

KLEEMAN, ANNA BARBARA — (Lt. 2, Blk. 25, Sec. 2) Mrs.
Fred Kleeman Sr. passed away Tuesday evening, December
25, 1945, after a week's illness in the hospital at
Syracuse. She was almost 82 years of age and had lived
in Kearny County since 1915, her husband passing away in
1941. Four children survive her departure, Ernest, Fred
Jr., Henry, and Mrs. Elsie Ploeger. Funeral service was
held Friday at 2:00 p.m. in the Lutheran Church at
Deerfield.

Anna Barbara (Gachstatter) Kleeman was born on March
20, 1864, at Sechselbach, Wurtemburg, Germany.

Soon after her birth she was received into the Covenant
of God through the holy sacrament of baptism. She was
later instructed in the chief parts of Christian doctrine
and also renewed her baptismal vow in the rite of
confirmation, thus becoming a communicant member of the
Lutheran Church. She arrived in New York on September
15, 1885.

She entered the holy estate of matrimony on July 4th,
1894, with Fred Kleeman at Phillipsburg, Kansas. To this
union seven children were born.

While in the United States she made her home at
Phillipsburg, Kansas, also in Wisconsin, and Missouri,

137

DEERFIELD CEMETERY

and again at Dodge City, Kansas. In the spring of 1915 she came to Kearny County, making her home on a farm north of Lakin.
She was preceded in death by her husband, one daughter, and two sons.
She is survived by three sons, Ernest, Henry, and Fred Kleeman, and one daughter, Mrs. Elmer Ploeger, and by ten grandchildren, also by her sister, Margerette Bishop of Phillipsburg, Kansas, by one son-in-law, three daughters-in-law, and other relatives and friends.
She fell asleep in Jesus on Christmas day, December 25, 1945. She reached the age of 81 years, 9 months, and 5 days.
Funeral services were held on Friday, December 28, 1945, at the Deerfield Lutheran Church with Pastor P.H.C. Stengel in charge. Interment was made in the Deerfield Cemetery.

KLEEMAN, EDNA ANNA - (Lt. 4, Blk. 25, Sec. 2) (The Lakin Independent, Oct. 20, 1922) Edna Anna, the eight day old daughter of Mr. and Mrs. Ernest Kleeman, passed away October 16th, 1922. The funeral services were held at the home Wednesday afternoon, and the little form was laid to rest in the Deerfield Cemetery. The bereaved family have the sympathy of a host of friends.

KLEEMAN, EDNA ROBERTA - (Lt. 2, Blk. 24, Sec. 2) Daughter of Henry and Nellie (Cole) Kleeman, born Oct. 20 and died Nov. 26, 1935. (The Lakin Independent, Dec. 6, 1935) Edna Roberta, infant daughter of Mr. and Mrs. Henry Kleeman, passed away November 26th. Funeral services were held November 27th at the Deerfield Lutheran Church. The child had not been well since her birth October 20th. Mr. and Mrs. Kleeman have the sympathy of friends in their loss and disappointment. They wish to extend thanks to neighbors and friends for every kind act and for sympathy shown them in their bereavement.

KLEEMAN, EDWIN H. - (Lt. 4, Blk. 34, Sec. 3) Funeral services for Edwin H. Kleeman was held Thursday, May 9, 1991, at the Immanuel Lutheran Church, Deerfield, with the Rev. Kenneth Haskell presiding. Burial in Deerfield Cemetery. Mr. Kleeman died May 4, 1991, at St. Catherine Hospital in Garden City.

Born February 9, 1914, at Plymouth, Nebraska, to Ernst and Maria Kleeman, he was a Kearny County resident for 72 years. He was a member of the Immanuel Lutheran Church of Deerfield.

Edwin was a retired farmer who spent a lifetime in his chosen occupation, except for the years he served his country with the United States Army. Ed served in the World War II campaign in North Africa and took part in the D-Day landing in France. It was on the fourth day on patrol after D-Day that Kleeman was captured by the Germans at St. Lo. Six of the men in the patrol were killed and six were captured. Kleeman himself was wounded by an exploding hand grenade and wore the Purple Heart.

Pfc. Kleeman escaped four times from the Germans and the fourth time he and his group made it stick. In April 1945, the First Division infantrymen and a group of those working with him on a German farm overpowered the guard and escaped. They found refuge with a German farmer who knew that the Allies were just about to enter the territory. It was there that they were officially liberated by the 86th Division.

He said that he got away three times before they ever got him to Germany but his punishment was not severe because as he put it, "I was never around long enough for them to find out who I was.

Kleeman was a life member of the Ex-POWs organization and a member and Past Commander of Post #6092 of Lakin. He was a former member and Past Commander of the Lakin American Legion Post #208. He also was a member of the Disabled American Veterans.

He is survived by two sisters: Esther Schoenborn of Mollala, Oregon, and Helen Huneke of Lincoln, Nebr.; and many nieces and nephews.

Greene-Schneider Funeral Home of Lakin was in charge of arrangements.

KLEEMAN, ERNST - (Lt. 4, Blk. 34, Sec. 3) Ernst Kleeman, 83, of Garden City, died Nov. 27, 1968, at his home after a short illness. Born Dec. 14, 1884, at Harlinghausen, Germany, he married Marie Franzmeier, Aug. 17,. 1911, in western Nebraska. She died July 10, 1924. He later married Emelia Seibel, Oct. 24, 1944, at Deerfield. He was a retired farmer and had been a resident here since 1946.

He was a member of the Deerfield Lutheran Church.

DEERFIELD CEMETERY

Survivors include the widow; son, Edwin, Lakin; daughters, Mrs. Esther Schoenborn, Molalla, Ore., Mrs. Helena Huneke, Oxford, Neb.; step son, Adolph Seibel, Boise, Idaho; step daughters, Mrs. Helen Klein, Bismark, N.D., Mrs. Mary Hayes, Foster, Ore., Mrs. Viola Kruger, Salem, Ore., Mrs. Anna Williams, Ketchum, Idaho; brother Frederick of Germany; six grandchildren; two great grandchildren.
Funeral was held Monday at 2 p.m., Rev. Norman Heironimus officiated. Burial at the Deerfield Cemetery.

KLEEMAN, ERNEST L. - (N/2 Lt. 2, Blk. 35, Sec. 3)
Funeral for Ernest L. Kleeman, 86, was held Thursday in Immanuel Lutheran Church, Deerfield, the Rev. Jerald Jeskewitz officiating. Burial at Deerfield Cemetery.
Mr. Kleeman died Sunday, Jan. 10, 1982, at Bob Wilson Memorial Hospital, Ulysses, after a short illness. He was a retired farmer and stockman and had lived in Kearny County since 1915.
He was born November 11, 1895, in Phillipsburg, Kansas, the son of Fred Kleeman and Anna Gackstatter Kleeman, moving to Kearny County in 1915. He was married to Dorothy Harbaugh, June 29, 1928, in Deerfield. They lived on their farm north of Lakin where he farmed extensively and raised cattle. He had been active on his farm until poor health caused his retirement.
He was a World War I veteran.
He was a member of the Immanuel Lutheran Church, Deerfield.
Survivors are his wife, of the home; a son, Darrel Kleeman, La Verne, Calif.; a daughter, Norma Jean Brengman, Lakin; a sister, Elsie Ploeger, Kendall; seven grandchildren and three great grandchildren.

KLEEMAN, FREDRICK CARL, JR. - (Lt. 3, Blk. 24, Sec. 2)
Fred C. Kleeman, 79, died January 25, 1977, at St. Catherine Hospital, Garden City. Born, Nov. 27, 1897, in Phillips County, he married Mary Bohl, October 14, 1921, in Kearny County. He was a retired farmer and Lakin resident since 1915. He was preceded in death by an infant son, Carl.
He was a member of Immanuel Lutheran Church, Deerfield.
Survivors include the widow; sons: Earl, Leonard, both of Lakin; daughters: Mrs. Edith Kelly, Englewood, Co., Mrs. Ethel Simshauser, Lakin; brothers: Henry, Ernst,

140

both of Lakin; sister: Mrs. Elsie Ploeger, Kendall; 13
grandchildren; three great grandchildren.
Funeral was held at the church; Rev. Merlin L. Reith.
Burial was in Deerfield Cemetery.

KLEEMAN, FRED H. - (Lt. 2, Blk. 25, Sec. 2) Born Jan.
25, 1869, in Westphalia, Germany, son of Ernest Henry and
Anna Maria Fitsemeier Kleeman. Died Aug. 18, 1941.
(The Lakin Independent, August 22, 1941) The funeral
of Fred Kleeman Sr. was held Friday afternoon. Services
at the home at 1:30 and continued at the Deerfield
Lutheran Church at 2:30. Interment made in Deerfield
Cemetery.
Mr. Kleeman was found dead in the wash house at his
home Monday with a bullet from a .38 revolver in his
head. When he had been missing for some time Mrs.
Kleeman became apprehensive and got Ernst Kleeman to help
look for her husband. After he was found Ernst brought
word to Coroner J. J. Nash.
Mr. Kleeman had been in poor health for a number of
years and required close attention.
(The Lakin Independent, August 29, 1942) Fred
Kleemann, Sr., was born January 25, 1869, at West Phalen,
Germany, and died near Lakin, Kansas, August 18, 1941,
reaching the age of 72 years, 6 months and 23 days.
Mr. Kleemann came to the United States of America in
the spring of 1885, settling at first at Clatonia,
Nebraska, with his uncle. In 1893 he moved to Phillips
County, Kansas. While here, on July 4, 1894, he entered
the estate of matrimony with Anna Gackstatter. To this
union seven children were born: Ernest, Fred Jr., Carl,
Anna, William, Henry, and Elsie. After living in
Phillips County until 1907, he moved to Ford County with
his family, from where he moved to Kearny in 1915. Here
he resided until his death. Three children, Carl, Anna,
and William, preceded their father in death. Mr.
Kleemann has been in ill health for over four and a half
years.
Mr. Kleemann was a faithful member of Immanuel Ev.
Lutheran Church at Deerfield. Up till he became ill, he
was a regular attendant at divine services and a frequent
guest at the Lord's Table. He served the congregation in
various ways, especially as an elder for a number of
years, always taking a great interest in its welfare.
He leaves to mourn his death: his wife; four children,
Ernest, Fred Jr., Henry, and Elsie; one brother, Ernest

DEERFIELD CEMETERY

of Lakin; two brothers in Germany; ten grandchildren; other relatives and friends.
Funeral services were conducted on Friday, August 22, by the Rev. A. O. Popp, who in the place of the regular pastor conducted a short service at the Kleemann home and then at the Lutheran Church at Deerfield. Interment was made in the Deerfield Cemetery.

KLEEMAN, HENRY A. - (Lt. 1, Blk. 35, Sec. 3) Henry A. Kleeman, 72, died Monday, May 1, 1978, at St. Catherine Hospital in Garden City after a long illness.
He was born on August 29, 1905, at St. James, Missouri. His family moved to a farm in Kearny County in 1915, where he continued to farm until his death.
On January 7, 1934, he married Nellie Cole at Lakin.
He was a member of the Deerfield Immanuel Lutheran Church.
Preceding him in death were four children and a brother, Fred.
Survivors include the widow, Nellie; two daughters, Mrs. Lewis (Agnes) Molz, Deerfield, and Mrs. John (Freida) Depe, Norman, Okla.; grandchildren: Irvin, Bonnie, Ann, Helen, and Lois Molz, and Roxanne, Kent and Jacquelyn Depe; one sister, Mrs. Elmer Ploeger, Kendall; and a brother, E. L. Kleeman, Lakin.
Funeral services were held at the Deerfield Immanuel Lutheran Church at 10 o'clock on May 4. Davis Funeral Home in charge, with Rev. Norman Heironimus officiating. Burial in Deerfield Cemetery.

KLEEMAN, IONA ANN - (Lt. 2, Blk. 24, Sec. 2) Funeral services for Iona Kleeman were held Tuesday afternoon at 3:00 at Immanuel Lutheran Church in Deerfield, the Rev. Henry Knoke officiating.
The casket bearers were: Cletus Ploeger, Virgil Hanneman, Carl Waechter and David Brownlee. Music was furnished by Mrs. Gilbert Merz, Mrs. Armin Kettler, Mrs. Herndon Campbell and Mrs. Harold Purdy, accompanied at the organ by Mrs. Calvin Scheuerman.
Iona Ann Kleeman, daughter of Henry and Nellie Kleeman, was born November 4, 1946, at Garden City, Kansas.
She was received into God's Kingdom of Grace through the sacrament of Holy Baptism on November 24, 1946.
She departed this life to enter God's Kingdom of Glory on June 14, 1952, at the age of five years, seven months

142

and ten days. Death was attributed to the rather rare disease of pancreatic fibrosis.

Iona was preceded in death by two sisters and one brother, who also were called home in infancy.

She leaves to mourn her passing: her deeply grieving parents; two sisters, Agnes and Frieda of the home; her maternal grandparents, Mr. and Mrs. E. R. Cole of Lakin; and many other relatives and a host of friends.

KLEEMAN, KARL or CARL - (Lt. 3, Blk. 24, Sec. 2) Karl Frederick Kleeman, the little son of Mr. and Mrs. Fred Kleeman Jr., passed away Sunday morning, March 7, 1925. He became ill Friday, after a short life of only 23 days. The funeral was held Monday afternoon at the Lutheran Church at Deerfield. Services conducted by Rev. Wahmeier, who preached in German and Rev. Karstenson who delivered a sermon in the English language. Interment was made in the Deerfield Cemetery.

KLEEMAN, LEO HERMAN - (Lt. 2, Blk. 24, Sec. 2) Leo Herman, infant son of Henry Kleeman and Nellie nee Cole, was born February 3, 1937, at Lakin, Kansas, and departed from this life, April 22, 1937, reaching the tender age of 2 months and 19 days. One sister, Edna Roberta, preceded him in death.

Leo Herman was baptized in the name of Triune of God on March 7, and was thus brought to his Savior, Jesus Christ, and made a child of God.

Soon after his birth he developed a cough which was very much aggravated by the dust storms, pneumonia finally causing his death.

Those mourning his early death are his parents, Mr. and Mrs. Henry Kleeman; one sister, Agnes Ruth; his grandparents, Mr. and Mrs. Fred Kleeman, Sr., and Mr. and Mrs. E. R. Cole; and other relatives.

Funeral services were conducted at the home and then in the Lutheran Church at Deerfield on Friday, April 23, with Rev. Walter J. F. Lebien in charge. Interment was made in the Deerfield Cemetery.

KLEEMAN, LEONA MAXINE - (Lt. 2, Blk. 24, Sec. 2) ts. March 24-May 21, 1938. Leona Maxine Kleeman was born March 25, 1938, at Lakin, Kansas, and departed this life at Garden City, Saturday, May 21, 1938, at the age of 1 month and 26 days. She was the daughter of Henry Kleemann and Nellie nee Cole. She was baptized in the

DEERFIELD CEMETERY

name of the Triune God and thus made a child of God on
April 10, 1938, in Immanuel Lutheran Church, Deerfield,
Kansas.
   Leona Maxine, soon after birth developed a cough which
later turned into acute bronchitis and then pneumonia.
She was rushed to St. Catherin'e Hospital, Garden City,
on May 12 where everything humanly possible was done for
her, but the Lord in His wisdom took her from this life
to Himself in heaven last Saturday. She was preceded in
death by one sister, Edna Roberta, and one brother, Leo
Herman.
   She leaves to mourn her early death, her deeply grieved
parents; one sister, Agnes Ruth; her grandparents, Mr.
and Mrs. Fred Kleemann Sr. and Mr. and Mrs. E. R. Cole;
other relatives and friends.
   Funeral services were conducted by the Rev. Walter J.
F. Lebien on May 23 with services at the Lutheran Church
and interment in Deerfield Cemetery.

KLEEMAN, MARY E. - (Lt. 3, Blk. 24, Sec. 2) Funeral for
Mary E. Kleeman, 92, was held Thursday at Immanuel
Lutheran Church, Lakin, the Rev. Robert Roberts
officiating. Burial at Deerfield Cemetery.
   She died May 23, 1993, at Kearny County Hospital,
Lakin.
   Born Feb. 1, 1901, at Hoisington, she was the daughter
of Adam and Madeline Knaus Bohl. She married Fred
Kleeman, Oct. 14, 1921, at Kearny County. He died Jan.
25, 1977.
   Mrs. Kleeman moved to Bazine, where she lived for a
short time before coming to Kearny County in 1906. She
grew up in north Kearny County in the Lydia area and
attended Columbia School in north Kearny County. The
Kleemans moved to Lakin in 1954.
   A homemaker, Mrs. Kleeman was a member of Immanuel
Lutheran Church, Lakin. Her hobbies were crocheting,
needlework, sewing and gardening.
   Survivors include two sons, Earl and Leonard, both of
Lakin; two daughters, Ethel Simshauser, Lakin, and Edith
Kelly, Orlando, Fla.; a brother, Fred Bohl, Lakin; 13
grandchildren; and 18 great grandchildren. She was
preceded in death by one son, two great grandsons, one
brother and four sisters.
   Garnand Funeral Home was in charge of arrangements.

DEERFIELD CEMETERY

KLEEMAN, MARY M. - (Lt. 4, Blk. 25, Sec. 2) (The Lakin Independent, July 18, 1924) After a brief illness of less than two days, Mrs. Ernst Kleeman died Thursday evening at her home north of Lakin.
Mary Franzmeier was born at Haborn, Nebraska, and at her death was 30 years, 5 months, and 25 days of age. She left three children, Esther, Edwin, and Helena, a husband, two brothers, and a sister, who arrived from Nebraska to attend the funeral.
Services were conducted Sunday by Rev. Karstensen at the Deerfield Lutheran Church, and her body was laid to rest in the Deerfield Cemetery.

KNOLL, KYLER JACOB - (Lt. 2, Blk. 69, Sec. 4) Funeral Mass for Kyler Jacob Knoll was held at Christ the King Catholic Church, Deerfield, the Rev. Mario Islas officiating. Burial at Deerfield Cemetery.
He was stillborn, Sept. 21, 1993, at St. Catherine Hospital. He was the son of Chris and Danna Nichols Knoll, Holcomb.
Survivors include his parents, of the home; his grandparents, Clarence and Sylvia Knoll, Deerfield, and Duane and Norma Nichols, Holcomb; his great grandparents, John and Ludwina Horning, Garden City, Arlene Nichols, Manter, and Allan and Juanita Neely, Manuel, Texas; and great great grandmother, Mabel Nichols, Johnson.
Garnand Funeral Home in charge of arrangements.

KNOLL, TARYAN NICOLE - (Lt. 2, Blk. 69, Sec. 4) Funeral Mass for Taryan Nicole Knoll was held at Christ the King Catholic Church, Deerfield, with Monsignor Nobert C. Temaat officiating. Burial at Deerfield Cemetery.
She died Sept. 15, 1994, at St. Catherine Hospital, Garden City. The daughter of Christopher Allen and Danna Suzette Nichols Knoll, she was born Sept. 15, 1994, at Garden City.
Survivors are her parents, Holcomb; a brother, Dylan Christopher Knoll, of the home; grandparents, Clarence and Sylvia Knoll, Deerfield, and Duane and Norma Nichols, Holcomb; great grandparents, John and Ludwina Horning, Garden City, and Arlene Nichols, Manter; and great great grandmother, Mabel Nichols, Johnson.
She was preceded in death by a brother, Kyler Jacob Knoll.
Garnand Funeral Home in charge of arrangements.

DEERFIELD CEMETERY

KOON, WALTER WILLIAM HARRISON - (Lt. 4, Blk. 54, Sec. 2)
(Funeral Records) Died Aug. 31, 1918, age 11 yrs., 10
mos., 10 days, fell from wagon. Father Wm. L. Koon,
mother Sophia Bell Russell. Charged to United States
Sugar and Land Co. Methodist minister Rev. Enyeart.
(The Kearny County Advocate, Lookout Hill News, Sept.
6, 1918) The friends of Walter Koon are very sorry to
hear of his death. Walter was a bright and promising boy
and we extend the heart felt sympathy to the bereaved
family.

KRAFT, ARLIE W. - (Lt. 3, Blk. 35, Sec. 3) Funeral for
Arlie W. Kraft, 85, lifetime Deerfield resident, was held
at 10:30 a.m. Saturday at the United Methodist Church,
Deerfield, with the Rev. Warren Hett officiating. Burial
at Deerfield Cemetery.
    Mr. Kraft died Thursday, March 27, 1997, at St.
Catherine Hospital, Garden City.
    He was born Dec. 17, 1911, at Deerfield, to Walter and
Emma Kersten Kraft, and attended Prairie View School in
Kearny County.
    After retiring from farming in the mid 1970s, he
enjoyed woodworking. He was a member of and served on
various boards at the United Methodist Church, a member
of Deerfield Lions Club and Prairie View Grange, and
served on the Deerfield School Board and Deerfield City
Council.
    On July 8, 1934, he married L. Faye Shull at Garden
City. She survives.
    He is also survived by two sons, Warren Kraft,
Syracuse, and Gary Kraft, Deerfield; two sisters, Opal
Drussel, Garden City, and Eileen Graham, Denver; five
grandchildren; and seven great grandchildren.

KRAUSE, LLOYD - (Lt. 3, Blk. 41, Sec. 3) Memorial
service for Lloyd A. Krause, 56, was held at the United
Methodist Church, Deerfield, the Rev. Harry Walz
officiating. A private family committal service.
    He died Oct. 8, 1991, at his home in Deerfield.
    He was born July 20, 1935, at Hillsboro. After moving
to Deerfield in 1941, he attended Deerfield Grade School
and later graduated from Deerfield High School in 1953.
    He graduated from Emporia State Teachers College in
1957 with a degree in music and received his masters
degree in 1973 from Wayne State University, Wayne, Neb.

DEERFIELD CEMETERY

He taught music in the United States for three years and then served two years in the Army in Korea. After the service, he began teaching for the Department of Defense in schools operated for miltary dependents. He taught music in Okinawa for five years, then transferred to elementary teaching and taught at Hahn, German, Turkey, Wiesbaden and Berlin, both in Germany. He retired, Aug. 20, 1991, after 33 years of teaching.

He received many awards and certificates in teaching. Besides school involvements, he actively participated in many German cultural and social functions.

He was a member of the United Methodist Church, Deerfield. His hobbies were music, teaching and traveling.

Survivors include his mother, Eva Morford, Deerfield; two sisters, Virginia DeWitt, Scott City and Eyvonne Crase, Garden City. He was preceded in death by his father and step-father.

Garnand Funeral Home in charge of arrangements.

KRIETE, F. H. - (Lt. 2, Blk. 56, Sec. 2) Fred H. Kriete was born at Mossville, Ill. His parents were Frederick Henry and Ruth Ann (Thompson) Kriete. He came to Kearny County with his parents in 1887. Born August 28, 1878, and died Dec. 31, 1956.

(The Lakin Independent, Jan. 4, 1937) Funeral services for Frederich Kriete, 78, were held in the Deerfield Immanuel Lutheran Church at 2 p.m. Wednesday.

Mr. Kriete, a long time resident of the Deerfield community, died in the Kearny County Hospital, Monday.

Surviving are a brother, Lew John Kriete, Chicago; a sister, Mrs. J. A. Powell, Great Bend; a nephew, Lee Smith; and a niece, Mrs. Ruth Smith, both of Great Bend. Burial was in the Deerfield Cemetery.

KRIETE, HENRY - (Lt. 2, Blk. 56, Sec. 2) (The Lakin Investigator, July 5, 1907) Henry Kriete was born in Hamilton County, Ohio, Dec. 23, 1846, and died at Deerfield, June 17, 1907, being 60 years of age. He was a war veteran, belonging to Co. D, 140th Regiment, Indiana Infantry. Was married December 22, 1875, to Ruth Thompson, of Peoria, Il.; moved to Kearny County about 18 years ago. His wife, four sons and one daughter survive to mourn their loss. The Saturday previous to his death he drove to Lakin to see his physician, returning home early in the evening and at once retired, called his wife

147

DEERFIELD CEMETERY

and told her his end was near and gave directions
concerning his financial affairs, soon became unconscious
and died Monday. His funeral was held at Deerfield
Thursday and buried in the cemetery at that place. Mr.
Kretie was a loving father and husband, and the family
have the sympathy of our community.

KRIETE, RUTH ANNE - (Lt. 2, Blk. 56, Sec. 2) (The Kearny
County Advocate, May 3, 1918) Ruth Anne Thompson was
born in Peoria, Illinois, May 6th, 1852, and died at
Deerfield, Kansas, April 24th, 1918, aged 65 years, 11
months and 18 days. She was married to Henry Kreite at
Peoria, Illinois, December 22nd, 1875. Six sons and two
daughters were born to them. The husband and one
daughter and two sons preceeded the mother in death. The
father departed this life, June 17th, 1907. Four sons
and a daughter survive to mourn the loss of a kind and
loving mother. At the age of sixteen she gave her heart
to God, and has always had faith in him, tho she had many
trials and temptations for almost fifty years. She had
been a member of the Methodist Church. In the year 1884
the family moved to Burrton, Kansas, and two years later
to Garden City. For 29 years the family have resided in
Kearny County, in the vicinity of Lakin and Deerfield.
The four sons and one daughter, living are Fred, and Will
of Deerfield, John Lewis of Chicago and Henry Clinton of
Humptulips, Washington, and Mrs. J. A. Powelson of Great
Bend, Kansas, all of whom were present except Henry, who
was unable to come. The last few days of her illness,
she had often said to her family and friends: "Be good
and true to him and he will take care of you."
   Mrs. Ruth A. Kriete, aged 66 years, died at her home
Wednesday evening from acute lobar pneumonia. Funeral
services were held at the Methodist Church, Sunday
afternoon, conducted by Rev. Enyeart, and interment made
in the Deerfield Cemetary.

KRIETE, WILLIAM BEN - (Lt. 2, Blk. 56, Sec. 2) (The
Lakin Independent, Nov. 23, 1923) The grim Angel of
Death has again stopped in our midst stealing away a
brother scarce in the prime of life. The fallen brother,
William Ben Kriete, was born at Deerfield, Kansas, April
22, 1889. His parents, Mr. and Mrs. Henry F. Kriete were
pioneer settlers in the community. The lad lived the
hard life of the pioneer family and on reaching manhood's
estate he chose the occupation of a stockman. In his

148

DEERFIELD CEMETERY

work he traveled over much of southwest Kansas and was
known as a man of honor whose word was never questioned.
While on a business mission to Wichita, uremic poison
followed by pneumonia seized him and after a battle of
two weeks, death came to relieve the sufferer on November
17, 1923.
The father in 1907 and mother in 1918 passed on to the
Land of Souls. There is left in sorrow to cherish his
memory three brothers: Henry, of Aberdeen, Washington;
Lewis, of Chicago; and Fred, of Deerfield; also a sister,
Mrs. J. A. Powelson, of Long Beach, California; with many
friends who miss the departed neighbor.
The deceased professed faith in Christ some years ago
and is now in the hands of a wonderful Father, who knows
men's motives as well as his acts.
Funeral services were held at the Deerfield M.E. Church
in charge of Rev. R. L. Wells. "Face to Face" and "It is
Well with My Soul" were sung by a double quartet. The
body was laid to rest in the Deerfield Cemetery. His
sister was the only one of the family not present at the
funeral.

KUEKER, POLLY K. - (Lt. 1, Blk. 67, Sec. 4) Polly
Kueker, 9, died Monday, December 29, 1975, in St.
Catherine Hospital, Garden City, after a long illness.
She was the daughter of Mr. and Mrs. Udell H. Kueker,
Deerfield.
She was born May 8, 1966, in Lakin and attended special
education classes in Lakin and was a member of Immanuel
Lutheran Church, Deerfield.
Survivors include the parents; a brother, Jonathan,
Holcomb; three sisters, Mrs. Meredith Morioka, Honolulu,
Hawaii, Mrs. Kristin Bowles, Talent, Ore., and Mrs.
Laurie Oshel, Pierceville; her grandmother, Mrs. Julia
Minor, Deerfield; and two nieces and three nephews.
Funeral was held at Immanuel Lutheran Church,
Deerfield, the Rev. Norman Heironimus officiating.
Burial in Deerfield Cemetery. Garnand Funeral Home in
charge.

KUEKER, THERESA - (Lt. 2, Blk. 60, Sec. 3) Theresa M.
Kueker was born Feb. 9, 1891, and departed this life
Thursday evening, Dec. 1, 1960, at the age of 69 years.
She was born at Marine, Ill., where she was also
received into Christ's Kingdom of Grace in holy baptism.

DEERFIELD CEMETERY

She was married to William C. Kueker on Nov. 6, 1910.
The William Kueker family came to western Kansas in 1915
which has been their home since that time, having farming
interests in Finney County and then later in Kearny
County.
Mrs. Kueker was a faithful member of the Lutheran
Church until released by our Lord into the Church
Triumphant above.
Surviving her are the husband, William C. Kueker; one
son, Udell of Deerfield; two daughters, Mrs. John Koch of
Garden City and Mrs. Clarence Meyer of Lakin; and eight
grandchildren.

KUEKER, UDELL H. - (Lt. 1, Blk. 67, Sec. 4)   Udell H.
Kueker, 69, died Friday, Jan. 22, 1982, at his home in
Deerfield. Born January 4, 1913, in Edwardsville, Ill.,
he married Myrtle Minor, March 9, 1947, in Deerfield.
Mr. Kueker retired from farming in 1960 and from Santa
Fe Motors four years ago.
He was a member of Immanuel Lutheran Church, Deerfield,
and was a charter member of the Lutheran Hospital
Association of Kearny County and served on the board.
Survivors are his wife, of the home; a son, Jonathan
Kueker, Holcomb; three daughters, Mrs. Roger (Laurie)
Oshel, Deerfield, Mrs. Randy (Kristin) Randall, Talent,
Ore., and Mrs. Meredith Morioka, Honolulu, Hawaii; two
sisters, Mrs. John (Evelyn) Koch, Garden City, and Mrs.
Clarence (Helen) Meyer, Harrisonville, Mo.; and seven
grandchildren. His parents and a daughter, Polly,
preceded him in death. Funeral was held in Immanuel
Lutheran Church, Deerfield, the Rev. Jerald C. Jeskewitz
officiating. Burial at Deerfield Cemetery. Garnand
Funeral Home in charge of arrangements.

KUEKER, WILLIAM C. - (Lt. 2, Blk. 60, Sec. 3)   t.s.
1885-1970. Funeral services for W. C. Kueker, 85, long
time Kearny County resident, was held Saturday at 10 a.m.
at the Immanuel Lutheran Church in Deerfield with Rev.
Norman Heironimus officiating. Burial was in the
Deerfield Cemetery.
Mr. Kueker was born August 20, 1884, in Illinois and
died at the Kearny County Hospital in Lakin, February 4,
1970. He was married to Theresa May, November 6, 1910,
in Troy, Ill. She died December 1, 1960.
He was a member of the Immanuel Lutheran Church in
Deerfield.

DEERFIELD CEMETERY

Survivors include a son, Udell Kueker, Deerfield, two
daughters, Mrs. John Koch, Garden City and Mrs. Clarence
Meyer, Harrisonville, Mo., nine grandchildren and six
great grandchildren.

LAFON, EUGENE C. - (N/2 Lt. 4, Blk. 64, Sec. 3) Eugene Charles LaFon, 71, Garden City, died at his home, Sept. 13, 1966, folowing a long illness. He was a retired farmer.
He was born Aug. 30, 1895, in Bosque County, Tex., and moved to Garden City in 1956 from Deerfield, where he had lived for nine years. He married Virginia Baxter, May 25, 1931, in Chickasha, Okla.
Mr. LaFon was a member of the Southern Baptist Church.
Surviving are the widow; a daughter, Mrs. Melvin Merz, of Deerfield; a step-son, Ralph Anderson, Lakin; eight grandchildren and one great grandchild.
Services were held at Phillips-White Funeral Home, the Rev. Robert Chisenhall officiating. Burial was in the Deerfield Cemetery.

LAFON, MINNIE V. - (Lt. 4, Blk. 64, Sec. 3) Funeral for Minnie V. LaFon, 87 , was held at 10:30 a.m. Saturday at High Plains Retirement Village, Lakin, P.M. Cousins, minister, officiating. Burial at Deerfield Cemetery. She died June 19, 1991, at High Plains Retirement Village, Lakin.
Born Minnie V. Baxter, Jan. 1, 1904, at Hunt County, Texas, she married Eugene Charles LaFon, May 25, 1931, at Chickasha, Okla. He preceded her in death. Mrs. LaFon was a retired nurse's aide and had been a Lakin resident since 1947, moving from Anadarko, Okla. She was a member of the Church of the Nazarene, Garden City.
Survivors include a son, Ralph Anderson, Lakin; a daughter, Jimmie Merz, Liberal; a sister, Evelyn Hammond, Purcell, Okla.; seven grandchildren; and 10 great grandchildren.
Greene-Schneider Funeral Home was in charge of arrangements.

LANDON, DANIEL ROSS - (Lt. 2, Blk. 71, Sec. 4) t.s. September 14, 1954-June 18, 1978. Daniel R. Landon, 23, was accidently electrocuted, Sunday, June 18, 1978, about noon while working on an electric drive sprinkler system at the family farm south of Deerfield in the sandhills.
The accident was reported to the Kearny County sheriff's office at 12 o'clock (MDT) and officers and an ambulance were dispatched to the scene. Landon was taken to the hospital in Lakin where he was pronounced dead on arrival.

Dan was born September 4, 1954, at Garden City and had lived in the Deerfield community all of his life. He attended schools there and graduated from Garden City Community College. He married Gloria Marie Miller on June 8, 1974, at Moscow.

Mr. Landon was a member of the First United Methodist Church, Deerfield.

Survivors include his wife of the home; a son, Cally Brice, a daughter, Angie Marie, both of the home; his parents, Mr. and Mrs. Bob L. Landon, Deerfield; a brother, Larry Landon, Garden City; two sisters, Victoria Landon, Garden City, and Mrs. Dixie Renstrom, Kalvesta; maternal grandmother, Mrs. Ester Fulton, Deerfield, and paternal grandmother, Mrs. Ruby Landon, Napa, Calif.

Funeral was held Wednesday at the church, the Rev. Harry Walz officiating. Burial in Deerfield Cemetery. Phillips-White Funeral Home in charge of arrangements.

LANDON, JAY - (Lt. 4, Blk. 44, Sec. 3)   Funeral services for Jay Landon, 65, was held at the Deerfield Methodist Church, with Rev. Denver Flowers conducting the services. Burial in the Deerfield Cemetery.

The well known retired farmer died Monday morning, March 2, 1953, in a Garden City hospital.

Death was attributed to a stroke which he suffered at his home early Saturday morning. He was taken to the hospital for treatment, but never recovered.

Jay Landon, son of Richard E. and Alice J. Landon, was born on a homestead ten miles south of Russell, Kansas, March 10, 1887. He attended grade school at nearby Mulberry School. His parents sold out and moved to a new farm near McCracken, Kansas, in 1901, where he attended school at EntreNous Rural High School.

He served with the American Expeditionary force in World War I, and remained with the army of Occupation in Germany for one year after the Armistice.

Jay returned after his discharge in 1919 and engaged in wheat farming near Galatia, Kansas, for two years.

In 1921 he purchased the farm eight miles north of Deerfield. Two years later he was married to Ruby Ellen Miller. To this union were born three sons, and three daughters. They made their home on this farm until about three years ago, when failing health forced Mr. Landon to leave the farm and move into Deerfield.

Survivors include his wife, of the home; three daughters, Peggy and Patty, of the home, and Deloris,

DEERFIELD CEMETERY

Surviving are the widower, Elmer; six children, Elmer,
Jr., Elaine, Darlene, Wayne, Marian, and Howard, all of
the home; her parents, Mrs. Madge Greefield of Wichita
and Willard Fischer of Winfield.
Phillips Funeral Home in charge of arrangements.

LEHMAN, MINNIE L. - (Lt. 3, Blk. 104, Sec. 1)   Minnie
Lucy Curless was born Aug. 26, 1894, in Finney County,
Kansas, to Abner Butler Curless and Lucy Jane (Quinn)
Curless and departed this life Feb. 29, 1960, at the age
of 65 years, six months and three days.
   She is survived by her husband, Percy D. Lehman of
Deerfield; five sons, Clifford A. of Westminster, Colo.,
Elmer of Deerfield, Kans., Dale, Wilmer and LaVerne of
Wichita; one daughter, Lucy Chase of Wichita; 18
grandchildren; two brothers; and one sister of
Mountainburg, Ark.; a brother of Hutchinson and many
nephews and nieces.

LEHMAN, PERCY DAVID - (Lt. 3, Blk. 104, Sec. 1) Percy
David Lehman, a retired railroad worker, died September
21, 1990, at the Kansas Masonic Home, Wichita. He was
the father of Elmer Lehman, Deerfield.
   Mr. Lehman was born January 3, 1893, at Rockford, Iowa,
and married Minnie Curless on September 6, 1914, at
Burrton. She died February 9, 1960.
   A Presbyterian, he was a past patron of Order of
Eastern Star and a member of the Railroad Maintenance
Union. He had worked for the Rock Island Railroad as a
water serviceman.
   Survivors in addition to the son at Deerfield are four
sons, Dale, Wichita, Clifford, Broomfield, Colo., Wilmer,
Haysville, and LaVerne, Arlington, Tx.; one daughter,
Lucy M. Chase, Wichita; and 18 grandchildren; 40 great
grandchildren; and nine great great grandchildren.
   Funeral, including Masonic services, were Monday
morning at 8:30 at the Kansas Masonic Home, Wichita, and
burial was at 3:30 Monday afternoon at the Deerfield
Cemetery.

LEHMAN, SOPHIA ESTHER - (Lt. 2, Blk. 81, Sec. 1) Sophia
Esther Lehman, 74, died Thursday, May 27, 1982, at St.
Catherine Hospital in Garden City after a long illness.
   Born Dec. 21, 1907, in Murdock, Okla., she married Zarl
Milton Claar, April 10, 1930, in Garden City. He died

Sept. 6, 1963. She married Percy Lehman, Jan. 3, 1979, in Deerfield.
In addition to her husband, survivors include two sons, Charles Claar and Ralph Claar, seven grandchildren and 13 great grandchildren. She also was preceded in death by four brothers, Fred, Charles, Joe and Herman Anderson, and two sisters, Osie Campbell and Louise West.
Mrs. Lehman was a member of the First United Methodist Church of Deerfield.
Funeral was held at the church, the Rev. Harry Walz officiating. Burial at Deerfield Cemetery. Garnand Funeral Home in charge of arrangements.

LEUBKE, WILMAR WILLIAM - (Lt. 3, Blk. 63, Sec. 3) Born Sept. 23, 1921, and died Oct. 10, 1961. Veteran of World War II.
(The Lakin Independent, Deerfield News, Oct. 19, 1961) Friends in this community extend heartfelt sympathy to Mrs. Wilmar Leubke and relatives in the death of Mr. Leubke, who passed away at Long Beach, Calif., Oct. 10.

LEWIS, GLENDA RAE - (Lt. 1, Blk. 26, Sec. 2) Glenda Rae Lewis, 38, Deerfield, died Tuesday, Dec. 23, 1980, at the Kearny County Hospital, Lakin, after a sudden illness. She was a homemaker and a part time employee of Kearny County SRS.
Born Feb. 28, 1942, in Garden City, she married Charles H. Lewis, Dec. 29, 1961, in Deerfield. She was a lifetime resident and a school and civic booster of the Deerfield community.
She was a member of Immanuel Lutheran Church and Capsula Club, both of Deerfield.
Her parents, Armin and Fern Kettler, and a brother, Armin Jr., preceded her in death.
Surviving are her husband and two sons, David and Brian of the home; three step-children, Becky Perry and Ramona and Randy Lewis, all of Gower, Mo.; a brother, Grant Kettler, Rensselaer, N.Y.; and grandmothers, Meta Kettler, Garden City, and Edna Mae Tibbitts, Sunnydale, California.
Funeral was at 10:30 a.m. Saturday at Immanuel Lutheran Church with Pastor Ben Bauer officiating. Burial in Deerfield Cemetery.

LILES, AGNES ANNA - (Lt. 3, Blk. 20, Sec. 3) ts. Agnes A. Liles, December 14, 1904-December 26, 1971. Daughter

DEERFIELD CEMETERY

of Aloys L. and Susan Zrubek, wife of William Liles.
Died Dec. 26, 1971, at her home in Pueblo, Co.
Burial was at 2 p.m. Wednesday in Deerfield Cemetery
for former local resident Mrs. Agnes Ann Liles.
She died unexpectedly at her residence in Pueblo,
Colo., Saturday, Dec. 26, 1971. Mrs. Liles had lived in
the Colorado city for the past 18 years. She was a
member of Lady Fireman's Lodge.
Survivors include the widower, William David Liles, of
the home; a son, Marlin Samuel Liles, Boulder, Colo.; two
brothers, Chris Zrubek, Fort Collins, Colo., and Henry
Zrubek, Dodge City; five sisters, Mrs. Barbara Lesher,
Wichita, Mrs. Ethel Steenis, Deerfield, Betty Zrubek,
Garden City, Mrs. Ethel Sharp, Garden City and Mrs.
Margaret Wilkerson, Vona, Colo.
Funeral was to be at Pueblo, with burial Wednesday
afternoon in Deerfield.

LOEWEN, HERMAN R. - (The Garden City Telegram, September
29, 1921) Herman Loewen, nineteen year old son of Mr.
and Mrs. Isaac Loewen died last Friday morning from the
kick of a horse that he received on Wednesday evening.
The young man was unhitching his team after a days work
in the field and as he stepped up to the side of one of
the horses to hang the bridle on the hame the animal
jumped forward and kicked young Loewen in the stomach.
After the accident the young man walked to the house and
told his parents. Medical aid was given him, but to no
avail, and Herman suffered a great deal until the end
came about 6:30 Friday morning. The horse, which made
the fatal kick, had been worked all summer and was never
known to kick before.
Funeral services were held Sunday afternoon at the
Baptist Church in this city and interment was made in the
Deerfield Cemetery.
Deceased leaves besides his father and mother, five
brothers and one sister. He was the oldest child of the
family, and a hard working young man of good habits.
Recently the Loewen family moved from the Burt ranch
northwest of this city to the Barney O'Conner ranch,
forty miles southwest of here.
The family have the sincere sympathy of the entire
community in the loss of their beloved son.
Herman R. Lowen, eldest son of Mr. and Mrs. Isaac
Loewen was born in Leigh, Kansas, November 10th, 1902,
and died September 23, 1921.

157

He practically grew to manhood in our midst. He has shown himself worthy of highest confidence, was a consistent member of the church, was pleased to have the pleasure of its help and companionship. He was a hard working true and manly boy. Those who knew him best loved him most.

His death came as a result of a kick from a horse on the Barney O'Connor ranch some 30 miles south west of town. He lived nearly 36 hours after the accident, his suffering was intense. though conscious practically to the last moment. Realizing that death was claiming him he was clear in his mind as to his state. With strong Christian faith he comforted his bereaved parents, assuring them of his abiding faith in the Savior and of his "Going to be with Him."

Appropriate funeral services were conducted at the Baptist Church, Sunday 1:30 p.m., by the pastor in the presence of an overflowing congregation of relatives and friends. The remains were taken to Deerfield burying grounds and laid to rest.

LOPEZ, BONIFACIO — (Lt. 3, Blk. 104, Sec. 1) t.s. 1891-1960. Bonifacio Lopez, 77, longtime Deerfield resident, died of injuries received in a two vehicle accident, Wednesday morning. Mr. Lopez succumbed at 11:50 a.m. Oct. 16, 1968, at the Kearny County Hospital from severe head and internal injuries.

The accident occured shortly before 10:00 a.m., about 1 1/2 miles east of Deerfield at the intersection of the county roads just south of the cemetery.

Mr. Lopez was driving a 1956 Buick coming south on the cemetery road when he collided with an empty beet truck driven by John Andrada, also of Deerfield. The truck was going east on the county road.

The injured men were brought to the Kearny County Hospital where Mr. Lopez died about two hours later. Mr. Andrada was treated and released.

Mr. Lopez came to Kearny County in 1920 and had lived here since that time.

He is survived by the widow; six sons, Ralph and Manuel of Deerfield, Paul and Frank of Garden City, Gabino of Saranac, N.Y., Eleno of Atchison, Kans.; two daughters, Mrs. Juan (Jessie) Perez of Lakin, and Mrs. Elmer (Hope) Lehman of Deerfield.

DEERFIELD CEMETERY

LOPEZ, FRANK - (Lt. 2, Blk. 104, Sec. 1) Rosary for
Frank Lopez, 50, was held at Garnand Funeral Home.
Funeral at St. Mary Catholic Church with the Rev. David
Dougherty and the Rev. Calvin Hartman officiating.
Burial in the Deerfield Cemetery.
    Mr. Lopez died Saturday, Aug. 8, 1981, at his home.
Born Jan. 29, 1931, at Deerfield, he married Lupe Duran,
Jan. 13, 1955, at Raton, N.M. He was a carpenter and had
also worked at Farmland. He was a lifelong resident of
the area.
    He attended the Methodist Church and was a member of
the Catholic Church, Deerfield, and an Army veteran of
the Korean conflict.
    Survivors include his wife, of the home; son, Ronnie,
San Jose, Calif.; daughter, Mrs. Albert (Josandra) Mesa,
Jr., 516 W. Thompson; five brothers, Paul, 314 W.
Edwards, Manuel and Ralph, both of Deerfield, Eleno,
Atchison, Gabino, Saranaz, N.Y.; two sisters, Mrs. Jessie
Perez, Lakin, and Mrs. Hope Lehman, Deerfield; a
grandson, and a granddaughter.

LOPEZ, GREGORY ANTHONY - (Lt. 2, Blk. 104, Sec. 1)
Stillborn baby of Ralph Lopez, June 13, 1964.

LOPEZ, KENT PAUL - (Lt. 2, Blk. 45, Sec. 3) Twin of
Rodney Frank, born Feb. 8, 1955, Kent Paul died Feb. 9,
1955. Parents were Manuel and Marlena Lopez.
    Graveside services were held this week for Kent Paul
and Rodney Frank Lopez, twin sons of Mr. and Mrs. Manuel
Lopez of Deerfield. The babies were born prematurely and
lived only a few hours.
    Burial was in Deerfield Cemetery.

LOPEZ, LUIS M. - (Lt. 4, Blk. 100, Sec. 1) Son of A. R.
Fleis and Antonia (Marquez) Lopez, born Oct. 11, 1883, at
Santa Leno of Rio Grande, Mexico. He died July 21, 1943.
Wife, Tiburcia Lopez.

LOPEZ, MANUEL - (Lt. 3, Blk. 34, Sec. 3) Manuel Lopez,
63, of Deerfield, died Monday morning, December 21, 1987,
when the truck he was driving was struck by a westbound
Amtrak train at the Garfield Street crossing in Lakin.
He was pronounced dead at the scene. He was born
November 8, 1924.
    According to the Kansas State Highway Patrol report the
accident happened at 7:25 a.m. (MST). The train was

159

DEERFIELD CEMETERY

westbound and traveling at a rate of 82 miles per hour, according to the KHP report.
The train engineer and fireman had minor injuries but refused treatment. There was no injuries among the 380 passengers on the train and no cars derailed. The damaged engine was removed from the train and in about two hours it proceeded on to La Junta powered by the remaining two engines.
Mr. Lopez, a longtime Kearny County road department employee, was driving a truck owned by the county.
Manuel Lopez, 63, died December 21, 1987, as the result of a vehicle train accident at Lakin. Born November 8, 1924, at Deerfield he married Marlena Winters, July 15, 1954.
Manuel was a heavy equipment operator for the Kearny County Road Department and was a lifetime Deerfield resident. His parents were Bonifacio and Maria Salas Lopez.
He was a member of Christ the King Church, Deerfield.
He was a World War II veteran, serving three years with an Army Airborne Division.
Survivors include his wife, Marlena, of the home; four sons, Gerard of Strasburg, Colo., Kyle, White Oak, Tx., Skitch, Henderson, Tx., Rory, Hays; one daughter, Julia Hamre, Madison, Wisc.; four brothers, Gabina of Saranac Lake, N.Y., Elena, Atchinson, Paul, Garden City, and Ralph, Deerfield; two sisters, Jessie Perez, Lakin, and Hope Lehman, Deerfield; five grandchildren and four step grandchildren.
He was preceded in death by two infant sons, Rodney Frank and Kent Paul, and a brother, Frank.
Funeral services were held Wednesday afternoon at St. Anthonys Catholic Church, Lakin, with Father Richard Kolega officiating. Interment in Deerfield Cemetery.

LOPEZ, MARIA S. - (Lt. 3, Blk. 104, Sec. 1) Mrs. Maria S. Lopez, 71, Deerfield, died Thursday morning, Sept. 30, 1971, at her home.
Born Sept. 23, 1900, in Mexico, she had lived here since 1920. She was preceded in death by her husband, Bonifacio (Bonnie) Lopez, in 1968.
She was a member of the St. Anthony Catholic Church, Lakin. Survivors include six sons, Eleno, Atchison, Gabino, Saranac Lake, N.Y., Manuel and Ralph, both Deerfield, and Paul and Frank, both Garden City; two daughters, Mrs. Juan (Jessie) Perez, Lakin, and Mrs.

DEERFIELD CEMETERY

Elmer (Hope) Lehman, Deerfield; a brother, Juan Sales, Mexico; 29 grandchildren and 25 great grandchildren.
Funeral was held at St. Anthony Catholic Church in Lakin. The Rev. Frank Laudick officiating. Burial in the Deerfield Cemetery.

LOPEZ, MARLENA - (Lt. 1, Blk. 34, Sec. 2) Funeral for Marlena Anne Lopez was held at St. Anthony's Catholic Church, Lakin, the Rev. Frank Laudick officiating. A rosary was said Monday at the church. Burial was in Deerfield Cemetery. Greene-Schneider Funeral Home, Lakin was in charge of arrangements.
She died May 15, 1990, at General Hospital, Saranac Lake, N.Y., after a short illness. Born Marlena Anne Winters, April 4, 1937, at Garden City, she married Manuel Lopez, July 15, 1954. He died December 21, 1987.
Mrs. Lopez was a librarian at Kearny County Library, Lakin, for the past 16 years, and had been a lifetime Deerfield resident. She was a graduate of Deerfield High School.
She was a member of St. Anthony's Catholic Church and the Altar Society, Lakin, and the Capsula Club, Deerfield.
Survivors include four sons, Gerard, Byers, Colo., Kyle and Skitch, Longview, Texas, and Rory, Deerfield; a daughter, Julia Lopez, Madison, Wisc.; a brother, Larry Winters, Calif.; and five grandchildren.

LOPEZ, RODNEY FRANK - (Lt. 2, Blk. 45, Sec. 3) Twin to Kent Paul Lopez, born Feb. 8, 1955, and died Feb. 10, 1955. Parents Manuel and Marlena Lopez.
Graveside services were held this week for Kent Paul and Rodney Frank Lopez, twin sons of Mr. and Mrs. Manuel Lopez of Deerfield. The babies were born prematurely and lived only a few hours.
Burial was in Deerfield Cemetery.

LORENZEN, THEODORE A. - (Lt. 2, Blk. 101, Sec. 1) Born July 20, 1940, and died June 18, 1962. Born in Colfax, Wash., father, Carl F. Lorenzen and mother, Vera E. Stengel Lorenzen.

LORENZEN, VERA ESTELLA - (Lt. 2, Blk. 101, Sec. 1) Graveside service was Saturday, April 11, at Deerfield Cemetery for Vera Estella Lorenzen. Mrs. Lorenzen, 63, a

DEERFIELD CEMETERY

former Deerfield resident, died Wednesday, April 8, 1981, at her home in Olathe, Colo.
Born Vera E. Stengel, Jan. 7, 1918, at Underwood, N.D., she married Carl F. Lorenzen, April 1, 1940, at Moscow, Idaho. She had been a Colorado resident for 13 years.
She was a member of Jehovahs Witness, Garden City.
Survivors include the husband, of the home, a son, Lory Lorenzen, Grand Junction, Colo.; two daughters, Mrs. Susan Elliott, Sherman, Texas, and Linda Stallinger, Delta, Colo.; five brothers, Theodore Stengel, CoeurdAlene, Idaho, Melvin Stengel, Tacoma, Wash., Marvin Stengel, Puyallup, Wash., Donald Stengel, Portland, Oregon, and Lewis Stengel, Underwood, N.D.; a sister, Mabel Adams, Puyallup, Washington, and nine grandchildren.

LYNCH, BLANCHE E. - (Lt. 3, Blk. 73, Sec. 1)   Born in 1882 and died in 1948.
(The Lakin Independent, April 30, 1948)   A short graveside service was held Wednesday at the Deerfield Cemetery for Mrs. William Lynch with Rev. W. A. Hawes in charge.
The Lynch family came here from Kingman in 1934 in the employ of the late J. W. Gillock.   Early in 1935 Mr. Lynch passed away.   The family returned to their former home in that same year.
Mrs. Lynch had been a sufferer from heart trouble for years but was only seriously ill one day.
She leaves to mourn her going, six children and six grandchildren.   They were all here for the services.
Mr. and Mrs. Chas. Barnhardt of Kingman and son; Mr. and Mrs. J. Verne Lynch of Corpus Christi, Texas; Pvt. William Lynch of Fort Knox, Kentucky; Mr. and Mrs. Chas Shulman (Vivian) of Hutchinson; Chief Petty Officer Ray Price, Mrs. Price (Dorothy) of Corpus Christi, Texas; and Lloyd Lynch of Hutchinson, Kansas.

LYNCH, WILLIAM ABNER - (Lt. 3, Blk. 73, Sec. 1)   William Abner Lynch was born January 27, 1876, at Ransom, Illinois, and died February 12, 1935, at his home in Deerfield, Kansas.   He had attained the age of 59 years and 10 days.
He lived in or near Ransom until 1915, when he came to Kansas and located near Wellington, where he lived for a number of years.   After living a short time in Kingman, he moved to Deerfield two years ago.

On June 17, 1915, he was married to Blanche Emma Barnhart. To this union were born five children, William, Laverne, Vivian, Lloyd, and Dorothy. One sister preceded him in death, July 2, 1927. He leaves to mourn his passing his wife, Mrs. Blanche Emma Lynch; five children; one stepson, Charles Heaton Barnhart; and a host of friends.

He was a member of the Methodist Church, but due to ill health was not active in community affairs.

He was a good worker and a good provider. He was an honorable man, well and favorably known in the community.

Funeral services were held in the Deerfield Methodist Church, Friday, February 15, 2:00 p.m., with Rev. Glen W. Palmer in charge. Burial was made in the Deerfield Cemetery.

DEERFIELD CEMETERY

MADDUX, ALMA I. - (Lt. 4, Blk. 73, Sec. 1) Alma Billings born in Brighton, Iowa, 1864, died April 16, 1954.

Alma Ida Maddux was the third daughter of Adelia Nichols Billings and Davis Billings who had migrated from New York State to Brighton, Ia., where she was born Nov. 1, 1864.

During the middle 1870's she moved with her family to Barton County, Mo., which was being opened to homesteaders at that time. This move was made to escape the rigors of the Iowa winters.

She attended school in Lamar, Mo., and later taught school in a nearby community. One of her pupils was Harlow Shapley, well known Harvard scientist.

On September 1888, she was married to Sherman T. Maddux at Lamar, Mo. They soon went to Bourbon County, Kans., where they lived until 1910, when they came to Kearny County where she lived on the same farm located eight miles northwest of Deerfield.

She and Mr. Maddux had been a part of the development of Kearny County through its pioneering stage to its present position of high standing as an agricultural community.

She had always been a home keeping woman and intensely interested in all problems affecting farm life, and the betterment of family culture and well being.

She is survived by three sons: L. A., Anson C. and Oscar N.; one daughter, May Maddux Smith, passed on in November of 1926. There are also six grandchildren: Howard, Maynard, Marilyn, Lyle, Phil and LeRoyce Ann and one great grandson, Gary Lynn. Her twin sister lives in California.

MADDUX, ANSON C. - (Lt. 3, Blk. 72, Sec. 4) Anson C. Maddux, 78, of Deerfield died Sunday, Feb. 27, 1977, at St. Catherine Hospital, Garden City.

Born Feb. 25, 1899, at Bronson, he married Christabelle Downing, July 31, 1928, at Deerfield. A farmer and stockman, he had lived in Deerfield 31 years. A graduate of Emporia State Teachers College, he taught school at Bancroft from 1928 to 1930. From 1930 until 1946, he was superintendent of schools at Holcomb.

He was a member of Deerfield United Methodist Church, Blue Lodge, Lakin, and 32nd Degree Mason, Wichita.

Survivors include the widow; two sons, Lyle, Topeka, and Phil, Deerfield; a daughter, LeRoyce Maddux, Deerfield; and six grandchildren.

DEERFIELD CEMETERY

Funeral was at 10:30 a.m. Wednesday, at the church, Dr. Ruben Reyes officiating. Burial was in Deerfield Cemetery.

MADDUX, CHRISTABELLE D. - (Lt. 3, Blk. 72, Sec. 4) Funeral for Christabelle D. Maddux, 88, was held at the United Methodist Church, Deerfield, the Rev. Donald J. Koehn officiating. Burial at Deerfield Cemetery. She died June 6, 1992, at St. Catherine Hospital, Garden City.

Born Christabelle D. Downing, Nov. 8, 1903, at Deerfield, she married Anson C. Maddux, July 31, 1928, in Deerfield. He died Feb. 27, 1977.

Mrs. Maddux attended Deerfield Grade School and graduated from Deerfield High School in 1922. She attended Southwestern College, Winfield, from 1922 to 1924 and taught one year in Garden City. She completed her education at Kansas State University in 1927 and taught one year in Roxbury. After her marriage she taught at Bancroft for two years. They moved to Holcomb in 1930 where she did substitute teaching until 1946 when she moved back to her childhood home for 10 years. In 1956, they built their home in Deerfield.

She was a member of the United Methodist Church, United Methodist Women, and Order of the Eastern Star, all of Deerfield.

Survivors include two sons, Lyle C., Topeka, and Phil A., Deerfield; a daughter, LeRoyce Ann Maddux, Deerfield; six grandchildren; two step grandchildren; seven great grandchildren; and three step great grandchildren. She also was preceded in death by two sisters and two brothers.

MADDUX, EDITH V. - (Lt. 2, Blk. 85, Sec. 4) Funeral for Edith V. Maddux, 78, was held at the First United Methodist Church, the Rev. Calvin Hartman officiating. Burial at Deerfield Cemetery. She died Wednesday, March 25, 1987, at St. Catherine Hospital.

Born Aug. 22, 1908, in McPherson County, she married Oscar N Maddux, Aug. 9, 1928, at Wellington. He died Dec. 24, 1973.

Mrs. Maddux moved to Deerfield from Cambridge in 1939 and lived there until moving to Garden City in 1974. She lived at 911 1/2 E. Fair, before moving to Garden Valley Retirement Village about a month ago.

She was a member of the First United Methodist Church, Garden City, Hawk Church Circle, Clothing Center and Quilters, and the Extension Homemakers Unit. She had various hobbies and liked to travel. During the 1940s, Mrs. Maddux and her family farmed and raised turkeys at the north end of Lake McKinney. They raised more than 2,000 head of turkeys per year. Survivors include two sons, Howard, Tulsa, Okla., and Maynard, Pine, Colo.; and daughter, Marilyn Holderman, Garden City; three brothers, Claude Lowe, Manhattan, the Rev. Ira Lowe, DeSoto, Texas, and Howard Lowe, Caldwell; three sisters, Winifred Smith, St. Petersburg, Fla., Ethel Asfahl, Enid, Okla., and Flossie Salee, Clearmont, Calif.; eight grandchildren and nine great grandchildren. She was preceded in death by a brother, and five sisters.

MADDUX, LAFAE A. - (Lt. 1, Blk. 73, Sec. 1) L. A. (Fay) Maddux, a Kearny County farmer-stockman, was born Feb. 6, 1897, at Fort Scott, son of Sherman T. and Alma I. Maddux.   He came to Kearny County as a boy and resided in the county for 45 years.
He succumbed Feb. 15, 1956, at the Kearny County Hospital.
Fay was preceded in death by his parents and one sister.   Survivors are two brothers, Oscar and Anson Maddux; and six nieces and nephews.
Funeral services were held at 2:00 o'clock, Saturday, Feb. 18, in the Deerfield Methodist Church with the Rev. Thomas A. Bandy officiating.   Interment was made in the Deerfield Cemetery.

MADDUX, OSCAR N. - (Lt. 2, Blk. 85, Sec. 4)   Oscar N. Maddux, 71, well known Deerfield resident, died Monday, Dec. 24, 1973, at St. Catherine Hospital after a short illness.
Born Nov. 29, 1902, in Bourbon County, he was married to Edith Lowe, August 9, 1928, at Wellington.   Mr. Maddux came to Kearny County with his parents when he was eight years old.
Besides a career as school teacher, he was a farmer and had lived on a farm until 1951 when he moved into Deerfield.   He was a graduate of Southwestern College of Winfield, and had taught school at Burden and was superintendent of schools at Cambridge for eight years.
Mr. Maddux was a member of the Deerfield United Methodist Church.

DEERFIELD CEMETERY

Survivors include the widow; two sons, Howard, Tulsa, Okla., and Maynard, Denver; a daughter, Mrs. Jack Holdeman, 2108 Parkwood, Garden City; a brother, Anson, Deerfield; eight grandchildren and one great grandchild. Funeral was at 2 p.m. Thursday at the Deerfield United Methodist Church, burial in Deerfield Cemetery.

MADDUX, SHERMAN T. - (Lt. 4, Blk. 73, Sec. 1)   Sherman T. Maddux, son of I. M. and Serena Maddux, was born near Carlyle, Clinton County, Illinois, September 16, 1864. When about 16 years of age, his parents moved to Lamar, Missouri, where he grew to manhood. Here he met and married Alma Billings, September 18, 1888. To this union four children were given, one daughter and three sons. The daughter, May Maddux Smith, having preceded her father in death. The wife and three sons survive him: L. A. of the home, O. N. of Deerfield, and A.C. of Holcomb. Besides this he leaves six grandchildren and a brother, C. W. Maddux of El Reno, Oklahoma.
    Although in failing health, his condition became more serious last week and he was taken to the hospital in Lakin, where he passed away Monday morning, June 28, 1943.
    In his passing the family loses a faithful father. His life was one of diligent application for the welfare of those about him. The deeds of men live after them and we aspire to maintain the good deeds. Mr. Maddux grew to manhood surrounded by church environment and developed a love for the hymns used by the church. Having spent nearly a third of a century in western Kansas, he has witnessed the good times and the bad, and through it all he knew how to face life as it came. He passed at the ripe age of 78 years, 9 months.

MAGILL, LILY - (Lt. 3, Blk. 74, Sec. 1)   Mrs. Lily Magill, 69, former Deerfield resident, died June 27, 1969, at Vallejo, Calif. She was born Sept. 13, 1899, at Kansas City, Mo. She moved with her parents to Deerfield in 1906, when they homesteaded in Kearny County. She graduated from Deerfield high school in 1920.
    She was married to Charles Magill, Jan. 21, 1921, at Clarkdale, Arizona. He died in 1961. She and her twin sister, Mrs. Rose Dickens, owned and operated the Twin Coffee Shop in Vallejo, Calif., for 18 years.
    She was a member of the First United Methodist Church and organ society of Vallejo.

DEERFIELD CEMETERY

She is survived by a son, Charles of Vallejo; three
sisters, Mrs. Adelyne Bechtel, Deerfield, Mrs. Rose
Dickens, Vallejo, and Mrs. Margaret Etchison, Venice,
Calif.; a brother Jake Thelen, Stockton; four
grandchildren and a great grandchild.
Funeral service was held at the First United Methodist
Church in Deerfield with Rev. Paul Brooks of Lakin
officiating. Burial was in the Deerfield Cemetery.

MAIER, ANNA CHRISTINA — (Lt. 3, Blk. 54, Sec. 2) Great
grandmother of Davis Williams. Born Jan. 19, 1824, and
died Oct. 18, 1911. She was a widow, died at Deerfield
of old age. She was of German nationality.

MANLEY, GEORGE — (Lt. 2, Blk. 84, Sec. 1) ts. 1858-1931.
(The Lakin Independent, May 8, 1931) George Manley was
born in Bunker Hill, Illinois, December 10, 1859, and
died at Deerfield, Kansas, May 4th, 1931, age 71 years, 5
months, and 24 days.
As a young man he came to Circleville, Kansas, where he
was united in marriage with Miss Jessie M. Eaden, March
7, 1900. Eighteen years later the family came to
Deerfield, where they have since made their home. Five
children were born to this union, two girls and three
boys, who, together with his wife, remain to mourn his
departure. The children are Mrs. J. H. Currier, Pomona,
California; Clifford G. Manley, Ralph S. Manley, and Carl
E. Manley, all of Deerfield; and Margaret Dorithy of
Ulysses.
The deceased became a member of the Christian Church in
1900 and remained loyal to that church until his death.
He was a highly respected Christian, faithful and regular
in attendance of church services as long as his health
permitted. He was also a member of the Woodmen lodge.
Mr. Manley was a good husband, a kind father, a highly
respected citizen, beloved by all who knew him. He left
a fine heritage to his children.
Funeral services were conducted by Rev. R. A. Corrie at
the Deerfield Methodist Church, Tuesday afternoon, May
5th. Burial was made in the Deerfield Cemetery.

MANLEY, JESSIE M. — (Lt. 2, Blk. 84, Sec. 1) Born in
1872 and died Keokuk, Iowa, Sept. 23, 1946.
(The Lakin Independent, Deerfield News, Sept. 27, 1946)
Friends have received word of the death of Mrs. Jessie
Manley at the home of her daughter, Mrs. Margaret Hall at

DEERFIELD CEMETERY

Kesurik, Iowa, September 23rd, at the age of 74 years. Mrs. Manley lived many years in or near Deerfield.

MARQUES, MIKE - (Lt. 3, Blk. 110, Sec. 1) Born in 1926, died May 5, 1935, age 8 yrs old. Son of Robert Marques. Died of pneumonia.
(The Garden City Telegram, Deerfield News, May 7, 1935) Mike Marques died of double pneumonia, Saturday, and was buried at Deerfield Cemetery, Sunday. He was in the first grade.

MARQUEZ, ANTONIO - ( ) 7 day old Mexican male died Nov. 29, 1934, at Deerfield of premature birth.

MARQUEZ, ELENA - (Lt. 4, Blk. 110, Sec. 1) 1932-1933. An 8 month old Mexican female died July 1, 1933, at Garden City of acute enterocolitis. Garnand in charge of arrangements.

MARTIN, ELLSWORTH DENTON - (Lt. 1, Blk. 75, Sec. 1) Ellsworth D. Martin, Deerfield resident for almost 35 years, died Saturady morning, May 23, 1953, at the Kearny County Hospital. Cause of death was carcinoma. He had been ill for a year.
He was born March 13, 1897, at Kinrass, Iowa, son of George B. and Nancy Martin. He came from Iowa to Deerfield about 35 years ago where he was employed as farmer and carpenter.
He married Rose Thompson in February 1919, at Deerfield, They moved to California in 1923, then returned to Deerfield in 1937.
Survivors include a daughter, Mrs. Kathleen McAdoo, Hobbs, New Mexico; three sisters, Mrs. Mable Herr of Deerfield, Mrs. Ethel Stullken of Lakin and Mrs. Leita Netser of North English, Iowa; two brothers, Harley Martin Yamhill, Oregon, and Ernest Martin of Garden City.
Funeral services were held at the Deerfield Methodist Church, Monday at 2 p.m. with the Rev. J. R. Guertner officiating. Burial was in the Deerfield Cemetery.

MARTIN, GERALDINE - (Lt. 1, Blk. 75, Sec. 1) (Davis Funeral Record) Died Mar. 8, 1920, age 25 days, father Ellsworth Martin, died of influenza.
(The Kearny County Advocate, March 12, 1920) Geraldine, infant daughter of Mr. and Mrs. Ellsworth D. Martin, born February 12, 1920, departed this life March

169

8th, being 25 days of age. She leaves to mourn their loss, father, mother and infant sister besides many other relatives.

The infant daughter, one of the twins of Mr. and Mrs. Ellsworth Martin, succumbed to an attack of pneumonia, passed away Monday. Funeral services were held at the home Tuesday and interment in the Deerfield Cemetery.

MARTIN, GORGE BURTON - (Lt. 3, Blk. 23, Sec. 2) Geo. B. Martin, son of Urias and Mary Martin, was born January 27, 1863, in Elkhart County, Indiana, and died at his home in Deerfield, February 17, 1932, age 69 years and 20 days.

When he was three years of age, his parents moved to Keokuk County, Iowa, where he resided until 1917, when he came to Deerfield, Kansas, to make his home where he lived until the end came.

He was married to Nancy J. Denton in the fall of 1886. To this union were born ten children. Those living are Mrs. Alma J. Deniston, Yoder, Colorado; Mrs. Mable Herr, Deerfield, Kansas; Mrs. Ethel Mannatt, Stuttgart, Arkansas; Earnest of Holcomb, Kansas; Harley of Coolidge, Kansas; Ellsworth of Los Angeles, California; and Leita, of the home. Besides these there were three deceased: Lula, who died at 2 years of age, Jay in young manhood, and Mrs. Joy Boyd.

Mr. Martin was the last to fall of his father's family of seven children. He had the privilege of ministering to all of them at the time of their decease: his father, his mother, one brother, and five sisters.

Mr. Martin was a member of the Masonic lodge in Iowa and became a charter member, March 1, 1923, of the local order. He continued a loyal member all these years, serving as treasurer for two terms. For many years until failing health prevented, he was an active member of the Odd Fellows and Modern Woodmen lodges.

Mr. Martin was a farmer until he came to Deerfield, where he engaged in the real estate business until failing health caused his retirement. He also served as county commissioner.

He was a loving husband and father, making his home his chief interest in life. He engaged actively in the welfare of his family and the community. He was kind of heart and loved to care for the sick and was full of kindly deeds to all who knew him. He was a highly repected citizen and will be greatly missed by his loved

DEERFIELD CEMETERY

ones and the community. Besides his loving care for his
family, Mr. and Mrs. Martin have made a home for the two
sons, Jay and Gail Boyd, of their daughter, Joy.

Besides his lifelong companion, he leaves to mourn his
loss his three sons and four daughters mentioned above,
sixteen granchildren, five great granchildren, and a host
of friends.

The funeral was held in the Methodist Church, February
20, 1932, conducted by Roy A. Corrie, the pastor, and the
interment made in the Deerfield Cemetery. Masonic
services were held at the grave.

MARTIN, NANCY - (Lt. 3, Blk. 23, Sec. 2) Mrs. Geo. B.
Martin, 82, long time resident of Deerfield, passed away
at the home of her daughter, Mrs. William Netzer, in
North English, Iowa, following a paralytic stroke. She
had been ill for several days.

Survivors are Mrs. Netzer and two other daughters, Mrs.
W. H. Herr of Deerfield and Mrs. Ed Stullken of Lakin;
and three sons, Harley of Yamhill, Oregon, Ellsworth of
Deerfield and Ernest of Garden City. Also surviving is a
twin brother, John Denton of Los Angeles, Calif.

Following services at North English, the body was
returned to Garden City, Wednesday, and services were
held at the Methodist Church at Deerfield on Friday
afternoon.

Mrs. Nancy Jane Martin, daughter of Stephen and Mary
Ann Denton, was born in Keokuk County, Iowa, Oct. 25,
1865, and departed this life, Jan. 24, 1947, at the age
of 81 years, 2 months, and 29 days, after having suffered
a stroke, Jan. 10, 1947.

She was united in marriage to George B. Martin on Nov.
25, 1886. To this union were born six daughters and four
sons: Mrs. Mabel Herr, Deerfield, Kansas; Mrs. Ethel
Stullken, Lakin, Kansas; Ernest Martin, Garden City,
Kansas; Harley Martin, Yamhill, Oregon; Ellsworth Martin,
Deerfield, Kansas; and Mrs. Leita Netser, North English,
Iowa. Mrs. Alma Deniston, Mrs. Joy Boyd, Jay Martin and
Leilah Martin are deceased. Her husband passed away Feb.
17, 1932.

Besides caring for her ten children, she also reared
two grandsons, Pfc. Jay M. Boyd in the Army Air Force and
Gail Boyd of Rockwell City, Ia.

She joined the Free Methodist Church at an early age
and led a devoted Christian life. She possessed a happy
disposition which won her many friends and was loved

dearly by her family. She spent the greater part of her
life in Iowa but in 1917 moved to Deerfield, Kansas,
where she remained until a little over a year ago. Due
to failing health, she sold her home and came back to
Iowa to make her home with Mr. and Mrs. Willie Netser and
Merlin Gail.
   She leaves three daughters, three sons, eighteen
grandchilren, twenty three great grandchildren, a twin
brother, John T. Denton of Los Angeles, Calif., six
nieces, six nephews, and a host of friends to mourn her
departure.
   Those from out of the county attending the funeral
service Friday were John Denton of Los Angeles, Calif.;
Mr. and Mrs. Harley Martin and daughter, Evelyn, of
Yamhill, Oregon; Mr. and Mrs. C. E. Martin and family of
Garden City; Mrs. and Mrs. Jack Hess and family and Mr.
and Mrs. Jim Martin and daughter of Coolidge; Mrs. Delia
Feris of Hutchinson, with her daughter, Clastine, and
husband of Minneola; Joe Hayden of Stafford; Rev. and
Mrs. R. L. Wells and Mrs. Futhey of Plains, Kansas. Rev.
Wells her former pastor, delivered the funeral sermon.

MARTINEZ, FEMALE - (   ) A female Mexican, 8 days old
died in Deerfield Township, September 28, 1921, of
hemorrhage of bowels.

MARTINEZ, ANTONIO - (Lt. 1, Blk. 110, Sec. 1) Son of
Carlos and Grace born in 1933 and died in 1933.

MARTINEZ, ESTHER - (Lt. 3, Blk. 27, Sec. 2) Born in 1915
and died April 9, 1933, at Deerfield of tuberculosis.
Garnand Funeral Home in charge of arrangements.

MARTINEZ, FELIX - (Lt. 4, Blk. 100, Sec. 1) Son of
Carlos and Grace Martinez, died June 26, 1929, by
drowning, age 3 yrs. Born May 18, 1926.

MARTINEZ, FRANCISCO - (Lt. 1, Blk. 110, Sec. 1) ts.
December 30, 1907-August 12, 1932.
   Son of Lusanna Martinez, born in Mexico, father Rufina.
Born Dec. 30, 1907, and died Aug. 12, 1932. (The Lakin
Independent, Aug. 19, 1932) Frank Martinez passed away
at the county hospital, Friday, August 12. He came here
from Mexico with his parents in 1920 and was 25 years of
age. He leaves a wife and son, besides his parents,

brothers and sisters. His burial was Saturday in the Deerfield Cemetery. The family wishes to thank all those who contributed to help with the necessary expenses, among whom are the Garden City Company, J. W. Wells, Deerfield State Bank, Independent Mercantile Company, Corbett store, W. E. Bechtel, W. L. Mullins, Carl Kersten, Harold Anschutz, Santa Fe Garage, E. M. Blake, J. F. Jones, H. N. Van Doren, E. W. Steenis, Deerfield Cafe, C. D. Anderson, and a host of Mexican friends.

MARTINEZ, FREDRICK COLERON - (Lt. 3, Blk. 27, Sec. 2) see Coleron, Fredrick.

MARTINEZ, INES C. - (Lt. 2, Blk. 45, Sec. 3) Ines Soto Martinez, 63, died at the Kearny County Hospital, March 5, 1967, after being a patient there only a few hours. He had been in ill health the past three months.
He was born in Sangulian Jalisco, Mexico, Dec. 10, 1904. He has been a farmer in the Deerfield area for many years.
He was a member of the Catholic Church. His only survivor in the United States is his widow, Dolores.
Rosary service was held at the Davis Funeral Home. Funeral service was at Christ the King Mission in Deerfield with Rev. F. C. Laudick officiating. Burial was in the Deerfield Cemetery.

MARTINEZ, JESUS - (Lt. 3, Blk. 27, Sec. 2) Born in 1885 and died in 1941. Jesus Mijiada Martinez, a 53 year old married female Mexican, died May 3, 1941, of cerebral hemorrhage at St. Catherine Hospital in Garden City, C. A. Wiley was the undertaker.

MARTINEZ, JUANITA A. - (Lt. 1, Blk. 128, Sec. 1) Juanita Alvarez de Martinez, 55, died Feb. 8, 1983, at the Kearny County Hospital, Lakin, after a long illness. She had been a Deerfield resident since 1965.
Born Juanita Lopez, March 29, 1928, at Los Laureles, Mexico, she married Vicente Martinez, March 22, 1946, in Mexico.
Survivors are her husband, of the home; four sons, Laco, and Jacinto, both of Garden City and Joe and Jesse, both of Deerfield; five daughters, Rosa Rodriquez, Dora Avila and Elva Martinez, Garden City, Oliva Garcia, Deerfield, and Evangelina, of the home; four brothers and

five sisters, all of Mexico, and 12 grandchildren. She
was preceded in death by a daughter, Alma Yolanda.
Rosary was at Davis Funeral Home, funeral at St.
Anthony Catholic Church, Lakin, the Rev. Austin Herrmann
officiating. Burial at Deerfield Cemetery.

MARTINEZ, RUFINA B. - (Lt. 1, Blk. 110, Sec. 1) (Death
Records) A female Mexican died Jan. 21, 1928, at
Deerfield of pneumonia, age 1 year.

MATHIAS, JAMES HENRY - (Lt. 2, Blk. 98, Sec. 4) James
Henry Mathias, 81, Deerfield, died Wednesday morning,
Feb. 18, 1976, in Garden Valley Retirement Village,
Garden City, following a six year illness. He was a
retired farmer stockman.
    Born June 19, 1894, in Stafford County, he moved to
Deerfield in August 1936, from Stanton County. He was
married to May Heimuller, Dec. 11, 1919, in Stafford.
    He was a member of the Friends Church, Stafford, the
American Legion in Garden City, and was a veteran of
World War I, serving in the U.S. Air force.
    Survivors include four daughters: Mrs. Leon (Nelle
Jane) Scheuerman, and Mrs. Richard (Nadine) Landon, both
of Deerfield, Mrs. Robert (LaVelle) O'Brien, Laurel, Md.,
and Mrs. Larry (Shirley) Graves, Staunton, Ill.; three
sons, Robert, Beaver, Okla., Rolland, Deerfield, and
Laddie, Garden City; 13 grandchildren, and 10 great
grandchildren. Four brothers and a sister preceded him
in death.
    Funeral was held in Phillips-White Funeral Home with
the Rev. Norman Heironimus officiating. Burial in the
Deerfield Cemetery.

MATHIAS, MAY - (Lt. 2, Blk. 98, Sec. 4) May Mathias, 94,
died September 4, 1991, at Terrace Garden Care Center,
Garden City.
    She was born September 10, 1896, at Lorraine, the
daughter of Edward and Iona Belle Elrod Heimiller. A
Garden City resident since 1987, moving from Deerfield,
she was a homemaker.
    She was a member of the Friends Church, Stafford.
    On December 11, 1919, she married James Mathias at
Stafford. He preceded her death.
    Other survivors include: three sons, Robert J.
Mathias, Hiwasse, Ark., Rolland J. Mathias and Laddie L.
Mathias, both of Garden City; four daughters, Nelle Jane

DEERFIELD CEMETERY

Scheuerman and Nadine Landon, both of Deerfield, LaVelle O'Brien, Laurel, Md., and Shirley Graves, Staunton, Ill.: 13 grandchildren; and 34 great grandchildren.

Funeral service was held Friday at the United Methodist Church, Deerfield, with the Rev. Don Koehn presiding. Burial in the Deerfield Cemetery.

MATHIAS, TIMOTHY - (Lt. 2, Blk. 98, Sec. 4) Timothy Robert Mathias, 26, died Nov. 9, 1986, at Enid State School, Enid, Okla. He was born Dec. 15, 1959, in Beaver, Okla.

He was a member of the United Methodist Church.

Survivors: Parents, Robert J. and Marjorie Mathias, Garden City; sisters, Deborah Nelson, Houston, Bee Ann Underwood, Forgan, Okla.; and paternal grandmother, Mae Mathias, Deerfield.

Funeral was held Thursday at Phillips-White Funeral Home, Garden City, the Rev. Nellie Holmes. Burial in Deerfield Cemetery.

MEADOWS, CHARLES - (Lt. 4, Blk. 61, Sec. 3) Born in 1879, died in 1951. Charles Meadows, a former resident of Deerfield, passed away at his home in Scott City, Wednesday afternoon, March 14, 1951.

Funeral services were held at the Baptist Church in Scott City at 2 p.m. Saturday. A short grave service was held at Deerfield at 3:30.

MEADOWS, EUGENIE (EDNA) - (Lt. 4, Blk. 61, Sec. 3) Mrs. Edna Meadows, 92, Deerfield, died Saturday, Oct. 2, 1971, at St., Catherine Hospital, Garden City, after a long illness.

Born April 29, 1879, in Smith County, she had been a lifetime resident of the Deerfield Community. She was married to Charles Meadows, June 4, 1902, at Wallace. He preceded her in death.

Mrs. Meadows was a member of the Baptist Church, Deerfield.

Survivors include three daughters, Miss Mabel E. Meadows, Mrs. Esther Fulton and Mrs. Ruth Downing, all of Deerfield; two sons, Robert, Los Angeles, and Edgar, Abilene, Tex.; 8 grandchildren and 21 great grandchildren.

Funeral service were held Tuesday at the First United Methodist Church in Deerfield, the Rev. Charles Hadley officated. Burial was in the Deerfield Cemetery.

DEERFIELD CEMETERY

MEADOWS, MABEL ELIZABETH - (Lt. 4, Blk. 61, Sec. 3) Funeral for Mabel Elizabeth Meadows, 79, Briar Hill Manor, Garden City, was held at the Deerfield United Methodist Church, the Rev. Nellie Holmes officiating. Burial was at Deerfield Cemetery. She died, Saturday, June 8, 1985, at St. Catherine Hospital after a long illness.

Born Nov. 16, 1905, in Wallace County, she graduated from Deerfield High School and attended Southwest College at Winfield. She was a graduate of the Concordia Hospital School of Nursing.

Before moving to Briar Hill Manor, she lived at Pershing Manor and at Deerfield.

She was a nurse at Condordia Hospital, Beloit Hospital, St. Catherine Hospital here, Kearny County Hospital at Lakin and the Hodgeman County Hospital at Jetmore. Her last years of nursing were spent at the Kansas State Hospital at Larned. When her health failed, she moved to Peshing Manor and later to Briar Hill Manor.

Surviving are two sisters, Mrs. Ester Fulton and Mrs. Ruth Downing, both of Deerfield. Two brothers, Robert C. and E. O. "Mike" Meadows, preceded her in death.

Phillips-White Funeral Home was in charge of arrangements.

MEADOWS, ROBERT C. - (Lt. 4, Blk. 61, Sec. 3) Robert Charles Meadows, 67, died unexpectedly Wednesday morning, Sept. 3, 1975, at St. Catherine Hospital.

Born May 10, 1908, at Sharon Springs, he married Dessie McVicars in 1937 at Newton. She died Dec. 24, 1969. Mr. Meadows was manager of the Thrifty Drug Co. in Los Angeles, Calif. for 35 years before retiring and moving to Garden City in 1971.

An Army veteran of World War II, he was a member of the American Legion.

Survivors include a brother, Edgar, Abilene, Tex.; and three sisters, Mrs. Ester Fulton, Mrs. Ruth Downing and Miss Mabel Meadows, all of Deerfield.

Funeral was held at the Phillips-White Funeral Home, the Rev. Norman Heironimus officiating. Burial in the Deerfield Cemetery.

MEARS, MINNIE B. - (Lt. 1, Blk. 21, Sec. 2) Mrs. Minnie Belle Mears, 75, a resident of Deerfield for the past 19 years, died December 31, 1950, in a Garden City hospital following an illness of three years. Mrs. Mears was born

DEERFIELD CEMETERY

March 4, 1875, at Monticello, Missouri. In her early childhood she moved with her family to near Cedarvale, Kansas.
She married R. B. Patton and spent her early married life in Grainola, Oklahoma. Mr. Patton died in 1914. In 1917, she married H. C. Mears. Following their marriage, the couple moved to a farm near Springfield, Missouri. Mr. Mears died in 1927.
Following the death of her second husband, Mrs. Mears moved to Deerfield in 1931. For the past 19 years she has made her home with her daughter, Mrs. W. T. Rooney, Jr., of Deerfield.
Mrs. Mears was an active member of the Methodist Church of Deerfield.
She is survived by two daughters, Mrs. Rooney and Mrs. H. C. Coleman of Los Angeles, California; and three sons, E. B. Patton of Burbank, California, P. S. Patton of Madison, Illinois, and H. A. Patton of Kirkwood, Missouri. One other daughter died in infancy.
Funeral services were held Wednesday in Garden City. Burial was in the Deerfield Cemetery.

MERZ, GILBERT C. - (Lt. 2, Blk. 82, Sec. 1) Graveside service for Gilbert Charles Merz, 56, Rt. 1, Garden City, was held Wednesday at the Deerfield Cemetery, the Rev. Terry Herzberg officiating.
He died Monday, July 29, 1985, at Humana Hospital, Dodge City, following a long illness. Born Jan. 18, 1929, at Deerfield, he married Maxine Corbett, Sept. 1, 1950, at Garden City.
A retired farmer, he was a member of the Immanuel Lutheran Church, Deerfield.
Surviving are his wife, of the home; two sons, David, Garden City and Danny, Dodge City; a daughter, Carol Schiffelbein, Holcomb; two brothers, John, Garden City, and Melvin, Liberal; three sisters, Edna Shurtz, Duarte, Calif., Ida Kooper, Arlington, and Laura Coerber, Deerfield; five grandchildren.
Garnand Funeral Home was in charge of arrangements.

MERZ, MAXINE - (Lt. 2, Blk. 82, Sec. 1) Funeral for Maxine Merz, 60, was held at Price and Sons Funeral Home, Garden City, the Rev. Erwin Meyer officiating. Burial at Deerfield Cemetery.
She died Dec. 28, 1992, at St. Francis Regional Medical Center, Wichita.

Born June 16, 1932, at Lakin, she was the daughter of Bert and Stella Netser Corbett. She married Gilbert C. Merz, Sept. 1, 1950, at Garden City. He died July 29, 1985, at Dodge City.

Mrs. Merz was an in-house personal care giver and had been a Garden City resident since 1967, moving from Deerfield.

She attended Trinity Lutheran Church.

Survivors include two sons, David and Danny, both of Garden City; a daughter, Carol Schiffelbein, Holcomb; three brothers, Sam Corbett, Deerfield, Fred Corbett, Garden City, and Gene Corbett, Iowa City, Iowa; a sister, Betty Stephens, Garden City and seven grandchildren.

MEXICAN - Died Oct. 15, 1929. Funeral record shows shipped in. (The Lakin Independent, Oct. 18, 1929) The wife of Abram Bonnon, Mexican, died suddenly at Scott City Monday morning and was brought to Deerfield for burial.

MEXICAN - (Funeral Records) Died Nov. 15, 1918, of influenza and pneumonia. Charged to Ben Tackett. Paid by Sugar Co.

MEXICAN - (Lakin Investigator, July 23, 1909) Last week Dr. Johnston was called to Deerfield to sew up a Mexican who had been carved up by one of his companions. The next day another was cut up and Sunday morning the first one was found dead on the railroad, about a mile east of Deerfield station. Coroner C. H. Waterman was notified, and accompanied by Justice L. P. Kimball and Dr. Johnston, went to the scene of the accident, empanelled a jury, who returned a verdict of "killed by the cars." The sugar company fired several of them first of the week as they had become unreliable and disorderly.

MEYER, ELIZABETH EPP - (Lt. 1, Blk. 54, Sec. 2) Elizabeth Epp was born January 28, 1854, in Marienburg, West Prussia, Germany. In 1881, she came to America and in the same year settled in Newton, Kansas. Shortly after her arrival here in America, she was married to Cornelius Penner at the age of twenty-seven. To this union two daughters were born, Mrs. Meta Kettler and Mrs. Elizabeth Becker of Trinidad, Colorado. In 1892 Mr. Penner died. In the year 1894 she, with her children, came to Kearny County. Here she was married to Mr.

DEERFIELD CEMETERY

William Meyer in the same year. They lived on the farm south of the river till 1907, when they moved to the town of Deerfield and retired. Mr. William Meyer died in the year 1915.

Our deceased sister was a faithful member of Immanuel Ev. Lutheran congregation ever since she came to Deerfield. The Holy Bible was more than an ornament in her home. She studied the Word of God; she searched the Scriptures and knew the truths upon which Christian faith and hope rest. Therefore, we did not find it difficult to comfort her in the days and hours of her life, especially during her illness. Even when the angel of death was beckoning her, and talked to her about Jesus as her Savior, she nodded her assent to this and clung to her Savior in true faith until her end.

In this faith in her Savior she passed away last Friday morning, April 11, 1930, at 8:30 at the age of 76 years, 2 months and 14 days.

The deceased leaves to mourn her departure: two daughters, Mrs. August Kettler of Deerfield and Mrs. August Becker of Trinidad, Colorado; five grandchildren; and other relatives and friends.

The funeral services were held Monday, April 14, at 2 o'clock, at the house, where the Rev. K. J. Karstensen of Lincolnville, her former pastor, spoke a few words of comfort and consolation to the bereaved. After which, services were conducted in the church in the German and English languages. Rev. K. J. Karstensen again spoke words of comfort and admonition to the mourners and all present. His sermon was based on Luke 10:42. The local pastor then addressed the bereaved, basing his sermon on John 14:2, which was chosen by the deceased as her funeral text.

After this service, the remains of the deceased were laid to rest beside her second husband in the Deerfield Cemetery.

"Blessed are the dead that die in the Lord from henceforth."

MEYER, HENRY WILHELM — (Lt. 2, Blk. 26, Sec. 2) Born 1875 and died July 6, 1947. (The Lakin Independent, Deerfield News, July 11, 1947) Friends of Mrs. Billy Myers and daughter, Mrs. Glenn McCue and family, extend their heartfelt sympathy in the loss of the husband and father, Billy Myers, whose death occurred early Sunday morning, following a stroke Wednesday of last week.

DEERFIELD CEMETERY

Henry Wilhelm Meyer was born in Corning, Missouri, on February 19, 1875. Soon after his birth he was received into the Covenant of God through the Holy Sacrement of Baptism, later he was also instructed in the chief parts of Christian doctrine and was received into communicant membership in the Lutheran Church through the rite of confirmation.

At the age of four years, Willie came with his parents to Kearny County, Kansas. The Meyers farmed on the Southside until 1936; then moved to Missouri, for one year, after which they resided in Deerfield.

In 1903, he entered the Holy Estate of Matrimony with Marie Slacik. This union was blessed with two daughters, Elfrieda and Rosina. Elfrieda preceded her father in to eternity.

Mr. Meyers was a charter voting member of the Lutheran congregation at Deerfield. He loved his church, faithfully attended devine services and was a frequent guest at the Lord's Table, clinging to his Savior in faith even unto the end.

He passed away peacefully on Sunday morning, July 6th, 1947.

He is survived by his widow, Mrs. Marie Meyer, and his daughter, Mrs. Glen McCue of Arriba, Colorado; by four grandchildren and one son-in-law; also by one brother, Fritz and one sister, Amanda Meyer of Deerfield, as well as other relatives and a host of friends.

He reached the age of 72 years, 4 months and 17 days.

Funeral services were held Wednesday morning from the Deerfield Lutheran Church with Pastor Paul H. C. Stengel officiating. Burial in the Deerfield Cematary.

MEYER, MARY E. - (Lt. 2, Blk. 26, Sec. 2) Marie (Slacik) Meyer was born August 31, 1875, in Corning, Missouri. Soon after her birth she was received into the covenant of God through the Holy Sacrament of Baptism. Later, having been instructed in the chief parts of Christian doctrine, she renewed her baptismal covenant through the rite of confirmation, becoming a faithful member of the Lutheran Church.

In 1903 she entered the Holy Estate of matrimony with Henry William Meyer. To this union two daughters were born: Elfrieda and Rosina.

She came to western Kansas in 1903, settling in Kearny County, near Deerfield. She made her home on the South Side until 1936 when she moved to Missouri for one year,

DEERFIELD CEMETERY

after which she returned to Deerfield. She lived here until 1945 when she left for Arriba, Colorado, to make her home with her daughter, Mrs. Glen McCue, because of failing health.

She fell asleep in Jesus on October 30, 1948, at Arriba, Colorado, having reached the age of 73 years, 1 month and 30 days.

She is preceded in death by her husband, the late Henry William Meyer and one daughter, Elfrieda Hendricks. She is survived by her daughter Rosina (Mrs. Glen McCue); four grandchildren and one son-in-law; also by one brother, Thomas Slacik, Corning, Missouri; and by two sisters, Mrs. Will Roethe, Pinckneyville, Illinois, and Mrs. Frank Coerber, Corning, Missouri; as well as by other relatives and friends.

Funeral services were held on November 3, 1948, at the Deerfield Lutheran Church with Pastor Paul H. C. Stengel in charge. Interment was made in the Deerfield Cemetery.

MEYER, STELLA CLARA RUBY — (Lt. 4, Blk. 45, Sec. 3) Mrs. Stella Meyer, 79, 206 N. 4th, Garden City, died Saturday afternoon, July 10, 1976, at her home.

She was born on April 23, 1897, at Lancaster, Mo., and had been a resident of Garden City since 1939. She moved here from Holcomb.

Mrs. Meyer was a member of the First Christian Church, American Legion, VFW, and Eagles Auxiliary.

She was married to Earl F. Sutton on Oct. 23, 1915, at Hutchinson. She was later married to Fred W. Meyer. He died Feb. 26, 1968.

Survivors include a son, Roy Sutton, of the home; three daughters, Mrs. Lola Welch and Mrs. Edith Fuller, both of Hutchinson, and Mrs. Lesta Holmes, Castle Rock, Colo.; a sister, Mrs. Carrie Hall, Grand Junction, Colo.; five grandchildren and four great grandchildren.

Funeral services were held at 10:30 a.m. Wednesday at the Phillips-White Funeral Home, the Rev. Alvin Daetwiler officiating.

MEYER, WILHELM — (Lt. 1, Blk. 54, Sec. 2) (The Kearny County Advocate, Mar. 19, 1915) The funeral services of Wilhelm Meyer, who passed away Thursday, March 11, were held at the Lutheran Church in Deerfield, Sunday, conducted by Rev. Pennecamp, after which interment was made in the Deerfield Cemetery. Mr. Meyer was born in Hanover, Germany, March 6th, 1845, and died March 11,

DEERFIELD CEMETERY

1915. He came to Lakin in 1879, and resided for a number
of years on his farm in Southside township, and moved to
Deerfield, where he resided until his death. He leaves a
wife, two daughters, a brother and sister who live in
Iowa, two nephews and a niece who reside in this county,
together with a host of friends to mourn his loss. The
Advocate extends sympathy to the grief stricken wife and
daughters, in this their hour of deepest sorrow.

MILLER, BEVERLY JANE - (Lt. 4, Blk. 62, Sec. 3) Wife of
Rex, killed with her husband in explosion of a cafe in
Monticello, Utah, on August 13, 1956.

MILLER, IDELL E. - (Lt. 1, Blk. 62, Sec. 3) Funeral for
Idell E. Miller, 92, was held at the First United
Methodist Church, Dr. Jerold Vogt officiating. Burial at
Deerfield Cemetery.
   She died March 22, 1992, at Garden Valley Retirement
Village.
   Born Idell E. Steen, May 8, 1899, at Westphalia, she
married Ralph H. Miller, April 27, 1921, at Westphalia.
He died in June 1977.
   Mrs. Miller was a homemaker and had been a Garden City
resident since 1947, moving from Deerfield.
   She was a member of the First United Methodist Church,
the Homemakers Sunday School class, United Methodist
Women, Hawk-Towns Circle, the Finney County Historical
Society, a charter member of the Knife and Fork Club, the
Priscilla Club, the Vogue Club and the 20th Century Book
Club, all at Garden City, and was a past member of the
Grange, Deerfield.
   Survivors include a son, Max R., Garden City; a
daughter, Shirley Tillotson, Ulysses; nine grandchildren;
and 14 great grandchildren.
   Price and Sons Funeral Home in charge of arrangements.

MILLER, JACQUELINE - (Lt. 4, Blk. 62, Sec. 3) Daughter
of Rex and Beverly Miller. Born Dec. 9, 1947, and was
killed with her parents in an explosion in a cafe in
Monticello, Utah. She died enroute to the hospital at
Grand Junction, Colo., Aug. 13, 1956.

MILLER, RALPH H. - (Lt. 1, Blk. 62, Sec. 3) Prominent
Kearny-Finney County resident, Ralph H. Miller, Garden
City, died Friday, June 24, 1977, at Briar Hill Manor
following a long illness. He was 85.

Born Sept. 11, 1891, at Bridgewater, Ohio, he married Idell E. Steen, April 17, 1921, at Westphalia.

Mr. Miller was a well known and active educator, farmer, stockman and businessman. He served two terms in the Kansas legislature, elected in 1939 and 1941. He was brought to Kearny County from Ohio when he was six months old. His father had come west in 1888 and had a tree claim in north Kearny County on which he built a "soddy."

Mr. Miller attended school in eastern Kansas and received a teaching certificate from Emporia Normal. He taught school for 20 years in Reno County, Garden City, Holcomb and Deerfield.

One of the organizers of the Production Credit Association, he served on the board and with the Garden City Co-op as secretary-treasurer for many years. Mr. Miller was a member of the First United Methodist Church and a veteran of World War I. He belonged to the American Legion, national and state Grange and the Homemaker Sunday school class.

Survivors include the widow of the home; a son, Max R. Miller, Deerfield; a daughter, Mrs. Shirley Tillotson of Ulysses; two brothers, Willard Rantoul, and Carl, Little Rock, Ark.; a sister, Pearl Dell, Holton; nine grandchildren; and two great grandchildren.

He was preceded in death by a son, Rex Miller, who died in 1956 and a granddaughter, Jackie, also in 1956.

Funeral was Monday morning at the First United Methodist Church, the Rev. J. Karl Jones officiating. Burial was in Deerfield Cemetery.

MILLER, REX LEON - (Lt. 4, Blk. 62, Sec. 3) Son of Ralph and Idell (Steen) Miller, born Jan. 19, 1922. Killed in an explosion of a cafe in Monticello, Utah, Aug. 13, 1956.

(The Lakin Independent, August 17, 1956) Funeral services for Mr. and Mrs. Rex Miller and their daughter, Jacqueline, will be held at 10 a.m. (MST) Friday morning in the high school auditorium in Deerfield. Services will be conducted by the Rev. Thomas A. Bandy of the Deerfield Methodist Church and the Rev. F. G. Smith, former pastor of the church. Burial in Deerfield Cemetery. The family suggests memorials be made for the family to the Deerfield church.

Kearny County folks were stunned this week to learn of the death of three members of the Rex Miller family of

DEERFIELD CEMETERY

Deerfield in an explosion which shattered a cafe in Monticello, Utah.

Dead are Mr. and Mrs. Rex Miller, 34, and their daughter, Jacqueline, 8. Their son, Gerald, 6, was injured.

The Millers were prominent in all types of community life in Deerfield and the county and were known far and wide in Southwest Kansas. They were the finest type young people and their death while vacationing, shocked and saddened everyone who knew them.

Rex, the son of Mr. and Mrs. Ralph Miller of Garden City, was a well known farmer in the Deerfield community. He was a member of the school board there and the Deerfield Methodist Church board of trustees. He served as county commissioner to fill out the term of the late John James.

Mrs. Miller was active in church and community work. The couple will be sorely missed in the social and civic life of the entire county.

Rex was born Jan. 19, 1922, in Garden City. He is survived by his parents, a brother, Max of Deerfield; and a sister, Mrs. Don Tillotson, of Larned.

Mrs. Miller was born Jan. 28, 1922, in Kansas City, Mo. She was formerly Beverly Jane Davis, daughter of Mr. and Mrs. Arthur Davis of Kansas City, prior to her marriage Dec. 7, 1943, to Mr. Miller.

She is survived by her parents and two sisters, Mrs. Louis Mannan of Independence, Mo., and Mrs. David Rowe of Lawrence.

It is the third time in three weeks death has brought sorrow to the Miller family, Mr. Miller's grandmother, Mrs. Alice Miller of Deerfield, died about two weeks ago. His great aunt, Mrs. A. A. Steen, of Garden City, died last week.

The blast in this southeastern Utah uranium mining town killed 15 and injured at least 28. More than 50 diners were in the Lariat Cafe at the height of the busy 7 o'clock dinner hour.

The Millers had left on a vacation trip to the West over the weekend.

The brick and cinderblock cafe was torn apart like a cardboard house by the blast.

The building was jammed with tourists, construction workers from nearby jobs, truckers and townspeople.

The cafe was on U.S. Highway 160 on the edge of town. Only its sign was left standing. The wreckage did not burn.

Some of the bodies were blown through the wall. Rescue workers found two cases of eggs in the rubble. They were not broken.

Two utility company employees, Jerry Fitch, 28, and Fran Urry, 18, both of Salt Lake City, survived. They had just begun to eat when the cafe flew apart. Said Fitch: "the first thing I noticed, I was up in the air. I just remember going straight up and coming down and seeing what I was coming down on." Fitch and Urry were blown out of the cafe and landed on the ground, unhurt.

The small Monticello hospital counted 28 injured. Others were flown to hospitals in Salt Lake City and to Cortez, Durango and Grand Junction, in Colorado.

The blast was believed caused by leaking gas. A resident, Steven Hazelwood, risked his life to shut off the gas system after the explosion.

Officials said the cafe had been connected only the day before to Monticello's new natural gas system.

The Red Cross flew blood and serum albumen from Salt Lake City, 240 miles northwest of here, to aid the injured. Doctors and nurses from towns as much as 100 miles away were rushed to the scene.

The explosion left a 30 foot deep hole in the center of where the small cinderblock cafe, owned by Mr. and Mrs. Harold Ramsdell, stood on the outskirts of the town. Mrs. Ramsdell was injured.

Automobile car lights lighted the small landing strip near the place so airplanes could land and take off with medical supplies and patients.

The two children, Gerald and Jacqueline, were rushed by plane to a hospital at Grand Jucntion, Colo. Jacqueline died enroute to the hospital. Gerald reportedly received slight head and neck injuries.

Mrs. Max Miller was flown to Grand Junction, Tuesday morning, to be with Gerald.

MINOR, JULIA O. - (Lt. 4, Blk. 64, Sec. 3) Funeral for Mrs. Julia O. Minor, 90, was held Friday at the United Methodist Church, the Rev. Ruben Reyes officiating. Burial in Deerfield Cemetery.

Mrs. Minor died January 31, 1978, at Garden Valley Retirement Village, Garden City.

DEERFIELD CEMETERY

Julis Onieda Baer was born in Kiowa County, Kansas, Aug. 19, 1887, the oldest child of Iola M. (Harmon) and W. L. Baer. She spent her early years in Kiowa County except for a few years spent in Greenwood County. She graduated from Friends Academy at Haviland in 1906. She married Manley B. Minor, Oct. 13, 1907, in Kiowa. He died, April 14, 1960. Mrs. Minor moved to Deerfield in 1925 from Lamar, Colo.

She was a member of the United Methodist Church and Garden Club, both of Deerfield.

Survivors include four daughters, Mrs. Udell H. (Myrtle) Kueker, Deerfield, Mrs. William R. (Corrine) Leimenstoll, West Palm Beach, Fla., Mrs. John P. (Barbara) Kingman, Fairfax, Va., and Mrs. Orin A. (Doris) Griesmyer, North Palm Beach, Fla.; eight grandchildren and 16 great grandchildren.

Garnand Funeral Chapel in charge of arrangements.

MINOR, MANLEY BRAKER - (Lt. 4, Blk. 64, Sec. 3) Manley Braker, son of Lewis and Sophia Minor, was born at Salisbury, Mo., on Jan. 6, 1878, and died at the Kearny County Hospital, April 14, 1960, following an illness of several years.

Mr. Minor was baptized in the Baptist Church in Salisbury, Mo. At the age of 21 he moved to Kansas and located in Haviland.

On Oct. 13, 1907, he was married to Julia Oneida Baer and to this union four daughters were born. The family lived in Haviland until 1922 when it moved to Lamar, Colo. In 1925 the family moved to Deerfield. Mr. Minor has resided in Deerfield since that time.

Mr. Minor was a salesman most of his life and was most recently associated with the Santa Fe Motor Company of Deerfield.

He is survived by his wife, Julia, and four daughters, Mrs. W. R. Leimenstoll, Waco, Tex., Mrs. O. A. Griesmyer, New York City, Mrs. J. P. Kingman, Falls Church, Va., and Mrs. Udell Kueker, Deerfield; two sisters, Mrs. Earl Williams of Florence, Colo., and Mrs. Josephine Rayburn, Anna, Ill.; eight grandchildren, three great grandchildren, and many other relatives and friends.

MITCHELL, MRS. ED. P. - (Lt. 4, Blk. 31, Sec. 2)

MOLZ, HENRY O. - (Lt. 2, Blk. 61, Sec. 3) Funeral for Henry Otto Molz, was held at 10:30 a.m. Saturday at the

DEERFIELD CEMETERY

Lutheran Church, Deerfield, the Rev. Ken Haskell officiating. Burial was in Deerfield Cemetery.

He died December 10, 1991, at St. Catherine Hospital, Garden City.

Born January 23, 1900, in Stanton County, he married Emma Marie Gropp, June 1, 1926, at Kendall.

Mr. Molz was a farmer and stockman and had been a Kearny County resident most of his life.

He was a member of the Deerfield Lutheran Church, served on various church boards and in various offices, and was a former Deerfield school board member.

Survivors include his wife, of the home; three sons, Lewis and Otis, both of Deerfield, and Ronald, Broomfield, Colo.; a daughter, Esther Esch, Fort Worth; 13 grandchildren; and 13 great grandchildren.

Greene-Schneider Funeral Home in charge of arrangements.

MONTOYA, JOSE - (S/2 Lt. 1, Blk. 128, Sec. 1) Funeral for Jose Montoya, 67, retired farm laborer, was held Monday at St. Anthony's Catholic Church in Lakin. Burial at Deerfield Cemetery.

He died Thursday, Aug. 21, 1986, at St. Catherine Hospital, Garden City.

He was born on Nov. 20, 1918, in Monero, New Mexico, the son of Mr. and Mrs. Jesus Montoya, he had lived in Deerfield nine years. Mr. Montoya was a member of the Catholic Church.

Survivors are a son, Lero Montoya of Oklahoma; a daughter, Jessie Monoya, Billings, Mont.; a brother, Alberto Montoya, Powell, Wyo.; and two sisters, Marie Lynch, Byron, Wyo., and Josie Montoya, Billings, Mont.

MOORES, FLORENCE JANE - (Lt. 3, Blk. 32, Sec. 2) (The Lakin Independent, Feb. 9, 1923) Florence Jane Moores, aged fifteen years, eight months and 12 days passed away, Tuesday, February 6th, 1923, at the C. W. Gibbs home, where she has been lovingly cared for since the death of her mother, when she was a child about two years old. She had been ill for a couple of weeks with pneumonia and for several days was in a very critical condition. The funeral was held at the Methodist Church in Lakin, on Thursday morning, with Rev. E. L. Nicholson in charge of the service. The remains were then taken to the Deerfield Cemetery where they were laid to rest beside her mother.

DEERFIELD CEMETERY

MORELAND, CARL - (Lt. 1, Blk. 14, Sec. 3) Carl Moreland, 88, of Deerfield died early Monday morning, Dec. 7, 1981, at St. Catherine Hospital in Garden City. A resident of Kearny County for 47 years he was a spiritual and community leader in the Deerfield and Lakin area.

Carl was born Oct. 30, 1893, in Topeka, Kansas, to John D. and Mary Elizabeth Moreland, the second of seven children. In 1902, Carl moved with his family from Topeka to Indian Territory, which became Oklahoma in 1906. Carl grew up on a farm near Freedom, Oklahoma, where he learned many aspects of farming.

On Dec. 28, 1913, Carl obeyed the gospel of the word of God which had a dramatic impact on his life and on those with whom he came into contact, and continues to this day.

In September 1918, Carl was drafted into the Armed Services where he served in the Medical Corps until his discharge in April 1919.

Carl returned to the farming community near Freedom, Okla. On August 17, 1919, Carl and Helen Annis were united in marriage. To this union were born eight children, 28 grandchildren and 21 great grandchildren.

In 1934, Carl moved his family from Mooreland, Okla., to Kearny County, Kansas. In 1937, Carl and his family moved to Deerfield, which was his place of residence until his death, with the exception of a brief stay in a nursing home in Garden City.

Carl and his wife, Helen, established a congregation of the Church of Christ, meeting first in their home and then in various locations in Deerfield and Lakin. Carl served as a minister to family and friends throughout his life, dedicating his life to the study of the bible, committing much to memory.

On September 5, 1942, Carl became freight and mail deliverer for the Santa Fe and U.S. Postal Service where he worked until retiring in October 1967.

Besides his wife, Helen, Carl leaves sons and daughters: Lois Tapp, Fairbanks, Alaska; Neil C. Moreland, minister, Ontario, Oregon; Iris Moreland Davis, Owasso, Oklahoma; Flora Beth Armstrong, Haven, Kansas; Melda Lou Moreland, Wichita, Kansas; Merle Lee Moreland, campus minister, Kilgore, Texas; John W. Moreland, campus minister, Boise, Idaho; also numerous grandchildren, and great grandchildren.

Funeral was held at the Church of Christ in Lakin. Officiating ministers were sons, Neil, John and Merle

DEERFIELD CEMETERY

Moreland and Leland Burch of Durham, Oklahoma. Pallbearers were Michael Armstrong, Ken Davis, Mark Davis, Michael Cottrell, Michael Bird and Marvin Estill.

MORELAND, GARY NEIL - (Lt. 4, Blk. 14, Sec. 3) Funeral services for Gary Neil Moreland, was held Thursday at the Deerfield High School Auditorium, the Rev. Herman Barnett, York, Neb., officiating. Burial in the Deerfield Cemetery.
   Mr. Moreland, died May 30, 1972, at St. Catherine Hospital, Garden City, of injuries suffered in an accident, May 23, at a county road intersection east of Deerfield.
   Born Feb. 5, 1952, in Lakin, he married Teresa Rae Jackson, July 19, 1970, in Juarez, Mexico.
   Survivors include the widow, Teresa; a son, Shawn of the home; his parents, Mr. and Mrs. Neil Moreland, Portales, N.M.; a sister, Mrs. Cynthia Bird; and his grandparents, Mr. and Mrs. Carl Moreland and Mr. and Mrs. Harold Bell all of Deerfield.

MORELAND, HARLEY D. - (Lt. 1, Blk. 14, Sec. 3) Funeral for Harley D. Moreland, 52, was held at the Church of Christ, Lakin, with the Rev. Jerry Seright officiating. Burial at the Deerfield Cemetery.
   Harley was born August 12, 1930, at Marlad, Okla., and died Monday, April 11, 1983, at Wesley Medical Center. Formerly of Deerfield, he was a resident of Heartland Development Center in Haven.
   He was a member of the Church of Christ, Lakin.
   Survivors are his mother, Helen M. Moreland, Deerfield; three brothers, Neil, Ontario, Ore., Merle, Kilgore, Texas, and John, Boise, Idaho; four sisters, Lois Tapp, Fairbanks, Alaska, Iris Davis, Owasso, Okla., Mrs. Bob (Flora) Armstrong, Portales, N.M., and Mrs. Allen (Melda) Dimick, Wichita. His father, Carl, died Dec. 7, 1981.
   Garnand Funeral Home in charge of arrangements.

MORELAND, HELEN M. - (Lt. 1, Blk. 14, Sec. 3) Helen M. Annis Moreland, 95, longtime Kearny County resident, died November 29, 1994, at Kearny County Hospital, Lakin.
   Born August 15, 1899, in Osborne County, she was the daughter of George Franklin and Flora Lou Rice Annis. When she was three, the family moved to Freedom, Okla., where she attended Unity School.

189

She married Carl Moreland on August 17, 1919, at Freedom. In 1934, they moved from Freedom to Kearny County. They moved to Deerfield in 1937. The couple estabished a congregation of the Church of Christ, meeting first in their home and then at various locations in Deerfield and Lakin. Her husband died December 7, 1981.

Mrs. Moreland was a cook for many years at the cafe in Deerfield, designed clothes in her home and took in laundry. A homemaker, she enjoyed quilting, crocheting, gardening and was active in her children's school activities.

She was a member of Church of Christ, Lakin, the Garden Club, Hobby Club, Extension Homemakers Unit and the Widows Card Club, all of Deerfield. She was past president of the Parent Teacher Association in Deerfield and had been a Bible school teacher.

Survivors are three sons, Neil Moreland, Ontario, Ore., Merle Moreland, Kilgore, Texas, and John Moreland, Memphis; four daughters, Lois Tapp, Fairbanks, Alaska, Iris Barnett, Pensacola, Fla., Flora Armstrong, Portales, N.M., and Melda Dimick, Wichita; 18 grandchildren; 43 great grandchildren; and five great great grandchildren.

She was preceded in death by her parents, her husband, a son, Harley Moreland, four brothers, two sisters and a grandchild.

Funeral was at 2 p.m. Saturday at Church of Christ, Lakin, officiated by Mrs. Moreland's three sons. Chaplain Pete Cousins assisted. Burial was in Deerfield Cemetery.

MORFORD, GLEN ARNETT - (Lt. 3, Blk. 41, Sec. 3) Funeral services for Glen A. Morford, was held at the United Methodist Church in Deerfield. Rev. Charles Hadley officiating. Burial in Deerfield Cemetery.

He was born Sept. 24, 1900, in Eldorado, Kansas, and was married to Eva Janzen, June 1, 1941. He was a retired mail carrier and had lived in Deerfield most of his life. He also owned the Deerfield Telephone Company at one time. He died at St. Catherine Hospital, Tuesday, February 9, 1971, after a short illness. He was 70 years old.

He was a member of the United Methodist Church in Deerfield and the Deerfield Grange.

Survivors are the widow, Eva, of the home; daughters, Mrs. Virginia DeWitt, Scott City, Mrs. Eyvonne Crase, Garden City; and a son, Lloyd Krause, Weisbaden, Germany.

MORRELL, FRANK - (Lt. 2, Blk. 20, Sec. 3)   Funeral for Frank Ecklon Morrell, 73, Syracuse, was held Friday at the United Methodist Church, Syracuse, the Rev. Dale Ellenberger officiating. Burial at Deerfield Cemetery.

He died Tuesday, March 3, 1987, at the Kearny County Hospital, Lakin.

Born April 16, 1913, at Freeport, Ill., he married Evelyn Zrubek Sharp, Aug. 3, 1976, at Miami, Okla. He was retired owner of the Sand and Gravel Co., Syracuse, and had been a Syracuse resident since 1930.

Mr. Morrell was a member of the Eagles Lodge, Garden City, and was an Air Force veteran of World War II.

Survivors include his wife, of the home; a son, Franklin, Wichita; a daughter, Francine Parker, Wellington, Colo.; a sister, Rose Morrell, Garden City; and one grandchild.

Greene Funeral Home, Syracuse, was in charge of arrangements.

MORRIS, BRIAN EUGENE - (Lt. 4, Blk, 78, Sec. 1)   Brian Eugene Morris, three year old son of Mr. and Mrs. Don Morris, was killed Aug. 6, 1973, in a two car accident.

Born March 31, 1970, at Garden City, he had lived here all his life.

Survivors in addition to his parents include his grandparents, Mr. and Mrs. Virgil Harsh, Holcomb, Mr. and Mrs. Boyd Morris, Dodge City, and Beverly Harding, Garden City; his great grandparents, Mr. and Mrs. E. M. Foreman, Holcomb, and Mr. and Mrs. Arthur Drussel, S. Star Rt.

Garnand Funeral Home was in charge of arrangements.

MULLINS, ELLA F. - (Lt. 2, Blk. 80, Sec. 1)   Ella Doyle Mullins, 96, a longtime Deerfield resident, died Oct. 30, 1965, at the Stormont-Vail Hospital, Topeka, after an extended illness. She had been living with her daughter, Mrs. Mary Pennekamp, Topeka, for the last four years.

She was born July 20, 1869, at Ridgeway, Va. She was married to James Samuel Doyle in 1887 at Spencer, Va. He preceded her in death, Nov. 11, 1910. She was also preceded in death by four sons.

Mrs. Mullins moved her family to Deerfield in 1914. She was married to W. L. Mullins in 1920.

Mrs. Mullins was a member of the Deerfield Methodist Church.

Survivors include the widower, W. L. Mullins, Lakin; four sons, H. W. Doyle, Tampa, Fla., R. H. Doyle, Bristow, Colo., R. G. Doyle, Buenos Aires, Argentina, and R. E. Doyle, Arcadia, Calif.; two daughters, Mrs. H. W. Jacobs, Colorado Springs, Colo. and Mrs. R. W. Pennekamp, Topeka; 11 grandchildren; 12 great grandchildren; and 2 great great grandchildren.

Funeral services were held at the Deerfield Methodist Church with the Revs. Wesley Davis and Robert Fleenor officiating. Burial was in the Deerfield Cemetery.

MULLINS, WILLIAM L. - (Lt. 2, Blk. 80, Sec. 1) Funeral services for William L. Mullins, 95, who died February 16, 1969, at the Kearny County Hospital, were held Feb. 19, at the United Methodist Church in Deerfield, Rev. Charles Hadley officiated. Burial was in the Deerfield Cemetery.

William Lee Mullins was born in Fayetteville, Arkansas, Feb. 5, 1874. He was a long time resident of Deerfield, owning and operating a produce house and filling station. He was married to Mrs. Ella Doyle in 1920 in Hutchinson. She died in 1965.

He was a member of the Deerfield Methodist Church.

He moved to Lakin in 1962, where he lived at the Pioneer Rest home.

He is survived by two stepdaughters, Mrs. Mary Pennekamp, Topeka, and Mrs. Bessie Jacobs, Colorado Springs; three step sons, Russell Doyle, Buenos Aires, Argentina, Harry Doyle, Tampa, Fla., and Raymond Doyle Bristol, Colo.

MUNOZ, ABUNDIA (ALUINDIO) - (Lt. 2, Blk. 21, Sec. 2) Mexican male, 58 years old, died Feb. 4, 1933, at Deerfield of carcinoma of prostate.

MUNOZ, CARMEN - (Lt. 2, Blk. 21, Sec. 2) Born Jan. 16, 1921, and died June 15, 1957. Born at Yates Center, Ks. Father Librado Beltran, mother Juna Rodriquez, husband Romoldo Munoz, children Lupe, Michael, and Mary.

MUNOZ, CAROLINA M. - (Lt. 3, Blk. 99, Sec. 1) ts. Nov. 5, 1917-July 4, 1985. Wake service for Carolina M. Munoz, 67, Garden City, was held at St. Mary Catholic

DEERFIELD CEMETERY

Church. Daughters of Isabella rosary followed and also a
Spanish rosary.
Funeral was held Saturday at St. Mary, the Rev. Tom
Vowell officiating. Burial at Deerfield Cemetery.
She died Thursday morning, July 4, 1985, at the High
Plains Retirement Village, Lakin. Born Jan. 5, 1917, at
Garden City, she married Louis C. Munoz, April 7, 1948,
in Garden City. He died Jan. 20, 1975.
Mrs. Munoz was a member of St. Mary Catholic Church,
the Daughters of Isabella, Cursillo Movement, RSVP and
the Senior Citizens.
Surviving are three sons, Abundio, Jorge, and Abelardo;
two brothrs, Ascencion Mora, Jr. and Andrew Mora; three
sisters, Justina Aguilera, Theresa Gallardo, and
Magdalena Cantu; and eight grandchildren.

MUNOZ, DELFINO - (Lt. 2, Blk. 21, Sec 2) Born July 14,
1917 and died September 8, 1925.

MUNOZ, LOUIS C. - (Lt. 3, Blk. 99, Sec. 1) Louis C.
Munoz, 65, died Monday evening, January 20, 1975, at St.
Catherine Hospital after a short illness.
He was born April 1, 1909, at Iola and moved with his
family to Deerfield where he farmed until 1958. In 1948
he married Carolina Mora in Garden City. When he retired
from farming in 1958, he and his wife moved to Garden
City where Mr. Munoz worked as a custodian for Garden
City Community College until his death.
Mr. Munoz was a member of St. Mary's Catholic Church in
Garden City.
Survivors include the widow, Carolina; three sons,
Jorge, Kansas City, Abundio, Garden City, and Abelardo,
of the home; a brother, Romaldo; a sister, Mrs. Merced
Aguilera both of Garden City and one granddaughter.
Funeral was held at St. Mary's Catholic Church, the
Rev. William Walter officiating. Garnand Funeral Chapel
in charge. Burial in the Deerfield Cemetery.

MUNOZ, MARIA C. - (Lt. 2, Blk. 21, Sec. 2) Mrs. Maria C.
Munoz, 89, died Wednesday noon, July 20, 1966, in St.
Catherine's Hospital, Garden City, after a six month
illness. Born July 2, 1877, in Mexico she moved to
Finney County in 1937. She married Aluindio Munoz in
Mexico. He died in 1933.
Member: St. Mary's Catholic Church, Altar Society,
Garden City.

Survivors: daughter, Mrs. Merceed Aguilera, Garden City; sons, Louis and Romaldo, both of Garden City; 48 grandchildren, 26 great grandchildren.

MURRAY, VALLEY L. - (Lt. 4, Blk. 43, Sec. 3) Valley L. Hemming Murray, age 69, of Deerfield, Kansas, was stricken at home Thursday evening, July 16, 1959, and passed away before she reached the hospital.

Born Sept. 7, 1889, at Thornton, Iowa, she moved to Kansas at an early age and lived near Ottawa, Kans. She was married to William T. Murray, Feb. 4, 1913. The Murrays moved to Western Kansas in 1921 and the Murray home has been one mile north of Deerfield for the last 30 years.

She leaves her husband, William, one daughter, Doris Scheuerman; two sisters, Verdie Hemming of Ottawa and Vilo Butell of Lawrence, Kans., and one brother, Glen Hemming of Ottawa; two grandchildren, many relatives and a host of friends.

Funeral services were held Saturday at 3:00 o'clock in Phillips Chapel in Garden City, Kans. Interment was in the Deerfield Cemetery.

MURRAY, WILLIAM T. - (Lt. 4, Blk. 43, Sec. 3) William Theodore Murray was born at Red Oak. Ia., Jan. 9, 1886, and passed away at the Kearny County Hospital, Sept. 7, 1959, at the age of 73 years. He lived in Franklin and Norton Counties before moving in 1921 to a farm north of Holcomb in Finney County. He had lived at his present farm home one mile north of Deerfield since 1929.

He served on the board of the Kearny County Irrigation Association for over 30 years, being its president for the past 20 years. He was a charter member of the Deerfield Grange and received his 25 year pin in 1956. He was the insurance agent for the organization. He was a member of the Deerfield Lions Club.

His wife preceded him in death July 16 of this year.

Survivors are one daughter, Mrs. Doris Scheuerman of Deerfield; three brothers, George of Puyallup, Wash., Joe of Coleville, Wash., and Harris of Pomona; one sister, Mrs. Verlie Simpson of Spokane, Wash., and two grandchildren; also many other relatives and a host of friends.

DEERFIELD CEMETERY

MCAFEE, HARRISON R. - (Lt. 1, Blk. 76, Sec. 1) Harrison
R. McAfee, son of William and Jane McAfee, was born Nov.
8, 1890, in Boxley, Ark. He died July 17, 1962.
The family moved to Oklahoma and in 1905 he came to
Kansas where he worked on the Oscar Downing (senior)
farm. Later another brother, Jap McAfee, came to Kansas
and the two of them farmed the land where he and his wife
lived at the time of his death.
He was a volunteer in World War I and served in the
110th Ammunition Train in France.
Just before leaving the States he was united in
marriage to Lulu Faye Downing at Lawton, Okla., Nov. 30,
1917.
To this union three children were born, Harrison Vern,
Oscar Wayne, and Lulu Muriel. Lula Muriel died when only
two months old, the sons were each a casualty of World
War II.
He was a member of the Deerfield Methodist Church,
Veterans of Foreign Wars, American Legion, Deerfield
Masonic Lodge, Deerfield Lions Club, and had served on
numerous boards and committees in the county.
Besides his wife he leaves to mourn his passing, three
sisters, Mrs. Carrie Brant, Mrs. Cordelia Cain, both of
Oklahoma; and Mrs. Meda Allsup of Wellington, Ks.; three
brothers, Jasper and Henry McAfee of California; and Joe
Johnson of Payett, Ida.; a daughter-in-law, Mrs. Wayne
MaAfee, and a granddaughter, Wynn; nieces, nephews and
many friends.
Funeral services were held at the Deerfield Methodist
Church, Rev. Robert Fleenor officiating. Burial in
Deerfield Cemetery.

MCAFEE, HARRISON VERN - (Lt. 1, Blk. 76, Sec. 1)
Harrison Vern McAffee was born July 21, 1920, in Garden
City, Kansas. Passed out of this life Dec. 12, 1941, in
Naval Hospital, Mare Island, California, age 21 years, 4
months and 21 days.
His childhood and early manhood was spent in the home
and schools of Deerfield. He was an honored graduate of
the Deerfield High School. At the age of 18 he passed
the rigid examinations and enlisted in the U.S. Marines,
serving his chosen profession and country well, until
called to a better country, where wars are no more.
When 12 years of age he gave his heart and life to
Christ and united with the Methodist Church of Deerfield,
Kansas. Our Heavenly Father tells us "I give unto them

195

eternal life and they shall never perish, neither shall any man pluck them out of my hand."

Vern leaves to mourn his passing, his much loved mother, father, and brother, Wayne, many other relatives and friends, both in his home country and far away places, where his duties as Marine Guard, on the cruiser, the U.S.S. Salt Lake City, took him.

Many honors were bestowed on him in his line of service, which he always received with the modesty that characterized him. Sergeant McAfee was being sent to San Diego as instructor in the sea school for marines in that city, when he was suddenly called to come home.

The funeral service was held in the Deerfield Methodist Church, the pastor Ira I. Woolard, being in charge. Interment being made in the Deerfield Cemetery. The body was escorted home by Sgt. J. L. Farris.

(The Lakin Independent, Dec. 19, 1941) Sgt. Verne McAfee, serving with the U.S. Marine Corps in the Pacific area, died Friday in the Mare Island naval base hospital of "intracranial" injuries, the cause of which has not been reported. Mare Island is located in San Francisco bay.

Sgt. McAfee is a son of Mr. and Mrs. Harrison McAfee of Deerfield and had been planning to spend the holidays with home folks. A telegram stating that his furlough has been cancelled came Friday morning and at 7:30 a.m. he was brought to the hospital where he died three hours later.

The body will be brought home to Deerfield for burial. Funeral arrangements cannot be made until arrival of the body which was to leave San Francisco on Wednesday. The American Legion will have charge of military graveside services.

This is the first Kearny County casualty since the breaking out of war. His father saw service overseas in the first world war.

MCAFEE, LULA MURIEL — (Lt. 1, Blk. 76, Sec. 1) ts. July 9, 1926-September 11, 1926.

Lula Muriel, daughter of Harrison R. and Lula Fay McAfee, was born July 9th, 1926, and died September 12, 1926, aged 2 months and 3 days.

Jesus said, "Suffer little children to come unto me," and our baby obeyed the loving call 3 o'clock Sunday afternoon.

DEERFIELD CEMETERY

We said--
            The bitterness of grief is gone
            Henceforward, we will think of her as one too
            good for selfish tears to stir
            A saint, who touched and blessed us, and then
            passed on;
            Our angel evermore to bend and take our
            brokern prayer to God for love's dear sake.
Funeral services were held Monday , September 13th, at
2:45 p.m., Rev. J. Q. Turner in charge.

MCAFEE, LULU (LOU) FAY - (Lt. 1, Blk. 76, Sec. 1)   ts.
1885-1963. Mrs. Lulu McAfee (Aunt Lou as she was known
to many of us) has lived among us as a symbol of courage.
It seemed as though heartbreak and pain were her constant
companion throughout her life.
    She was born Sept. 23, 1885, in Camp Point, Ill. As a
small girl she was placed in an orphanage. A. R. Downing
was in Illinois on business and went to the orphanage and
got her. He came bringing her home in his arms as a
surprise to the family. Now there was a little girl in
the home of all boys. Here she grew to young womanhood.
Then she made her home with Oscar J. Downing Sr. family.
    The time of marriage found her among the many new war
brides of World War I. She traveled to Lawton, Okla., to
become the wife of Harrison R. McAfee, Sept. 30, 1917.
They had one week together before her husband was shipped
overseas for the remainder of the war.
    Three children came to bless the home. One daughter
and two sons. The daughter died in infancy, thus making
the family span the two worlds of time and eternity.
    The black clouds of war came over the land again. The
cream of the crop of young men and women again were
answering the call of their country. The two sons,
Vernon and Wayne, answered this call. As each young man
left his home the unspoken word was that he could have to
pay the supreme sacrifice. These two boys answered this
call to the complete end being listed as those that had
given the supreme sacrifice for their country.
    Aunt Lou bore with patience and endurance of a good
soldier, the crippling disease of arthritis. This
greatly hampered her activities, but not her spirit. Her
concern was always for those about her that needed a
comforting hand or a word of encouragement.
    She was left as the last member of her home in July of
1962, when her husband joined the family circle of

DEERFIELD CEMETERY

eternity. Since that day she has looked forward to the day that she could be reunited with her family.

At the time of her death she held the record of being the only member of our church that joined before the 20th century. She joined the church in 1897 and was a continuous member till her death, Oct. 2, 1963.

She leaves behind one granddaughter, Wynn McAfee; two brothers of the home she came into, Clarence and Ed Downing of Garden City, and many friends.

MCAFEE, OSCAR WAYNE - (Lt. 4, Blk. 76, Sec. 1) Sgt. Oscar Wayne McAfee, son of Mr. and Mrs. Harrison McAfee, was born September 8, 1921, at Garden City, Kansas, and departed this life in the vicinity of St. Lo., France, on July 11, 1944, having reached the age of 22 years, 10 months, and 3 days.

He grew up in and near Deerfield, where he was an active member of the Methodist Church. He attended the Deerfield grade school and high school, graduating with the class of '39. He was associated with his father in farming until he entered military service. He was united in marriage with Eloris Scheuerman on August 23, 1942, and left for service with the U.S. Army three days later.

He took his basic training at Camp Roberts, California, and joined the 127th Regiment of the 35th Infantry Division in December 1942, at El Segundo, California. While stationed at San Luis Obispo, California, he became a member of the Lutheran Church by the rite of confirmation on March 14, 1943.

Other places of military training were Camp Rucker, Alabama, maneuvers in Tennessee, Camp Butner, North Carolina, maneuvers in West Virginia and on May 4, 1944, the 137th moved to Camp Kilmer, New Jersey. They sailed on the morning of May 11, 1944, and landed in England on May 24. They were stationed at Newquay, England, until July 6-7, when the regiment sailed and landed on French soil at Omaha Beach on July 7, 8 and 9.

He is survived by his wife, Eloris and a daughter, Lola Wynn, now three years of age; also his parents, Mr. and Mrs. Harrison McAfee, and a number of other relatives and friends.

Funeral services were conducted Tuesday, February 10, at the Deerfield high school auditorium with Rev. P.H.C. Stengel of the Lutheran Church in charge. The VFW and American Legion were in charge of military honors. Interment was made at the Deerfield Cemetery.

198

DEERFIELD CEMETERY

Pallbearers were Ernest Lindberg, Great Bend; Clifford Knight, Caldwell; Tom Sutton and Guy Murray, Emporia; Guy Martin, Wellington; and Arthur Boman, Pierceville; all former army buddies of Sgt. McAfee and members of the 35th Division. Sgt. Freeman Louden of Kansas City was the army escort.

Included among those attending the funeral from out of town were Mr. and Mrs. Wm. J. Scheuerman, Mrs. Emma Appel of LaCrosse, Kansas; Miss Bertha Scheuerman of Bison, Kansas; Mr. and Mrs. Merlin Dirks and daughter of Albert, Kansas; Mrs. Lester Hagerman of Timken, Kansas; Mrs. Alva Weathers, Mr. and Mrs. Ernest Lindberg of Great Bend; Miss Venita Beth Downing of Winfield; Mr. and Mrs. Robert Corbett, Las Vegas, New Mexico; Mr. and Mrs. Louis Grosjean, Mr. Tom Sherry and Mrs. Tom Tuggle of Scott City; Mr. Oliver Drussel and Rev. M. E. Hickman of Cimarron.

Despite a near-blizzard more than 500 people attended the funeral and memorial services held for Sgt. McAfee, one of Kearny County's war heroes, was killed in France shortly after D-Day.

Friends and comrades of the deceased gathered to pay a final tribute in services at the high school and at military services by the combined VFW and American Legion organizations at the cemetary, as a high wind swept a blizzard into Kearny County.

(The Lakin Independent, Feb. 6, 1944) The body of Sgt. Wayne McAfee, World War II casualty, killed in the invasion of France, arrived in Garden City Monday morning at 9:45 o'clock, according to word received by his parents, Mr. and Mrs. Harrison R. McAfee of Deerfield.

The military escort who accompanied the body of McAfee from the American Graves Registration Distribution center in Kansas City, Mo., to Garden City was selected and trained to represent the government on the mission.

The Garden City VFW and American Legion posts had delegations to meet the train Monday and Kearny County posts took part in the burial services.

(The Lakin Independent, March 7, 1947) A posthumously awarded Silver Star medal was received last week by Mrs. Wayne McAfee of Deerfield, who is the widow of Sgt. Wayne McAfee, who was killed in action near St. Lo, France, in July of 1944.

The citation received by Mrs. McAfee read as follows:

Citation for the Silver Star-- For gallantry in action in the vicinity of St. Lo, Normandy, France, 2 July,

1944. In the initial attack of Company "B", harassing enemy machine gun fire impeded the progress of the unit. Sergeant McAfee, accompanied by three others, voluntarily went forward in an attempt to destroy an enemy machine gun emplacement in a hedgerow one hundred yards to its right. Despite enemy fire of all types, the patrol was successful in reaching the emplacement, where Sgt. McAfee destroyed the machine gun position by using three hand grenades, killing two enemy machine gunners and wounding two, whom he took as prisoners. Returning to his unit, Sergeant McAfee, his patrol and prisoners were discovered by an enemy observer, fire was directed on them and Sergeant McAfee, the two prisoners and two members of the patrol were killed.

Sgt. McAfee's gallantry in action, his courage and devotion to duty are in accord with the high tradition of the military service.

In addition to the Silver Star, Sgt. McAfee was entitled to the following decorations: American Theatre Ribbon, Victory medal, European-African-Middle Eastern Theatre ribbon with two bronze service stars, Good conduct medal, expert carbine and rifle badges combat infantry-man badge and the Purple Heart.

Sgt. McAfee was attached to the 35th Infantry Division overseas.

MCGINN, CLARA E. - (Lt. 1, Blk. 28, Sec. 2) Funeral for Mrs. Clara E. McGinn was held Saturday at the United Methodist Church, Deerfield, the Rev. Harry Walz officiating. Burial was in Deerfield Cemetery.

Mrs. McGinn, 81, died Thursday, February 8, 1979, at the Fort Dodge Hospital, Fort Dodge, following a long illness.

Born Clara E. Gass on December 12, 1897, at Peoria, Ill., she married Robert O. McGinn on January 12, 1921, at Garden City. He died on March 11, 1976.

She was a member of the United Methodist Church and the Garden Club, both of Deerfield, and a past worthy matron of the O.E.S., Lakin.

Survivors include a son, Willard, Garden City; a daughter, Mrs. Ruth Holsten, Ensign; three brothers, Bill Gass, Dallas, Texas, Albert Gass, Garden City, and Harry Gass, Lakin; a sister, Mrs. Rudy Hoglund, Albuquerque, N.M.; 10 grandchildren and six great grandchildren.

MCGINN, LOLA MAY - (Lt. 1, Blk. 51, Sec. 2) Died before
1918 at the age of 7 years. Bob McGinn's sister.

MCGINN, MILDRED FAYE - (Lt. 4, Blk. 28, Sec. 2) Daughter
of Robert O. and Clara (Gass) McGinn born and died Nov.
30, 1921.

MCGINN, ROBERT O. - (Lt. 1, Blk. 28, Sec. 2) Robert O.
McGinn, 81, died March 11, 1976, at Halsey Hall, Fort
Dodge. A resident of the Deerfield area most of his
adult life, Mr. McGinn was a retired farmer and well
driller. He and his wife moved to Fort Dodge about a
year ago.
    Born Jan. 12, 1895, in Paola, he moved to Deerfield
from Wichita. He married Clara E. Goss, Jan. 12, 1921,
in Garden City. They had celebrated their 55th wedding
anniversary in January.
    Mr. McGinn served in the Army in France during World
War I. He was a member of Masonic Lodge, Lakin.
    Survivors are the widow, of Fort Dodge; a son, Willard,
Garden City; a daughter, Mrs. Harold (Ruth) Holsteen,
Ensign; a brother, Pat McGinn, Denver, Colo., 10
grandchildren and 4 great grandchildren.
    Funeral was held Saturday at 2 p.m., at Deerfield
United Methodist Church, with Dr. Ruben Reyes
officiating. Burial at the Deerfield Cemetery, where
American Legion and Masonic graveside services were
conducted.

MCKEDY, DORA ELLEN - (Lt. 2, Blk. 19, Sec. 3) Mrs. Dora
Ellen McKedy, 66, Deerfield, died May 5, 1973, at St.
Catherine Hospital, Garden City, after a long illness.
    Born Feb. 14, 1907, at Vici, Okla., daughter of Bessie
Barnes Dennett and A. J. Dennett, she was married to
Russell McKedy, December 12, 1926, at Taloga, Okla. They
moved from Towner, Colo., to Deerfield in 1954, where
they operated a cafe on Highway U.S. 50.
    Survivors include the widower; four sons, Fred,
Colorado Springs, Colo., Charles, Andrews Air Force Base,
Md., Frank, Garden City, and Leon, Ulysses; a daughter,
Mrs. Ruby Scrivner, Manter; three brothers, Roy Dennett,
New Plymouth, Idaho, Ray and Otis, both Vici, Okla.;
three sisters, Mrs. Nora Young, Kirkwood, Okla., Mrs.
Beulah Harsha, Chico, Calif., and Mrs. Jo Miles, Florida;
and 12 grandchildren.

DEERFIELD CEMETERY

Funeral was held at Immanuel Lutheran Church, Deerfield, the Rev. Norman Heironimus officiating. Burial in Deerfield Cemetery.

MCKEDY, RUSSEL GEORGE - (Lt. 2, Blk. 19, Sec. 3) Russell G. McKedy, 72, died unexpectedly, June 6, 1973, in the home of his son Frank, in Garden City, Kansas.
Mr. McKedy moved to Deerfield from Towner, Colo, in 1954. He was a retired cafe operator. He was born Feb. 7, 1901, in Hilda, Mo., and married Dora Ellen Dennett, Dec. 12, 1926, in Tolga, Okla. Mrs. McKedy preceded him in death on May 5, 1973.
Survivors include a daughter, Ruby L. Scrivner, Manter; four sons; Fred L., Colorado Springs, Charles R., Andrews AFB, Maryland, Frank E., Garden City and Leon H., Ulysses; two sisters, Louise Ingrem, Cosmopolise, Wash., and Ruth Williams, San Jose, Calif.; two brothers, Fred, Langdale, Okla., and Elgie, Ordway, Colo.; 12 grandchildren.
Funeral services were held June 9, at Immanuel Lutheran Church in Deerfield with the Rev. Norman Heironimus officiating. Burial in The Deerfield Cemetery.

MCMICHAEL, LLOYD J. - (Lt. 4, Blk. 27, Sec. 2) Funeral for Lloyd J. "Mike" McMichael, 72, 414 Davis, Garden City, was held at Trinity Lutheran Church, the Rev. Vernon E. Oestmann officiating. Military graveside rites was conducted by American Legion Harry H. Renick Post #9. Burial in Deerfield Cemetery.
Mr. McMichael died Nov. 17, 1993, at St. Catherine Hospital.
He was born Aug. 1, 1921, in Madison County, Iowa, the son of Thomas McMichael and Mary McKinney McMichael. He graduated from high school in Des Moines, Iowa, and was a graduate of Bradley University, Peoria, Ill. He married Esther Kettler, June 18, 1948, at Deerfield. She survives.
A Garden City resident since 1976, moving from Canon City, Colo., he was a retired jeweler and watch maker. He owned and operated Lloyd Jewelry for 25 years in Canon City, and was also co-owner of Good News Christian Bookstore in Garden City.
Mr. McMichael was a member of Trinity Lutheran Church, and was a U.S. Army and Air Force World War II veteran. He enjoyed gardening and was active in church activities.

Additional survivors include a son, David James McMichael, and a grandson, Ryan McMichael, both of Canon City. Preceding him in death were his parents and three brothers, Vernon, Wilber and Carl.

MCMILLAN, DORA - (Lt. 3, Blk. 22, Sec. 2) ts. 1896-1938.
Dora Beulah Woodard was born at Pittsburg, Kansas, on August 14, 1895, and departed this life on March 4, 1938, at her home near Deerfield, Kansas, from an acute heart attack. She was 42 years, 6 months, and 20 days of age.
At the age of five years she moved with her family to Rocky Ford, Colorado, and later to Allison, Colorado. She attended the schools of Tiffany, Colorado.
On August 27, 1913, she was married to Frank McMillan. With their two sons, Frank Jr., 14, and James Dale, 11, they later moved to Deerfield. Two nieces, Misses Bessie and Edith McMillan, lived with the family for several years.
She also leaves three brothers, Will Woodard of Pagosa Springs, Colorado, and David and John Woodard, both of Alamosa, Colorado; two sisters, Mrs. Alice McCoy of Pagosa Springs, and Mrs. Myrtle Crider of Oxnard, California; and one aunt, Mrs. O'Connor.
Mrs. McMillan was a loving wife and mother. She served her family faithfully and well. Her many friends will miss her friendly spirit and helping hand which was always extended to those in need.
The funeral was held Tuesday afternoon from the Deerfield M. E. Church, the pastor, Rev. Glen Palmer, in charge. Burial was made in the Deerfield Cemetery.

MCMILLAN, FRANK - (Lt. 3, Blk. 22, Sec. 2) Born in 1886 and died in 1958.
Frank McMillan, Granada, Colo., a former Deerfield resident, passed away on May 30, 1958, at the hospital at Lamar, Colo., and was buried at Deerfield, June 2. Friends in the community extend sympathy to the bereaved family.

MCNELLIS, JOHN MAURICE - (Lt. 4, Blk. 75, Sec. 1) John Maurice McNellis, the only son of John and Maud Holloway McNellis, was born in Lakin, Kansas, June 6, 1903, and passed away at his farm home, January 26, 1958, at the age of 54 years, 7 months and 20 days. He was preceded in death by his parents and two sisters, Mary and Helen.

DEERFIELD CEMETERY

On January 5, 1927, at Garden City, Kansas, he was united in marriage to Evelyn Smith. To this union was born a son, Manley, and a daughter, Marion Jo.

He leaves to mourn his passing, his wife, the son and daughter, two grandsons, Jimmy and Kelly, an uncle, Doc McNellis, of Deerfield, and a nephew, Jack Couch of Syracuse, Kansas, other relatives and a host of friends.

MCNELLIS, MANLEY - (Lt. 4, Blk. 75, Sec. 1) Manley McNellis, known as "Doc", son of John and Mary McNellis, was born at Mt. Pleasant, Iowa, Nov. 26, 1874, and passed away at the Kearny County Hospital, Aug. 1, 1962, at the age of 87 years, 8 months and 6 days.

In 1886 he came to Western Kansas with his parents, and resided in or around Deerfield since that time.

He and Maud Helen McNellis, who departed this life in January 1939, were married in September 1916.

He leaves to mourn his passing: one nephew, Bert Hart of Kansas City, Mo.; three step grandchildren, Jesse M. McNellis of Lawrence, Kansas., Mrs. Jim Johnson of Deerfield, and Jack Couch of Syracuse, Kans.; four great grandsons, Jimmy Johnson, Kelly Johnson, Darwin Couch and John McNellis; and one great granddaughter, Nikki Couch; other relatives and many friends.

Each man is unique and "Doc" through his multitude of friends and neighbors all over Western Kansas, exemplified how trust and open friendship are repaid in kind.

MCNELLIS, MAUDE - (Lt. 4, Blk. 75, Sec. 1) (Lakin Independent, January 6, 1939) Maude Helen McNellis, daughter of Jacob and Mary Holloway, was born in Pennsylvania, October 1, 1874, and departed this life at her home north of Deerfield, January 1, 1939, at the age of 65 years and 3 months.

In 1886 she came with her parents from Freeport, Illinois, to western Kansas, where they located in Garden City and later took a claim in Kearny County. Here she resided since, except for nine years residence in Denver, Colo., where she was soloist in the Trinity Methodist Church. Later she affiliated with the Methodist Church in Deerfield.

In February 1898, she was married to John McNellis, who departed this life September 1910. To this union three children were born, Mary Priscilla, John Maurice, and

DEERFIELD CEMETERY

Maude Helen, two of whom are now living. In September 1916, she was united in marriage to Manley McNellis. She was a wonderful mother and a loyal friend, sacrificing her life for the comfort of her loved ones. She was a great lover of music and vitally interested in world affairs. During her long illness her interest never wavered. She kept herself unusually well informed through her radio and by constant reading.

She leaves to mourn her passing: her husband, Manley McNellis; one son, Maurice McNellis of Bellflower, Calif.; a daughter, Helen Couch of Syracuse, Kans.; three grandchildren; other relatives and many friends.

The funeral service was held in the Deerfield Methodist Church, conducted by Rev. Markwell, a former pastor. Interment was made in Deerfield Cemetery.

DEERFIELD CEMETERY

NELSON, BABY - (Lt. 1, Blk. 49, Sec. 2) (The Kearny County Advocate, June 25, 1915) The five weeks old son of Mr. and Mrs. Benjamin Nelson died at the home of his parents on South Main, Thursday, and the interment made at the Deerfield Cemetry. The bereaved parents have the sympathy of the entire community in the loss of their son.

NELSON, HOMER - (Lt. 1, Blk. 49, Sec. 2) (Lakin Investigator, Deerfield News, Nov. 12, 1909) Homer, the three year old son of Mr. and Mrs. Ben Nelson, died of tonsilitis and croup Friday about noon. The funeral was held at the residence Saturday morning.

NEWTON, HARRY E. - (Lt. 4, Blk. 82, Sec. 1) ts. 1878-1947. Harry Earl Newton was born in Harrisburg, Penn., May 2, 1877, and departed this life in Deerfield, Kansas, Jan. 30, 1947, at the age of 6Y years, 8 months and 28 days.

He was united in marriage with Miss Jo Sutton, in Williamsburg, Kentucky, in 1902. To this union three children were born, all of whom survive. They are: Edward S. Newton, Deerfield, Kansas; Richard D. Newton, Deming, N. Mex.; and Mrs. Mildred E. Brown of Richmond, Calif.

Besides the immediate family, the deceased is survived by one sister, Mrs. Hazel Hewitt of Marion, Ind.; one brother, Merl Newton of Ormsby, Penn.; six grandchildren and two great grandchildren. The wife and mother preceded her husband in death in Van Buren, Ind., in June 1914, leaving the care and rearing of the children to the father. Their deep affection for him is an honor to his memory.

Mr. Newton was a man of integrity of character, clean in personal habits. Though his work in the oil business for many years, and later in other industrial enterprises, brought him into touch with men of all types, he did not become addicted to many of the unwholesome practices of men.

While his family and friends will miss him and mourn his going, he would not have undue grieving for his going.

Funeral services were held at the Phillips Funeral Home, Garden City, Monday at 2:30 p.m. in charge of Rev. M. E. Hickman, and interment was made in Deerfield Cemetery.

DEERFIELD CEMETERY

Mr. Newton had just returned to Deerfield, following a six weeks stay in a Garden City hospital and his death was caused by a serious diabetic condition aggravated by gas fumes from the flame of an oven burner which was left on at the home of his son, Ed Newton, manager of the Deerfield Petroleum Company. Others in the household received only slight headaches from the gas fumes.

NEWTON, MARY ALMIRA - (Lt. 4, Blk. 82, Sec. 1) Funeral service for Mrs. Mary Almira Newton, former Deerfield resident were held Saturday afternoon at the Phillips-White Funeral Home, Garden City, the Rev. Michael Clark officiating. Burial was in Deerfield Cemetery.
   Mrs. Newton died Tuesday, January 21, 1975, at Kerrville, Tex.
   Born July 16, 1906, at Pauls Valley, Okla., she married Edward S. Newton in 1923. They celebrated their 50th anniversary in Lakin in December of 1973 when their daughter and her family, the J. D. Bolingers, entertained in their home. They lived in Deerfield from 1946 until 1953, when they moved to Oklahoma. They have been living in Kerrville, since 1961.
   Mrs. Newton was a member of the Presbyterian Church.
   Survivors include the widower of the home; a daughter, Mr. Pauline Bolinger, Lakin; her mother, Mrs. G. C. Blackford, Mound, Okla.; two brothers, Jim Blackford, and George Blackford, both of Collingsdale, Okla.; a sister, Mrs, J. W. Marquis, Wichita; three grandchildren; and three great grandchildren.

DEERFIELD CEMETERY

OCHS, SOLOMON - (Lt. 3, Blk. 52, Sec. 2) (Funeral
Records) Died Aug. 22, 1918, age 1 yr., 10 mos., 26 days,
child of Mary and Henry Ochs, died of amebic dysentery.

ORBACH, H. RAYMOND - (Lt. 4, Blk. 21, Sec. 2) Child of
Kevin Raymond and Margaret Anne (Grauberger) Orbach, died
Jan. 24, 1969. Born January 24, 1969, at Ulysses.
Funeral at graveside, January 25, by Rev. Heironimus.

ORLOFF, PETER P. - (Lt. 4, Blk. 58, Sec. 2) Born Oct.
22, 1868, Uhland, Denmark, came to Kearny County in 1893,
died in Kearny County Hospital, Jan. 16, 1938.
    Peter Orloff, fourth child of Peter Orloff and his
wife, Anna, nee Andersen, was born October 22, 1868, in
Uhland, Denmark. As a child he was received into God's
covenant of grace through baptism and later he renewed
his baptismal vow in the rite of confirmation in the
Lutheran Church in Denmark.
    In about 1893 he, together with his twin sister and
family, emigrated to America. After living about one
year in New York he came west and finally settled at
Deerfield, Kansas, about 1894, where he resided till his
death.
    Mr. Orloff was well known in this community as a fine
and kind gentleman, accommodating, fair and friendly in
all his dealings, and was respected and honored as such
by everyone. He was always keenly interested in the
welfare of Deerfield and the community. At the time of
his death he was a member of the city council.
    Mr. Orloff enjoyed comparatively good health until last
fall when he became ill with heart attacks. He reached
the age of 69 years, 2 months, and 23 days. He was
preceded in death by his parents, one brother, and one
sister.
    His passing is mourned by three sisters, Mrs. Anna Wind
of Hartford, Conn., Miss Andrea Orloff of Pelham, N. Y.,
Mrs. Minne Johansen of Decatur, Ill.; three brothers,
Christ, George, and Andrew, all of Denmark; other
relatives and many friends.
    Funeral services were held at the Lutheran Church with
Rev. Walter J.F. Lebien in charge, assisted by the
Lutheran choir. Interment was in the Deerfield Cemetery.
The following served as pallbearers: Wm. H. Herr,
Orville Smith, L. R. Wagner, George A. Buell, Lewis
Keeler, and Glenn Steward.
(City Death Records show date of death as Jan. 15, 1938.)

208

DEERFIELD CEMETERY

OROZCO, JACOB WALTER - (Lt. 2, Blk. 38, Sec. 3) Jacob
Walter Orozco was born and died March 14, 1992, at Kearny
County Hospital, Lakin.
Survivors include his parents, Daniel L. and Theresa
Clymer Orozco, Garden City; two sisters, MiKayla and
Tonya Orozco, both of the home; grandparents, Mike and
Helen Orozco, Garden City, and Dolly Clymer, Deerfield;
and great grandmother, Rosie Moore, Clinton, Okla.
Graveside service was Sunday at the Deerfield Cemetery,
Deerfield, with the Rev. Gilbert Herrman presiding.
Greene-Schneider Funeral Home, Lakin, was in charge of
arrangements.

ORTEGA, CIPRIANO - (Lt. 2, Blk. 126, Sec. 1) Cipriano
(Joe) Ortega, 51, died at the Kearny County Hospital
after a short illness, Thursday morning, November 13,
1969. He had been in ill health for several years and
had been living at the Pioneer Rest Home in Lakin. He
was born in Glendale, Ariz., June 11, 1918.
Survivors include four children living in Topeka,
Ralph, Lloyd, Joseph and Patricia; four sisters, Mrs.
Romona Rodriques and Mrs. Teresa Gongalez of Garden City,
Mrs. Shirley Cruz, Deerfield, and Mrs. Lupe Villanuera,
Van Nuys, Calif.; and a brother, Frank Ortega, Lakin.
Rosary service was Friday evening at the Davis Funeral
Home. Funeral service was Saturday morning at St.
Anthony Catholic Church with Rev. F. C. Laudick
officiating.

ORTEGA, FRANK - (Lt. 3, Blk. 109, Sec. 1) Funeral for
Frank Ortega, 71, was at 9 a.m. (MDT) Tuesday at St.
Anthony Catholic Church, Lakin, the Rev. Austin Herrmann
officiating. Rosary was at 6:30 p.m. Monday at St.
Anthony. Burial at Deerfield Cemetery.
He died Saturday, August 3, 1985, at Kearny County
Hospital, Lakin. Born Oct. 24, 1913, in California, he
was a retired farm laborer and had been a resident of
Deerfield for 60 years.
Mr. Ortega was a member of the Christ the King Church,
Deerfield, and was an Army veteran of World War II.
Survivors include four sisters, Ramona Rodriguez,
Teresa Gonzales, and Shirley Cruz, all of Garden City,
and Lupe Villanuera, Santa Ana, California.
Davis Funeral Home, Lakin, in charge.

DEERFIELD CEMETERY

ORTEGA, JUAN DOMINGO - (Lt. 3, Blk. 110, Sec. 1)   Died
Aug. 30, 1935, age 26 days.

ORTEGA, RAFEL (RAQUARL) - (Lt. 1, Blk. 125, Sec. 1)   Died
July 6, 1940, age 61 yrs. Born in 1872.

ORTEGA, VICTORIA - (Lt. 2, Blk. 126, Sec. 1)   Born in
1891 and died March 12, 1954. Mother of Mrs. Shirley
Cruz.

OWSTON, JOHNNIE W. - (Lt. 2, Blk. 49, Sec. 2)   Born Feb.
15, 1908, in East Hibbard Twp., and died March 16, 1909.
Son of W. W. Owston.
   The baby boy of W. W. Owston, living near the Finney
Couny line in Kearny County, died Tuesday of spinal
meningitis.   The other children are now sick with
whooping cough.

DEERFIELD CEMETERY

PARKER, MYRTLE — (Lt. 4, Blk. 55, Sec. 2) (The Lakin
Independent, April 25, 1958) Myrtle B. Downing Parker
was born Jan. 10, 1876, near Burnettsville, Ind., and
departed this life April 18, 1958, in the Scott County
hospital.
     She came with her parents, John Madison and Belle
Tedford, to this part of the country when she was ten
years old. She grew to young womanhood in the Hartland
community, and taught school for eight years.
     In 1900, she was married to Oscar J. Downing, and they
resided in the Deerfield community all of their lives
together, taking an active part in church and community
affairs. To this union five children were born:
Christabele Maddux, Oscar J. Downing, Madison T. Downing,
all of Deerfield; Muriel Downing, deceased; and LeRoyce
Grosjean of Scott City, Kans.
     She was preceded in death by her daughter, Muriel, in
1918, and by her husbasnd, Oscar J. Downing, in 1932.
     After her husband's death, she made a home for herself
and her son, Madison, on her farm north of Deerfield.
After her son's marriage, she moved to Emporia, Kansas,
to be near her daughter, LeRoyce, who was teaching in the
Neosho Rapids high school.
     A short time later, she moved to Garden City, where she
worked as receptionist for Garnand Funeral Home.
     In the fall of 1940, she was married to R. B. Parker of
Denver, Colo., and lived there for over 17 years, where
she and Mr. Parker were very active in church work.
     She became seriously ill last December and in January
it became necessary for her children to bring her to the
Kearny County Hospital in Lakin, Kans.
     On April 7, she was taken to Scott City, Kans., to the
home of her daughter, LeRoyce, and husband, Louis
Grosjean, where she was privileged to stay only a few
days before she was taken to the Scott County hospital
where she passed away April 18, 1958.
     Left to mourn her death are her husband, her four
children, nine living grandchildren, and five great
grandchildren, her sister, Etta Whitmer, and husband
Charles of Denver, Colo., also her sister-in-law, Lou
Downing McAfee and Harrison McAfee, who both lived in the
Downing home for many years.
     Others to mourn her passing are five step-children of
Denver, Colo., and a host of friends.

DEERFIELD CEMETERY

PELNAR, ELIZABETH - (Lt. 4, Blk. 28, Sec. 2) Elizabeth Morris Pelnar, age 77, died at Holcomb, Kansas, Dec. 2, 1929, of diabetes. Garnand was the undertaker.

Mrs. Elizabeth Morris Pelnar, age 77, died Dec. 1, 1929, at her home, 7 miles northwest of Holcomb, following several months illness of sugar diabetes. Mrs. Pelnar was a native of Wales and came to this country with her father at the age of 2 months, her mother dying when she was but a few weeks old.

Services were held at Holcomb and were conducted by Rev. Francis Sherman of the Episcopal Church of Cimarron.

Mrs. Pelnar is survived by her husband, John Joseph Pelnar; four sons, A. R. Pelnar, Chicago; Jacob Pelnar, Delafield, Wisconsin; Lester and John Pelnar of Holcomb, and a daughter, Mrs. J. F. Fitzroy of Pueblo, Colorado. A son, Joe, of Holcomb, preceded his mother in death, two months ago. He died from injuries received when his coat was caught in the machinery of a beet dump near Lowe.

PELNAR, JACOB - (Lt. 1, Blk. 28, Sec. 2) Son of John and Sarah Pelnar. Jacob Roy Pelnar died, July 6, 1941, of an accidental gunshot wound of chest at rural Lowe, Sherlock Twp., Finney County. He was a single, white male, age 22. C. A. Wiley was the undertaker.

Jacob Roy Pelnar, 22, was killed early Sunday morning at the home of his uncle, Lester Pelnar, at Lowe station, when a bullet from a .22 caliber rifle entered his chest and pierced his heart. County officials said today there would be no inquest and termed the shooting "accidental."

The shooting occurred about 3:00 a.m. Sunday morning, officials estimated. Pelnar was heard groaning shortly after that time. Relatives in the house heard the groaning and went to his aid.

Pelnar still was breathing, it was said, when his relatives reached the scene. A Garden City physician was called and not until he arrived was it known that the victim had been shot. He was dead by the time the physician arrived.

Officials at the sheriff's office said Pelnar had crawled some distance from the point where he was shot and in the darkness the gun was not noticed immediately. The wound was clean and no blood was visible on the outside of Pelnar's clothing, they added.

Pelnar was said to have had a weak heart and relatives supposed it was a heart attack until the physician arrived and discovered the bullet wound. The rifle was

DEERFIELD CEMETERY

found by the aid of a flashlight a few feet away from the body.

Officers said Pelnar had been in Garden City since the morning of the Fourth and went to the dance at Holcomb Saturday night. As yet is has not been discovered how Pelnar reached his home at Lowe following the dance. Officers surmised that since no one could be found who had given Pelnar a ride to his home, he must have walked there following the dance.

Pelnar, who had been reared by Mr. and Mrs. Lester Pelnar, was heard by Mrs. Pelnar as he came into the yard, officers said. Then according to the officers' report, she did not hear anything further until Pelnar moaned for help. No one, it seems, heard the shot fired.

County officials said there was evidence that Pelnar looked into the chicken house at his home, as if he had heard something there and was investigating the noise. There seemed to have been an indication that Pelnar tripped over something in the yard. It was surmised that such a fall might have discharged the rifle into Pelnar's breast.

Friends of Pelnar, who had seen him at the dance, said he was said to have been in good spirits and friends discounted any suicide theory.

Officers aaid there was no indication of foul play and that there would be no inquest unless the family desired one. This afternoon officers said the family had not requested such and that the death certificate would be filled out with death attributed to accidental means.

Pelnar is survived by his mother, Mrs. Sarah Pelnar, Garden City; two sisters, Mrs. Josephine Cunningham, Dodge City, and Mrs. Marjorie Delgado, of rural Finney County; and four brothers, Lester, John, Robert and George Pelnar, all of Garden City or Lowe.

Funeral services were held in the Wiley Funeral home Tuesday afternoon with Rev. Joseph Young in charge. Burial at Deerfield.

PELNAR, JOHN - (Lt. 1, Blk. 28, Sec. 2) John Evan Pelnar, 45, died Sept. 7, 1932, at Holcomb, Kansas, of myocarditis. Garnand was the undertaker.

John E. Pelnar, 45, who lived near Holcomb, died Sept. 7, 1932, after a six months illness of anemia and heart conplications. John Pelnar, with his brother Lester Pelnar, were well known well drillers in Western Kansas. He had lived in Finney County for many years.

213

DEERFIELD CEMETERY

Pelnar became ill several months ago and for the past two months has been lingering at the point of death.

He is survived by a wife and seven children; three brothers, Lester of Deerfield, Alfred of Chicago; Jacob of Delafield, Wisc.; and a sister, Mrs. Jess Fitzroy of Pueblo. Burial in Deerfield Cemetery.

PELNAR, JOSEPH SR. - (Lt. 4, Blk. 28, Sec. 2) Joseph John Pelnar, 85, died May 14, 1930, in Sherlock Twp., Finney County, Kansas, of chronic nephritis. Married. Wiley undertaker.

(The Lakin Independent, May 23, 1930) Joseph Pelnar Sr., was laid to rest last Friday in the Deerfield Cemetery. Mr. Pelnar had been ill for several months. He died at a Garden City hospital, and the funeral was held by his pastor.

PELNAR, JOSEPH W. - (Lt. 4, Blk. 28, Sec. 2) Born in 1884 and died in 1929. Joseph Wesley Pelnar, age 44 years died Nov. 11, 1929, of traumatic pneumonia. He was married. Garnand was the undertaker.

Joseph W. Pelnar, 45, died November 11, 1929, at 9 o'clock at a local hospital from injuries received, two weeks ago, while loading beets at the Wolf beet dump, 4 miles west of Peterson. The funeral services were held November 13, at 2:30 at the Holcomb school house. Rev. Sherman, pastor of the Episcopal Church at Cimarron, officiated.

Mr. Pelnar was well known in this community, having come to Finney County 20 years ago with his parents. He was married in 1917 to Miss Rose McGinn and has been in the employ of the Garden City Sugar Company for several years, residing 7 miles northwest of Holcomb. He was a member of the Episcopal Church and a member of the Masonic lodge at Deerfield. This order was in charge of the services at the cemetery.

His wife, Mrs. Rose Pelnar, and their adopted daughter, Roberta Ruth, age 3; his parents, Mr. and Mrs. Joseph Pelnar, residing 12 miles northwest of Garden City; one sister, Mrs. J. S. Fitzroy of Pueblo, Colorado; and four brothers, A. R. Pelnar, Chicago, Illinois, Jacob Pelnar, Delafield, Wisconsin, Lester and John Pelnar of Holcomb survive him.

PELNAR, LESTER - (Lt. 4, Blk. 51, Sec. 2) Born in 1882 in Wisconsin and died in 1966. Lester Pelnar, 33, of Deerfield and Mary Stebbins, 18, were married Dec. 10, 1916.

PELNAR, MARY - (Lt. 4, Blk. 51, Sec. 2)   Born Oct. 7, 1899, and died May 1, 1950. Mrs. Lester Pelnar, 50, of Holcomb, died about 12:10 a.m. Monday in St. Catherine Hospital. Funeral services were at 9:30 a.m. Thursday at St Thomas Episcopal Church with the Rev. Joseph S. Young officiating. Burial in Deerfield Cemetery. Mrs. Pelnar was born Oct. 7, 1899, at St. Peter, Kansas. She was a member of the Episcopal Church.

PELNAR, SARAH - (Lt. 1, Blk. 28, Sec. 2)   Sarah Eliza Pelnar was born Jan. 10, 1893, her father was Alexander Craig Killion and her mother Eliza Hobbins Killion.
      Mrs. Sarah Eliza Killion Pelnar, 67, 212 Spencer, Garden City, died early August 9, 1960, at St. Catherine Hospital. She had been an invalid for the past five years, and a resident for 47 years here.
      Mrs. Pelnar was born Jan. 10, 1893, at Glendale, Wisc., and was married in Illinois in 1913 to John E. Pelnar, who died in 1932.
      She was a member of the St. Thomas Episcopal Church.
      Survivors include three sons, John A. Pelnar, Garden City, Charles L. Pelnar, Sublette, and George Paul Pelnar, Wichita; two daughters, Mrs. Josephine Cunningham, Wichita, and Miss Marjorie Pelnar, Garden City; a sister, Mrs. Myrtle Sensen, Spring Valley, Wisc.; and nine grandchildren also remain.
      Garnand Chapel in charge of arrangements.

PEREZ, ANTONIO - Stillborn Sept. 24, 1935.

PEREZ, JESUS - (Lt. 1, Blk. 125, Sec. 1)   ts. 1936-1940. Son of Mauro and Maria (Ortega) Perez, age 3 yrs., 6 mo., 6 days, killed under moving train.
      (The Lakin Independent, July 5, 1940) Jesus Perez is dead, his mother has one foot cut off, all because their pet kitten bounded from their car and ran beneath a slowly moving freight train in the Lakin yards Monday morning.
      The boy's father, Manro Perez, had left his family in the parked car while he went to the coal bin for a sack of coal purchased from the Darr Elevator.

DEERFIELD CEMETERY

As the four-year old Mexican boy ran under the car to catch his kitten, his mother ran to rescue her son from danger. She stepped over the rail. Her foot was cut off while the youngster was ground beneath the wheels. The Perez family lives at Deerfield. Mrs. Perez is in the hospital where her injured leg is healing. The boy was buried Tuesday at Deerfield. The kitten escaped without injury.

PEREZ, MARIA - (Lt. 1, Blk. 125, Sec. 1) ts. 1917-1941. Died Dec. 10, 1941, age 23 yrs. Wife of Mauro Perez, daughter of Raquarl and Vita (Gonzalez) Ortega both of which were born in Silao, Old Mexico. Maria was born Dec. 17, 1918, at Bomi, Calif.

PHILPOT, MALE CHILD - (Funeral record) Died May 9, 1932.

PLOEGER, CLARENCE - (Lt. 1, Blk. 23, Sec. 2) Funeral for longtime Kearny County resident Clarence Ploeger, of Deerfield, was Thursday at the Immanuel Lutheran Church, Deerfield, the Rev. Jerald C. Jeskewitz officiating. Burial at Deerfield Cemetery.
He died Monday, September 23, 1985, at the Kearny County Hospital, Lakin.
Born August 23, 1909, Dexter, Mo., he married Katherine Grauberger, April 20, 1932, in Lincolville. She died June 26, 1985.
He moved to Kearny County from Missouri in 1925. A retired farmer, Mr. Ploeger was a member of the Immanuel Lutheran Church, Deerfield, where he was a past church elder and a member of the 1950 building committee.
Surviving are two sons, Cletus and Ervin, both of Deerfield; two daughters, Luella Curtis, Satanta, and Ardith Steele, Littleton, Colo; a brother, Herbert, Deerfield; 11 grandchildren and five great grandchildren.

PLOEGER, ELMER W. - (Lt. 1, Blk. 84, Sec. 1) Funeral for Elmer William Henry Ploeger, 83, was held at the United Methodist Church, Lakin, the Rev. Nathan Morgan officiating. Burial was in Deerfield Cemetery, Deerfield. He died January 5, 1990, at Hamilton County Hospital, Syracuse. Born April 21, 1906, at Treloar, Mo., he married Elsie Augusta Kleeman, March 24, 1935, north of Lakin.
Mr. Ploeger was a farmer and rancher and had been a Kendall resident since 1916. He was a member of the

DEERFIELD CEMETERY

United Methodist Church, Kendall, past president and
secretary of the Wheatland Electric board, where he was a
30 year member, was a past member of the Kendall school
board, was on the board of directors for the WheatBelt
Credit Union, Lakin, was a former 4-H leader, and was
founder of the Loyal Neighbors Hall, Kendall.
Survivors include his wife, of the home; two daughters,
Anna Graber and Emma Horton, Kendall; six grandchildren;
and four great grandchildren.

PLOEGER, ELSIE - (Lt. 1, Blk. 84, Sec. 1) Elsie A.
Ploeger, 88, of Kendall, died Tuesday, June 25, 1996, at
the Kearny County Hospital in Lakin.
She was born February 3, 1908, in St. James, Missouri,
to Anna Gackstatter and Fred Kleeman, Sr. Elsie lived in
Dodge City for a short time before moving with her family
to just north of Lakin in 1916. She graduated from Lakin
High School in 1928. She then attended Emporia State
Teachers College, where she received her Normal Training.
She returned to the Lakin area and taught school for
seven years at North Kearny School.
Elsie married Elmer Ploeger on March 24, 1935, in
Kearny County, Ks. After their marriage, they moved to a
farm north of Kendall. They lived their entire married
life at that farm until 1988, when they moved to Lakin.
Elmer died on January 5, 1990. Elsie enjoyed hand and
needlework and gardening.
She was a member of the United Methodist Church and
United Methodist Women and the Chatterbox Club, all of
Kendall.
Survivors include her daughters and their husbands,
Anna and John Graber, and Emma and Harvey Horton, all of
Kendall; six grandchildren, Janice and Don Simon,
Syraucse, Bryan and Becky Graber, Kendall, Fanci and
Billy Coyle, Aledo, Texas, Wade and Marcey Horton, Garden
City, John and Lora Horton, Kendall, Brett and Michelle
Horton, Lafayette, Indiana; and twelve great
grandchildren.
Elsie was preceded in death by her parents, three
brothers, Earnest Kleeman, Fred Kleeman and Henry
Kleeman.
Garnand Funeral Home of Lakin in charge of the
arrangements. Funeral services were held Friday, June
28, 1996, at 10:00 a.m. in the Lakin United Methodist
Church with Rev. Leroy Smoot officiating. Burial in the
Deerfield Cemetery.

PLOEGER, HERBERT S. - (Lt. 1, Blk. 23, Sec. 2) Herbert
Simon Ploeger, 76, died August 26, 1990, at St. Francis
Regional Medical Center, Wichita. He was born August 13,
1914, at Treloar, Mo., the son of Theodore W. and Emily
C. Stock Ploeger. A Deerfield resident since 1945,
moving from Kendall, he was a retired farmer.
He was a member of the Kansas Wheat Growers Association
and the Lutheran Church, Deerfield.
Survivors include: two nephews, and two nieces.
Funeral service was held at 10:30 a.m., Wednesday at
the Lutheran Church, Deerfield, with the Rev. Kenneth
Haskell presiding. Burial in Deerfield Cemetery.

PLOEGER, KATIE - (Lt. 1, Blk. 23, Sec. 2) Funeral for
lifetime Deerfield resident Katie Ploeger, 76, was at
10:30 a.m. Saturday at the Immanuel Lutheran Church,
Deerfield, the Rev. Jerald Jeskewitz officiating. Burial
at Deerfield Cemetery.
She died Wednesday, June 26, 1985, at Kearny County
Hospital, Lakin. Born April 20, 1909, in Deerfield, she
married Clarence Ploeger, April 10, 1932, at
Lincolnville.
Mrs. Ploeger was a homemaker and a housewife and a
lifetime member of the Immanuel Lutheran Church in
Deerfield.
Surviving are her husband, of the home; two sons, Ervin
and Cletus, both of Deerfield; two daughters, Luella
Curtis, Satanta, and Ardith Steele, Littleton, Colo.; two
brothers, Carl Grauberger, Deerfield, and George
Grauberger, Fort Collins, Colo.; seven sisters, Marie
Uhrich, Oakley, Elizabeth Boxberger, WaKeeney, Mollie
Hanneman, Garden City, Eva Hanneman, Fort Collins, Colo.,
Lydia Bisterfelt, Liberal, Anna Elliott, Deerfield, and
Pauline Winters, Holyoke, Colo.; 11 grandchildren and 5
great grandchildren.

PLOEGER, LAURA M. - (Lt. 1, Blk. 84, Sec. 1) ts.
1879-1945. Mrs. Wm. Ploeger of Florence community, north
of Kendall, died at the Syracuse hospital, Tuesday, after
a lingering illness.
Laura Marie Louise Nieweg (Ploeger) was born October
26, 1878, at Holstein, Missouri. Soon after her birth
she was received into God's covenant of grace through the
holy sacrament of baptism. After having been instructed
in the chief parts of Christian doctrine she renewed her
baptismal vow in the rite of confirmation in the year of

1894, thus becoming a communicant member of the Lutheran Church.

On April 8, 1904, she entered the holy estate of matrimony with William Ploeger at Holstein, Missouri. To this union two sons were born. She moved to Kansas with her family in 1916 and made her home on a farm north of Kendall.

She is preceded in death by one son and her husband who departed this life on Easter Sunday, April 1, 1945. She is survived by one son, Elmer Ploeger, one daughter-in-law, two grandchildren, one brother, Fred Nieweg of St. Charles, Missouri, and many other relatives and friends.

She fell asleep in Jesus on October 30, 1945, at the Syracuse hospital, reaching the age of 66 years and 4 days.

Funeral services were held November 2 from the Lutheran Church with Pastor P.H.C. Stengel in charge and interment was made in the Deerfield Cemetery.

PLOEGER, LAVERNA E. - (Lt. 1, Blk. 23, Sec. 2) Laverna Emilie Ploeger was born August 14, 1937, at Syracuse, Kansas, and departed this life, Saturday, May 14, 1938, at her home north of Kendall, at the age of nine months. She was the daughter of Mr. Clarence Ploeger and Katie nee Grauberger. She was baptized in the name of the Triune God on August 31, 1937, and thus was accepted into God's covenant of grace and made a child of God.

Laverna Emilie was not well and strong since birth, but by the grace of God and through the kind and loving care of her dear parents, she seemed to be growing stronger and there was hope that the Lord would spare her to dear parents. But the Lord, in His loving kindness, willed it otherwise. Laverna Emilie contracted a sort of pneumonia last Thursday and the Lord took her unto Himself Saturday afternoon.

Laverna Emilie leaves to mourn her early departure, her deeply grieved parents; one sister, Luella; one brother, Cletus; and many other relatives and friends.

PLOEGER, THEODORE WILLIAM - (Lt. 1, Blk. 23, Sec. 2) Father of Clarence and Herbert Ploeger. Born May 5, 1879, and died Feb. 17, 1957. His father was William Ploeger and mother, Friederike Fahrmeyer Ploeger. He was born in Holsten, Mo. He was a member of the Immanuel Lutheran Church in Deerfield.

(Garden City Telegram, Feb. 18, 1957) Theodore William Pleger, 77, died Sunday at his home two miles North of Deerfield.

A Holstein, Mo., native, Mr. Ploeger has lived here for a dozen years.

Survivors include two sons, Clarence and Herbert, both of Deerfield.

Funeral was at 2 p.m. Wednesday at Immanuel Lutheran Church with Rev. Henry Knoke officiating. Burial at Deerfield Cemetery.

PLOEGER, WILLIAM H. - (Lt. 1, Blk. 84, Sec. 1) William H. Ploeger, north of Kendall in Florence neighborhood, passed away Sunday, April 1st, 1945. The end came suddenly and unexpectedly just after he had finished his morning chores. Funeral services Thursday afternoon in the Deerfield Lutheran Church and burial in Deerfield Cemetery.

It has pleased the Lord of Life and Death to call out of time into eternity the soul of William Henry Ploeger. He was born June 23, 1874, at Holstein, Mo. Soon after his birth he was received into the Covenant of God through the Holy Sacrament of Baptism; and in the year 1889, after a thorough instruction in the chief parts of Christian doctrine, he renewed his baptismal vow in the rite of confirmation, thus becoming a member of the Lutheran Church of which church he remained faithful until death.

April 7, 1904, he entered the Holy Estate of Matrimony with Laura Nieweg. To this union two sons were born.

He moved to Kansas in 1916 and made his home on a farm in the Kendall community. Here he engaged in general farming and stockraising.

It was on Easter Sunday, April 1, 1945, that the Lord suddenly called him to his heavenly home. He is preceded in death by one son.

He leaves to mourn his departure his grief-stricken widow, Mrs. Laura Ploeger; one son, Elmer Ploeger; two granddaughters and a daughter-in-law; also one brother, Theo. Ploeger of Kendall; and four sisters, Mina Stuecken of Warrenton, Mo., Matilda Stuecken of Franklin, Mo., Emilia Sass of Nevada, Mo., and Hulda Steiger of Hawk Point, Mo.; as well as many other relatives and friends.

He reached the age of 70 years, 9 months and 9 days, "and when he lifted up his eyes he saw no man save Jesus only."

DEERFIELD CEMETERY

Funeral services were held April 5, 1945, at the Deerfield Lutheran Church with pastor Paul H.C. Stengel in charge. Burial was in the Deerfield Cemetery.

PRUITT, HERMAN JAMES - (N/2 Lt. 3, Blk. 90, Sec. 4) Herman James "Jim" Pruitt, 71, of Deerfield, died Monday, December 26, 1994, at Kearny County Hospital. A 46 year resident of Deerfield, he was retired from Kansas Nebraska Gas Co.
He was born June 16, 1923, at Dexter, New Mexico, the son of Charles C. and Emma Elizabeth Bishop Pruitt.
Jim was a World War II Air Force veteran. He was a B-24 air gunner in the service.
He married Evelyn Scott on May 13, 1944, in Tonopah, Nevada. She survives. They moved to Deerfield in 1948 from Longview, Texas. Jim worked for the Santa Fe Motor Company at Deerfield for 30 years. He then worked for Kansas Nebraska Gas Co. for 10 years, retiring in June, 1988.
He was a member of the United Methodist Church in Deerfield, the Deerfield Lions Club and the VFW post in Garden City. His hobbies were making jewelry, rock collecting, fishing, hunting, and traveling.
Survivors include his wife, Evelyn, of the home; a son, Scott Pruitt, Panama City Beach, Fla.; daughters: Carol Hudon, Yuma, Ariz., Chris Gilbert, Lakin, Connie Pruitt, Deerfield, Cathy Burgardt, Lakin; brother, Eugene Pruitt, Tacna, Ariz.; sister, Marie Minker, San Simon, Ariz.; 12 grandchildren and two great grandchildren.
He was preceded in death by his parents, one brother and one sister, and two grandchildren.
Funeral services were held Thursday, December 19, at 10:30 a.m. at the United Methodist Church, Deerfield, with the Rev. Donald J. Koehn officiating. Burial in the Deerfield Cemetery with military graveside rites.

PURDY, RUTH ARLENE - (Lt. 1, Blk. 87, Sec. 4) Longtime Deerfield resident, Ruth Arlene Purdy, 69, died September 15, 1994, at her home in rural Deerfield.
Ruth was born April 17, 1925, in Garden City, Kansas, the daughter of Charles and Rose Weimers Bentrup. She graduated from Deerfield High School in 1943 and attended Nurse's Training at Denver General Hospital.
Ruth was a member of Immanuel Lutheran Church, Deerfield, until 1979, then the Word of Life Church, Garden City.

DEERFIELD CEMETERY

She married Harold Purdy on September 3, 1951, at Cheyenne Wells, Colorado. He survives.

Other survivors include two sons, Larry Gene Purdy and Jed Purdy, both of Deerfield; three daughters, Jerilyn Combs, Bailey, Colo., Rhonda Stenner, Salina, and Rebecca Brownlee, Syracuse; four brothers, Henry Bentrup, Garden City, Carl Bentrup, Paul Bentrup, and Eldor Bentrup, all of Deerfield; and ten grandchildren.

She was preceded in death by her parents and one brother, Walter Bentrup.

Burial was September 15 at Deerfield Cemetery. Memorial services were held Thursday, September 22, at 2 p.m. at Deerfield Community Building.

DEERFIELD CEMETERY

RAMIREZ, JUANA R. - (Lt. 3, Blk. 110, Sec. 1) ts. May 3, 1890-April 15, 1943. Female, Mexican, married, native, died in Sherlock Twp., Finney County, Kansas, of some form of heart disease. She was 52 years of age. Bryant Garnand was the undertaker.

RAMIREZ, PEDRO R. - (Lt. 4, Blk. 109, Sec. 1) Pedro R. Ramirez, 71, died at St. Catherine Hospital in Garden City, February 8, 1985. He was a resident of Deerfield where he had lived for 15 years.
Born August 19, 1913, in Mexico, the son of Quillerma Ramirez and Metividad Renteria Ramirez. He married Consuelo Garcia, May 22, 1949, in San Angelo, Texas.
He was a veteran of W.W. II, serving in the U.S. Army.
He was a member of Christ the King Church in Deerfield.
He was a former mechanic and had been a mill operator at Western Alfalfa Co. in Deerfield.
He is survived by his widow of the home; a son, Pete R. Ramirez, Jr.; four daughters, Elsa Ramirez, Elma Martinez, and Lupe Ramirez, all of the home and Grace Morales, San Angelo, Texas; one brother, Alfredo Ramirez, Big Spring, Texas; and a sister, Aurora Cantu, Denver, Colo.
Funeral Mass was at St. Anthony Catholic Church, Monday, February 11, 1985, with the Reverend F. C. Laudick C.PP.S. officiating. Burial was in the Deerfield Cemetery.

REESE, TOSHA DANAE - (Lt. 3, Blk. 38, Sec. 3) Tosha Danae Reese, one month, died August 12, 1989, at her home at Hays. She was born July 3, 1989, at Hadley Regional Medical Center, Hays.
Survivors: parents, Harold Reese and Sherry Eberhart Reese, of the home; grandparents, Mr. and Mrs. Roger Brunson, Holcomb, Mr. and Mrs. LaVern Eberhart, Deerfield; great grandparents, Mr. and Mrs. Vernon Eberhart, Garden City, Mr. and Mrs. Bill Mitchell, Hays, Mr. and Mrs. Mearl Brunson, Garden City, and Mrs. Agnis Brown, Garden City; and great great grandmother, Wilma Mardis, St. Louis.
Funeral was at 1 p.m. Monday at United Methodist Church, Deerfield, the Rev. Donald J. Koehn. Burial in Deerfield Cemetery. Greene-Schneider Funeral Home, Lakin, in charge of arrangements.

DEERFIELD CEMETERY

REINERT, HARRY H. - (Lt. 2, Blk. 64, Sec. 3) Funeral services for Harry H. Reinert were held Sunday afternoon at 2 o'clock at the Deerfield Methodist Church with Rev. C. M. Fogelman, Jr., officiating. Burial was in the Deerfield Cemetery.

Harry H. Reinert was born March 1, 1895, in Benton County, Mo. He died April 25, 1968, at St. Catherine Hospital in Garden City, after a three year illness, at the age of 73 years, 1 month and 25 days. He was married to Pearl Brock, Jan. 1, 1918, in Gray County. He was a farmer and moved to a farm west of Deerfield in 1950. He was a member of the Deerfield Methodist Church.

He is survived by the widow of the home; a son, Leslie, of Syracuse; three daughters, Mrs. Opal Bruington, Montezuma, Mrs. Dollie Hodges, Denver, and Mrs. Leona Randolph, Lakin; two brothers, Floyd and Ervin, both of Montezuma; two sisters, Mrs. Lillie Lepol, Colorado Springs, and Mrs. Ella Gamble, Montezuma; 12 grandchildren.

REINERT, PEARL - (Lt. 2, Blk. 64, Sec. 3) Pearl Reinert 96, died Thursday, April 11, 1996, at the Kearny County Hospital in Lakin.

She was born Sept. 15, 1899, in Gray County, the daughter of James W. and Lattie L. Edwards Brock, and attended Jumbo School in Gray County.

On Jan. 1, 1918, she married Harry H. Reinert at her parents' home in Gray County. After their marriage they moved to a farm near Cimarron. In 1933 they moved to Meade County, and in 1950 they moved to a farm west of Deerfield, where she has lived since.

Her husband died April 25, 1968. She was also preceded in death by a daughter, Zella Padget, two grandchildren, one great great grandson, two brothers, William Brock and Harold Brock, and two sisters, Esther Linder and Beulah Brock.

Mrs. Reinert was a member of United Methodist Church in Deerfield, United Methodist Women and volunteered at the Budget Shop in Lakin. A homemaker, she enjoyed playing the piano, singing, writing music and poetry, babysitting, seamstress work and cooking.

She is survived by a son, Leslie Reinert, Syracuse; three daughters, Opal Bruington, Montezuma, Dollie Hodges, Denver, and Leona Randolph, Lakin; two brothers, George Brock, Albany, Ore., and Edwin Brock, San Luis Obispo, Calif.; three sisters, Edith Marrs, Fowler, Ollie

DEERFIELD CEMETERY

Gooden, Meade, and Gladys Blake, Dodge City; 11 grandchildren; 23 great grandchildren; and two great great grandchildren.
Funeral was held at 2 p.m. April 15, at the United Methodist Church, Deerfield, with the Rev. Donald J. Koehn officiating. Burial at Deerfield Cemetery.

RICH, THELMA GRACE - (Lt. 3, Blk. 18, Sec. 3) Thelma Grace Rich, 73, of Deerfield, died September 29, 1989, at High Plains Retirement Village, Lakin. She had been a resident of Deerfield since February 1989, moving from Moberly, Mo.
Mrs. Rich, a homemaker, was born on November 3, 1915, at Harrison, Maine. She was a member of the Methodist faith.
Survivors are a son, Duwayne Rich, Deerfield; two daughters, Roberta Henks, Hutchinson, and Rosalie McNutt, Cairo, Mo.; 13 grandchildren and several great grandchildren.
Funeral was at 2 p.m. Monday at the Deerfield United Methodist Church, with the Rev. Donald J. Koehn officiating. Burial in the Deerfield Cemetery.

RICH, WALLACE P. - (Lt. 3, Blk. 18 , Sec. 3) Wallace P. Rich, 80, formerly of Deerfield, died September 23, 1995, at his home, Kimberling City, Mo.
He was born May 7, 1915, at Highland Park, Mich., the son of Walter P. and Sadie Covey Rich. A Kimberling City resident since March 1995, moving from Lampe, Mo., he was a farmer.
He attended the Methodist church, Swink, Colorado.
Survivors include: a son, Duwayne E., Deerfield; two daughters, Roberta Mae Henks, Branson West, Mo., and Rosalee J. McNutt, Cape Fair, Mo.; a sister, Blanch Lorene Love, La Junta, Colo.; 13 grandchildren; and 28 great grandchildren.
Graveside service was at 2 p.m. Tuesday in Deerfield Cemetery, with the Rev. Don Koehn presiding.

RICH, WILLIAM P. - (Lt. 4, Blk. 18, Sec. 3) William P. "Bill" Rich, 21, died October 8, 1984, at the Kearny County Hospital, after a sudden illness. Born October 20, 1962, at Garden City, he was a farmer and had been a Deerfield resident since 1970, moving from Johnson.
He was a member of Deerfield United Methodist Church.

Survivors: parents, Duwayne and Margaret Rich, Deerfield; brothers, David and Jimmy, both of Deerfield; sisters, Joyce Rich and Betty Jo Hampton, both of Garden City; grandparents, Floyd and Velda Marie Pantier, LaJunta, Colo., Wallace and Thelma Rich, Moberly, Mo. Funeral was at 4 p.m. Thursday at the church, the Rev. Nellie Holmes. Burial at the Deerfield Cemetery.

RICHARDS, G.C.W. - (Lt. 1, Blk. 75, Sec. 1) ts. 1855-1934. Dr. G.C.W. Richards died at his home in Deerfield, Kansas, Friday, July 13th, 1934. The deceased had been in failing health for several months and everything possible was done for him but to no avail. Dr. Richards was the pioneer physician of this county and his services was not only confined to Kearny County, but in neighboring counties and there never was a call made for him that he did not respond. It made no difference whether it was hot or cold, a short or long drive, he made the trips, and in the early days it was hard driving in bad weather, but the doctor, always arrived at his destination. The deceased leaves a wife, together with a host of friends to mourn his departure, and The Advocate extends heartfelt sympathy to the bereaved wife in the loss of her loved one. Funeral services was held here Saturday aftenoon and his remains were laid to rest in the Deerfield Cemetery.

RIFFEL, ALEXANDER - (Lt. 1, Blk. 52, Sec. 2) Alexander "Alex" Riffel, 82, died September 28, 1990, at Garden Valley Retirement Village, Garden City. He was born May 9, 1908, at Lakin, the son of George H. and Mary Winick Riffel. A resident of Garden City since 1945, moving from Kearny County, he was a retired journeyman lineman for the Wheatland Electric Cooperative Inc., formerly Southwest Kansas Power Co.
He belonged to the Lutheran faith and was a member of the Fraternal Order of the Eagles No. 3124 and the John J. Haskal Veterans of Foreign Wars Post 2279, both at Garden City. He was a U.S. Army veteran of World War II.
Survivors include: a brother, Harry, LaJunta, Colo.; and several nephews and nieces.
Funeral service was at 2 p.m. Wednesday at Price and Sons Funeral Home, Garden City, with Pastor Vernon Oestmann presiding. Burial in Deerfield Cemetery.

DEERFIELD CEMETERY

RIFFEL, GEORGE H. SR. - (Lt. 1, Blk. 52, Sec. 2) George Henry Riffel, Sr., was born in Galga, Russia, June 1, 1870. He passed away at his home northwest of Deerfield, January 9, 1941, at the age of 70 years, 7 months, and 9 days. He had been in failing health for many years. His ailment had robbed him of his mental keenness as well as of his physical strength.

His father passed away when Mr. Riffel was a boy six years old; his mother a few years later. He made his home with an uncle after the death of his parents.

In 1894 he was united in marriage to Mary Kathrine Wienick. They made their home near the Volga River in Russia until they moved to America in 1904. They came direct to Woodbine, Dickinson County, Kansas. After living there a short time they moved to Rush County where they lived until they moved to Kearny County in 1906, where they took up a homestead on which they lived at the time of his death.

To this union 11 children were born.

He leaves to mourn his passing: his wife; six sons, George Jr., Harry, and Alex, of Lakin, Kansas, Jake of Union City, Michigan, Rudolph of Fort Warren, Wyoming, and Fred of Cripple Creek, Colorado; four daughters, Mrs. Cathrine Jones of Lakin, Mrs. George Dinger of Zenda, Kansas, Mrs. Dan Brack and Mrs. Clayton Brack of Leoti, Kansas, Mrs. Jack Norris of Pratt, Kansas, preceded her father in death a few months.

He also leaves two sisters, Mary Cathrine and Susanna, and a brother, Henry, who are living in Russia, many grandchildren and other relatives and friends remain.

He was confirmed in the Lutheran Church in Russia at the early age of 13.

The funeral services were held in the Methodist Church, Deerfield, the pastor, Rev. Woolard, being assisted by Rev. Cain of Leoti, pastor of the Baptist Church. The music was furnished by a male quartet composed of the Gillock men: Joe D., Will J., Monroe and O. J. Downing.

Interment was made in the Deerfield Cemetery.

RODRIGUEZ, JOSE R. - (Lt. 2, Blk. 126, Sec. 1) Funeral for Joe R. Rodriguez was held Wednesday at the St. Mary Catholic Church, the Rev. James Schrader officiating. Burial in Deerfield Cemetery.

Mr. Rodriguez, 91, 1411 St. John, Garden City, died Monday, Sept. 17, 1979, at St. Catherine Hospital.

Born on Sept. 2, 1888, in Calvillo, Aguascalientes, Mexico, he married Maria Luna in 1912 in Mexico. She died in 1956. He had lived in the Garden City area since 1914.

He was a member of the St. Mary Catholic Church. Survivors include a son, Robert L. Rodriguez, 1411 St. John; nine grandchildren and 10 great grandchildren.

A wake service was held Tuesday at the Garnand Funeral Chapel.

RODRIGUEZ, MARIA LUNA - (Lt. 2, Blk. 126, Sec. 1) Mrs. Maria Luna Rodriquez, 65, a longtime resident of Kearny County, died Nov. 17, 1956, at the Lakin hospital. Death followed a lengthy illness.

Mrs. Rodriquez, had been a resident of Deerfield for 35 years and had lived in Lakin the past year. She was born in Mexico, May 10, 1891. She was a member of St. Mary's Church.

Surviving are the husband, Jose, of Lakin; one son, Robert and four grandchildren.

Rosary at Phillips Chapel, Monday and funeral services Tuesday at St. Mary's Church. Burial in the Deerfield Cemetery.

RODRIQUEZ, ROBERT JR. - (Lt. 1, Blk. 125, Sec. 1) Born Sept. 29, 1949, and died Oct. 1, 1949.

Graveside services were conducted Tuesday morning, October 4, 1949, in the Deerfield Cemetery for Robert Rodriquez, Jr., 3 day old son of Mr. and Mrs. Robert Rodriquez of Deerfield, who died over the weekend in a local hospital.

ROGERS, AARON S. - (Lt. 1, Blk. 17, Sec. 3) Funeral for Aaron Scott Rogers, 3 months, Holcomb, was held at Calvary Assembly Church, the Rev. Ray Raley officiating. Burial at Deerfield Cemetery.

He died Jan. 5, 1993, at St. Catherine Hospital, Garden City.

Born Sept. 6, 1992, at Garden City, he was the 3 month old son of Steve and Jana Porter Rogers, Holcomb.

Survivors include his parents, of the home; three brothers, Brandon Rogers, Jason Rogers, and Matthew Rogers, all of the home; his grandparents, Kathy Porter; and his great grandmother, Nora Montgomery.

DEERFIELD CEMETERY

ROMAN, MANUELA - (Lt. 2, Blk. 99, Sec. 1) ts. December 25, 1932-January 25, 1933.
Mexican female, premature, January 25, 1933, died in Sherlock Twp., Finney County, Kansas. Undertaker, Garnand.

ROMMEL, JACOB - Jacob Rommel, son of Mr. and Mrs. John George Rommel, was born in Fort Collins, Colorado, July 26, 1913, and was accidentally killed near Portland, Oregon, February 11, 1935, when a limb struck him while he was felling trees. His age was 21 years, 6 months, and 15 days.
He moved with his family to Kansas in 1914, where he had since resided. He moved to the Deerfield community about two years ago.
He leaves his parents, Mr. and Mrs. John George Rommel; four brothers, Fred, George, Samuel, and David; and two sisters, Amelia and Alice.
The entire community joins in extending their heart felt sympathy to his family in this, their time of sorrow.
Mr. Rommel was a member of the Congregational Church at Alamota, Kansas. He was an honest and sincere young man.
Funeral services were held in German at the Rommel home east of Deerfield at 12:30 Wednesday. Rev. Hoersch of Bazine, Kansas, was in charge. At 1:00 a combination English and German service was held at the Methodist Church in Deerfield with Rev. Hoersch and Rev. Palmer in charge. Interment was made in the Deerfield Cemetery.

ROONEY, ROBERT - (Lt. 1, Blk. 28, Sec. 2) Son of W. T. Jr. and Mamie Rooney, born June 11 and died June 12, 1936.
(The Lakin Independent, June 19, 1936) On Thursday morning, June 11, a little son was born to Mr. and Mrs. W. T. Rooney. The little one lived only a few hours and was laid to rest Saturday morning with a beautiful little service by Rev. Palmer and songs by the high school girls and Mrs. Palmer. We are deeply sorry for them in their loss.

ROONEY, WILLIAM TECUMSEH - (Lt. 1, Blk. 22, Sec. 2) W. T. (Bill) Jr., 59, Garden City, prominent farmer, stockman and businessman, died unexpectedly of a heart attack at St. Catherine Hospital, March 28, 1968.

Born Oct. 4, 1908, at Haddam, he graduated from the University of Kansas Medical School in 1930, where he was a member of the Phi Beta Phi medical fraternity.

In the early 1930's, he moved to Kearny County and made his home on a ranch north of Deerfield. He married Mamie (Pat) Patton, April 13, 1935, in Raton, N.M.

The Rooneys moved into Deerfield in 1941, and to Garden City in 1952. Mr. Rooney owned and operated the Wolf Elevator in addition to being a farmer and stockman.

He was a member of the Community Church, Elks Lodge, and the Garden City Country Club.

Surviving are the widow, of the home; three sons, William T. Rooney III, 1613 York, Stephen Rooney, of the home, and Ronald Rooney, St. Louis, Mo.; a daughter Mrs. Linda R. Haliby, New York City, N.Y.; two brothers, George Rooney, Belleville, and Capt. Paul Rooney, Shrewsburg, Mass.; four sisters, Mrs. Anne Sherman, San Anselmo, Calif., Mrs. Mable Cahill, Phoenix, Ariz., Mrs. Helen Bledsoe, Hugo, Colo., May Rooney, Haddam; and six grandchildren. He was preceded in death by a son, Robert, June 11, 1936, and two brothers and two sisters.

Funeral service was held Saturday morning at the Community Church in Garden City with the Rev. Malcom C. Bertram officiating. Burial was in the Deerfield Cemetery.

ROSS, GRACE F. GROSS — (Lt. 2, Blk. 105, Sec. 1)   A private family funeral for Grace F. Gross Ross, 81, was Saturday at Garnand Funeral Chapel, Lakin, the Rev. Nathan Morgan officiating with a public graveside service following at Deerfield Cemetery.

She died June 15, 1993, at St. Francis Regional Medical Center, Wichita.

Born November 16, 1911, at Sherman County, she was the daughter of Frank and Mabel Sorenson Chilton. She married Harry Gross in Cheyene Wells, Colorado. He died January 11, 1967. She married Donald Ross, September 2, 1978, at Lakin. He died February 21, 1985.

Mrs. Ross lived in various places throughout her life including Garden City and Deerfield and moved to Lakin in 1988. While in Garden City, she was the administrator of Shadylawn Nursing Home.

She was a member of the Deerfield United Methodist Church. Her hobbies were quilting, reading, and garage sales.

DEERFIELD CEMETERY

Survivors include two daughters, Ann Mason, Lakin, and
Kathy Leavitt, Garden City; one son, Steve Gross, Olathe;
10 grandchildren; and six great grandchildren. She was
preceded in death by one grandson and one granddaughter.

RUSSELL, CHESTER WILLIAM - (Lt. 1, Blk. 53, Sec. 2)
Chester William Russell, son of Albert and Edith Russell,
was born April 2nd, 1925, at Deerfield, Kansas. Died
October 18th, 1925, at 8 o'clock p.m. after an illness of
about one month. His age was six months and sixteen
days.
He leaves to mourn his departure his father and mother,
two brothers and two sisters, three grandparents, and
other relatives and friends.
The funeral was conducted by Rev. B. E. Willoughby on
Monday at 2 p.m. from the Methodist Church in Deerfield,
and the remains were laid to rest in the Deerfield
Cemetery.

RUSSELL, DORA EULANE - (Lt. 1, Blk. 53, Sec. 2) Born in
1931 and died Nov. 12, 1932, of intestinal influenza.
Undertaker: Wiley.

RUSSELL, ETHEL DELILAH - (Lt. 4, Blk. 54, Sec. 2) ts.
August 19, 1882-November 20, 1918.
Died Nov. 20, 1918, age 36 yrs., 3 mos., 1 day. Father
Wm. Albert Russell, from Berry Co. Mich., mother Rebecca
Lucretia Woodrow from Jackson Co., Ohio. Died of
influenza followed by bronchial pneumonia.

RUSSELL, LESLIE A. - (Lt. 4, Blk. 53, Sec. 2) Funeral
for Leslie A. Russell, 75, who was also known as "Skeet"
and "Red" was held Tuesday at Garnand Funeral Home with
the Rev. Randy Caddell officiating. Burial at Deerfield
Cemetery with military rites conducted by the Garden City
Area Veterans group.
Mr. Russell died Friday, July 26, 1996, at Veterans
Administration Hospital, Denver.
Born at Deerfield on March 6, 1921, to Albert M. and
Lula Edith Heinlen Russell, he attended Deerfield
schools.
He enlisted in the U.S. Army and served 13 years in the
service during World War II and the Korean conflict, part
of this time as a drill instructor. After his discharge,
he moved to Garden City where he worked in construction,
farming and for Brookover Feed Yard.

Mr. Russell moved to Washington where he worked in the raspberry patches and as a lumberjack. He returned to Garden City in 1959 and began work as a caretaker of Richard Quint's rental property. He later worked as a vehicle serviceman for the Kansas Department of Transportation. After his retirement, he moved to Springfield, Colo., in 1985.

He was a member of the Veterans of Foreign Wars Post of Springfield and enjoyed doing puzzles and reading.

On April 10, 1948, he married Virginia M. Page at Garden City. She survives.

Other survivors are four sons, Chester Russell, Garden City, L. Dale Russell, Moreno Valley, Calif., Mike Russell, Lamar, Colo., and Bill Russell, Paris Tenn.; two daughters, Rebecca Thomas, Moreno Valley, and Mary Harrison, Garden City; two brothers, Bob Russell, Garden City, and J. D. Russell, Wichita; three sisters, Velma Castor, Fruita, Colo., Edna McBeth, Canon City, Colo., and Mae Vaughn, Lamar, 22 grandchildren; and six great grandchildren.

He was preceded in death by two sons, Roger and James, two great grandchildren, four brothers and one sister.

RUSSELL, LULA EDITH HEINLEN — (Lt. 4, Blk. 42, Sec. 3) Born March 14, 1902 and died Jan. 31, 1995.

(The Garden City Telegram, Feb. 2, 1995) Funeral for Lula Edith Russell, 93, longtime Garden City resident, before moving to Colorado, was held at Church of Jesus Christ of Latter-day Saints at Burlington, Colo. Burial at Deerfield Cemetery on Saturday.

Mrs. Russell died Feb. 1, 1995, at Burlington Hospital.

The daughter of James and Alberta Heinlen, she married Albert Russell on March 3, 1920, at Garden City. He preceded her in death.

Mrs. Russell had served as administrator for the Fellowship Baptist Senior Center for five years. She was a resident of Grace Manor Nursing Home in Burlington.

She is survived by three daughters, Edna McBeth, Canyon City, Colo., Velma Castor, Fruita, Colo., Mae Vaughn, Burlington; three sons, Leslie Russell, Springfield, Colo., Robert Russell, Garden City and John Russell, Wichita; and numerous grandchildren, great grandchildren and great great grandchildren.

Hendricks-Love Mortuary, Burlington, in charge of arrangements.

DEERFIELD CEMETERY

RUSSELL, M. ALBERT - (Lt. 4, Blk. 53, Sec. 2) ts.
1897-1959. Born in 1897 and died in 1957. Santa Fe
Laborer. Wife, Edith. Children: Walter, Leslie, Edna,
Velma, Kenneth, Bobby, Orval and Lula Mae.

RUSSELL, REBECCA L. - (Lt. 1, Blk. 53, Sec. 2) (The
Garden City Telegram, Monday, July 14, 1941) Services
for Mrs. Rebecca Lucretia Russell, a resident of Garden
City for the past twenty seven years and a Kansas
pioneer, were held this afternoon at the Church of God,
the Rev. L. W. Irons in charge.
    Mrs. Russell, 76, lived at 315 N. Tenth St. in Garden
City, where she had lain ill for four days previous to
her death, July 13, 1941. She was born April 8, 1865, in
Jackson County, Ohio, coming to Kingman County, Kansas,
and marrying William A. Russell there in 1881.
    Survivors including children and members of her
immediate family are Bell Dunn, Walla Walla, Wash.; John
J. Russell, Wichita; Mrs. Dora Harsh, Sheldon, Mo.; Mrs.
M. Albert Russell, Garden City; Mrs. Minnie Young and
John Woodrow, Enid, Okla.; and Mary Lockey, Cheney,
Kansas.
    Interment was made at the Deerfield Cemetery, the
Garnand Funeral home was in charge of arrangements.

RUSSELL, WILLIAM A. - (Lt. 1, Blk. 53, Sec. 2) Born in
1858 and died in 1928. Wife: Rebecca L.

RYBA, FLORENCE V. - (Lt. 3, Blk. 34, Sec. 3) Daughter of
Ralph and Vera (Hittle) DeWitt, mother of Marlena
(Winters) Lopez, Born June 27, 1916, at Medicine Lodge,
Ks. and died Dec. 17, 1972, at Wichita, Ks.

DEERFIELD CEMETERY

SAUNDERS, SARAH - (Lt. 3, Blk. 32, Sec. 2) (Kearny County Advocate, Sept. 15, 1911) Mrs. Sarah Saunders, of Deerfield, died Sunday, August 10th, and was buried in the Deerfield Cemetery, Monday the 11th. She, for months, had been failing with tubercular trouble. A few weeeks ago she was converted in her home and was baptized by Rev. Newsom and received into the Methodist Church. She leaves four small children who were taken by neighbors and friends to care for.

SCALF, DANIEL - (Lt. 3, Blk. 60, Sec. 3) (The Kearny County Advocate, May 9, 1930) Mr. Daniel Scalf passed away Monday at the home of his son, James. Mr. Scalf has been sick for several months and for several weeks has been gradually growing weaker. Funeral services were held at the Methodist Church in Deerfield and interment in the Deerfield Cemetery.
(Lakin Independent, May 16, 1930) Daniel Scalf was born in Illinois, August 5, 1857. At the age of twenty six years he was married to Winnie Booth in Washington County, Iowa. To this union were born four children, two of whom lived to grow up: J. V. Scalf and Mrs. C. C. Berry, both of Lakin. Mr. Scalf died near Deerfield on May 5 at the age of seventy-two years and eight months. He was a kind father and loved to be at home. He also was a hard working man and labored as long as he had strength.

SCHAAF, ANNA M. - (Lt. 4, Blk. 23, Sec. 2) Anna M. Coerber, daughter of Carl A.M. and Marie (Kliever) Coerber was born Dec. 1, 1890, in Butler Co. Came to Kearny County in 1892 with her parents.
Mrs. Anna M. Schaaf, 75, died Wednesday afternoon, October 26, 1966, in Scott County Hospital. Born Dec. 1, 1890, in Harvey County, she came to Kearny County as a girl, and married C. Fred_ Schaaf, Sept. 5, 1917, at Deerfield. He died in 1930. She moved to Scott City from Kansas City in 1961 to make her home with her daughter.
Member: Holy Cross Lutheran Church, Scott City.
Survivors: Son, Oscar, Eugene, Ore.; daughters, Mrs. Clarence Bron, Scott City; Mrs. Roy Cornelison, Vienna, Va., and Mrs. Carl Hiteshew, Verona, N.J.; five sisters, 14 grandchildren.

Funeral: 2 p.m. Saturday at the church; Rev. K. J. Karstensen. Burial: Deerfield Cemetery. Call: Weinmann-Price Funeral Home, Scott City.

SCHAAF, C. FREDERICK - (Lt. 4, Blk. 23, Sec. 2) (The Kearny County Advocate, Feb. 28, 1930) C. Fredrick Schaaf was born on July 28th, 1878, at Seneca, Kansas. In 1905 he settled at Deerfield, Kansas, and removed to Wichita in 1924 where the family resided at 406 Sheridan Avenue. He was baptized and confirmed in the Evangelical Lutheran Church. While he and his family resided at Deerfield, he was a faithful member of Immanuel Evangelical Lutheran Church, and held the office as Elder of the congregation for a number of years. Coming to Wichita with his family he affiliated with Immanuel Evangelical Lutheran Church and at the time of his death was a member of the school board of the congregation. He died on February 17th, 1930, at 3:30 p.m., at the age of 51 years, 6 months and 19 days. He is survived by his wife, Anna; four children, Oscar, Alberta, Kathryn and Mildred Ann; three brothers and four sisters, Ernest Schaaf, of Palmer, Kansas, Mrs. S. F. Mueller, of Morril, Kansas, William Schaaf, of Coaldale, Colorado, Mrs. H. H. Kruger, of Dodge City, Kansas, Rev. Carl Schaaf, of Chickasha, Oklahoma, and Misses Elsie and Frieda Schaaf of San Diego, California.
Burial services for the deceased were held at Wichita on February 19, at 10:00 a.m., and then he was brought to Deerfield, Kansas, where burial services were held at the Lutheran Church on Thursday at 2:00 p.m. Services were conducted by Rev. Deffner, of Wichita, who was assisted by the local Lutheran pastor, Rev. Walter Lebien. Interment in the Deerfield Cemetery.
"Blessed are the dead that die in the Lord from henceforth."

SCHAAF, DANIEL - (Lt. 3, Blk. 28, Sec. 2) Daniel was born in Waldfischbach, Germany, Jan. 30, 1849, came to Kearny County in 1910 and died at Deerfield, Feb. 25, 1922. He was a retired farmer. His wife was Minnie Marie.

SCHAAF, DANIEL GOTTLIEB AUGUST - (Lt. 3, Blk. 28, Sec. 2) (The Kearny County Advocate, Oct. 5, 1928) (The Garden City Telegram, Oct. 4, 1928) Daniel Gottlieb August Schaaf was born at Bern, Nemaha County, Kansas, on April

23, 1888. In the year 1909 he came to Deerfield with his parents. A few years later he purchased his farm about nine miles north of Deerfield, where he spent the remainder of his life. On September 6th, 1920, he was united in holy wedlock with Margareth Gernand at Emporia, Kansas. To this union three children were born: Herbert Martin, Gertrude Helen, and Arthur Eugene. On the morning of September 29th, 1928, he met with an automobile accident and died a few hours later at 1:30 p.m. in the Lakin hospital, at the age of 40 years, 5 months and 6 days.

Mr. Schaaf had just cranked his car and stepped around to the side of it when he was struck by a car driven by a Pennsylvania tourist who brought him into town. He had a concussion of the brain and never regained consciousness.

Mr. Schaaf was a member of the Evangelical Lutheran Church, in which he was baptised and confirmed. Since January of this year, he has been serving as one of the elders in the local Lutheran congregation.

Funeral services were held at the home and at the Lutheran Church. At the home the pastor based his remarks on the seventh petition of the Lord's Prayer, "Deliver us from evil." At the church the subject of the funeral discourse was: "What is the Christian's view of a violent death?" Text: Isaiah 57:1-2. After these services the departed was laid to rest in the Deerfield Cemetery.

He leaves to mourn his death a loving wife, Mrs. Margareth Schaaf; the three children, Herbert, Gertrude, and Arthur; four brothers, Ernest Schaaf of Palmer, Kansas, Fred Schaaf of Coaldale, Colorado, Rev. Karl Schaaf of Chickasha, Oklahoma; four sisters, Mrs. Esther Mueller of Morril, Kansas, Mrs. Anna Krueger of Dodge City, Kansas, and the Misses Elsie and Frieda Schaaf of Wichita, and besides, a number of other relatives and a host of friends.

Thus we have bidden farewell to one whom we esteem and love. The hand that wounds will also know how to bind and heal. Though bowed down in grief, we humble ourselves under the Mighty Hand of God and say:

> My Jesus, as Thou wilt!
> O, may Thy will be mine;
> Into Thy Hand of love
> I would my all resign.
> Through sorrow or through joy,
> Conduct me as Thine own;

DEERFIELD CEMETERY

And help me still to say,
My Lord, Thy will be done.

Dan Schaaf, a young and energetic farmer, living about four miles north of Deerfield was fatally injured Saturday when he was struck by a motor car on the highway at the edge of town. He died several hours later in the Hastings hospital here. Mr. Schaaf had just cranked his car and when he stepped from in front of it, an approaching automobile struck him, causing concussion of the brain. The driver of the car, who was from Pennsylvania brought him to town. Mr. Schaaf is survived by a wife and four small children.

Coroner Nash empanelled a jury who returned a verdict of "unavoidable accident."

SCHAAF, MINNIE MARIE — (Lt. 3, Blk. 28, Sec. 2) (The Kearny County Advocate, Nov. 25, 1927) Mrs. Minnie Marie Schaaf, nee Wesselhoeft, was born on the 27th day of April 1858, in West Prussia, Germany. At the age of eight she came to American and lived in Chicago and Wisconsin for a short time and then moved to Nemeha County, Kansas, with her parents. In the year 1875 she was married to Mr. Daniel Schaaf. After being married forty eight years, her husband passed away on February 26th, 1922. This union was blessed with ten children, five sons and five daughters. One daughter, Mrs. Louisa Bentrup, preceeded her parents in death. In 1909 Mrs. Schaaf moved to Deerfield with her husband and family. About three years ago she went to Wichita to live with her children.

The children who mourn her death, but who are thankful that God has delivered their mother from pain and suffering, are: Ernest Schaaf, Palmer, Kansas, C. F. Schaaf, Wichita, Kansas, William Schaaf, Coaldale, Colorado, Rev. K. Schaaf, Chickasha, Oklahoma, Mrs. Esther Mueller, Morrill, Kansas, Mrs. Anna Krueger, Dodge City, Kansas, Misses Elsie and Frieda Schaaf, Wichita, Kansas.

Mrs. Schaaf died Tuesday afternoon, November 15, 1927, at the age of 69 years, 6 months and 18 days. On Thursday morning funeral services were held in the Lutheran Church of Wichita. On Friday afternoon services was again held in the Lutheran Church at Deerfield, after which she was laid to rest in the Deerfield Cemetery.

We lay away our loved ones here,
As ripened grain into the ground,

237

DEERFIELD CEMETERY

And in the places once so dear,
Their presence will no more be found.
Yet ever nearer draws the time,
When we with all our own shall come,
As garnered sheaves at harvest time
To the eternal Harvest home.

SCHAGUN, CHARLES FEAREND - (Lt. 2, Blk. 47, Sec. 2) (The Kearny County Advocate, May 7, 1908) Chas. F. Shagun was born in Germany, at Didlaken, near Insterburg, Feb. 16, 1857, and died in Deerfield, Kansas, April 28, 1908, aged 51 years, 2 months and 11 days, of pneumonia.

All of his married life was spent in Kansas, and for 13 years he lived in Deerfield, 10 of which he worked for the Santa Fe.

He leaves a wife and three small children, a brother-in-law and a sister and family to mourn his departure. 'I wish to return sincere thanks to my many friends and neighbors for their kindness and assistance in the sickness and death of my husband. Mrs. Bertha Shagun and Children.'

SCHAGUN, FRED - (Lt. 2, Blk. 47, Sec. 2) (The Lakin Investigator, July 3, 1908) Fred Shagun, son of the widow Shagun, of Deerfield, was drowned in Lake McKinnie, on Thursday afternoon last. He was fishing and waded out in the water to unfasten his line and got beyond his depth. He was 13 years of age, but being unable to swim, lost his life. His body was recovered.

(The Kearny County Advocate, July 9, 1908) The oldest son of Mrs. Schagun, of Deerfield, a boy about 14 years old, was drowned in Lake McKinnie last Thursday. He and his younger brother were fishing, and he went into the water and got into one of the channels where the water was several feet deep, and drowned before help could reach him. The funeral was held on Friday.

He was born April 5, 1894 and died July 2, 1908.

SCHEUERMAN, CALVIN H. - (Lt. 1, Blk. 81, Sec. 1) Calvin H. Scheuerman, 72, lifetime Kearny County resident, died Thursday, Feb. 13, 1997, at his home in Deerfield.

Born Nov. 13, 1924, at Garden City, he was the son of Henry E. and Dora Bisterfelt Scheuerman. He attended Deerfield schools and graduated from Deerfield High School.

DEERFIELD CEMETERY

Mr. Scheuerman was a member of Immanuel Lutheran Church of Lakin, a charter member and past president of Deerfield Lions Club, member of Kearny County Fair Board and Kearny County Extension Council, served on the board of directors of Kearny County Farmers Irrigation Association, and was supervisor on the Kearny County Conservation District Board for 37 years.

A lifelong farmer, he received the National Endowment for Soil and Conservation Award and the KACD Outstanding Supervisor Award, both in 1990, and the Kansas Good Earth Family Award in 1991. He enjoyed traveling and had visited most of the United States.

On Sept. 1, 1946, he married Doris Murray at Deerfield. She died Oct. 28, 1987. He was also preceded in death by a brother, Elmer Bisterfelt.

He married Burnalee Loomis on Nov. 3, 1990, at Topeka. She survives.

Other survivors are a son, Hal Scheuerman, Deerfield; a daughter, Linda Doll, Garden City; three stepchildren, Jewel Robinson, Larry Maddux and Kim Maddux, all of Topeka; a brother, Leon Scheuerman, Deerfield; three sisters, Eloris McAfee, Garden City, Mabel Abby, Pasadena, Texas, and Betty Krueger, LaPort, Texas; two grandchildren; and two stepgrandchildren.

Funeral was Monday at 10 a.m. at Immanuel Lutheran Church, Lakin. Robert Roberts, pastor, officiating. Burial at Deerfield Cemetery.

SCHEUERMAN, DORIS V. - (Lt. 1, Blk. 81, Sec. 1) Funeral for Doris V. Scheuerman, 61, was at 10:30 a.m., Saturday, at Immanuel Lutheran Church, Deerfield, the Rev. James A. Baker officiating. Burial was in Deerfield Cemetery.

She died Oct. 28, 1987, at St. Catherine Hospital, Garden City. Born Doris V. Murray, Feb. 13, 1926, at Holcomb, she married Calvin H. Scheuerman, Sept. 1, 1946, at Deerfield.

She was a homemaker and had been a resident of Deerfield since the age of three, moving from Holcomb.

Mrs. Scheuerman was a member of Immanuel Lutheran Church, Deerfield, Garden City Piano Teachers League, and Kansas Association of Conservation District Auxiliary. She was church organist for many years and gave piano lessons. Her hobby was music.

Survivors include her husband, of the home; a son, Hal Scheuerman, Deerfield, and a daughter, Linda Doll, Eminence Rt., Garden City.

DEERFIELD CEMETERY

Garnand Funeral Home was in charge of arrangements.

SCHEUERMAN, HENRY E. - (Lt. 1, Blk. 81, Sec. 1) Henry E. Scheuerman was born at Bison, Kan., on December 6, 1885. As an infant he was received into God's covenant of grace though the sacrament of holy baptism. As an adult he was instructed in the chief parts of Christian doctrine and received into membership with the Deerfield Lutheran Church by the rite of confirmation during the pastorate of the Rev. K. Karstensen.

May 30, 1909, he entered the holy estate of matrimony with Miss Dora Bisterfelt at Bunker Hill, Kan. This union was blessed with five children, two sons, and three daughters. A nephew, Elmer Bisterfelt, was reared and loved as a son in the Scheuerman home.

It was in the year 1923 that the Scheuermans moved to Kearny County. Living on the well-ordered and modernly-equipped farm north of Deerfield, Mr. Scheuerman experienced the truth of the Lord's promise: "I will bless the labor of his hands." Yet he realized that the greatest blessings are not the material but the spiritual blessings, and these he valued most highly. He loved the word of God and His church. He was faithful in his attendance upon the means of grace. The church recognized his ability for leadership, and as the senior member of the board of elders his judgments were respected, his devotion and zeal in the work of the church, his concern for the welfare of the congregation were well worthy of emulation.

He departed this life on May 8, 1946, believing and trusting in Jesus, his Savior, whom he loved and served. He reached the age of 60 years, 5 months and 2 days.

He leaves to mourn his passing: his grief stricken widow, Mrs. Dora Scheuerman; his sons, Leon and Calvin; his daughters, Mrs. Eloris McAfee, Betty and Mabel Scheuerman; his granddaughter, Lola Wynn McAfee; his daughter-in-law, Mrs. Leon Scheuerman, nee Nelle Jane Mathias; his nephew, Elmer Bisterfelt, and wife, Lydia, nee Grauberger, and their children, Dorothy Ann and Janice Bisterfelt; his brothers, John, George, Jacob, David and William Scheuerman; his sisters, Elizabeth Schwindt, Katherine Flagler, Mary Staley, Emma Appel, Sara Newhauser, Martha Hanhardt, and Clara Rodie; as well as many other relatives and friends.

DEERFIELD CEMETERY

Funeral services were held from the Lutheran Church at Deerfield on May 12, with Pastor Paul H.C. Stengel in charge. Interment was made in the Deerfield Cemetery. "Whether we live, we live unto the Lord; and whether we die, we die unto the Lord; whether we live, therefore, or die, we are the Lord's. For to this end Christ both died, and rose, and revived, that He might be the Lord both of the dead and living." Rom. 14, 8-9.

SCHEUERMAN, KATHERINE DORA - (Lt. 1, Blk. 81, Sec. 1) Katherine Dorothea Bisterfeldt, 90, daughter of John Jacob and Dorothea (Bisterfeldt) Bisterfeldt, was born on April 19, 1891, at Wilson, Kansas, and passed away on April 14, 1982, at St. Catherine Hospital in Garden City, Kansas, after a long illness.

Dora, as she was called, married Henry E. Scheuerman, son of Conrad and Anna Elizabeth (Krum) Scheuerman, on May 30, 1909, at Bison, Kansas. To this union was born five children.

Dora and her husband, Henry, raised her nephew, Elmer Bisterfelt, after his parents passed away. Dora and Henry and their family of two children and Elmer, moved to their farm north of Deerfield, Kansas, arriving on May 23, 1923, Henry passed away on May 9, 1946.

In May 1950, Dora moved to Garden City, Kansas, to make her home with her daughter, Eloris McAfee.

She was a member of Trinity Lutheran Church, Senior Citizens, and the Lutheran Women's Missionary League, all of Garden City.

Survivors include two sons, Leon and Calvin, both of Deerfield; three daughters, Eloris McAfee, Garden City, Betty Johnson, Deer Park, Texas, and Mabel Abbey, Pasadena, Texas; her nephew, Elmer Bisterfelt, Liberal, Kansas; two brothers, Ben Bisterfeldt, LaCrosse, Kansas, and Henry Bisterfeldt, Lyons, Colorado; two sisters, Mary Green, Gering, Nebraska, and Amelia Story, Colorado Springs, Colorado; two half brothers, Bill Bisterfeldt. LaCrosse, Kansas, and George Bisterfeldt, Santa Clara, California; one half sister, Elma Karst, Hutchinson, Kansas; two step sisters, Martha Wilhelm, Hoisington, Kansas, and Eva Bisterfeldt, Lyons, Colo.; 15 grandchildren, and 15 great grandchildren. Her parents, two sisters, two brothers and one half brother preceded her in death.

Funeral services were held in Garden City, Kansas, on April 17, at 10:00 a.m. at the Trinity Lutheran Church,

DEERFIELD CEMETERY

Pastor Merlin Reith officiating. Burial was in the Deerfield Cemetery.

SCHMIDT, FRED GEORGE - (Lt. 3, Blk. 105, Sec. 1)
Graveside service was held at Deerfield Cemetery, June 28
at 10:00 a.m. for Frederick George Schmidt, 78, who died
in Cortez, Colo., June 25, 1967. Funeral services were
in Colorado Springs, June 27, at the Chapel of Memories,
Pastor Robert C. Jacobson officiating.
The Schmidt family lived in Kearny County, north of
Lakin, from 1932 to 1940, moving into town where they
lived until 1945. Mrs. Schmidt died in 1944. His
daughter, Mrs. Mollie Hullett, also preceded him in
death.
Mr. Schmidt was born Dec. 12, 1888, in Frane, Russia.
Surviving him are three sons, Alec and Carl F.,
Colorado Springs, and L. E. Schmidt of Cody, Wyo., ten
grandchildren and 20 great grandchildren.

SCHMIDT, KATHERINE E. - (Lt. 3, Blk. 105, Sec. 1)
Briefly before her death, Catherine Schmidt expressed her
dying wish and thought in these words: "Jerusalem, thou
city fair and high, Would God I were in thee. My longing
heart fain, fain to thee would fly. Far over vail and
mountain, Far over field and plain, It haste to seek its
fountain and quit this world of pain. A moments space
and I shall surely be released from earthly ties. God's
chariots shall bear my soul to thee, through all these
lower skies. To yonder shining regions, where blessed
saints do roam, while fairest angel legions now bid me
welcome home." With this beautiful desire she passed
away at 11:00 a.m., August 1, 1944, at the early age of
56 years, 11 months, and 24 days.
She was born August 7, 1887, in Frank, Russia. As her
father was a pastor in the colony, she was presented to
the Lord in Holy Baptism at an early age. He also
instructed her in the Word of God and confirmed her in
the faith. When she was 19 years of age, she came to
America with her parents, settling at first in LaCross,
Kansas. There she lived but six months. After that, her
home was in the vicinity of Garden City. Her father and
mother, being very godly people, was her guiding spirit.
On Nov. 17, 1907, she was joined in holy wedlock with
Mr. Fred Schmidt. The Lord blessed the labor of their
hands so that she, with her husband, had extensive
holdings of property at home and in bordering

242

communities. And in as much as their family life was
concerned, she with her husband enjoyed the companionship
of four children; three sons, Alexander, Syracuse, Kans.,
Carl, Coolidge, Kans., Leslie, Worland, Wyoming; a
daughter, Mrs. Mollie Hullett, Lakin, Kans. These
children together with four brothers, Carl and Jake
Kisselman, Denver, Colo.; Alexander Kisselman, Portland,
Oregon; S/Sgt. Wm. Kisselman, with U.S.A. army; one
sister, Mrs. Molly Kaufman of Denver, Colo.; 8
grandchildren, with the bereaved husband, are left to
mourn the deceased.
   The deceased was a member of the Lutheran Church. It
was one of her great delights to go to church to join in
the singing of spiritual hymns, or hear them sung. In
these hymns she found one of the great comforts she so
much needed in her time of illness. Mrs. Schmidt had
been of ill health during the last 15 years. However,
her illness took a decided change for the worse since
February 1 of this year. From that time forth, she had
been bedridden most of the time. For some time she was
confined to the hospital at Lakin, was later removed to a
hospital at Garden City, but when her condition became
hopeless, she was taken to her home, at Lakin, where she
chose to meet her Lord. Everything was done for her that
doctors, a loving husband, children, and especially her
daughter and daughter-in-law could do for her. May the
Lord reward them for their kindness shown unto a loving
Mother.
   Many a time she was encouraged in her illness by her
pastor with the Word of God and the Sacrament. May she
now enjoy the fruition of her faith. We take leave from
her, as we say, for her and our encouragement and
comfort, "God be with you, 'till we meet again."

SHARP, WILLIAM HAL - (Lt. 2, Blk. 20, Sec. 3) William
Hal Sharp, Jr., 52, cabinet maker, died Saturday morning,
July 9, 1966, at St. Catherine's Hospital, Garden City;
after being in ill health about a year. Born July 17,
1913, at Independence, he married Evelyn Zrubek, May 1,
1937, at Wichita. He moved to Garden City, July 5.
   Member: First Baptist Church, Willow Springs, Mo.;
Sunflower Masonic Lodge No. 86 and Midian Shrine,
Wichita.
   Survivors: The widow of the home; son, William M.,
Springfield, Mo.; sister, Mrs. Homer Wilson, Atlanta,

DEERFIELD CEMETERY

Ga.; parents, Mr. and Mrs. William Sharp, Willow Springs,
Mo.; one grandson.

SHEPHERD, RALPH - (Lt. 2, Blk. 30, Sec. 2) Ralph E.
Shepherd, son of Mr. and Mrs. F. A. Shepherd, was born
August 9, 1894, at Guthrie, Oklahoma. He enlisted in the
National Guard, State of Kansas, June 13, 1917, at
Deerfield, Kansas, and was assigned to Company F, 2d
Infantry Regiment, at which time he gave his home address
as Deerfield, Kansas.

On August 5, 1917, Private Shepherd was mustered into
the active Federal service at Larned, Kansas. He was
sent to Camp Doniphan, Fort Sill, Oklahoma, where he was
transferred to Company F, 137th Infantry, on March 26,
1918. Private Shepherd departed the United States with
his organization on April 25, 1918, for duty in France.
He was on detached service with the 35th Division Remount
Detachment, American Expeditionary Forces in France from
July 12, 1918, to August 11, 1918. Shortly after
returning to his unit, Private Shepherd was killed in
action September 28, 1918, in France.

Private Shepherd was authorized the Purple Heart for
having made the supreme sacrifice on September 28, 1918,
and the World War I Victory Medal with Clasps for
Meuse-Argonne and Defensive Sector.

Ralph was a good horseman and was sent to Italy from
his location in France to buy horses for the army. He
had just returned to his company shortly before he was
killed. His body was returned to Deerfield where he was
buried in the Deerfield Cemetery.

Shepherd-Moore Post No. 208, American Legion, Kearny
County, was named for the first and last men from the
county to lose their lives in World War I.

Private Ralph E. Shepherd, son of Mr. and Mrs. Theo. A.
Shepherd, was born at Guthrie, Okla., Aug. 9, 1894. He
graduated at Granada, Colo., in 1912. Moved with his
parents to Deerfield, Kans., in 1913, and enlisted in the
service of his country, June 13, 1917, at Deerfield.
Trained at Larned, then in Camp Doniphan, Okla., in Co.
F, 137 Inf., 35th Division. Made the supreme sacrifice
Sept 29, 1918, in the Argonne Forest, faithful to the
flag he loved.

His body was brought to Deerfield, Kans., Sept 13,
Military services were held at the M. E. church on
Wednesday, September 14, at 2 p.m.   Rev. Thomas A.
Claggett, pastor of the Presbyterian Church at Garden

244

DEERFIELD CEMETERY

City, an overseas chaplain of the 35th Division, and the
Ralph Shepherd Post No. 271 of Deerfield, conducted the
services.

"Our Comrade"
We cannot say, we will not say,
He is dead, he's just away;
With a happy smile, and a wave of his hand
He has wandered into an unknown land,
Leaving us dreaming how sweetly fair,
It needs must be since he lingers there.

SHIPLEY, DOROTHY E. - (Lt. 1, Blk. 41, Sec. 3) Dorothy
E. Shipley, 57, died February 15, 1993, at her home, 1204
Hattie, Garden City.
    She was born Nov. 18, 1935, at Rolla, Mo., the daughter
of Raymond A. and Elsie Marie Borlisch Wishon. A Garden
City resident since 1948, she was a homemaker.
    She was a member of the Grandview Congregation of
Jehovah's Witnesses. Her hobbies included sewing, hand
crafts and reading.
    On July 13, 1952, she married Floyd Shipley at Raton,
N.M. He survives.
    Other survivors include two sons, Warren F. II, 409
Evans, and Frank E., Calhan, Colo.; two daughters, Teresa
M. Craig, Wichita, and Terry A. Gunderson, Dodge City;
her mother, Elsie Wishon, Burnside Drive; three brothers,
Raymond "Bud" Wishon Jr., Holcomb, Chester Wishon,
Hampton, Va., and Arnold Wishon, 606 E. Burnside Drive;
five sisters, Deloris Miller, 1706 N. Main, Loretta
Wishon, Burnside Drive, Marietta Burtis, 510 W. Chestnut;
Leeta Dingus and Patricia Baier, both of Holcomb; and
eight grandchildren.
    Funeral was held at 2 p.m., Friday at Garnand Funeral
Chapel, with the Grandview Congregation of Jehovah's
Witnesses presiding. Burial in the Deerfield Cemetery.

SHRIVER, OLIVER W. - (S/2 Lt. 4, Blk. 36, Sec. 3) Oliver
W. Shriver, Deerfield, died Thursday, March 22, 1984, at
the Kearny County Hospital in Lakin. He was a retired
farmer and stockman.
    He was born December 26, 1903, at Clearwater, Kansas,
the son of Arza and Ruby (Coulson) Shriver. He came to
Kearny County in 1928. On June 27, 1936, Oliver married
Hazel A. Steenis at Garden City. After farming north of
Deerfield for 50 years, he retired and moved to Deerfield
City in 1974.

DEERFIELD CEMETERY

Oliver took an active part in community improvement, striving to improve community pride through various projects.

He attended the Deerfield United Methodist Church, Elks Lodge and Eagles Lodge, both of Garden City, Kearny County Historical Society, Lakin, Kansas Genealogical Society, Dodge City Chapter, Cornerstone Genealogical Society, Green County, Pa., the Marion, W. Va., Historical Society and the Deerfield Grange.

Oliver is survived by his wife, Hazel, and numerous relatives and friends.

He was preceded in death by his parents and two brothers, Herschel A. and William C., and a cousin, Ruby Hatfield Hosler, reared in the Shriver home.

Funeral services were held in the Deerfield United Methodist Church at 11:00 a.m. (CST), on Monday, March 26, 1984, with Rev. Nellie Holmes officiating. Burial in the Deerfield Cemetery.

Oliver was born at Clearwater, Kansas, the third son of Arza and Ruby Shriver. His parents were lifelong farmers and livestock people raising registered cattle, hogs, dogs, competing at the State Fair at Hutchinson with these animals. His father always insisted that the boys settle their differences with boxing gloves, which may have left its mark on Oliver in that he learned to live with right or wrong decisions, not looking back, but always forward. He often was quick with decisions throughout his life.

Oliver was six years old when the family moved from Kingman County to Barber County, Kansas, where he grew up as a young man in the family farm home. He had a tremendous capacity for hard physical work and loved animals, plants, and wildlife.

In the late teens his parents bought land near Hooker, Oklahoma; later trading this land for land near Moscow, Kansas, at which time Oliver and his father entered into a farming partnership, Oliver being the "suitcase" farmer during the summer months and returning to the family farm near Lake City, Kansas, in the winter to help his father feed cattle and hogs.

In the late 20's Oliver bought out the partnership and moved to Deerfield, Kansas. He also became interested at that time in aviation. He and his friend, Fred Fulton, owned an airplane, flying out of Garden City airport. This venture ended when they loaned their airplane to a barnstormer who brought it back in pieces. Oliver continued to have a yen for aviation all his life.

In 1929 Oliver grew a tremendous crop of wheat, had a new line of machinery with quite a lot of debt, which he was a long time paying off with 28 cent per bushel wheat. But he continued farming undaunted by the "dirty thirties" and raised his next big crop in 1939, working off the farm during this period of time to survive, always believing in the ultimate prosperity and opportunities of and in Western Kansas.

Oliver was mechanically minded, a trait necessary to survive and succeed in the farming business.

On June 27, 1936, Oliver married Hazel Steenis and they immediately moved to the Rector farm north of Deerfield, where they were to spend about 40 years, acquiring land, developing irrigation and growing with the times.

Oliver, like his father Arza, was not afraid to try something new, and often made decision in his business planning contrary to what most people were doing, knowing that often times the majority would be wrong, and he would cash in on the contrary opinion. Several times during his life time he cashed in on cheap grain and livestock to take advantage of windfall profits. He knew how to roll with the punches. He was a self-educated man.

Oliver tried many new ideas in farming and stock raising, crops like safflower, and irrigated brome grass pastures; machinery, and labor and time saving methods in cattle feeding.

Oliver acknowledged his belief in Christ at an early age. His father and mother were charter members of the Christian Church at Clearwater, Kansas. In the 1840's his grandparents, Abram and Elizabeth (Wilson) Shriver, were early members and active in the construction of the Mt. Pleasant Methodist Church in Greene County, Pa.

His grandfather, Charles Wilson, was on the church board and was one of that group to receive the deed to the land for the new Methodist church at Kirby, Greene County, Pa., in the 1830's. Rev. Adam Baird Gilliland, great great grandfather, was the minister of the Presbyterian Church at Hamilton, Ohio, for 42 years.

SINGLETON, BABY - (Lt. 2, Blk. 76, Sec. 1)   Maybe 1919.

SKAGGS, JAMES FLOYD - (Lt. 4, Blk. 41, Sec. 3)   James Floyd Skaggs, 41, Deerfield, died unexpectedly Monday

DEERFIELD CEMETERY

evening, March 2, 1970, in St. Catherine Hospital, Garden
City, following a sudden illness.
He was employed by Max Miller at Deerfield. He was
born Sept. 16, 1928, in Garfield County, Okla., and had
been a resident of Kearny County for 16 years, moving
there from Lamar, Colo.
He was a member of Deerfield Methodist Church, Eagles
Lodge and was president of Lake McKinney Boating Assn.
He also was active in Boy Scouts.
He was united in marriage to Geraldine Johnson, June 8,
1949, at Kendall.
In addition to his widow, he is survived by two sons,
James, of the US Army in Ethiopia, and Bobbie of the
home; two daughters, Mrs. Rose Landers, Garden City, and
Patricia, of the home; his parents, Mr. and Mrs. Floyd
Skaggs, Garden City; a brother, Calvin, U.S. Air Force in
Guam; two sisters, Mrs. Vivian Krug, and Mrs. Dorothy
Knoll, both of Garden City, and one grandchild.

SMITH, MRS. A. H. - (Lt. 2, Blk. 58, Sec. 2) Mrs. A. H.
Smith died at her home 10 miles northwest of the city
last Monday, Sept. 6, 1909. The funeral sermon was
preached by Rev. E. H. Jones. Burial was in Deerfield
Cemetery.
(Kearny County Advocate, Doings at Deerfield, Sept. 16,
1909) Mrs. Smith of north of Holcomb, was buried in our
cemetery on Wednesday of last week.

SMITH, CLARA BELLE - (Lt. 2, Blk. 74, Sec. 1) Clara Bell
Couch was born in Columbus, Ohio, April 14, 1864, and
departed this life July 25, 1946, at Hutchinson, at the
age of 82 years, 3 months and 9 days.
At the age of six, she moved with her parents to
Illinois.
In 1884 she was united in marriage to John A. Smith.
Later Mr. and Mrs. Smith moved to Kansas and established
their home. To this union five children were born:
William Allison, who died in 1925; Lewis M., of El
Modeno, California; Ira D. of Avondale, Colorado; Mrs.
Maggie Kersten and Orville A. of Deerfield, Kansas.
Besides the immediate family, she is survived by three
grandchildren. Mr. Smith died, June 6th, 1939.
At an early age, the deceased united with the Methodist
Church, of which she remained an active member until her
health failed. She was a resident of Deerfield for many
years, where she has a host of friends.

DEERFIELD CEMETERY

SMITH, GORDON - (Lt. 1, Blk. 74, Sec. 1) Son of Lewis Marion and Louise Marie (Corbett) Smith, born at Deerfield, June 26, 1917, and died May 21, 1919.

SMITH, JOHN A. - (Lt. 2, Blk. 74, Sec. 1) Born Sept. 3, 1857, and died June 5, 1939, father of William A., Orville A., and Maggie (Smith-Kersten) Coy.
(The Lakin Independent, June 9, 1939) J. A. Smith passed away at his home Monday afternoon at 5:00 p.m. Mr. Smith had been failing in health for several months but was taken down a few days ago. He had been a resident of Deerfield a number of years and the entire community extends deepest sympathy to the bereaved family.

SMITH, MAY - (Lt. 2, Blk. 74, Sec. 1) The community was shocked Saturday morning when the sad news was received of the death of Mrs. May Maddux Smith. Her clothing caught fire from an explosion of coal oil poured on live coals in the stove. She was a graduate of the Deerfield High School. She was well known and loved by all and was a good Christian woman. Our loss is heaven's gain. The school was dismissed in the afternoon. The pallbearers were Wasson McClain, Oscar Downing, Ray Jones, Will James, Jim Wilford, and Madison Downing. A beloved young woman has gone, but is not forgotten.
Anson Maddux returned Wednesday to Emporia, after attending his sister's funeral, and Oscar returned to Burden, Kansas, where he is teaching school.
May Maddux was born in Bourbon County, Kansas, May 24, 1905; died at her home Saturday at half past eleven, December 4, 1926, after a few hours of suffering caused by accidental burning.
On March 30, 1926, she was married to Orville A. Smith of Deerfield, Kansas. To this couple was granted only a few months of wedded happiness.
In early girlhood May was converted and for the remainder of her life she was a loyal and consistent member of the Methodist Church of our community.
For many years May worked in our Sunday School and Epworth League, and will be greatly missed by all who knew and loved her.
When death finally came, a blessed relief from her suffering, and she woke in a painless, tearless Paradise where angels wait and will truthfully say, "She did what

DEERFIELD CEMETERY

she could," and what higher tribute could be paid to her
life.
  She leaves to mourn her going her young husband,
father, mother, three brothers, and a host of friends and
other relatives.
  The funeral services were held in the Methodist Church
at Deerfield Monday, December 6th, at 2 p.m., Rev. J. Q.
Turner, the pastor, in charge, A large crowd was
present. There were many beautiful flowers. The body
was laid to rest in the Deerfield Cemetery.

SMITH, MYRTLE G. - (Lt. 1, Blk. 74, Sec. 1) ts. Oct. 2,
1900, May 2, 1991. Funeral for Myrtle G. Goodwin Smith,
95, was at 2 p.m., Sunday, at High Plains Retirement
Village, Lakin, the Rev. Donald Koehn officiating.
Burial was in Deerfield Cemetery. She died May 2, 1991,
at High Plains Retirement Village.
  Born Myrtle G. Goodwin, October 2, 1895, at Moorefield,
she married Orville Smith. He preceded her in death.
  Mrs. Smith was a homemaker and had been a a resident of
the Lakin-Deerfield area since 1933.
  She was a member of the United Methodist Church, Garden
Club and Order of the Eastern Star, Deerfield.
  She is survived by many nephews and nieces.
  Greene-Schneider Funeral Home, Lakin, was in charge of
arrangements.

SMITH, ORVILLE A. - (Lt. 1, Blk. 74, Sec. 1) ts. Dec.
24, 1901-Feb. 16, 1981. Funeral for Orville A. Smith,
79, Deerfield, was held at 2 p.m. Monday at Deerfield
Methodist Church, the Rev. Harry Walz officiating.
Burial in Deerfield Cemetery.
  Mr. Smith died Thursday, February 12, 1981, in St.
Catherine Hospital, Garden City.
  Born Dec. 24, 1901, in Cedar Vale, he married Myrtle
Goodwin. His wife survives. Other survivors are several
nieces and nephews.
  Mr. Smith farmed and worked at alfalfa plants and later
was janitor for Deerfield schools. A resident of
Deerfield most of his life, he had been living at Briar
Hill Manor, Garden City, since 1978.
  He was a member of Deerfield Methodist Church and
Masonic Lodge.

SMITH, SAMUEL L. - (N/2 Lt. 2, Blk. 33, Sec. 3) ts.
8-16-1885-2-26-1953. Born Sept. 26, 1886, at Chase, Ks.

DEERFIELD CEMETERY

Died Feb. 16, 1953, age 66 years, 4 months, and 10 days. He hadn't lived in this area for years.

SMITH, WILLIAM ALLISON - (Lt. 2, Blk. 74, Sec. 1) ts. June 28, 1886-May 28, 1925. Another of America's one hundred per cent men and fine citizen fell asleep on the morning of May 28th, 1925, in Lewis, Kansas. William Allison Smith, a son of Mr. and Mrs. J. A. Smith of Deerfield, Kansas, entered upon that sleep from which none awaken until they are called by the voice of Him who has taken the sting out of death and made it but sleep for all those who fall in Him.

Brother Smith was born at Fairview, Illinois, June 29th, 1888, thus making him only 38 years, 10 months and 29 days of age at the date of his death. As in many other like cases, we are apt to wonder why such a citizen as William Allison Smith, a man so cheerful in disposition, a good musician, a man who was a friend to all, and to whom all who made his acquaintance were friends, was taken just in the prime of life, and on such short notice. But when we remember that God doeth all things well, knowing far better than we what is best, we uncover our heads, and, though it seems hard for us to part with such a friend, we say, "Thy will, not ours, be done."

Mr. Smith came to Sedgwick County, Kansas, with his parents from his birthplace at Fairview, Illinois, in June 1887, and lived there until 1907, when the family came to west Finney County, where they resided for one and one half years, then removing to Deerfield in Kearny County.

He was dedicated to God in Holy Baptism by his parents in infancy, and so became a preparatory member of the M. E. church, which was the church of his parents' choice.

He was also a member of the following organizations: the Organization of Railroad Telegraphers, and the Hunters Club of Deerfield, Kansas. He was a lover of outdoor sports and spent many delightful hours in hunting with his friends who enjoyed the same. He has been engaged in Santa Fe service since July 29th, 1918, at the following places: Halstead, Mission, Belpre, and Lewis.

He was indeed a good musician, and was for some time a member of the orchestra of the M. E. Church of Deerfield.

It is indeed gratifying to the relatives, since he must go, that he did not suffer long. He performed his regular duties as night operator at the station the night of the 27th, and returned to his room at the residence of F. B. Newton complaining with a pain in his chest. The doctor was called, but death came before he arrived. Heart failure is given as the cause of death.

He leaves his father, mother, three brothers, one sister, two nieces, and one nephew, besides a host of friends to mourn his loss. The names of the brothers and sister are Lewis M. Smith of El Modena, California; Ira D. of Pierceville, Kansas; Mrs. Maggie Kersten of Deerfield, Kansas; and Orville A. Smith of Deerfield. All of these were at the funeral except Lewis M. of El Modena, California.

The number of his friends could easily be judged by the amount of flowers, which were very beautiful, and the attendance at the funeral, it being the largest crowd ever seen at a funeral in Deerfield.

The funeral services were conducted by the pastor of the M. E. Church, Deerfield, Rev. Robert L. Foster, at 2:00 o'clock Sunday afternoon, May 31, and the body lain to rest in the Deerfield Cemetery. Farewell, dear friend, we will meet you in the morning.

SMITH, WILLIAM ROBERT - (Lt. 3, Blk. 45, Sec. 3) William R. (Bob) Smith, 83, 602 E. Santa Fe, Garden City, died April 6, 1967, at St. Catherine Hospital. He had been in failing health for the past year. He was a retired water well driller.

Born May 13, 1883, in Chase County, Mr. Smith homesteaded south of Kendall in 1915. He married Ethel Crawford, April 9, 1931, in Dodge City, and for a number of years they farmed northwest of Holcomb, moving to Garden City in 1941. He worked here for Henkle Drilling Co. and for Swearengen Drilling Co., retiring in 1953 due to poor eyesight.

He was a member of the Assembly of God Church.

Surviving are the widow; three sons, William Lee, 707 Garden City Ave., Garden City, Elmer Ray, 309 Emerson, Garden City, and Theodore H., Ticonderoga, N.Y.; two daughters, Mrs. Faye Williamson, 710 Summitt, and Mrs. Edith Anderson, 207 S. 8th, Garden City; two stepsons, Donald Crawford, Alliance, Ohio, and Harvey Crawford, Okla. City, Okla.; a step-daughter, Mrs. Lucy Ann Romans, Hawaii; a brother, Arthur Smith, Rosamond, Calif.; 38 grandchildren; 42 great grandchildren; and 9 step grandchildren.

DEERFIELD CEMETERY

Funeral was held at 2 p.m. Monday at the Garnand Funeral Chapel, the Rev. Paul Bryant officiating. Burial at the Deerfield Cemetery.

SMYTH, MARTHA MERRCUIA – (Lt. 1, Blk. 83, Sec. 1)   Died at Dodge City, age 67, buried Aug. 25, 1927.

SMYTH, MATTHEW – (Lt. 1, Blk. 83, Sec. 1)   Mathew Smyth passed away last Thursday, August 15, 1935, at the county hospital. He was 77 years and 16 days old. Mr. Smyth formerly lived near Deerfield, and burial was made Friday in the Deerfield Cemetery beside his wife, who preceded him in death.
He was born July 29, 1858, at Lancaster, Mo. Wife Martha Smyth, parents Robert J. and Ellen Mary (Frazer) Smyth, both born in Ireland.

SOWER, FRED MARION – (Lt. 2, Blk. 48, Sec. 2)   ts. 4-30-1859 11-24-1937. Born April 30, 1859, at Ottumwa, Iowa, son of William Sower. Came to Kearny County in 1886, married in 1884, to Louise Virginia McCracken. Died Nov. 23, 1937, at the Kearny County Hospital.
(The Kearny County Advocate, Nov. 26, 1937) Fred Sower died Tuesday night after a short illness. He was brought to the hospital last week and his family summoned when the seriousness of his illness became apparent.
(The Kearny County Advocate, Dec. 10, 1937) Frederick M. Sower was born at Ottumwa, Iowa, on April 30, 1859, and departed this life at Lakin, Kansas, on November 23, 1937, at 8:00 o'clock. He had attained the age of 78 years, 6 months and 23 days. He came to Kansas in his young manhood and has lived in the vicinity of Deerfield since 1885.
On February 27, 1884, he was united in marriage to Louise Virginia McCracken, who died November 10, 1910. On December 4, 1913, he was united in marriage to Nettie Thompson. He leaves his wife, Mrs. Sower of Deerfield, his son, Jas. W. Sower of Bayfield, Colorado; seven grandchidren, Floyd, Ned, Fred, Cecil, Kenneth, Milton and Shirley Jo Sower; three great grandchildren, Jean, Vern and Jimmie Wayne Sower; three step-sons Frank, Arthur and Harry Thompson; and three step-daughters, Mae Kell, Carrie Bond and Rose Martin.
Mr. Sower was an active member of the Masonic Lodge and the O.E.S. and a worker for community enterprise. He will be missed as a good neighbor and friend. Through

the pioneer days Mr. Sower made his contribution to the great west. Today his many friends and acquaintances join the family in their grief.

Funeral services were conducted from the Deerfield Methodist Church, Thursday, November 25, at 3:00 pm. His six grandsons, all brothers, served as pall bearers. Rev. Glenn W. Palmer, pastor of the church, was in charge. Masonic rites were performed at the grave.

SOWER, LOUISA VIRGINIA - (Lt. 2, Blk. 48, Sec. 2) (Lakin Investigator, Nov. 18, 1910) After suffering intensely for many weeks, Mrs. Fred M. Sower passed away at her home in Deerfield, November 10, 1910, at 4:45 p.m.

Mrs. Louisa Virginia Sower, whose maiden name was McCrocken, was born in Geneso, Il., October 13, 1860; married to Fred M. Sower, February 27, 1884, at Griswold, Cart County, Iowa; moved to western Kansas in 1885. Two children blessed this union, William Wood, who died at the age of two years and six months, and James Wayne, who survives.

The deceased was a member of the Presbyterian Church uniting with the church in early life. Mrs. Sower was a great sufferer, but bore it all patiently, and death came as a gracious relief, sitting on the couch talking to her husband when death called, and she passed quietly away with out a seeming struggle.

The funeral service was held at the residence, conducted by Rev. Robinson, and the remains laid to rest in Deerfield. Husband and son have the heartfelt sympathy of their many friends.

STARK, JULIAN - (The Lakin Investigator, May 15, 1908) On the morning of April 30, 1908, five miles north of Deerfield, Kans., a stranger that was traveling on foot going west, his destination being the mines of Colorado, died suddenly at the place where he had stayed all night. In the morning, after breakfast, he went to the water closet, and, not returning as soon as the family thought he should, they went to investigate and found him dead. He stayed two nights at John Maier's and complained of stomach trouble. On Saturday he came to the place where he died. The writer of this together with several of the neighbors laid the remains in the Deerfield Cemetery. It was ascertained by papers found on his person, that his name was Julian Stark, of Lexington, Mo., and that he has a brother living in Mallory, Okla. He was about 60 years

DEERFIELD CEMETERY

of age, medium height, and chin-whiskers, slightly gray.
He was a Russian, having been in this country for about
fifteen years. He had with him a few clothes, a pocket
knife and a pocket book containing 52 cts. His friends
were notified of his death.

STEENIS, DALLAS E. - (Lt. 1, Blk. 82, Sec. 1) Dallas E.
Steenis, 57, longtime Deerfield farmer, stockman and
civic leader, died last Friday night, August 14, 1970, at
th K.U. Medical Center, following a short illness.
   Dal was born November 4, 1912, at Creston, Nebr. He
moved to the Deerfield community in 1928 from Nebraska.
He married Ethel Zrubek at Garden City on April 18, 1944.
   He was a member of the United Methodist Church,
Deerfield; Lakin V.F.W.; SW Irrigation Asso., Kansas
Wheat Grower's Association, Deerfield Grange 1925, and a
W.W. II veteran of the Air Force.
   He is survived by his widow, two daughters; Miss Betty
Steenis of the home; Mrs. Marilyn Sue Morgan, Hugoton; a
sister, Mrs. Dale E. Goddard, Wichita; his mother, Mrs.
Ethel Steenis, Lakin; and two grandchildren. Two
brothers preceded him in death.
   Funeral services were held at the Deerfield Methodist
Church, Rev. Charles Hadley officiating. Burial was in
the Deerfield Cemetery.

STEENIS, DENNIS A. - (Lt. 4, Blk. 74, Sec. 1) Dennis A.
Steenis born Jan. 6, 1856, at Appleton, Wisc. Died Jan.
28, 1940, at Deerfield farm home of myocarditis.
   (The Garden City Telegram, Monday, Jan. 29, 1940)
Dennis A. Steenis, who had lived for approximately 26
years in the Deerfield community, died at his home 3
miles North of Deerfield, Sunday evening, Jan. 28, 1940.
   He is survived by three sons and one daughter, Jack J.
Steenis, Richard Steenis and Mrs. Josephine Steward, all
of Deerfield and James Steenis, Hartford, Kansas.
   Funeral services were held Wednesday afternoon at the
Methodist Church in Deerfield. Burial in the Deerfield
Cemetery. Rev. Ira O. Woolard in charge of the services.

STEENIS, EDITH SARAH - (Lt. 3, Bl, 75, Sec. 1) Mrs.
Edith Steenis, 88, died Monday, February 25, 1974, at
Kearny County Hospital.
   Born Sept 17, 1885, at Emporia, she was married to Jack
Steenis, Jan. 2, 1907, at Hartford. He died in 1957.

255

DEERFIELD CEMETERY

The Steenises came to Kearny County in 1913 and moved to Oregon in 1946. She returned to Lakin in October 1971, and was residing at Lakin Manor. Mrs. Steenis was a member of Deerfield United Methodist Church and of Deerfield Grange. Survivors include three daughters, Mrs. Hazel Shriver and Mrs. Josephine Walker, both of Deerfield, and Mrs. Rowena Urie, Redmond, Ore.; seven grandchildren; and 19 great grandchildren. Funeral was held at the Deerfield United Methodist Church, the Rev. Charles Hadley officiating. Burial in Deerfield Cemetery.

STEENIS, EDWARD W. - (Lt. 1, Blk. 82, Sec. 1) On February 13, 1945, Edward W. Steenis passed away at a Garden City hospital, after a short illness. Although he had been in poor health for many years, he was always industrious, and willing to help his neighbors and friends.
"Eddie" was born on May 16, 1884, at Creston, Nebraska, where he grew to manhood. He and Ethel Newman were married at Columbus, Nebraska, on March 13, 1906. To this union were born four children: Doris Goddard of Garden City; Dallas Steenis of Deerfield; and two sons who preceded their father in death.
Eddie worked as a rural mail carrier for ten years, later managing a lumber, coal and grain company. In 1928, the family moved to Deerfield where he was occupied in the oil business, later in farming and livestock raising. His greatest interest, however, was always in his two children, whom he helped and counseled in all their undertakings.
He was united with the church in 1914, later transferring his membership to the Methodist Church at Deerfield.
He is survived by his wife, two children, and his mother, Mrs. C. C. Chase, of Denver, Colorado.

STEENIS, ETHEL S. - (Lt. 1, Blk. 82, Sec. 1) Funeral for long time Deerfield resident Mrs. Ethel Steenis, 88, was held Tuesday at Deerfield United Methodist Church, Dr. Ruben Reyes officiating. Burial in Deerfield Cemetery.
Mrs. Steenis died Saturday, Dec. 11, 1976, at River View Manor, Oxford. Born Feb. 27, 1888, in Ainsworth, Neb., in early childhood she moved with her parents to a farm near Portland, Oreg., where they lived until she was

12 years of age. After her father's death in Oregon, the family moved to Creston, Neb., where she attended school. On March 16, 1906, she married Edward Steenis at Columbus, Neb. He died in February of 1945. Mrs. Steenis had lived in Deerfield since 1929.

A member of the Deerfield Methodist Church, Mrs. Steenis had been active in Methodist church work since 1904. She worked with the church women's association.

Mrs. Steenis suffered a stroke in December 1961, and was hospitalized three months in Garden City. She was taken to Lakin Manor at Lakin and lived there until its closing in July 1976. At that time she moved to River View Manor, Oxford.

Survivors include a daughter, Mrs. Dale F. (Doris) Goddard, Wichita; a sister, Mrs. Olga Pollock, Arnold, Calif.; four grandchildren; and eight great grandchildren. A son, Dal, died in August 1970, and two sons died in infancy.

STEENIS, JOHN JOHN (Jack) – (Lt. 3, Blk. 75, Sec. 1) Funeral services for John J. Steenis, longtime rural resident of the Deerfield community, was held Tuesday at 2:30 p.m. MST, in the Deerfield Methodist Church. He was 75.

Mr. Steenis died Saturday, September 21, 1957, in the Lakin hospital following a long illness. Since 1947 he has lived in Redmond, Ore.

He was born at Menasha, Wisc., Dec. 16, 1882. In 1911 he moved to Garden City and then two years later to a farm north of Deerfield. He had been retired for the past seventeen years.

Mr. Steenis had been visiting his family in the Deerfield community since mid-summer. He was a member of the Deerfield Masonic Lodge and a charter member of the Deerfield Grange.

Surviving are his wife, Edith; three daughters, Mrs. Oliver Shriver and Mrs. Carl Jones, both of Deerfield, and Mrs. Albert Urie of Redmond; a brother, Richard Steenis of Wadsworth; a sister, Mrs. Samuel Bowman of Deerfield; 7 grandchildren and 4 great grandchildren.

Services were in charge of the Rev. Robert Fleenor. Burial in Deerfield Cemetery. Phillips was in charge of arrangements.

STEENIS, KATIE – (Lt. 4, Blk. 74, Sec. 1) Katie Toennessen Steenis was born June 19, 1860, in Milwaukee,

Wisconsin, and passed away at her home north of Deerfield, Kansas, October 18, 1941, at the age of 81 years and 4 months.

She moved from Milwaukee with her parents to Menasha, Wisconsin, where she grew to womanhood. She was confirmed in the Catholic Church and remained in this faith to the time of her death. She was married in the Catholic Church to Dennis A. Steenis, October 13, 1880. This happy union lasted more than 59 years. To this union five children were born, three sons and two daughters.

In 1888 they moved to Nebraska, residing there until 1906, when they moved to Hartford, Kansas, where they lived for five years, moving then to their home north of Deerfield where they have lived the past 30 years.

She is survived by one daughter, Josephine Steward of the home; three sons, Jack and Richard of the home community and Leonard of Hartford, Kansas; two sisters, Mrs. Susie Stilp and Mrs. Anna Laemmerich; one brother, John Toennessen, all of Menasha, Wisconsin.

She leaves also six granddaughters, two grandsons, and twelve great grandchildren. One daughter, Cora Maye Erwin, and her husband preceded her in death.

Mrs. Steenis in her quiet, unassuming way and manner was a faithful wife, a true mother, and a loyal friend to all. A woman who was truly loved in her home and community, being always Christlike in her life.

Her funeral was held from the Methodist Church in Deerfield, the pastor, Rev. Woolard, in charge.

STENNER, IVAN - (Lt. 2, Blk. 83, Sec. 1) Ruth and Harold Purdy received word that their son-in-law, Ivan Stenner of Salina, had passed away Sunday, December 29, 1991, at Asbury Hospital in Salina. He married Rhonda Purdy in 1978 and she survives him. Ivan was born in Wisconsin in 1932. He was a member of the Emmanuel Four Square Gospel Church of Salina. The funeral was held at the church December 31, with the pastor, Loren Houltbert officiating and interment was at the Deerfield Cemetery.

STEWARD, GLENN E. - (Lt. 3, Blk. 75, Sec. 1) Glen E. Steward, 68, a resident of Deerfield for many years, died suddenly Monday afternoon, Oct. 26, 1952, in the Kearny County Hospital at Lakin. Death was attributed to a cerebral hemorrhage.

Glen was striken while walking along the street in Deerfield, Monday morning. He was rushed to the hospital at Lakin, but lived only a few hours.
Steward was born September 17, 1884, at Greeley, Kansas. He had been a resident of the Deerfield community for nearly 40 years.
He was a retired farmer. He is survived by his wife, Dolly, of the home; one daughter, Mrs. Donald Burden and one son, Denny, both of Deerfield; a nephew, Don Irwin, also of Deerfield; and four grandchildren.
Funeral services were held at Deerfield, Thursday at 2:30 p.m. Masonic services were held at the graveside in the Deerfield Cemetery.
Glenn E. Steward was born at Greeley, Kansas, on September 17, 1884, the youngest child of Andrew J. and Mary E. Steward; and passed away at Lakin, Kansas, October 27, 1952.
After the death of his parents, which occurred when he was four years old, Glenn was reared in the home of an aunt and uncle, Mr. and Mrs. W. A. Pease of Hartford, Kansas. He spent his childhood and young manhood in this vicinity.
Glenn was married to Josephine Steenis on March 1, 1910, and moved with his family to Deerfield one year later. He resided here until his death, with the exception of one year spent at Woodburn, Oregon. Glenn gave liberally of his time and means to his community, having served on the board of education, as county committeeman of the Triple A, Kearny County Hospital board, and was serving on the Deerfield City Council at the time of his death.
He was a member of the Deerfield Methodist Church; also a faithful member of the Deerfield Grange and Deerfield Masonic Lodge and the Order of the Eastern Star.
He is survived by his wife, Josephine; two children, Carol Steward Burden of Lakin,, Kansas, and Dennis Steward of Deerfield, also Don Erwin of the home who was raised as a son; four grandchildren, Dolores Steward, and Judy, Jimmy and Jerry Burden; one sister, Mrs. Earl Thompson of Lubbock, Texas, and other relatives and a host of friends.

STEWART, RAYMOND B. - (Lt. 2, Blk. 77, Sec. 1) Born in 1910 and died in 1928.

DEERFIELD CEMETERY

STULLKEN, ETHEL H. - (Lt. 3, Blk. 23, Sec. 2) Ethel H. Stullken was born October 27, 1889, near Kinross, Iowa, and passed away Feb. 7, 1965. She was the daughter of Mr. and Mrs. G. B. Martin. On May 25, 1944, she was married to Ed H. Stullken, who passed away on March 17, 1952. She is survived by one daughter, Mrs. Evalyn Hannagan of Manhattan, Kans., and two stepsons, Ralph D. of Sand Springs, Okla., and Everett of Guymon, Okla.; one brother, Ernest C. Martin of Garden City and one sister, Mrs. Leita Netser of Kinross, Iowa; four grandchildren and six great grandchildren, and a number of nieces and nephews of whom she has been very fond.
    Mrs. Stullken was a member of the Presbyterian Church, VFW Auxiliary, Lakin Woman's Club, Green Thumb Garden Club of Deerfield, charter member of the LaFlora Club of Lakin and member of a hobby club which she helped to organize.
    Services were held Tuesday morning, Feb. 9, with Rev. Sid Raymond in charge. Burial was in the Deerfield Cemetery.

SUTTON, EARL F. - (Lt. 4, Blk. 45, Sec. 3) ts. 1891-1967.   Earl Franklin Sutton, 77, Truth or Consequences, N.M., died Monday, January 30, 1967, at his home after an eight weeks illness.
    Born June 3, 1889, in Missouri, he had been retired as a Santa Fe Trailways Truck Driver after 20 years of service.
    He was a member of the Christian Church.
    Surviving are his wife, Margaret, of the home; one son, Roy Sutton, North Platte, Neb., formerly of Garden City; three daughters, Mrs. Lola F. Welch, formerly of Garden City, and Mrs. Edith Fuller, both of Hutchinson, and Mrs. Lesta Holmes, Castle Rock, Colo.; a sister, Mrs. Alice Link, Lyons; 7 grandchildren; and 3 great grandchildren.
    Funeral was at 2 p.m. at the Phillips-White Funeral Home, with the Rev. E. P. Roger officiating. Burial at the Deerfield Cemetery.

SUTTON, ERNEST F. - (Lt. 4, Blk. 45, Sec. 3) Fourth degree manslaughter charges were filed against a Scott City man Friday in the death of Ernest S. Sutton, 40, Garden City, following a fist fight Thursday night.
    Archie Lee Sickelbauer waived preliminary hearing in Finney County Court, Friday, and was bound over to district court for trial on a $1500 bond.

DEERFIELD CEMETERY

Acting Police Chief Richard Rohleber quoted Sickelbauer as saying that he struck Sutton during a fight at the Walter Foreman home in Garden City. The officer said the men apparently had been drinking and got into an argument. Sickelbauer claimed he used only his fists. Three other men attending the party were witnesses. They were Fred Frisby, Lakin; Robert Rivenburg, Garden City and Foreman.

Rohleber said the exact cause of death has not yet been determined.

The fight occurred around 7:45 p.m. Thursday, August 2, 1962. Sutton was dead when officers arrived at the house a short time later.

Sutton had lived in Garden City 20 years. He was a truck driver.

He was born March 19, 1922, at Greensburg. He was a veteran of World War II, serving in the Marine Corps, and was a member of the John J. Haskell VFW Post No. 2279 at Garden City.

Survivors include his mother, Mrs. Stella Meyer, Garden City; his father, Earl F. Sutton, Great Bend; a brother, Roy R., Great Bend; three sisters, Mrs. Lola Welch and Mrs. Edith Fuller, Hutchinson, and Mrs. Lesta Lou Holmes, Castle Rock, Colo.

Funeral was held at 1:30 p.m. Monday in the Phillips Funeral Home in Garden City. Rev. Arthur F. Fleming officiating with burial in the Deerfield Cemetery.

SUTTON, ESTHER JOAN FULTON - (Lt. 1, Blk. 70, Sec. 4) Mrs. Esther Jean Sutton, 43, former resident of Deerfield, died Sunday, July 7, 1974, at Mercy Hospital, Denver, following a long illness.

She was born August 1, 1930, and was married to John Roarks Sutton, April 16, 1953, at Deerfield. She was a resident of the Denver area prior to her move to Aurora, Colo., where she had lived three years.

She was a member of the First United Methodist Church, Aurora, and is a graduate of the University of Denver.

Surviving are the widower, a son, Jon F., of the home; her mother, Mrs. Ester O. Fulton, Deerfield; two brothers, Robert Fulton, Deerfield, and James Fulton, Springfield, Mo.; and two sisters, Mrs. Mary Lois Smith, Liberal, and Mrs. Faith Landon, Deerfield.

A son and a daughter preceded her in death.

DEERFIELD CEMETERY

SUTTON, ROY R. - (Lt. 4, Blk. 45, Sec. 3)   Graveside
service for Roy Robert Sutton, 70, formerly of Garden
City, was held at Deerfield Cemetery, Deerfield, with the
Rev. Leroy Smoot officiating.
    Mr. Sutton, of Hutchinson, died March 9, 1996, at
Silver Oak Health Center, Hutchinson.
    He was born May 15, 1925, at Greensburg, the son of
Earl Franklin and Stella S. Meyers Sutton.
    A Hutchinson resident since 1993, formerly of Garden
City and Topeka, Mr. Sutton was a retired employee of
Meyers Cream Dairy, Garden City.
    He is survived by a son, Robert L., Garden City; and a
sister, Lesta L. Holmes, Westcliffe, Colo.
    Elliott Mortuary, Hutchinson, is in charge of
arrangements.

SWORDS, LINNA FAYE - (Lt. 4, Blk. 63, Sec. 3)   Funeral
service for Linna Faye Swords, 84, Lakin, was held
Tuesday at Church of Jesus Christ of Latter Day Saints,
Garden City, President Errol Burns officiating.   Burial
in Deerfied Cemetery.
    She died Feb. 19, 1988, at High Plains Retirement
Village, Lakin.
    Born Linna Faye Henebergh, August 1, 1903, at Kendall,
she married Ralph Joseph Swords, July 6, 1919, at
Syracuse. He died Aug. 2, 1959.
    Mrs. Swords was a homemaker and had been a Lakin
resident, moving from Garden City. She attended early
schooling at Kendall until she was married. She lived in
Syracuse until 1942, moving to Deerfield where she
operated the Corner Grocery until 1959. She then moved
to Phoenix, Ariz., for three years. She later moved to
Garden City in 1977.
    She was a member of Church of Jesus Christ of Latter
Day Saints, Daughters of American Revolution, Royal
Neighbors of America, Relief Society of the Church,
Genealogical Society, all of Garden City, and Garden
Club, Deerfield.
    Survivors include two sons, Dr. Ralph (Sonny) Swords,
Garden City, and Garry Swords, Ozawkie, Ks.; seven
daughters, Leatrice Shaw, Garden City, Alameda Barnett,
Olathe, Rosemary Shipley, New Plymouth, Idaho, Barbara
Ann Jones, Deerfield, Martha Baber, Oklahoma City, Peggy
Maddux, Russell, and Kay Menhusen, Anthony; 24
grandchildren; and 13 great grandchildren.
    Garnand Funeral Home was in charge of arrangements.

DEERFIELD CEMETERY

SWORDS, RALPH JOSEPH - (Lt. 4, Blk. 63, Sec. 3) Ralph J.
Swords, life long resident of Hamilton and Kearny county,
first born of William J. and Rose May (Else) Swords, was
born at Syracuse, Kansas, Feb. 19, 1899, and departed
this life Aug. 2, 1959, at the Kearny County Hospital,
Lakin.
On July 6, 1919, he was united in marriage to Linna
Faye Henebergh and to this union was born ten children,
three sons and seven daughters.
He is survived by his wife, Linna Faye; daughters:
Leatrice Shaw, Garden City, Kans., Alameda Barnett,
Shawnee, Kans., Rosemary Shipley, St. Ann, Mo., Barbara
Ann Jones, Deerfield, Kans., Martha Faye Swords, Oklahoma
City, Okla.; William, Ralph Jr., Peggy, Kaye and Garry
Lynn of the home. His mother, Rose May Swords, Ottawa,
Kans.; one brother, Steven R. Swords, Mound City, Mo.;
two sisters, Mrs. Clifford Hobbs and Miss Martha Swords,
Ottawa, Kans. Four grandsons, four granddaughters, one
niece, one nephew and many other relatives and friends.
He had been a member of the First Christian Church of
Syracuse, for 34 years, and attended schools in Syracuse
and Kendall.
He worked many years for the Santa Fe railroad as call
boy, warehouse clerk and yard switchman. Later he was
employed as district clerk of the State Highway
department for two years. He also engaged in farming.
On November 16, 1942, he purchased the Corner Grocer,
Deerfield, Kans., and moved his family from Syracuse in
June 1943.
He has served his community in many ways including the
Deerfield City council and Deerfield high school board of
education.
He was a loyal friend, a faithful husband, a devoted
father.
        May there be green pastures waiting,
            And some whitefaced cattle too;
        May the horses you love be at the gate
            To greet you as you pass through.

SWORDS, WILLIAM ADOLPHUS - (Lt. 4, Blk. 63, Sec. 3) Born
August 29, 1926, at Syracuse, Ks., and died Nov. 11,
1972, at Garden City, Ks. Son of Ralph Sr. and Linna
Faye (Henebergh) Swords. Veteran of U.S. Navy in WWII.
William A. Swords, 46, Deerfield, died unexpectedly
Saturday night, Nov. 11, 1972, at St. Catherine Hospital,

DEERFIELD CEMETERY

Garden City, after an apparent heart attack. He was owner of the Corner Grocery in Deerfield.

Born Aug. 29, 1926, in Syraucse, he had been a resident of Deerfield since 1942. He was a member of the Christian Church, Syracuse, the VFW, and Associated Grocers. Survivors include his mother, Mrs. Faye Swords, Deerfield; two brothers, Dr. Ralph Swords, 603 E. Edwards, Garden City, and Garry Swords, Deerfield; 7 sisters, Mrs. Martha Babe, Oklahoma City, Okla., Mrs. Leatrice Shaw, 1610 Jan, Garden City, Mrs. Alameda Barnett, Overland Park, Mrs. Rosemary Shipley, Bridgeton, Mo., Mrs. Barbara Jones, Deerfield, Peggy Swords, Arkansas City, and Mrs. Kaye Menhusen, Stafford.

Funeral was held Wednesday at the United Methodist Church, Deerfield, the Rev. Charles Hadley officiating. Burial in Deerfield Cemetery.

DEERFIELD CEMETERY

TABOR, CHESTER LLOYD - (Lt. 3, Blk. 102, Sec. 1) Chester Lloyd Tabor, 50, 1118 N. 12th, Garden City, died January 26, 1973, at his home of a self-inflicted gunshot wound. Born Nov. 20, 1922, at Springfield, Colo., Mr. Tabor moved from Gray County to a farm northeast of Holcomb with his parents. The family moved to Oregon and then back to Garden City, and had lived in this area for about 40 years.
Mr. Tabor was a retired pipeline construction worker. Survivors include his father, George E. Tabor, Garden City and a sister, Mrs. Pauline Johnson, Deerfield. Funeral was held at the Garnand Funeral Chapel, the Rev. Ron Van Hee officiating. Burial in Deerfield Cemetery.

TABOR, GEORGE ELMER - (Lt. 3, Blk. 102, Sec. 1) Funeral for George Elmer Tabor was Tuesday afternoon at the Fellowship Baptist Church. Burial was in Deerfield Cemetery with military rites.
Mr. Tabor, 82, formerly of 1118 N. 12, Garden City, died Sunday, April 1, 1979, at Briar Hill Manor.
Born on April 8, 1896, in Jacksboro, Texas, he married Mildred Kitch on Dec. 22, 1921, at Springfield, Colo. She died on Aug. 19, 1970.
Mr. Tabor was a retired farmer, having farmed for 23 years in the Holcomb area. He was a member of the Fellowship Baptist Church and served in the army in World War I.
Survivors include a daughter, Mrs. Pauline Johnson, Deerfield; four brothers, Theodore, Garden City, Alvie, Merced, Calif., Curt, Delta, Colo., and Woody, Sioux City, Iowa; and three sisters, Mrs. Ruby Mason, Springfield, Colo., and Mrs. Blanche Walker and Mrs. Linnie Hartman, both of Sioux City, Iowa.
One son, Lloyd, preceded him in death in January 1973.
Garnand Funeral Home was in charge of arrangements.

TABOR, MILDRED L. - (Lt. 3, Blk. 102, Sec. 1) ts. 1901-1970. Mrs. Mildred L. Tabor, 67, died Wednesday morning, Aug. 19, 1970, at St. Catherine Hospital, Garden City, after a short illness.
Born Oct. 2, 1902, at Abbyville, she was married to George E. Tabor, Dec. 22, 1921, at Springfield, Colo. She had lived in this area for about 49 years.
She was a member of the Fellowship Baptist Church.

DEERFIELD CEMETERY

Survivors include the widower, Lakin; son, Chester Lloyd, Garden City; daughter, Mrs. Pauline Johnson, Deerfield; brothers, Fred N. Kitch, Arkansas City, Kans., Frank T. Kitch, Garden City; sister, Mrs. J. S. Warden, Oregon City, Ore.

Funeral was held at the church; Rev. Paul Lackore. Burial was in the Deerfied Cemetery, Deerfield.

TACKETT, BENJAMIN F. - (Lt. 2, Blk. 31, Sec. 2) Benjamin F. Tackett, 70, died Jan. 6, 1966, at the Sabo Park Manor Nursing Home, Lakin, after a 4 1/2 year illness.

He was born Aug. 4, 1886, at Stockton, Mo., and married Myrtle Bechtel, April 19, 1907, at Stockton.

They moved to Kearny County near Deerfield in 1915 where he worked as a fieldman for the Great Western Sugar Co. He started farming for himself when the company began renting land and farmed until his retirement in 1950.

Mr. Tackett, who was preceded in death by two sons, was a member of the Deerfield Masonic Lodge.

Survivors include the widow, Mrytle, Deerfield; three sons, Earl, Joe and Lloyd, all of Deerfield; 11 grandchildren and 7 great grandchildren.

Funeral was at the Garnand Funeral Chapel with the Rev. Wesley Davis officiating. Burial was in the Deerfield Cemetery.

TACKETT, EARL - (Lt. 3, Blk. 31, Sec. 2) Funeral for Earl Tackett, 56, Deerfield, was held Tuesday at the Deerfield Methodist Church with the Rev. Wesley Davis officiating. Burial was in the Deerfield Cemetery.

Mr. Tackett died Saturday evening, Dec. 3, 1966, at St. Catherine Hospital, Garden City, after a lengthy illness. Born Jan. 15, 1910, Stockton, Mo. He married Bessie Ellen Wells on May 15, 1932, at Lakin. He was a farmer and had been a resident of Deerfield since moving from Emporia in 1915.

He was a member of the Deerfield Methodist Church.

Surviving are the widow; two sons, Douglas of Garden City, and Stanley of Deerfield; a daughter, Myrtle, Deerfield; two brothers, Joe of Garden City, and Lloyd, Deerfield; his mother, Mrs. Myrtle Tackett, Deerfield; and six grandchildren. A son, Robert, preceded him in death in April 1965.

DEERFIELD CEMETERY

TACKETT, JOE EUGENE - (Lt. 2, Blk. 31, Sec. 2) Joe
Eugene Tackett, son of Benjamin Tackett and Myrtle
Bechtel Tackett, was born March 11, 1914, at Emporia,
Kansas. He died at the Kearny County Hospital, February
18, 1970, at the age of 55 years, 11 months, 7 days. He
had been a long time resident of Deerfield where he had
farmed.
He was a WWII veteran receiving an honorable discharge,
September 15, 1945. Citations and decorations received
were the Purple Heart, Service Medal, American Defense
Service Medal and Bronze Service Arrowhead.
Survivors are his mother, Mrs. Ben Tackett, and
brother, Lloyd, of Deerfield.
Graveside service was held at the Deerfield Cemetery
with VFW members of McAfee Stebens Post No. 6092 in
charge of the service. Chaplain B. C. Nash officiated.

TACKETT, JOSHUA - (Lt. 4, Blk. 69, Sec. 4) Graveside
services for Josh Tackett were held Friday, Feb. 13, at
the Deerfield Cemetery, Dr. Ruben Reyes officiating.
The son of Mr. and Mrs. Stanley Ray Tackett was
stillborn at St. Catherine's Hospital, Garden City,
Tuesday, February 10, 1976,
Survivors include his parents of Deerfield; and
grandparents, Opal R. Bryon, LaJunta, Colo, Dale L.
Bryon, Pritchett, Colo., and Mr. and Mrs. E. Stanley
Tackett, Deerfield; great grandparents are Mrs. Bessie
Tackett, Deerfield, and Mr. and Mrs. Harold Bell,
Deerfield; and great great grandmother Mrs. Myrtle
Tackett.

TACKETT, LLOYD L. - (S/2 Lt. 3, Blk. 36, Sec. 3)
Graveside service for Lloyd L. Tackett, 64, was at 11
a.m. Tuesday, at Deerfield Cemetery, the Rev. Austin
Herrman, St. Anthony Catholic Church, Lakin, officiating.
He died Saturday, July 27, 1985, at Kearny County
Hospital following a long illness.
Born March 28, 1921, at Deerfield, Mr. Tackett lived
here all his life. He was a farmer and a member of the
Eagles Lodge in Garden City.
Preceding him in death were his parents and four
brothers. Survivors include nieces and nephews.
Davis Funeral Home, Lakin, was in charge of
arrangements.

DEERFIELD CEMETERY

TACKETT, MYRTLE A. - (Lt. 2, Blk. 31, Sec. 2)   Mrs.
Myrtle A. Tackett, 92, died Sunday morning, Nov. 26,
1978, at Bob Wilson Memorial Hospital, Ulysses, following
a week long ilness.
   She had been a resident of the Western Prairie Nursing
Home in Ulysses for the past two and a half years.
   Born Sept. 5, 1886, at Stockton, Mo., she married Ben
F. Tackett on April 19, 1907, in Stockton. He died Jan.
8, 1966.
   Mrs. Tackett was a member of the Deerfield Baptist
Church and had been a resident of Deerfield for 63 years.
   Survivors include a son, Lloyd Tackett, Deerfield.
   Graveside services were held at 10 a.m. Tuesday at
Deerfield Cemetery, the Rev. Milan Lambertson
officiating.

TACKETT, ROBERT K. - (Lt. 3, Blk. 31, Sec. 2)   Funeral
services were held Wednesday afternoon for Robert K.
Tackett, 24, who died Sunday afternoon, April 25, 1965,
at St. Catherine Hospital in Garden City after an illness
of three months due to cancer.
   Services were held at the Deerfield Methodist Church
with the Rev. Wesley Davis officiating. Burial was in
Deerfield Cemetery.
   Bob was born at Lakin on Dec. 26, 1940, and lived in
Deerfield all of his life. He had been employed by the
Wakefield Drilling Company.
   Tackett married Judy Cox at Deerfield on April 5, 1963.
He was a member of the Deerfield Methodist Church and
served in the U.S. Navy as a machinist from 1958 through
1961.
   He had worked for the Kearny County Road Department for
1 and 1/2 years, and was also a former employee of Garden
City Coop.
   Survivors include the widow, Judy, of the home; a
daughter, Pamela Sue Ellen of the home; a sister, Myrtle
Tackett of Deerfield; two brothers, Earl Stanley of
Deerfield and D. Douglas of Garden City; his parents, Mr.
and Mrs. Earl Tackett of Deerfield, and his paternal
grandparents, Mr. and Mrs. Benjamin Tackett of Deerfield.

TACKETT, WILLARD G. - (Lt. 2, Blk. 31, Sec. 2)   Willard
Tackett was found dead Saturday morning a half mile north
of Deerfield where his car turned over at the turn of the
road. The body was some distance from the car where he
evidently had walked before he died from internal

DEERFIELD CEMETERY

injuries. A post mortem examination made Sunday morning
disclosed that his liver had burst, apparently as a
result of the accident.
Tackett was employed by Dan Ratzlaff and living on the
old Weber place south of the sand hills. His parents,
Mr. and Mrs. Ben Tackett, live a mile and half north of
Deerfield and he may have been on his way there when he
failed to make the turn and the fatal accident occurred,
early Saturday morning, between one o'clock and seven
o'clock. He was found by August Winter on his way to
Deerfield to open his barber shop.
Willard Gray Tackett, third son of Mr. and Mrs. Ben
Tackett, was born April 14, 1918, at Deerfield, Kansas.
Passed away July 26, 1941, at the age of 23 years, 3
months, and 12 days.
April 14, 1936, he was united in marriage at Lamar,
Colorado, to Wilma Newberry of Garden City, Kansas. To
this union were born two children, Anita Jean and William
Gerald.
Besides the wife, daughter, and son, he leaves to mourn
his going his father and mother, grandfather and
grandmother, three brothers, and other relatives and
friends.

THELEN, CATHERINE - (Lt. 3, Blk. 74, Sec. 1) ts.
1864-1932. (The Lakin Independent, January 15, 1932)
Katherine Feldman was born at Cole Camp, Missouri, July
7th, 1862, and passed to her reward on January 4th, 1932,
age 69 years, 5 months, and 27 days.
She grew to womanhood in Cole Camp and then took up her
residence at Kansas City, where she met William F.
Thelen, to whom she was united in marriage on December
9th, 1886. To this union were born eleven children, of
whom two died in infancy. The nine living to mourn the
loss of their mother are: Mrs. Mary Cody, Edwardsville,
Kansas, Jacoby H. Thelen, Webster, Kansas, Mrs. Maggie
Etchison, San Francisco, California, Mrs. Ruth Warren,
Beverly, Kansas, Mrs. Gusty Warden, Las Vegas, Nevada,
Mrs. Adelyne Bechtel, Deerfield, Mrs. Lily Magill,
Clarkdale, Arizona, Mrs. Rose Dickens, Deerfield, and
Matthew Thelen of Clementan, Arizona. There are
seventeen grandchildren and four great grandchildren.
She also leaves two sisters and one brother; her husband
having preceded her in death.
Mrs. Thelen was confirmed in the Lutheran Church when a
girl and held her membership in that church until 1915,

DEERFIELD CEMETERY

when she united with the Methodist Church at Deerfield. She was a faithful Christian woman, regular in her church attendance, and an inspiration to her family and friends.

THELEN, WILLIAM FREDERICK - (Lt 3, Blk. 74, Sec. 1) William Frederick Thelen was born in Genefus, Germany, November 13, 1850; passed away at his home December 9, 1926, at 5 o'clock, at the age of 76 years and 26 days.

For the last three years he suffered from a cancer and was confined to his bed since the twentieth of August.

He came to America with his parents when he was three years old. When his country was in war with the South, he was too young to enlist, but as soon as he was 21 he enlisted and served five years.

On December 9, 1886, he was united in marriage to Miss Katherine Feldman, being married forty years to the day. To this union eleven children were born, two dying in infancy. Those living are: Mrs. Mary Cody, Edwardsville, Kansas; Jacob Thelen, home address; Mrs. Margaret Etchison, Santa Monica, California; Mrs. Ruth Warren, Beverly, Kansas; Mrs. Gusty Warden, Los Angeles, California; Adelyne Thelen, home address; Mrs. Rose Purdy, home address; Mrs. Lily Magill, Clarksdale, Arizona; and Matthew Thelen of Cleamenseau, Arizona.

He also leaves to mourn his going one sister, Mrs. Mary Houston of Syracuse, New York, and one brother, Phil Thelen of Kansas City, thirteen grandchildren and many nieces and nephews, and a host of friends.

The funeral services were held at the home Sunday, December 12th, at 2 p.m., Rev. J. Q. Turner the pastor in charge. The body was laid to rest in the Deerfield Cemetery.

THOMAS, MAVIS A. - (Lt. 1, Blk, 24, Sec. 2) Mavis A. Thomas, 59, of Guthrie, Okla., died Thursday, Oct. 24, 1996, at Mercy Health Center, Oklahoma City.

Born at Lakin on Dec. 17, 1936, she was the daughter of A. M. and Maude Goodman Gillock.

She was a graduate of Panhandle State University at Goodwell, Okla., and had been a resident of Dodge City since 1979. She had worked at Bank of the Southwest, Dodge City, and had been a small business owner and a school teacher.

She married Jim Thomas in August 1993, at Dodge City, where they lived until moving to Guthrie in 1996.

270

DEERFIELD CEMETERY

Mrs. Thomas was a member of First Christian Church of
Dodge City and participated in the church choir, was a
member of Dodge City Round-Up, Christian Women's Club,
and served on the board of directors of Manhattan
Christian College and Dodge City Crisis Center.
She had been active in American Association of
University Women, Dodge City Women's Chamber of Commerce,
Dodge City Book Club, Soroptimist Club, Panhandle State
University Alumni Association and was a charter member of
the Boot Hill Association.
Survivors include her husband; two sons, Greg Jones,
Oklahoma City, and Sid Jones, Edmond, Okla.; two
daughters, Paula Scott, Edmond, and Hiedi Buss, Hunter,
Okla.; her mother, Deerfield, two brothers, Myron Gillock
and Gordon Gillock, both of Deerfield; a sister, Neva
Quakenbush, Garden City,; and eight grandchildren. She
was preceded in death by her father and a brother, Truman
Gillock.
Funeral was held Monday at First Christian Church,
Dodge City, with Larry Williams officiating. Committal
service at Deerfield Cemetery.

THOMSEN, ELINE KATRINE - (Lt. 2, Blk. 57, Sec. 2) Mrs.
Aline Catherine Thomsen, daughter of Christian and
Catherine Lassan, passed away at the Bailey Hospital at
Garden City, February 24th, 1933, after her last illness
of six days. She was taken sick Sunday and was operated
on in the afternoon and lived five days.. She was born
January 4, 1859, at Varda, Denmark, and died February 24,
1933. She was brought to Christ in her infancy through
the Sacrament of Baptism. In 1873 she renewed her
baptismal covenant by the rite of confirmation in the
Lutheran Church. She was united in Holy Wedlock to Hans
Thomsen in 1885. This union was blessed with six
children, two preceded her in death.
She leaves to mourn, her husband; one daughter in
Alberta, Canada; three sons, Carl, of Alamo, Texas,
Francis and Bryan of Deerfield; two sisters in Denmark,
one sister and brother in California; one sister in New
York; and one brother in Alaska; eleven grandchildren and
other relatives and friends.
Funeral services was conducted by Rev. Walter J. F.
Lebien, Sunday afternoon from the Lutheran Church and
interment was made in the Deerfield Cemetery.

271

THOMSEN, HANS - (Lt. 2, Blk. 57, Sec. 2) ts. inscription shows 1859-1938. Kearny County History shows born Aug. 23, 1857, at Varde, Denmark, and died June 21, 1938, at Wenatchee, Washington.

On June 21, 1938, Hans Thomsen of Deerfield passed away in Wenatchee, Washington, at the age of 79 years, 9 months, and 28 days. He was a member of the Lutheran Church and was born in Denmark. He leaves his three sons, Carl Thomsen of Alamo, Texas, who with his wife and family were in Wenatchee, Francis Thomsen of Deerfield, and Bryan Thomsen of Mansfield, Washington, and one daughter, Mrs. Mary Chaffin of Delburn, Alberta, Canada. There are ten grandchildren and six great grandchildren.

Funeral services were held Thursday afternoon at 2:00 in the Deerfield Methodist Church with Rev. Palmer in charge.

THOMPSON, THOMAS CHRISTIAN - (Lt. 2, Blk. 57, Sec. 2) ts. September 5, 1891-February 17, 1909. (The Lakin Investigator, Feb. 26, 1909) The community was saddened by the death, last week of Christian Thompson, whose parents live north of Deerfield, in the Knauston neighborhood. Pneumonia was the cause of his death, and he was only sick about a week. Mr. Lawson conducted the services at the house, and Rev. Kirkpatrick, of Garden City, conducted the services at the Deerfield Cemetery. The bereaved family have the sympathy of the entire community.

Son of H. & E. K. Thompson, born Sept 5, 1881, and died Feb. 17, 1909. Kearny County History shows born 1888.

TURNEY, INFANT - (Lt. 3, Blk. 31, Sec. 2) Infant son of R. H. and Mabel Turney, born May 2 and died May 3, 1911.

TURRENTINE, CHRISTOPHER AARON - (Lt. 4, Blk. 17, Sec. 3) Christopher Aaron Turrentine, 16, died June 19, 1994, at St Catherine Hospital, Garden City.

The son of Craig and Janice Grimsley Turrentine, he was born Dec. 3, 1977, at Garden City.

He was a member of the United Methodist Church, Deerfield. He belonged to band, pep band, student council and was a member of the football, track and basketball teams, all at Lakin High School. A lifetime Deerfield resident, he enjoyed weight lifting, music and sports.

DEERFIELD CEMETERY

Survivors include his parents, Deerfield; two brothers, James Turrentine and Dylan Turrentine, both of the home; a sister, Caitlin Turrentine, of the home; and grandparents, Bill and Phyllis Turrentine, Garden City, and Marie Grimsley, Satanta.

Funeral was held Thursday at the United Methodist Church, Deerfield, the Rev. Donald Koehn officiating. Burial at Deerfield Cemetery.

Three 16 year olds, Christopher Turrentine, Deerfield, Andria D. Rice and Jayme Jo Nelson, both of Lakin, were killed in a crash with a semi truck and trailer loaded with two combines. Driver of the semi, Jim Hauck, 25, Dickinson, N.D., was treated and released from St. Catherine Hospital.

Kansas Highway Patrol said Turrentine was eastbound on U.S. 50 highway. Rice and Nelson were passengers in the 1994 Chevrolet Suburban. Hauck was westbound in the semi, pulling the trailer and two combines. The patrol said the two vehicles collided near the center line. The Suburban came to rest facing north in the eastbound lane on the highway. The semi stopped facing west on the north shoulder. The patrol report, from Trooper Randy Mosher, did not mention whether any of those involved in the accident were wearing seat belts. The Suburban was demolished in the crash. The semi, a 1982 Freightliner, along with the trailer and combines, had a total of $10,000 damage.

McClain said the teens will be remembered as good students and citizens who were popular with their school mates. All three attended Lakin High School.

DEERFIELD CEMETERY

UNKNOWN - (The Lakin Investigator, June 15, 1901) Early Monday morning the body of a man was found near the railroad track at Deerfield. It was terribly mangled and the coroner decided that it was unnecessary to hold an inquest, as he had without doubt been crushed by the cars. There was no means by which identification was possible and the body was buried in the Deerfield Cemetery.

UNKNOWN - (Lt. 4, Blk. 56, Sec. 2) There are three unknown burials in this lot. One is probably Neva Onita Epps who died Sept. 28, 1920. Another one has a marker with a metal tag with the word "HEAD O. G. Lockard Funeral Director, Hope, Kansas". This one was moved from J. W. Wells lot in 1918 by Nash Funeral Home because Wilbur Wells was disturbed when it was discovered that this body was buried on his lot, probably in 1904. The Ladies Aid let them move this body to their lot.

UPHOFF, BARBARA DIENER - (Lt. 1, Blk. 25, Sec. 2) Barbara Diener was born August 1, 1870, at Joliet, Illinois. Soon after her birth, on August 28, she became a child of God through the Sacrament of Holy Baptism. After a few years she with her parents moved to Nebraska, where her parents sent her to school to receive a Christian education. She renewed her baptismal vow at her confirmation on May 17, 1885, at Meridian, Nebraska. At the age of 21, on October 6, 1891, she entered the estate of matrimony with Diedrich Uphoff at Gladstone, Nebraska. On December 22, 1892, she, with her husband and children, moved to Deerfield, Kansas. To this union 10 children were born: 6 sons, Carl J., Diedrich Paul, George Henry, August Henry, Leonhard Benhard, and Edwin Lewis; 4 daughters, Margaret Ida, Christina Anna, Viola Sophrona, and Odelia Amelia. Of these 2 sons preceded their mother into eternity, namely, Carl and Paul.

Our deceased sister was a faithful member of Imanuel Ev. Lutheran Church ever since she came to Deerfield. She was a diligent reader of God's Word and frequently communed with God in prayer. As soon as she was taken to the hospital she asked for the Bible and her prayerbook. Due to this I found it not difficult to comfort her during her last illness as she always loved to hear the Word of God read to her and she also asked me to pray with her. A week before her death she requested to partake of the Lord's Supper once more with her dear

husband and children, and this request was gladly
granted. Our departed sister remained faithul unto the
end which came on Tuesday, April 19, 1930, at 2:30 p.m.,
at the age of 59 years, 8 months and 28 days.

Mrs. Uphoff is survived by her husband, Diedrich
Uphoff; and eight children: Ida Uphoff of Garden City,
George Uphoff, Mrs. Charley Wendlandt of Gladstone,
Nebraska, August Uphoff, Mrs. John Siebenneicher, of
Gilead, Nebraska, Odelia Uphoff of Wichita, Kansas,
Lonard Uphoff and Edwin Uphoff; and by six sisters: Mrs.
Henry Naimann, Mrs. Henry Menssen, Miss Augusta Diener,
Mrs. John Itzen, Mrs. M. J. Harms, Miss Nora Diener, all
of Nebraska. Also her mother-in-law, Mrs. Jurgen Uphoff,
of Nebraska.

Funeral services were conducted in Garnand's funeral
parlor at Garden City, and from there the funeral
procession came to Deerfield, where services were
conducted by the Rev. Walter J F. Lebien. In German the
pastor spoke on Phil 1:21, the text which the deceased
requested as her funeral text. Her mortal remains were
laid to rest in the Deerfield Cemetery.

UPHOFF, DIEDRICH G. - (Lt. 1, Blk. 25, Sec. 2) Diedrich
Gerhard Uphoff, son of Mr. and Mrs. Jurgen Uphoff, was
born July 26, 1865, at Peoria, Ill. and died at
Gladstone, Neb., April 13, 1946, at the age of 80 years,
8 months and 18 days.

He was baptized in the Lutheran Church by Pastor
Limston at Peoria on August 27, 1865, and was confirmed
on April 2, 1882, at Woodford, Ill., by Pastor Theo.
Pessel.

On October 6, 1891, he was married to Barbara Diener at
Gladstone, Neb., and to this union were born ten
children, six sons and four daughters.

He leaves to mourn his passing: four sons and four
daughters: Ida Uphoff, North Hollywood, Calif.; George
Uphoff and Mrs. Odelia Jones, Garden City, Kan.; Mrs.
Christina Wendlandt and Mrs. Viola Siebenneicher,
Gladstone, Neb.; August Uphoff, Deerfield, Kan.; Leonard
Uphoff, Long Beach, Calif.; and Edwin Uphoff, Laramie,
Wyo.; twenty-two granchildren and five great
grandchildren. One sister, Mrs. C. H. Ude of Gladstone,
Neb., also survives him. His wife and two sons preceded
him in death.

"Blessed are the dead, which die in the Lord from
henceforth."

DEERFIELD CEMETERY

UPHOFF, GEORGE - (Lt. 1, Blk. 25, Sec. 2) Born Sept. 23, 1897, in Missouri and died June 6, 1952, at Garden City, Ks.

Geo. Uphoff, a former resident of Deerfield, passed away Saturday in Garden City after many months of illness. Friends in this community extend sympathy to the Uphoff family.

George Henry Uphoff, a resident of Western Kansas since 1921, died June 6, 1952, in a local convalescent home, after an illness of more than a year.

He became ill about a year and a half ago and was treated at the University of Kansas Medical Center last November. Since that time he has been confined to his bed most of the time. He had been in the local convalescent home since the latter part of November.

Upholf was born Sept. 23, 1879, at Norbin, Mo. He moved to Western Kansas from Gladstone, Neb., in 1921, locating in Deerfield. He lived and farmed in the Deerfield community until 1939, when he moved to Holly, Colo. He lived there one year and then moved to Garden City, where he took over the operation of the Garden City Bowling Club. He operated that business until 1943. He then entered the construction business in Garden City, continuing in that line until he became ill about a year and a half ago.

He was a member of the Trinity Lutheran Church of Garden City.

He is survived by his wife, Ruth, of 611 North Ninth, Garden City; one son, Darol Gene of Pasadena, Calif.; one daughter, Mrs. Marjorie Van Fosen, Sidney, Ohio; four sisters, Ida Uphoff, Van Nuys, Calif., Christina Wnedlandt, Hebron, Nebr., Viola Siebenneicher, Fairbury, Nebr., and Odelia Jones of Garden City; three brothers, August of Redmond, Ore., Leonard of Van Nuys, Calif., and Edwin of Laramie, Wyo.; and five grandchildren.

Funeral services Wednesday afternoon. Burial in Deerfield Cemetery.

UPHOFF, IDA HELEN MILLER - (Lt. 1, Blk. 25, Sec. 2) Ida Helen Miller Uphoff was born June 22, 1894, at Bloomfield, Nebraska, and departed this life Tuesday evening, February 23, 1937, at Garden City, Kansas. She was the second child of Henry Hafner and his wife, Emma, nee Eliasson. She was baptized February 12, 1898, and confirmed March 20, 1910, after having been instructed in the chief parts of Christian doctrine. Two brothers,

DEERFIELD CEMETERY

John M. and Albert C. Hafner, preceded our deceased into death.

December 9, 1922, she entered holy matrimony with George Uphoff at Garden City, Kansas. Two children were born to this union, Marjorie Helen, now 13 years old, and Darol Gene, 9 years old.

Our deceased sister spent her youth at Bloomfield, Nebraska, living there till 1912, when she moved with her parents to California. Here she made her home till 1922, when she came to Garden City to wed George Uphoff, and she has made her home in and near Deerfield, Kansas, till her death.

Mrs. Uphoff had been failing in health for the past eight years, many times being seriously ill. During all this time she was a patient sufferer, trusting in her Lord and Savior until her death.

She leaves to mourn her loss: her husband; two children, Marjorie and Darol; her parents, Mr. and Mrs. Henry Hafner of Bloomfield, Nebraska; two brothers and two sisters, Charles Hafner of Bloomfield, Nebraska, Helen Hafner of Albany, New York, Henrietta Morhart of Burns, Oregon, and Harold Hafner of Lincoln, Nebraska; her father-in-law, Dietrich Uphoff of Deerfield; and the following brothers and sisters-in-law: Ida Uphoff of Deerfield, Mrs. C. Wenlandt of Gladstone, Nebraska, Aug. Uphoff of Deerfield, Mrs. John Siebenneicher of Gilead, Nebraska, Mrs. John Jones of Hutchinson, Kansas, Leonard Uphoff of Lakin, and Edwin Uphoff of Savory, Wyoming; and many other relatives and a host of friends.

Funeral services were held on February 26, with Rev. Walter J.F. Lebien in charge, assisted by a singing group consisting of Mrs. John Hanneman, Miss Minnie Coerber, and Henry Bentrup. Interment was made in the Deerfield Cemetery. Those serving as pallbearers were: P. L. Dillon, Oliver Shriver, C. A. Humphrey, Roy Graham, Paul Jones, Dallas Steenis.

> I fall asleep in Jesus' wounds,
> There pardon for my sins abounds;
> Yea, Jesus' blood and righteousness
> My jewels are, my glorious dress,
> Wherein before my God I stand,
> When I shall reach the heavenly land.
> With peace and joy I now depart,
> God's child I am with all my heart;
> I thank thee, death, thou leadest me
> To that true life where I would be.

DEERFIELD CEMETERY

So cleansed by Christ I fear not death,
Lord Jesus, strengthen Thou my faith!

VALDEZ, URBANO 'SAM' - (Lt. 2, Blk. 129, Sec. 1) Urbano "Sam" Valdez, 51, died September 3, 1993, at St. Catherine Hospital, Garden City.
He was born May 26, 1942, at Durango, Mexico, the son of Jose Isabel and Maria De Los Angeles Ochoa Valdez. A Deerfield resident since 1983, moving from Lawrenceville, Ill., he worked in the slaughter department at the Iowa Beef Plant.
He was a member of Christ the King Catholic Church, Deerfield, and the Moose Lodge, Garden City.
On August 14, 1976, he married Sarah O. Armstrong at Lawrenceville, Ill. She survives.
Other survivors include: two sons, Jesus, Houston, and Jose, of the home; two daughters, Martina Valdez, Mexico, and Jessica Valdez, of the home; a stepson, Curtis Buchanan, Chicago; a stepdaughter, Sarah Jennings, Chicago; a brother, Ismael, Houston; nine sisters, Sofia Valdez, Lioncia Valdez, Maria Del Refugio Valdez, Carmen Valdez, Margarita Valdez, Enedina Valdez, Gloria Valdez, Alejandra Valdez and Petra Valdez, all of Mexico; and nine grandchildren.
Vigil service was at Christ the King Catholic Church, Deerfield. Funeral Mass was held Wednesday at the church, with Father Mario Eslas and the Rev. Dan Mitchell presiding. Garnand Funeral Home, Lakin, was in charge of arrangements. Burial in the Deerfield Cemetery.

VERMILLION, BURL L. - (Pottersfield) (Funeral Records) Died Dec. 14, 1918, age 27 yrs., 10 mos., 27 days. Married, farm hand, died of influenza and pneumonia. Came from Illinois. Funeral charged to Kearny County.

DEERFIELD CEMETERY

WALKER, JOSEPHINE - (Lt. 4, Blk. 83, Sec. 1) Pearl Josephine Walker, 70, died at Kearny County Hospital in Lakin, Sunday, December 27, 1981, after a long illness.
Josephine, daughter of Jack and Edith (Brewer) Steenis, was born September 24, 1911, at the farm home north of Garden City, Kansas, and in 1913 moved with her parents to Deerfield where she lived the remainder of her life.
She and George Carl Jones were married on October 9, 1929. They reared a family of five children, sharing with and supporting them in school activities, 4-H, basketball trips to surrounding towns and to the state tournaments. Jo, too, returned to school and completed the requirements for her Deerfield High school diploma in 1957. She then assumed the bookkeeping duties at Jones Motor Company for her husband. Carl died in 1963 after a lengthy ilness.
Josephine then served for many years as secretary in the administrative offices of the Deerfield school system where she was again working with young people. In 1969 she became clerk of Unified School District #216 and was a member of this governing body for six years.
On June 9, 1967, Josephine (Jo) was married to Harold Walker. They shared an interest in many church and community activities and were especially active in helping to establish the Kearny County Senior Citizens center and program. Jo was always active in her home life, in church and community affairs and programs, including church choir, Sunday School, church services, United Methodist Women, 4-H service leader, Book club and other social clubs, secretarial offices and board member positions.
Survivors are her husband, of the home; three sons, Keith, Lakin, Douglas, Valley Center, and Gary, Tyrone, Okla.; two daughters, Betty Young, Bend, Ore., and Carol Salvati, San Diego, Calif.; a step-son, Clayton Walker, South Chicago, Ill.; three step daughters, Diana Hoffmann, Aurora, Colo., Wanda Christensen, Garden City, and Sheri Jo Medley, Grainfield; two sisters, Rowena Urie, Redmond, Ore., and Hazel Shriver, Deerfield; 25 grandchildrn, and one great grandchild.
Funeral was held at 10:30 a.m. Wednesday at the United Methodist Church, Deerfield, the Rev. Harry Walz officiating. Burial at Deerfield Cemetery.

DEERFIELD CEMETERY

WANDS, GEORGE M. - (Lt. 3, Blk. 26, Sec. 2) (The Lakin Independent, Oct. 4, 1935) George M. Wands was born near Paola on December 12, 1875, and departed this life September 27, 1935, at his home in Deerfield, Kansas. He was 59 years, 9 months, and 15 days of age.
He was united in marriage on January 19, 1904, at Kansas City, Missouri, to Miss Lillie Hall. To this union were born two children, Owen and Martha. Owen preceded him in death on September 24, 1932.
Mr. and Mrs. Wands spent most of their lives in Kansas, but they have also lived in Missouri, Montana, and Colorado. Mr. Wands' adult years were spent following the trade of blacksmith. He has lived in Deerfield since 1921.
He has two brothers, F. M. Wands of Penrose, Colorado, an J. D. Wands of Sedalia, Missouri; two sisters, Mrs. Ola Braden of Portersville, California, and Mrs. Ellen McGinn of Deerfield, Kansas.
Mr. Wands was a member of the Mason Lodge, a Methodist by preference, and a respected member of the community. He was a great lover of home and family, never caring to be away without them. He will be missed by a host of friends and acquaintances.
He was always very friendly with his customers when they came into his place of business and would always take time to visit with them. He was fair in his dealings with his fellowman and always met his obligations promptly. By his going the community has lost a good citizen, father, and husband.
Funeral services were held at the Methodist Church at Deerfield on Sunday, September 29. Rev. R. A. Corrie, a former Deerfield pastor, was in charge. Interment was made in the Deerfield Cemetery.

WANDS, GEO. OWEN - (Lt. 3, Blk. 26, Sec. 2) Geo. Owen Wands, son of Mr. and Mrs. G. M. Wands of Deerfield, Kansas, was born September 21, 1915, at Pueblo, Colorado, and passed away at the Lakin hospital August 24, 1932. Age 16 years, 11 months, and 3 days.
At the age of six years he moved with his parents to Deerfield, Kansas, where, with his parents, he has since made his home.
Owen belonged to the Deerfield High School class of 1933, so would have graduated next spring.

281

He was highly respected and greatly beloved by his classmates and teachers alike. He was a member of Mrs. Hetzer's S.S. class of the Methodist Church. He was held in the highest esteem by all who knew him. Strong, vigorous, optimistic, and reliable, he made a favorable impression on all his acquaintances. He was adored and beloved by his grief-stricken parents and sister. His short and well spent life will always remain as a wholesome and refreshing memory of the people of Deerfield. It is so sad that one so young and so hopeful should be cut down so young, but oh! it is so splendid that his life was well spent. The funeral was held Friday, August 26, at the Deerfield Methodist Church, conducted by the pastor, Roy A. Corrie. Interment was made in the Deerfield Cemetery.

WARD, GEORGE W. - (Lt. 3, Blk. 101, Sec. 1) George W. Ward, 89, died at the Kearny County Hospital, Tuesday morning, March 5, 1963. He had been in poor health for several years.

Mr. Ward had made his home at the Pioneer Rest home the past five years. He had been a Kearny County resident for 33 years.

Mr. Ward was born March 17, 1873, in Greenfield, Ala. He was a member of the Baptist Church. His daughter, Mrs. Paul Jones of Deerfield is the only survivor. His wife died 52 years ago.

Funeral services was held at the Davis Funeral Home, Thursday morning, March 7, at 10 o'clock. Rev. Robert Fleenor, pastor of the Methodist Church in Deerfield officiating. Burial in the Deerfield Cemetery.

WARD, JEREMY LEE - (Lt. 2, Blk. 127, Sec. 1) Graveside service for Jeremy Lee Ward was held at Deerfield Cemetery, with Deacon Harold Stickney officiating. The son of Crystal Lynn Saiz and Jeremy Richard Ward, Jeremy was stillborn, March 5, 1996, at St. Catherine Hospital in Garden City.

He is survived by his parents, both of Deerfield; his grandparents, Robert and Lois Oropeza, and Kelly Tudrick, all of Deerfield, and Rick Ward, Lakin; and his great grandparents, Arthur and Amilla Urteaga, Deerfield, and Norm and Lois Matthews, Lakin.

Garnand Funeral Home, Garden City, was in charge of arrangements.

DEERFIELD CEMETERY

WEATHERRED, DUANE - (Lt. 1, Blk. 90, Sec. 4) Duane Weatherred, 66, died March 4, 1995, at St. Catherine Hospital in Garden City.
Born in Scott City on Feb. 26, 1929, he was the son of Rusty and Alice Benedict Weatherred. He attended school in Wiley, Colo., and was a graduate of Lamar High School.
Mr. Weatherred worked for Marx Master Bakery for more than 20 years before moving to Kearny County in 1966. From 1970 until 1988, he had a candy and tobacco wholesale distributorship and was known as "The Candy Man." Since 1988, he has worked in the maintenance department of Deerfield USD 216.
Mr. Weatherred was a member of United Methodist Church of Deerfield, Deerfield Lions Club and the Deerfield Recreation Board.
On Oct. 31, 1947, he married Wanda Grauberger at Clayton, N.M. She survives.
Other survivors are four sons, Don Springer, Lamar, Colo., Jim Weatherred, Fort Collins, Colo., Rich Weatherred, Deerfield, and Mike Weatherred, Emporia; three daughters, Judy Banek, Aurora, Colo., Barbara Jarboe, Lakin, and Karen Waechter, Ulysses; his mother, Deerfield; a brother, Bob Weatherred, Albuquerque, N.M.; two sisters, Caryol Heckman, McClave, Colo., and Lois Venn, Alt, Colo.; 15 grandchildren; and one great grandchild. He was preceded in death by his father and a sister, Annalee Weatherred.
Funeral was held Wednesday at United Methodist Church of Deerfield, the Rev. Donald J. Koehn officiating. Burial at the Deerfield Cemetery.

WELCH, REVA JEAN - (Lt. 2, Blk. 78, Sec. 1) Funeral for Reva Jean Welch, 46,, Garden City, was held Tuesday at Trinty Lutheran Church, the Rev. Vernon Oestmann officiating. Burial at Deerfield Cemetery. She died Feb. 17, 1990, at St. Catherine Hospital, Garden City.
Born Reva Jean Rigdon, Sept. 5, 1943, at Kansas City, she was a homemaker. She had been a Garden City resident for 17 months, moving from Moorefield, Neb.
She graduated from Cainsville, Mo., High School in 1961. She was raised as a member of the Nazarene Church.
Survivors include a son, Bradley, Curtis, Neb.; her mother, V. Ruth Anderson, Garden City; four brothers, Eugene Rigdon, St. George, Utah, Warren Rigdon, Phoenix, Ariz., Charles Anderson, Garden City, and James Anderson, Mattituck, N.Y.; seven sisters, Georgia Carter, Memphis,

DEERFIELD CEMETERY

Tenn., Frances Skipton, Stella McGinn, both of Garden City, Laura Slattery, St. Joseph, Mo., Mary Skipton, Deerfield, Judy VanVacter, Kansas City, Mo., and Mary Sue Stanfield, Simi Valley, Calif.; and one granddaughter. She was preceded in death by her father and one brother.

WELLS, ELIZABETH - (Lt. 1, Blk. 50, Sec. 2)   (The Herington Times, Herington, Dickinson County, Kansas, Thursday, Mch. 28, 1918)   Mrs. C. H. Wells died at her home just east of the city yesterday morning of heart failure following a long illness.   She has been very low for several months and her death was not unexpected.   The funeral was held this morning at 10:30 o'clock with Rev. Hatfield, pastor of the Presbyterian Church, officiating.

(The Herinton Times, Herington, Dickinson County, Kansas, Thursday, April 4, 1918)   Elizabeth Caroline Wininger was born near Nashville, Tennessee, August 3rd, 1841.   She was married three times, her first marriage being to George Loughmiller in 1856, her second to John F. Hale in 1866 and her third, Mch. 3rd, 1882, to Charles H. Wells.   She is survived by three children, Mrs. Chloe Davis of Cheyenne, Wyoming, John R. Hale and Julian Wilbur Wells, both of Deerfield, Kansas.

Mrs. Wells became a Christian in early life.   After coming to Herington many years ago she united with the Presbyterian Church.   She lived a devout Christian life and had many friends in this community.   The funeral was held at the home east of Herington last Thursday morning, after which the body was taken to Deerfield, Kansas, for interment.

WEST, FRANK G. - (Lt. 4, Blk. 30, Sec. 2)   A long time resident of Garden City and Deerfield died at St. Catherine Hospital.   Frank G. West, 79, 1301 New York Ave., Garden City, died February 7, 1967, after an illness of two weeks.   He was a retired carpenter and contractor.

Mr. West had lived in Garden City since 1940, moving there from Deerfield where he and his family had moved in 1914.   He was born in Barry County, Mo., on Oct. 31, 1887, and married the former Nelle Barnes in Manhattan on April 25, 1918.

He was an active member of the First Methodist Church, the Methodist Men, Homemaker Sunday School Class, American Legion and Senior Citizens.   He was a veteran of World War I.

284

DEERFIELD CEMETERY

Surviving are the widow; four sons, Duane E. West, Garden City, Madison F. West, Wichita, Kenneth B. West, Nashville, Tenn., and the Rev. Howard W. West, Manhattan; a daughter, Mrs. H. Alan Lee, Manhattan; a sister, Mary I. West, Pierce City, Mo.; and a brother, Luther M. West, Pierce City. Mo.

WEST, MILDRED MAXINE - (Lt. 4, Blk. 30, Sec. 2) Daughter of Frank and Nelle West, born March 13, 1919, and died April 13, 1919.

WEST, NELLE MAE - (Lt. 4, Blk. 30, Sec. 2) Nelle May West, 81, Garden Valley Retirement Village, died Monday, April 25, 1977, at St. Catherine Hospital.
    She was born May 30, 1895, at Phillipi, W. V., and moved to Kansas in 1907, living at Holcomb and Deerfield. She married Frank G. West, April 25, 1918, at Manhattan. He died in 1967.
    In August 1940, she and her family moved to Garden City. She was a member of First United Methodist Church, a charter and life member of Womans's Society of Christian Service, Quilter group and Homemakers Sunday School class. She was past president of Harmony E.H.U. and past president of Legion Auxiliary of Harry H. Renick American Legion Post.
    She is survived by four sons: Madison, Wichita, Kenneth, Nashvill, Tenn., Howard, Longmont, Colo., and Duane, Garden City; a daughter, Mrs. H. Alan (Janice) Lee, Manhattan; 17 grandchildren and four great grandchildren.
    Funeral was held Thursday at the church, the Rev. Leonard Clark officiating. Burial at Deerfield Cemetery.

WHITEHURST, CLAUDE CONLEE - (Lt. 4, Blk. 50, Sec. 2) Born Jan. 5, 1878, at Bacchow, Mo. and died Feb. 3, 1964, at Merced, Calif.
    (The Garden City Telegram, Feb. 5, 1964) Claude C. Whitehurst, former Garden City and Deerfield resident, died Monday at Winton, Calif.
    Two sons, Aubrey and Lynn Whitehurst of Garden City left today for Pasadena, Calif., where they will meet two sisters, Mrs. Leonard Hahn and Mrs. Mildred Clampitt. They will drive to Winton for the funeral.

WHITEHURST, H. V. - (Lt. 4, Blk. 50, Sec. 2) Born April 2, 1894, and died Feb. 14, 1963.

WHITEHURST, JAMES ALLEN - (Lt. 4, Blk. 50, Sec. 2)   Born in 1855 and died in 1926, wife Mary Whitehurst.   Died April 27, 1926, 70 years of age, widower.   Died of softening of brain. Undertaker, Garnand. He was born in Illinois. His father was born in Scotland and his mother in Illinois. He had a son, Harry.

WHITEHURST, JUANITA GENEVA - (Lt. 4, Blk. 50, Sec. 2) Born Jan. 12, 1917, and died Jan. 26, 1918.

WHITEHURST, MARY ISABEL - (Lt. 4, Blk. 50, Sec. 2) (Funeral Records)   Died Oct. 30, 1917, of Brights Disease, in Southside Township, age 62 yrs., 7 mos., 23 days, Mother Mary Crowder, father John Coulee.

WILCOX, BABY - (Lt. 4, Blk. 49, Sec. 2)

WILCOX, NORA PEARL - (Lt. 4, Blk. 49, Sec. 2) (Kearny County Advocate, Deerfield Doings, May 19, 1910)   Pearl Allen was born in 1889, and died May 10, 1910, aged 21 years, 19 days. She moved to Deerfield in 1906, and was united in marriage to A. R. Wilcox, June 4, 1907. They moved south of the river for her health, but death claimed her for his own. She leaves a husband, father and mother, four brothers and four sisters, and a host of friends to mourn her loss.

(Lakin Investigator, Deerfield News, May 13, 1910)   The funeral of Mrs. A. R. Wilcox was held Thursday. She passed away suddenly, Tuesday night, and her death was unexpected. Rev. Irwin conducted funeral services.

(Lakin Investigator, May 20, 1910)   We mentioned, briefly, in our last issue, the death of Mrs. A. R. Wilcox, and her burial on Thursday of last week. Rev. Irwin preached the funeral sermon at the M. E. Church, to a large audience, who followed the corpse to the Deerfield Cemetery. Nora Pearl Allen Wilcox was born December 3, 1888, and married to A. R. Wilcox, June 4, 1907, and death occurred May 10, 1910. Mr. and Mrs. W. A. Wilcox, and F. M. Wilcox, of Dodge City and M. R. Allen, of Great Bend, were here to attend the funeral.

WILLIAMS, ALICE P. - (Lt. 2, Blk. 43, Sec. 3)   Alice P. Williams, 84, died December 13, 1991, at the High Plains Retirement Village, Lakin.   She was born October 11, 1907, at Holdredge, Nebraska, the daughter of George and

DEERFIELD CEMETERY

Isabel Hurrel Pepoon. A resident of Kearny County most of her life, she was a homemaker.
She was a member of the First Presbyterian Church, past member of Eastern Star, and was a member of the Pioneer Grange, all at Lakin, and was a member of the Deerfield Hobby Club, Deerfield.
On May 11, 1929, she married Davis A. Williams in Kearny County. He died September 10, 1983.
Survivors include: a son, Ralph, Meridian, Miss.; a daughter, Kathryn Jones, Lamar, Colo.; five grandchildren; eight great grandchildren; and one great great grandchild.
Funeral service was held at the First Presbyterian Church, Lakin, with the Revs. Tom Armstrong and Laurie Armstrong presiding. Burial in the Deerfield Cemetery. Greene-Schneider Funeral Home of Lakin in charge of arrangements.

WILLIAMS, ANNA - (Lt. 3, Blk. 54, Sec. 2) (Lakin Investigator, Sept. 17, 1909) Mrs. John Williams died at her home, Saturday night at nine o'clock, after an illness of four weeks, with typhoid fever. She was 28 years old and leaves a husband and three children to mourn her death. She was taken to the Deerfield Cemetery for interment. Not being able to get the pastor the funeral sermon will be given Sunday, 19th, at 3 o'clock at the M. E. Church.
Anna Entz was born in Saline County, Missouri, March 17, 1880. She departed this life September 10, 1909, after a four weeks illness, of typhoid fever. In November 1904, she was married to John Williams. A husband, mother, three children, one brother and one sister are left to mourn her departure. From early life Mrs. Williams lived a consistent Christian life. She first became a member of the Lutheran church, and about one year ago united with the Christian church, of which she was a member at the time of her death. A faithful wife and good mother, a thoughtful neighbor, she will be greatly missed in the home and community.
(Kearny County Advocate, Sept. 16, 1909) The saddest event we have had to chronicle for some time is the death of Mrs. Anna Williams wife of John Williams, last Saturday evening, about 9 o'clock. She had been suffering for some time with the dread typhus, and while here death was not wholly unexpected it comes as a shock to the entire commity. She leaves three small children,

287

the youngest of which a babe of about eight months, is in the grip of the same disease, but at last reports it was seemingly improving. The funeral was held Tuesday at the Methodist Church conducted by Mr. Freshwater.

WILLIAMS, ARLENE - (Lt. 2, Blk. 54, Sec. 2) Mrs. Arlene Williams, daughter of Davis and Josephine Williams, was born in Centretown, Missouri, June 23, 1872. At the age of twenty-six years she was married to Griffin Pace to which union was born one son. Being left a widow, she came to Claflin, Kansas, and later was married to James Williams who preceded her in death. About 1921 she moved to Deerfield, Kansas, where she has since resided. She united with the Methodist Church in Deerfield in 1921 and lived a devoted Christian life until her death.

She had been in failing health for several years and six weeks ago suffered a stroke. She was taken to the Kearny County Hospital where she received the best of care but failed to recover. She departed this life on Sunday, June 4, 1944.

Mrs. Williams was one of a family of nine children, three of whom preceded her in death. She leaves to mourn her going, her son, Ben, of the home; two brothers, Bob of Delta, Colo., and Harry of Columbia, Mo.; three sisters, Mrs Joe Johnson of Pleasant Green, Mo., Mrs. Mary Beck of Clifton City, Mo., and Mrs. Elizabeth Thompson of Sedalia, Mo. Also several nieces and nephews and many friends and neighbors.

Mrs. Williams was a good mother, a splendid home maker and neighbor and will be greatly missed by her many friends.

Services were conducted by Rev. Rolla Wells of Syracuse, at the Methodist Church in Deerfield on Wednesday, June 7, 1944. Rev. Wells was a former pastor of Deerfield. Pallbearers were J. J. Steenis, Joe Gillock, Harrison McAfee, Glen Steward, E. R. Eyman, and Wayne Sower. Interment was in the Deerfield Cemetery.

WILLIAMS, BENJAMIN - (Lt. 2, Blk. 54, Sec. 2) (Lakin Independent, July 6, 1961) Benjamin Franklin Williams, 67, died Friday, June 30, 1961, at the Pioneer Nursing Home here of a heart attack. He had lived here for about the past two years.

Mr. Williams was born in 1893 in Sedalia, Mo. He moved to Deerfield in 1915.

DEERFIELD CEMETERY

Survivors include two cousins, Davis Williams, Deerfield, and Clarence Williams, Lakin. Funeral was held Sunday in the Deerfield Methodist Church. The Rev. Robert Fleenor officiated. Burial was in the Deerfield Cemetery. Funeral record shows birth date as 12-23-99.

WILLIAMS, DAVIS ANTON - (Lt. 2, Blk. 43, Sec. 3) Funeral for Davis Anton Williams, 78, was held at the United Presbyterian Church, Lakin, with the Rev. Bruce Hurley officiating. Burial at the Deerfield Cemetery. Mr. Williams died Saturday, Sept. 10, 1983, while attending his garden at his home. He was a farmer and had been a Kearny County resident for 65 years.

Born March 15, 1905, at Pleasant Green, Mo., he married Alice Pepoon, June 11, 1929, at Lakin.

He was a member of the United Presbyterian Church and Pioneer Grange, both of Lakin, and the Lions Club, Deerfield.

Survivors are his wife, of the home; a son, Ralph, Meridian, Miss.; a daughter, Kathryn Jones, Lakin; sister, Katheryn Hadd, Rapid City, S.D.; seven grandchildren and three great grandchildren.

Davis Funeral Home was in charge of arrangements.

WILLIAMS, ELSIE LUCILE - (Lt. 3, Blk. 54, Sec. 2) Daughter of Davis and Alice Williams, died March 8, 1936.

WILLIAMS, JAMES - (Lt. 2, Blk. 54, Sec. 2) He died in 1921. He was the second husband of Arlene Williams Pace.

WILLIAMS, URY ETTA - (Lt. 2, Blk. 54, Sec. 2) (Lakin Investigator, Nov. 5, 1909) The next to the youngest child of Mr. and Mrs. Robert Williams died Monday at three o'clock. It was taken sick at about ten o'clock, and a doctor was called, but all of his efforts were in vain. The funeral was held at the Methodist Church, Wednesday afternoon at two o'clock. Born Mar 7, 1908, and died Nov. 1, 1909.

WILLIAMS, WILLIE - (Lt. 3, Blk. 54, Sec 2) ts. January 15-September 20, 1909. (Lakin Investigator, Oct. 1, 1909) The eight months old baby of Mr. John Williams died, Saturday, September 25, and the funeral was held Sunday at the Methodist Church and the burial was in the Deerfield Cemetery.

DEERFIELD CEMETERY

(Kearny County Advocate, Sept. 30, 1909) The little son of John Williams died Friday night of brain fever. The funeral was held at the M. E. Church Sunday afternoon. He was born Jan. 15, 1909.

WILLS, JESSIE - (Lakin Investigator, Jan. 24, 1907) Miss Wills, 19 year old daughter of Mr. and Mrs. Carl Wills, died Tuesday nite at the residence of R. Beckett in Deerfield. She had almost recovered from a severe illness when she was attacked by pneumonia, and her system could notwithstand it. She has hosts of friends. She was interred at Deerfield.

WILLSON, CLARA LANG - (Lt. 4, Blk. 43, Sec. 3) Mrs. Clara Lang Willson, 89, died Tuesday night, Dec. 14, 1971, at the Kearny County Hospital, Lakin, after a long illness. Born, July 22, 1882, near Clifton, she was married to Ray Walter Willson, Dec. 5, 1906, at Clifton. He died Aug. 15, 1961. She moved to Deerfield from Garden City in 1920.

She was a member of the Deerfield United Methodist Church and the Order of Eastern Star, Lakin.

Survivors include sons: Victor, Garden City, Preston, Pico Rivera, Calif.; daughters: Mrs. Bill McElroy, Garden City, Mrs. Carl Hulen, Hemet, Calif.; 12 grandchildren; 16 great grandchildren.

Funeral was at the Deerfield Methodist Church. Rev. Charles Hadley officiating. Burial in Deerfield Cemetery.

WILLSON, RAY WALTER - (Lt. 4, Blk. 43, Sec. 3) Ray Walter Willson was born to J.A.N. and Martha Jane Willson, September 21, 1882, in Utica, Kans. He was the youngest of seven children, all of whom have proceeded him in death.

He moved from Utica, Kans., to Garden City, Kans. A short time later he moved to Kearny County where he has lived for the past 41 years. He moved from the farm and made his home in Deerfield the last seven years.

He was united in marriage to Clara Lang at Clifton, Kans., on Dec. 5, 1906. To this union four children were born: Chelsea McElroy of Englewood, Colo.; Erma Hulen of Compton, Calif.; Preston of Pico-Rivera, Calif.; Victor of Garden City.

He was a lifelong member of the Methodist Church and faithful in his attendance at church and Sunday school. He was also a member of the Masons for 55 years, the OES and Grange.

He loved to fish and had a stroke while fishing at Lake McKinney on July 31. He was taken to the Garden City hospital where he passed away early in the morning of August 15, 1961.

He leaves to mourn his passing, his wife and four children, 12 grandchildren, five great grandchildren, many nieces and nephews, and a host of friends.

WILSON, LULU EDITH - (Lt. 4, Blk. 42, Sec. 3)   see Lulu Edith Russell

WINTER, ALDEN M. - (S/2 Lt. 2, Blk. 42, Sec. 3) ts. Jan. 12, 1922-Nov. 29, 1982. Funeral for Alden M. Winter, 60, Holyoke, Colo, was held Friday at the Immanuel Lutheran Church, Deerfield, Pastor Gary Rahe of Holyoke officiating. Burial at Deerfield Cemetery.

Mr. Winter died Monday, Nov. 29, 1982, at Holyoke, after a short illness. A carpenter, he had been a resident of Holyoke for a year, moving there from Colorado Springs. He was a former resident of Garden City, moving to Colorado Springs, in the early 1950s. He married Pauline Grauberger.

He was a veteran of World War II.

Survivors are his wife, of the home; two sons, Robert Winter, Holyoke, and Donald Winter, Rehoboth, Mass.; a daughter, Janet Green, Colorado Springs; a brother, Marvin Winter, Garden City; two sisters, Maxine Drennan of California, and Margaret Egbert of Garden City; and six grandchildren.

Thompson Mortuary of Holyoke in charge of arrangements.

WINTER, ALVINA - (Lt. 2, Blk. 29, Sec. 2) Mrs. Alvina L. Winter, 73, stepmother of Marvin Winter, 1912 "C", Garden City and Mrs. Margaret Egbert, 107 W. Walnut, died July 4, 1974, at South Hospital, Hutchinson, following a two week illness.

She was born April 13, 1901, at Drake, Mo. She married August F. Winter, Feb. 5, 1948, in Hutchinson, and he died December 2, 1962. She moved from Deerfield to Hutchinson in 1948.

She was a member of Our Redeemer Lutheran Church, Hutchinson.

DEERFIELD CEMETERY

Surviving are a daughter, Mrs. Joan A. Wells, Cortez, Colo.; another stepson, Alden Winter, Colorado Springs, Colo.; another stepdaughter, Mrs. Dorothy Drennan, Belle Gardens, Calif.; three sisters, Mrs. Mary Klingsick, Washington, Mo., Mrs. Amanda Liesemeyer, and Mrs. Lena Scheer, Owensville, Mo.; 14 grandchildren and 8 great grandchildren.

Funeral was held on Monday at the church, the Rev. K. J. Karstenson officiating. Graveside services at Deerfield, the Rev. R. C. Greene officiating.

WINTER, ARTHUR F. - (Lt. 2, Blk. 29, Sec. 2) Infant son of August F. and Dorothy E. Winter, died March 18, 1921.

WINTER, AUGUST F. - (Lt. 2, Blk. 29, Sec. 2) August F. Winter, 66, a former Deerfield resident, died Sunday, December 2, 1962, in California. He was born on June 5, 1896. He moved from Deerfield to Hutchinson in 1948. He married Alvina Lottmann, Feb. 5, 1948, at Hutchinson.

Survivors are the widow; sons, Marvin and Alden, Woodland Park, Calif.; daughters, Mrs. Dorothy Lubkee, South Gate, Calif. and Mrs. Margaret Egbert, Pierceville; a stepdaughter, Mrs. Joan Keenan, Hutchinson; a brother, George, Granite City, Ill.; a sister, Mrs. Anna Rosel, Lakin and 11 grandchildren.

Funeral services were held in Hutchinson, Friday, and in the Deerfield Lutheran Church, Saturday afternoon. Burial in Deerfield Cemetery.

WINTER, BECKY ELIZABETH - (Lt. 2, Blk. 63, Sec. 3) (The Garden City Telegram, March 27, 1963) Graveside services for Becky Elizabeth Winter, infant daughter of Mr. and Mrs. Marvin Winter, rural Holcomb was at 1 p.m. CST, Thursday in the Deerfield Cemetery, the Rev. Clarence Born, Scott City, officiating.

She was born Monday, March 25, 1963, at St. Catherine Hospital and died Tuesday evening.

Survivors are the parents, three brothers, Marvin Eugene II, Carl Raymond and Thomas Allan; a sister, DeLorse Irene; the paternal grandmother, Mrs. Alvina Winter and the maternal grandparents, Mr. and Mrs. Neal Hodges, Lyons.

WINTER, DOROTHY E. - (Lt. 2, Blk. 29, Sec. 2) Dorothy Kettler Winter was born December 4, 1900, at Block, Kansas. As an infant she was received into God's

DEERFIELD CEMETERY

Covenant of Grace through the holy sacrament of baptism. Later, making her home near Deerfield, she was instructed in the chief parts of Christian doctrine and renewed her baptismal vow in the rite of confirmation, thus becoming a communicant member of Immanuel Lutheran Church, Deerfield, Kansas.

September 17, 1919, she was united in marriage with Mr. August Winter. This union was blessed with five children, one son, Arthur, passing away in infancy.

In December 1944, the Winters moved to Parsons, Kansas, and had their church membership transferred to the Lutheran congregation of that place. Mrs. Winter was a devote Christian woman, a faithful wife, a loving mother, a trusted friend. She was taken to her heavenly home on December 31, 1946, reaching the age of 46 years and 26 days.

She leaves to mourn her loss, her grief stricken husband, August Winter; her daughters, Mrs. Leubke of Los Angeles, Calif., and Mrs. Francis Egbert Jr. of Pierceville, Kansas; her sons, Alden of Parsons and Marvin of the home; one grandson, Donald; one daughter-in-law and two sons-in-law; her sisters, Mrs. Herman Coerber, Deerfield, Mrs. Gustave Schultz, Divine, Texas, Mrs. Orville Keyser of San Jose, Calif., and Mrs. Herman Kuhlman of Leoti, Kansas; also her brothers, Chris and August Kettler of Deerfield as well as many other relatives and friends.

Funeral services were held in Immanuel Lutheran Church wih Pastor Paul H.C. Stengel in charge. Interment was made in the Deerfield Cemetery.

WINTER, MARVIN — (Lt. 2, Blk. 63, Sec. 3) Funeral for Marvin E. Winter, 61, was held at 2:30 p.m. Sunday at Trinity Lutheran Church, the Rev. Vernon E. Oestmann officiating. Burial at Deerfield Cemetery.

He died Oct. 17, 1991, at St. Francis Hospital, Wichita. Born March 1, 1930, at Hutchinson, he married Irene Hodges in Sept. 1949, at Dennis.

Mr. Winter was an assistant foreman for Acra Plant. He moved to Deerfield as a young child and attended Deerfield schools. He moved to Dennis in 1947 and attended schools there. After their marriage, the Winters lived in Hutchinson and Lyons and then moved to Garden City in 1960 from Lyons.

DEERFIELD CEMETERY

He was a member of Trinity Lutheran Church, Wild West
Camping Club and Good Sam R.V. Club, all of Garden City.
His hobbies were mechanics, camping and welding.
Survivors include his wife, of the home; five sons,
Marvin Jr., Liberal, Carl, Kalispell, Mont., Tom, Garden
City, Fred, Attica, and Gregory Dean, Stafford; a
daughter, Dolores Winter, Stafford; three sisters, Maxine
Drennan, Henet, Calif., Margaret Egbert, Garden City, and
Joan, Cortez, Colo.; seven grandchildren; and one great
granddaughter. He was preceded in death by his parents,
a daughter, two brothers, and one granddaughter.

WISHON, MARION JOSEPH - (Lt. 1, Blk. 65, Sec. 3) Marion
(Joe) Wishon, 32, 606 E. Burnside, Garden City, died
Friday, July 18, 1980, at Bucklin Hospital, Bucklin. Mr.
Wishon suffered an electrical shock while setting up a
pump rig near Bucklin.
Born Aug. 25, 1947, at Rolla, Mo., he married Marilyn
Maxine Parrish, Oct. 19, 1964, at Dodge City.
Mr. Wishon had worked at Farmland Foods for 12 years
before joining Miller Gear Head and Pump as a pump setter
two weeks ago.
Survivors include his wife, of the home; four sons, Joe
Shane, Jason, Michael and Joshua, all of the home; two
daughters, Rebekah and Leslie Ann, of the home; his
mother, Elsie Wishon, Garden City; three brothers,
Raymond (Bud), Holcomb, Arnold, Garden City and Chester,
Hampton, Va.; six sisters, Loretta Wishon, Mrs. Floyd
(Dorothy) Shipley, Mrs. Ornad (Delores) Miller, Mrs.
Spencer (Marietta) Burtis, all of Garden City, Mrs.
Clarence (Leeta) Dingus, Holcomb, and Mrs. John G. (Pat)
Baier, Holcomb.
Funeral was held at Garnand Funeral Chapel, Frank
Crotts officiating. Burial at Deerfield Cemetery.

WISHON, RAYMOND A. - (Lt. 1, Blk. 65, Sec. 3) Raymond A.
Wishon, 69, died Jan. 9, 1971, at Garden City after a
long illness.
Born Nov. 9, 1910, in Rolla, Mo., he married Elsie
Marie Borlisch, April 12, 1930, in Rolla, Mo. He was a
carpenter and moved here in 1948.
Survivors include the widow; sons: Raymond (Bud), Jr.,
Marion and Arnold L., Garden City, Chester E., Hampton,
Va.; daughters: Mrs. Orand Miller, Garden City, Mrs.
Floyd Shipley, Fort Louis, Wash, Mrs. Clarence Dingus,
Holcomb, Mrs. Johnny G. Baier, Mrs. Richard Dunn and Mrs.

DEERFIELD CEMETERY

Spencer H. Burtis, Garden City; brothers: Elvia L., Grove, Okla., Charles E., Rolla, Mo., Roy A., Arizona; sisters: Mrs. Jim Kates, Grove, Okla., Mrs. Joe Kemper, St. Louis, Mo., Mrs. Pauline Whittaker, Rolla, Mo.; 27 grandchildren. Funeral was held at 2 p.m. Tuesday at the Garnand Funeral Chapel; Rev. Frank Crotts. Burial in the Deerfield Cemetery.

WOLF, DAISY MABY - (Lt. 1, Blk. 55, Sec. 2) June 18-19, 1912. Daughter of Chet A. and Ida Stebens Wolf.

WOOD, ELIZABETH A. - (Lt. 4, Blk. 22, Sec. 2) Born in 1858 and died in 1953. Mother of Mrs. C. L. Vastine.

WOOD, GEORGE THOMAS - (Lt. 4, Blk. 22 Sec. 2) George Thomas Wood was born near Prince Frederick, Calvert County, Maryland, on May 1, 1842, and passed away at Deerfield, Kansas, May 13, 1938, at the age of 96 years and 12 days. He had been in declining health for some time and on February 5 suffered a stroke of paralysis.

When a young man he assisted his widowed mother in running her farm and caring for his younger brothers and sisters until they were nearly grown. During the Civil War he worked on a government steamboat which carried U.S. soldiers and supplies. He later engaged in farming in Illinois, Iowa, Nebraska, and Kansas, coming to Kansas in 1882.

He owned and operated a general store for a time but most of his life was spent in farming, at which he was quite successful, having owned a number of fine farms. He retired in 1928 and in the financial crash of the following year the most of his lifetime's savings was wiped out, and he and his wife have since made their home with their daughter, Mrs. C. L. Vastine, and Mr. Vastine, northwest of Deerfield.

He was a member of the Masonic Lodge and also the A.O.U.W., a kind and loving husband and father, a highly respected citizen.

September 4, 1877, he was united in marriage to Elizabeth Ann Holmes and they celebrated their 60th wedding anniversary last year. To this union four children were born, one son, Franklin, dying in infancy.

He is survived by his wife, Mrs. Geo. T. Wood; and three children, Walter A. Wood, Marienthal, Kansas, Mrs. Anna M. Hogsett, Brownell, Kansas, Mrs. Nellie E.

DEERFIELD CEMETERY

Vastine, Deerfield, Kansas; a sister, Mrs. Priscilla J. Bowen, Barstow, Maryland; six grandchildren; three great grandchildren; and many other relatives and friends.

Funeral services were held at the Deerfield M.E. Church Monday afternoon with the pastor, Rev. Glen W. Palmer, in charge and interment made in the Deerfield Cemetery.

WOODBURN, RONALD LYNN — (Lt. 3, Blk. 33, Sec. 3) Son of C.F. and N.F. Woodburn died in 1927.

DEERFIELD CEMETERY

YODER, EDITH A. - (Lt. 1, Blk. 53, Sec. 2) April 22, 1942, Aug. 21, 1942. White female, 3 months old, died at 212 W. Santa Fe St., Garden City, Kansas, of enterocolitis malnutrition. Bryant Garnand was the undertaker.

YODER, WILLIAM SYLVESTER - (Lt. 4, Blk. 53, Sec. 2) Born June 11, 1918, and died of a skull fracture, July 23, 1946, funeral held July 26, Garnand's in charge.

(Garden City Telegram, July 25, 1946) Funeral services for William Sylvester Joder, former Garden City resident, son-in-law of Mr. and Mrs. M. A. Russell, will be held Friday afternoon in Garnand Chapel at 2 o'clock, the Rev. B. A. Hartnett will officiate.

Joder died in a Colby hospital Tuesday night as the result of injuries received when a car-lift fell while he was servicing a car at his Winona, Kansas, filling station. He is survived by his widow, Velma; 3 children, Gary, Lois and Donna Jean; his parents; and four brothers. Burial will be in Deerfield Cemetery.

DEERFIELD CEMETERY

ZRUBEK, ALEXANDER FRED - (Lt. 1, Blk. 21, Sec. 2) Alexander Fred Zrubek, son of Aloys and Susan Zrubek, was born March 13, 1900, near Everest in Brown County, Kansas, and departed from this life, July 19, 1939, at the age of 39 years, 4 months and 6 days.

He moved with his parents to Rawlins County, Kansas, in 1907, where he grew to manhood. In 1922 he came to Kearny County and settled on a farm six miles north of Deerfield where he resided until the time of his death.

He was preceded in death by his father and an infant brother. He leaves to mourn his sudden departure: his mother; six sisters, Agnes, Bessie, and Ethel of the home, Mrs. Margaret Wilkinson, Vona, Colorado, Mrs. Barbara Lesher, Augusta, Kansas, Mrs. Evelyn Sharp, Excelsior Springs, Missouri; two brothers, Henry of Pratt, Kansas, and Chris of Beardsley, Kansas; and a host of relatives and friends.

He was a kind and devoted son and brother and will be greatly missed by all.

Funeral services were held Saturday morning at the home conducted by the Rev. Father Wibbles of the Catholic Church. Interment was made in the Deerfield Cemetery.

Card of Thanks: Mrs. Susan Zrubek, Agnes, Bessie, and Ethel; Mr. and Mrs. Roy Wilkinson and family; Mr. and Mrs. Henry Zrubek and daughter; Mr. and Mrs. Chris Zrubek and family; Mr. and Mrs. Earl Lesher and son; Mr. and Mrs. Wm. Sharp.

Alexander F. Zrubek, 39, was the victim of a fatal accident Wednesday afternoon while disking weeds with a one-way. He evidently fell from his machine, the disks passing over his body. Then the tractor kept going in a circle and ran over him again until his form was badly lacerated.

Mr. Zrubek, a single man, lived with his mother and sisters on a farm about ten miles north of Deerfield.

ZRUBEK, ALOYS L. - (Lt. 1, Blk. 21, Sec. 2) Aloys Zrubek son of Leopold and Barbara Marak (Panek) Zrubek, born Oct. 10, 1873, at Everest, Ks., married in 1894 at Greeley, Ks. to Susan Sobba. He died May 8, 1926, in Rawlins County, Ks.

He purchased Section 3-23-35 in 1920, giving as down payment a herd of horses. Bohemian anc., grade school education, Catholic school.

DEERFIELD CEMETERY

Children: Margaret Francis, Henry Adolph, Alex Fred, Chris Frank, Agnes Ann, Barbara Francis, Evelyn Kathryn, Bessie May, Paul, and Ethel Marie.

ZRUBEK, BESSIE M. - (Lt. 3, Blk. 20, Sec. 3) Funeral for Bessie M. Zrubek, 79, Garden City, was held Wednesday afternoon at Price and Sons Funeral Home, Garden City, the Rev. Gilbert Herrman officiating. Burial was in Deerfield Cemetery.
She died December 21, 1992, at Kearny County Hospital, Lakin. Born January 23, 1913, in Rawlins County, she was the daughter of Aloys and Susan Sobba Zrubek.
Miss Zrubek was a bookkeeper for Collins Furniture Store, Garden City, for 41 years. She taught school for 10 years in Rawlins and Kearny counties. She had been a Garden City resident since 1943, moving from Kearny County. She graduated from McDonald High School in 1930.
She was a member of the Catholic faith and was very active in the Women's Chamber of Commerce, Garden City.
Survivors include three sisters, Barbara Lesher, Wichita, Evelyn Morrell, Garden City, and Ethel Steenis, Deerfield. She was preceded in death by four brothers and two sisters.

ZRUBEK, HENRY A. - (Lt. 3, Blk. 20, Sec. 3) Henry A. Zrubek, 73, Dodge City, former Garden City businessman, died at his home unexpectedly Wednesday evening, April 12, 1972.
Born Sept. 15, 1898, at Everest, Mr. Zrubek operated an implement business in Garden City for a number of years before moving to Pratt in 1929. He moved to Dodge City in 1951 and established the Ark Valley Inc. implement manufacturing company.
He was a member of the Western Kansas Manufacturers Inc., charter member of the Western Kansas Caravan, member of Elks, Dodge City Chamber of Commerce, Coronado Car Club and the Packard Motor Club.
Survivors include the widow, Reeda, of the home; a son, William Henry, of the home; a daughter, Mrs. Donna Louden, Dayton, Ohio; a brother, Chris, Ft. Collins, Colo.; five sisters, Mrs. Margaret Wilkinson, Vona, Colo., Mrs. Earl Lesher, Wichita, Mrs. Evelyn Sharp, Bessie Zrubeck, Garden City, and Mrs. Ethel Steenis, Deerfield; and three grandchildren.

DEERFIELD CEMETERY

Funeral was held Saturday at the Hulpieu-Swaim Chapel, Dodge City, the Rev. William H. Travis officiating. Burial at the Deerfield Cemetery.

ZRUBEK, SUSAN - (Lt. 1, Blk. 21, Sec. 2) Susan Sobba was the daughter of Christopher and Margaret (Hastert) Sobba, born Jan. 24, 1874, Verl Westplanter, Germany, died May 26, 1945, at Greeley, Ks. Married Aloys Zrubek, 1894. (The Lakin Independent, Deerfield News, June 1, 1945) Mrs. Dallas Steenis' mother, Mrs. Susan Zubeck, passed away Saturday at her home in Garden City after many months of illness. Friends extend sympathy to Mrs. Steenis and other members of the family.

ZUBECK, BESSIE - (Lt. 4, Blk. 24, Sec. 2) Daughter of Joe and Josephine Zubeck, died July 18, 1925.

ZUBECK, CHARLES - (Lt. 4, Blk. 24, Sec. 2) Son of Joe and Josephine Zubeck, died April 13, 1924, at 5 yrs. of age.

ZUBECK, DENA - (S/2 Lt. 1, Blk. 19, Sec. 3) Funeral for Dena Zubeck, 64, was at 10:00 a.m. Friday, November 12, 1982, at the Kingdom Hall, Garden City, with Frank Crotts officiating. Burial was at the Deerfield Cemetery.
Mrs. Zubeck died of cancer, Tuesday, November 9, 1982, at her home near Deerfield.
Born Dena Martin, December 10, 1917, at Sylvia, she came to Garden City in 1932. She was married to Jimmie Zubeck, November 25, 1939, at Cimarron. To the marriage three children were born, Ginger, Glenda, and Jimmy. After raising her family she became a popular sales clerk at the Crazy House from 1971 to March of 1982.
She was a member of Jehovah's Witnesses, Garden City.
Survivors are her husband, of the home; a son, Jim D. Zubeck, Garden City; two daughters, Ginger Sonderegger, Leoti, and Glenda Schwartz, Garden City; a brother, Leo Martin, Larned; four sisters, Virginia Gray, Cunningham, Frances Whitman and Beverly Branscorn, both of Hutchinson, and Betty Schreibvogel, Lakin; and five grandchildren, Judy, Jill, and Joell Sonderegger, and John and Janelle Schwartz.

ZUBECK, FRANK - (Lt. 1, Blk. 19, Sec. 3) Frank Zubeck, 88, died Wednesday, December 28, 1994, at Fresno, California.

He was born October 21, 1906, in Michigan, the son of Czechoslovakian immigrants, Joe and Josephine Zubeck. The family moved to Ohio, and then to Deerfield when Frank was six years old. He then resided at Deerfield until he was 81, when he moved to California to reside with his children.

Mr. Zubeck was a farmer, and farmed sugar beets, wheat and maize for 20 years, 10 of those being at the Finney/Kearny County line. In 1947, he went to work for the Santa Fe Motor Company (now Deerfield Ag) where he worked for 30 years assembling farm equipment. He retired in 1978.

Mr. Zubeck had a keen interest in people watching, and enjoyed having a cup of coffee and observing folks around him. He liked boats, airplanes and trains, and in recent years he particularly enjoyed a cruse to Mexico, trips to Hawaii, and a train trip down the California coastline. Family trips in the motor home to Las Vegas or Lake Tahoe were fun for all. He enjoyed trips to the mountains, trips to the beach, and business trips with his daughter.

Even though he lived in California for seven years, his heart remained in Kansas. He was a devoted reader of The Lakin Independent newspaper. He grew a "Kansas" garden in California, using seed corn, maize and wheat from Kansas. He returned four years ago to Deerfield for a wonderful visit. He was much loved by his friends and family, and is greatly missed.

He is survived by his children, Norma, Regina, Cherry and Allan, and by his former wife, Bertha Guillory; by grandhildren, Norman and Tina; and by great grandchildren, Justin, Ryan, Janel and Kendra, all of Fresno, California. He is survived by brothers, Bob Zubeck and Jim Zubeck, of Deerfield; and by eight nieces and nephews.

Funeral arrangements were handled by Lisle Funeral Home of Fresno, California, and Garnand Funeral Home of Garden City. A memorial service was held at the Deerfield Methodist Church on Saturday, January 7, and burial was at the Deerfield Cemetery.

ZUBECK, JOE - (Lt. 4, Blk. 24, Sec. 2)   ts. 1885-1937. (The Kearny County Advocate, Oct. 15, 1937) A car wreck 3 miles east of Deerfield claimed the life of Joe Zubeck, Deerfield farmer, when his 1936 Chevrolet collided with an Oldsmobile driven by Garrett Bishop of Resada,

California. Zubeck died almost instantly of a broken neck and a fractured skull.

It is believed that Bishop will survive despite brain concussion and a fractured right hip, and severe cuts on the knees. He regained consciousness Monday and is reported to have said that he does not remember anything about the accident.

Both cars were going at a high speed and collided head on. Zubeck is survived by his wife and six sons, all of Deerfield. Funeral services were conducted Monday by the Rev. L. W. Irons of the Garden City Church of God.

(The Lakin Independent, October 15, 1937) Jos. Zubeck, 52, farmer who lived near Deerfield, is dead and Garrett Bishop of Reseda, California, is in critical condition at St Catherine's Hospital as the result of a head-on motor car collision late Saturday night, six miles west of Holcomb on Highway US 50.

Both men were driving alone. Zubeck's machine, a 1936 model Chevrolet coach, and Bishop's car, a 1935 Oldsmobile sedan, both were turned into piles of junk by the impact.

Zubeck, who farmed on land owned by the Garden City Company and who has lived in the vicinity of Deerfield for 15 years, is believed to have died a few minutes after the crash. Dr. H. C. Sartorius, county health officer, said he suffered a broken neck and a fractured skull.

The attending physician said Bishop has an excellent chance to recover, although he is certain to be in the hospital for at least two months. Bishop suffered a brain concussion, a fractured and dislocated right hip and severe knee lacerations.

Bishop, who was in a stupor throughout Sunday, regained his senses for the first time today. He said he cannot recall any details of the accident.

Sheriff J. C. Standly, who arrived on the scene shortly after the accident, said today he believed neither driver saw the other until they were but a few feet apart. There were no tire marks on the pavement, he said.

Standly expressed the opinion that both men were traveling at a high rate of speed. He asserted that the crash was almost full head-on and said it is remarkable that Bishop escaped death.

It was reported, but the report could not be confirmed, that Zubeck swung over past the center of the highway

DEERFIELD CEMETERY

because a truck, whose driver had stopped to repair its lights, was parked at the edge on the pavement. Zubeck was returning to his home from Garden City at the time of the crash. Bishop was driving from Reseda, Calif., to Weldon, Ia., where he planned to meet his wife and return her to California.

Funeral services for Zubeck were conducted this afternoon at the Garnand Funeral Home with Rev. L.W. Irons of the Garden City Church of God officiating. The body will be taken to Deerfield for burial.

Zubeck is survived by his wife and six sons. The sons are: Tom, Joe, Frank, James, John and Robert, all of Deerfield.

Zubeck, a native of Czechoslovakia, came to the United States 33 years ago. He has been a farmer and cattleman fo 30 years.

ZUBECK, JOHN - (Lt. 1, Blk. 19, Sec. 3)   John George Zubeck, 74, died suddenly Tuesday, September 11, 1990, at his home in Garden City, Kansas. Graveside services were held at the Deerfield Cemetery with Military Services conducted by the John J. Haskell VFW Post No. 2279. Rev. Don Koehn was in charge of the Christian prayers, Bible reading and last words.

John was born September 21, 1915, near Deerfield, to Joseph and Josephine Zubeck. He attended school at Deerfield. John was a farmer until 1941 when he was drafted to serve his country. World War II was very intense at the time John entered the service and he never received a furlough home. Injured twice in battle as an infantry soldier, he was treated in field hospitals and returned to the front lines. He served in North Africa and the push through Italy with the U.S. Army 168th Infantry. Received the Purple Heart with one bronze oak leaf cluster, bronze arrowhead, the good conduct medal and American defense service ribbon.

John returned home July 1945, to Deerfield where he worked for Harley Rector and the Santa Fe Motor Co. in Deerfield.

John moved to Garden City and was a welder for East Side Iron until he became ill in 1976. He stayed in the VA hospital and domiciliary until 1980, when he returned to Garden City to live in his own place until his death.

John was one of six boys: Frank, Tom, Jimmie, Joe and Bob. The three surviving brothers are Frank Zubeck of

303

DEERFIELD CEMETERY

Fresno, Calif., and Jimmie and Bob Zubeck of Deerfield, and many nieces and nephews.

ZUBECK, JOSEPH JR. - (Lt. 1, Blk. 19, Sec. 3) Funeral for Joseph Zubeck Jr., 72, was held at the Garnand Funeral Chapel, the Rev. Leland DeMent officiating. Burial at Deerfield Cemetery.
Mr. Zubeck died Thursday, June 16, 1983, at St. Catherine Hospital. He was a retired carpenter/farmer.
Born Nov. 13, 1910, at Paulding, Ohio, he married Nora Cook, August 13, 1936, at Colorado Springs.
He moved to Kansas from Ohio when three years old with his parents. He moved to Garden City from Deerfield in 1970.
Surviving are two daughters, Kathaleen Porter and Patsy Brimm both of Garden City; four brothers, Frank, Jim and Bobby, all of Deerfield, and John, Garden City; seven grandchildren and three great grandchildren. Two brothers and two sisters preceded him in death.

ZUBECK, JOSEPHINE - (Lt. 4, Blk. 24, Sec. 2) Mrs. Josephine Zubeck, 76, died Wednesday afternoon, June 26, 1963, in the Kearny County Hospital.
She was born Sept. 22, 1886, in Prague, Czechoslovakia. She came to Pittsburgh, Pa., in 1904 and in 1911 to a farm south of Deerfield.
She was married to Joseph Zubeck, Jan. 29, 1905, at Flint, Mich. He died Oct. 9, 1937.
Two sons and two daughters also preceded her in death. Survivors include six sons, Tom, Frank, Jim and Bob Zubeck, all of Deerfield; Joe of Gardendale and John of Garden City; 12 grandchildren and six great grandchildren.
Funeral was Saturday at 10 a.m. in Garnand chapel. The Rev. Robert Fleenor of the Deerfield Methodist Church officiated. Burial was in the Deerfield Cemetery.

ZUBECK, MARY - (Lt. 4, Blk. 24, Sec. 2) Daughter of Joe Zubeck, died Dec. 24, 1928, 7 months, 19 days old, of pneumonia.

FAIRVIEW CEMETERY

This small cemetery is located in the northwest corner of Kearny County. Ulysses Grant McCoy and Mary E. McCoy, his wife, deeded to The Trustees of the Fairview Cemetary Association, January 21, 1910, a tract, 17 rods square, in SE/c of SE/4 of Section 6, Township 21, Range 37 in Kearny County, by a deed recorded in Deed Book 14, page 283. There were 45 designated burial plots.

(The Kearny County Advocate, April 23, 1908) A meeting was held at Fairview last Wednesday night to organize a Burial Association. D. H. Braden was elected Chairman, Grant McCoy Secretary, Al Wilson, Mr. Stanley and Ira Brown, Trustees. A site for a cemetery and meeting house was chosen on Grant McCoy's farm. The next meeting will be held on Wednesday evening, May 6th. Let all interested attend.

(The Kearny County Advocate, April 30, 1908) The Fairview Cemetery Association completed laying out and fencing the Cemetery, Tuesday.

(Lakin Investigator, May 15, 1908) The farmers of Fairview Neighborhood have organized a cemetery association. There are 19 members. They have their plot layed out, fenced and sowed to blue grass. Grant McCoy gave three acres of land on the southeast corner of his place.

(Kearny County Advocate, September 17, 1908) There will be a meeting of the Burial Association on Wednesday evening, September 23rd, at 8 o'clock at Fairview school house. Want all members to be present for there is some important business to attend to. We invite our neighbors and friends to join us in this good work for you know not when the good Lord will call some of your dear ones and you will need a place to lay them at rest. D. H. Braden, Chairman.

(The Lakin Independent, April 27, 1923) The new Immanuel Presbyterian Church was dedicated last Thursday in an all day service. Rev. R. L. Price of Syracuse preached a helpful sermon on "Loyalty" at 10:30, and following the sermon Rev. D. C. Smith presided at the Communion service. Rev. E. L. Brandner of Coolidge preached in the afternoon at 2:30, taking as his theme the Parable of the Good Samaritan, after which Rev. D. C.

FAIRVIEW CEMETERY

Smith read the service dedicating the church building to God, as a place of worship.

On Friday evening the members of the Presbyterian Christian Endeavor Society drove up to the new church and conducted a helpful and inspiring service.

This new church building is located 30 miles northwest of Lakin, in a neighborhood not supplied by any other church services and will fill a much felt need.

(Author"s Note) The church is now long gone. The marker reads: Immanuel Presbyterian Church, Organized March 1921, Disorganized April 1959, Sunday School begun 1910. The cemetery is under the care of Kearny County Cemetery District No. 3.

FAIRVIEW CEMETERY

CLOW - (no information found only John F. Clow homesteaded the SE/4 of Sec. 3, Twp. 21, Range 38, Patent Jan. 23, 1913. He sold it April 27, 1918.)

DOWNS, BABY BOY Leil - (The Lakin Independent, July 1, 1932) A baby boy was born to Mr. and Mrs. Emil Downs Monday, the 20th. The tiny baby lived until Saturday. Funeral services were held at the church Sunday afternoon, conducted by Rev. E. L. Brandner.

DOWNS, BABY BOY Hugh - (The Lakin Independent, Nov. 15, 1935) Funeral services were held at the Fairview church Saturday afternoon for Mr. and Mrs. Jack Downs's 26 day old baby boy; Rev. Brandner in charge. The little fellow died at the Scott City hospital, where he had been given the best of care since his birth. The Fairview community join in extending sympathy to Mr. and Mrs. Jack Downs in the loss of their first born baby.

DOWNS, IRA - Ira Downs, another Fairview pioneer, passed away Saturday, Sept. 6, 1958, at the Wichita County Hospital where he had spent 13 months and a few days. Funeral services were held at the Presbyterian Church at Leoti, Monday afternoon, and interment was in the Fairview Cemetery. Mr. Downs was 85 years old. The family spent many years in the Fairview community enduring the hardships and inconvience of pioneer life. The Fairview folks extend sympathy to the family.

Old friends and neighbors in former years from Garden City that attended the services at Leoti were Mr. and Mrs. Clare Whitaker, Mrs. Emma Brewer, Mr. and Mrs. A. J. Rupp and Mrs. C. W. Rosebrook, and Mr. and Mrs. Robert Rosebrook from Dodge City.

Ira Downs, son of William and Margaret Ashlock Downs, was born January 7, 1873, in Wyandotte County, Kansas, near Kansas City. Soon after he was born his parents moved to Clay County where he grew up and went to school. He married Permelia (Millie) Harriet Bates, February 22, 1898. Later the family moved to Kearny County, then back to Clay County for a few years and back to Kearny County in 1916.

Ira Downs, son of William Downs and Margaret Ashlock, was born January 7, 1873, in Wyandotte County, Kansas, near Kansas City, and died September 6, 1958, at the Wichita County hospital.

He is survived by five sons: Lloyd and Jack of Wichita; Emil of Plains; Vernon and Horace, of Leoti; and two daughters: Mrs. Laura Hahn and Mrs. Vardie Buck of Leoti.

DOWNS, IRA J. "JACK" - Memorial service for former Leoti resident Ira J. "Jack" Downs, 82, Arlington, Texas, was held at 2:30 p.m. Friday at the First Presbyterian Church, Leoti, the Rev. Dave Smith officiating. Burial at Fairview Cemetery, north Kearny County.
He died March 13, 1988, at Arlington.
Born Nov. 25, 1905, in Wakefield, he married Elsie E. Brown, July 14, 1934. She died Oct. 28, 1960. He married Dorothy Johnson, Oct. 1, 1966, in Texas.
Mr. Downs was a retired carpenter and machinist, and had been a Texas resident since 1963, moving from Wichita and was a former Leoti resident.
He was a member of the Elks Lodge, Arlington.
Survivors include his wife, of the home; a daughter, Laura L. Shaffer, Grand Lake, Colo.; a stepson, Robert Johnson, San Antonio, Texas; two brothers, Emil Downs, Plains, and Horace Downs, Leoti; two sisters, Laura Hahn and Vardie Buck, both of Leoti; and four grandchildren.

DOWNS, LOIE IREL - Born July 15, 1918, and died Oct. 26, 1921, daughter of Ira and Millie Downs. Died of spinal meningitis.

DOWNS, MILLIE - Mrs. Ira (Purmelia Harriet Bates) Downs passed away Wednesday morning, July 13th, 1938, at the family home. Funeral was held at the home and she was laid to rest in Fairview Cemetery, Friday evening. Her death was a blessed relief for her as she had been in frail health for a number of years. All those years of suffering she had been tenderly cared for at the home by her family. Her devotion and self sacrifice for her family and neighbors was beautiful. The terrible deluge of rain Friday afternoon made it impossible for scores of friends to be present at the funeral service. Friends far and near extend sympathy to Mr. Downs and his family.
Mr. and Mrs. Emil Downs and family of Plains and Jack and Lloyd Downs of Wichita came home to attend their mother's funeral. Jack and Lloyd returned to Wichita Sunday evening and Emil and family left for Plains Monday morning.
Mrs. Downs was born August 13, 1877.

FAIRVIEW CEMETERY

EDENBURN, PETER - (Death Records)   Peter Edenburn, a white male, 91 years, 10 months, and 3 days old, died July 4, 1912, in Kearny County of senility.   He was a widower. B. F. Clayton undertaker.   He was a Civil War Veteran.

HAHN, AUGUST, SR. - August Hahn, Sr., was born Dec. 21, 1876, in Adeenhart, Germany, and departed this life Dec. 28, 1955, at the age of 79 years and seven days. He left Germany at the age of 15 and settled near Peoria, Ill. While living in Illinois he was united in marriage to Caroline Catherine Lay, June 11, 1898.   To this union four children were born.   He later moved to Reno County, Kans., where he lived for several years. In September of 1905, Mr. Hahn, with his wife and three eldest children, came to Kearny County, Kans., where they settled on a homestead.   The youngest daughter, Violet, was born on the homestead where Mr. Hahn resided until a few weeks before his death.
One son, Samuel, two brothers and one sister preceded him in death.
When a young man he was baptized in the Lutheran faith. He was always interested in Sunday School and church and attended regularly at Immanuel Lutheran Church until Mrs. Hahn's health failed.
Mr. Hahn was a quiet, unassuming man, devoted to his children and grandchildren. He was a good neighbor, ever ready to help when one was in need.
Mr. and Mrs. Hahn celebrated their 50th wedding anniversary, June 11, 1948.
Mr. Hahn enjoyed fair health for his age until a few months ago when his health began to fail. His condition grew steadily worse until Wednesday afternoon when death came.
In the passing of Mr. Hahn, Fairview has lost one of its early pioneer settlers.
He leaves to mourn his passing, his invalid wife, who in her feeble condition, is not aware of her husbands death; one son, August, Jr., of Leoti; two daughters, Mrs. Lillie Burns of Nice, Calif., and Mrs. Violet Henry of Sacramento, Calif.; two sisters in Illinois; 23 grandchildren; 22 great grandchildren and a host of other relatives and friends.
Services were held at the Fairview Church, Sunday afternoon, Jan. 1, Rev. Wilty was in charge. A quartet consisting of Mr. and Mrs. Duard Hill, Mrs. Horace Downs

and Vern Miles with Mrs. Miles at the piano furnished the
music. Pallbearers were A. E. and G. J. Anderson, G. H.
Hylton, Tobe Koehn, Howard Clevenger and Alvin Bishop.
Interment was in the Fairview Cemetery.

HAHN, CAROLINA - Carolina Kathrine (Lye) Hahn was born
May 24, 1876, in Bush, Germany, and passed away June 22,
1959, at Stella's Nursing Home in Garden City, Kansas.
She came to the United States of America, in April 1896.
When a child she was baptized in the Lutheran faith.
    She was married to August Hahn, Sr., on June 11, 1898,
at Peoria, Ill., to this union four children were born.
She was preceded in death by a son, Samuel, in 1912, and
her husband in December 1955. In 1905 she, her husband
and family came to Western Kansas where they took up a
homestead in Kearny County. They lived here until
passing away.
    Mrs. Hahn attended the Immanuel Presbyterian Church of
Fairview community as long as her health permitted.
After her husband passed away she was cared for in the
homes of her grandson, Orval Hahn, and son, August Hahn,
until taken to Stella's Nursing Home in Garden City,
where she passed away.
    She was a quiet person, devoted to her family and
friends and loved by all who knew her.
    She is survived by a son, August Hahn, Jr., of Leoti,
Kansas; two daughters, Mrs. Lillie Burns of Nice, Calif.,
and Mrs. Violet Henry of Del Paso Heights, Calif. She
also leaves 23 grandchildren and 30 great grandchildren
and a host of other relatives and friends. She was laid
to rest at the Immanuel Fairview Cemetery on Friday
afternoon at three o'clock.
    Friends and relatives attending from out of town were
Mrs. Cecil Henry, Del Paso Heights, Calif.; Mrs.
Katherine Jones, Mrs. Leroy Jones, Lakin, Kansas; Mrs.
Lawrence Ferrell and Mrs. Kenneth Peters, Ulysses,
Kansas; Angie E. Rouge, and Mr. and Mrs. L. L. Lusing,
all of Garden City, Kansas.

HAHN, JOSEPH - 2/7/1908, first burial. He was moved from
the Lutheran Cemetery.
    Joey, as he was known, was a son of Carl and Mary Hahn,
died Feb 7, 1908, age 9 yrs., of lung fever.

HAHN, BOY Sammy - (Kearny County Advocate, Aug. 2, 1912)
A sad accident occured in the family of August Hahn, of

FAIRVIEW CEMETERY

the Fairview neighborhood last week. A ten year old son
was run over by a run away team attached to a wheat barge
and the little fellow only lived two hours. The father
was away from home at the time. The family has the
sincere sympathy of the entire community,
He was born Sept. 26, 1900.

HETZER, TWINS - Twins of Mr. and Mrs. George Hetzer.

KUNKLE, INFANT - Infant of Tom Kunkle.

MCCOY, HARVEY - (The Kearny County Advocate, April 23,
1908) Little Harvey McCoy has passed through, "The blind
cave of eternal night"
   "Ere sin could blight or sorrow fade,
   Death came with friendly care;
   The opening bud to Heaven conveyed
   And bade it blossom there."
   Miss Lucile McCoy who has been attending school at
Kansas City came home Thursday on account of the death of
her brother.
   We extend to Grant McCoy and family of north Kearny our
heartfelt sympaty in the loss of their little three year
old son, Harvey, who died April 8th. It is a sad loss to
them, and there is a deep response of sympathy from other
hearts that have suffered in the same way. (Later moved.)

MCCOY, JAMES HARVEY - James Harvey McCoy, son of Abraham
and Susie McCoy, was born in Newville, Cumberland County,
Pennsylvania, June 27th, 1868, and died in Leoti, Wichita
County, Kansas, December 30th, 1921, being fifty three
years, six months and three days old at the time of his
death. He came with his parents to Wilson, Kansas, in
1878. He was married to Eva Elkins, September 8th, 1894,
at her home near Dorrance, Kansas.
   He lived at Wilson, Kansas, until the year of 1906,
when he moved with his family to Kearny County, Kansas,
where he has since resided.
   He joined the Methodist Church in his youth and
remained a faithful and devoted Christian up to the time
of his death. He united with the Presbyterian Church
here and was elected and ordained an Elder, March 27th,
1910.
   He was always ready and willing to do his duty and help
any one in any way he could.

311

FAIRVIEW CEMETERY

He is survived by his wife and five children, Ira, Mertie, Verne, Ray and Vera; one sister, Mrs. Grace Stanley of LaCrosse, Kansas; three brothers, Grant and Howard of Wilson, Kansas, and Walter of Herrington, Kansas. He was a kind father and a loving husband and his friends were numbered by the ones who knew him. The funeral was held at the family home Sunday afternoon and the remains laid to rest in the Lydia Cemetary.

(The Advocate, Jan. 6, 1922)   James H. McCoy, a prominent and highly respected citizen of northwest Kearny, had taken a load of grain to Leoti to the elevator Dec. 30th, for Mr. Ned Sylvia. He left the team standing just east of the elevator while he went inside the office. The noon whistle blew and the team became frightened. Mr. McCoy ran to catch the lines and tripped and fell under the wagon, the wheels passing over his chest killing him instantly.

(Later moved to Lakin Cemetery.)

PEARL, FRED - (Lakin Independent, Fairview News, June 27, 1924) This community was saddened by the death of Fred Pearl, which occurred at his home Wednesday noon, after a short illness. He was buried Friday in the Fairview Cemetery.

ROSEBROOK, ROSALIE - Born Aug. 14, 1913, and died June 10, 1914, of whooping cough and pneumonia. Daughter of C. W. and Hannah Rosebrook.

WADLEY, CLIFFORD INFANT - (Lot 21) Clifford Dean Wadley, son of Rufus J. and Rita Brewer Wadley, was born Sept. 13, 1924, and died Sept 15, 1924, at the home of his grandparents, Floyd and Emma A. Brewer, at Lydia. Surviving are his grandparents, Suan Wadley and Floyd and Emma Brewer and two uncles: John and Ben Wadley.

WINTERS, NOMA - Daughter of Mr. and Mrs. J. A. Winters, born June 17, 1905, and died July 4, 1908. (Later moved to Lakin Cemetery.)

MISCELLANEOUS KEARNY COUNTY BURIALS

At one time there were several rural cemeteries in Kearny County. Many of those bodies have been removed to other cemeteries. In the earlier days homesteaders and families were buried on their own land.

Located on the southeast corner of Section 20-21-35 was a cemetery of about 2 acres. It was used from 1886 through the nineties. This is where Charlotte A. Kaye is buried.

Another cemetery of about a half acre was established in 1886 on the northeast corner of Section 3-22-25. This is where Herbert E. Tedrow is buried.

Another cemetery known as the Riffel Cemetery was located on the northeast corner of NW/4 of Section 17-21-35.

The Kearny cemetery was located in the neighborhood of the abandoned townsite of Kearny which was on NE/4 16-22-37 in 1887.

The town of Omaha was located in Section 13-23-37 in 1888.

I have found the following deaths mentioned in old newspapers and hope they will be of interest to someone.

MISCELLANEOUS KEARNY COUNTY BURIALS

ANDERSON, GIRL - In 1877 a little girl of a Mr. Anderson, an emigrant, died of skunk bite where they camped on the Santa Fe trail west of Lakin. The little child was buried south of the railroad near the railroad fence, and for many years the little grave, marked by a pile of stones, could be seen west of the stockyards.

APPLEBY, THOMAS W. - (Pioneer Democrat, August 28, 1886) Died August 27th, 1886, Thomas W. Appleby, aged 25 years. The deceased came to Lakin nearly three years ago. By his business integrity, and good character he had gained the high esteem of all who knew him, and the entire community are alike pained to learn of his death. Rev. J. R. Lowrance delivered the funeral sermon at 2:30 o'clock this afternoon.

BARINGER, - (The Lakin Index, Sept. 12, 1891) We learn from county attorney Kelso, that old man Baringer, a prosperous farmer living four miles north of Kendall, died at his home on Saturay night or Sunday morning last. He was about 70 years of age, and was in Kendall on Saturday evening last, apparently in good health. While in town he invited his friend, Wm. Hanah, to come out to his place Sunday and eat watermelons. Arriving there Sunday morning, Mr. Hanah was surprised to find the house all shut up, and on gaining an entrance was astonished to find the old man lying on his bed dead. Old man Baringer was a prosperous farmer outside of irrigation. Last year he raised fully 700 bushels of wheat, and this year had a fine crop of 80 acres, and was probably the only farmer in the north part of the county who had bearing peach trees on his farm. He has been living in this county about six years, and is said to have been an old Confederate soldier. A coffin was sent up from this place on Monday last, in which to bury him. We understand that he came to this county from California.

BEATTY, DERIUS - (The Lakin Index, April 28, 1893) Derius Beatty, one of the early settlers of this county, died at his home, north of Lakin, on Friday last. He was born April 17, 1812, and died April 21, 1893, being six days less that 81 years of age. He was a member of the Separate Baptist Church, having become attached to that church previous to the death of his wife, some 19 years since. He was born in Kentucky and removed from there when a boy to Indiana, and in the spring of 1886 came to this city. He was the father of nine children, five of whom are left to mourn his loss, together with 23 grandchildren and 22 great grandchildren During his illness he said "I am a worn out old man, but if we will put our trust in Jesus, he will bring us out all safe in the end." He felt that he was warned of his approaching end two weeks before his death by a dream. He told his friends that "he was taking a walk and he saw a fine mansion. He knocked at the door which was opened to him and there he saw his departed wife as natural as life." He was taken seriously ill a few days after relating this dream to his son-in-law. He called for his son, Joseph, to raise him up in his bed and died quietly in his son's arms.

Rev. Oliver conducted religious services at the home, Sunday afternoon, and the body was buried on his place by the side of a grand-son, in the presence of a large number of relatives and friends. (Derius Beaty homesteaded the NE/4 of Sec. 18-23-36.)

BOATRIGHT, JAMES - (Kearny County Advocate, Sept. 25, 1914) James Boatright, a well known farmer living four miles north of town, received a death blow, while milking a cow, on his farm, Sunday morning, by a severe kick from the animal, striking him in the groin and directly over the solar plexus. Dr. Johnston gave prompt attention to his injuries, but death ensued on Monday afternoon. Mr. Boatright was one of our active, industrious and respected farmers and his sudden and untimely death gave a shock to his many friends. He was the candidate of the Socialist party for sheriff, and came to this county some seven years ago from near Fort Scott, Kansas. He was a prominent member of the I.O.O.F., and will be missed from his lodge room, and his sudden absence sincerely mourned. Funeral services were held Wednesday afternoon at the Methodist Church, Rev. Gibbons preaching the sermon, and the interment made by the odd fellows, which he was an honored member.

BOYLE, JAMES - (Lakin Herald, Finney County Kansas, Oct. 28, 1882) On Wednesday night, James Boyle, one of our old settlers, was taken suddenly ill, the effects of a kick from a horse and died the same evening. Aged 45.

(Lakin Herald, Nov. 4, 1882) When James Boyle died in our town a few days ago, he was without money enough to defray his funeral expenses, though having steady

MISCELLANEOUS KEARNY COUNTY BURIALS

employment from the AT & SF railroad, he forgot that
there was a time to come when sickness and death will
visit us. He boarded with Mrs. Morgan for a long time
and though in debt to that lady, she kindly paid all his
funeral expenses showing the kindness of woman to man.

COOPER, GIRL - (The Lakin Investigator, June 11, 1904) A
little daughter of Mr. Cooper of Deerfield, died very
suddenly last Wednesday. The child was about 3 years old
and was sick only about a day.

DAY, ARCHIE - (Kearny County Advocate, March 20, 1886)
Mr. and Mrs. Sidney Day buried their infant child,
Archie, aged seven months, on Sunday last. Rev. H. M.
Carr held funeral services over the remains of the little
one, which was largely attended by sympathizing friends.

DILLON, MABEL - (The Lakin Herald, July 25, 1881) Died
on the 18th of accidental shooting, Mable Dillon, aged 3
years, daughter of Jos. Dillon. Funeral services were
performed by the Rev. Mr. Platt of Garden City.

DISSTLER, WM. - (The Kearny County Advocate, April 16,
1891) Found dead was the report that reached Hartland
last Friday. Wm. Disstler, of Kearny Township was found
dead in his house by one of his neighbors last Thursday
evening. Coroner Richards summoned a jury, and after an
examination of the premises and body, reported that
deceased died from natural causes. Wm. Disstler had been
a resident of this county for over four years. He came
originally from Germany and settled in Pratt County, and
from there to this county, where him an his three boys
settled, his sons proving up their land and left, the old
man being left alone. He was probably 75 years old and
had been apparently in good health. Coroner Richards
thinks he had been dead some ten to fifteen days. His
sons have been notified. He was buried on his claim.
    (The Lakin Index, April 18, 1891) An old German, known
as "Deitchler," living in Kearny Township, some ten miles
northwest of Lakin, was found dead on his claim, on
Thursday of last week. Decomposition had set in and it
was supposed that he had been dead for several days. The
old man was unable to speak English in any manner,
whatever, and for a year or more had been a charge on the
township, until ex-commissioner Johnson ordered his food
rations stopped. It is said that he had provisions in

his house, and his death is not attributable to lack of food, but being alone and some distance from any neighbors, no doubt died during a sick spell. He is said to have had considerable means when he came to the county three or four years ago, but his wife and boys left him a year ago, and since that time has had to have his temporal wants supplied. He had a wagon and team and his entire effects are not more than $100. He was probably 65 years of age, and has no relatives in the county.

FRIESNER, WALTER - (Kearny County Advocate, April 13, 1889) Walter Friesner, whose sickness were mentioned last week, died on Friday last. Our sympathies are extended to the bereaved parents. Card of thanks signed by Mr. and Mrs. J. S. Friesner.

GOLDEN, GIRL - (The Kearny County Coyote, May 19, 1888) The six year old daughter of Mrs. Ellen Golden, of 22-36, died a few days ago with congestion of the brain. The child was buried in 21-35. The mother has the sympathy of all her friends and neighbors in her sad bereavement.

GULICK, GARRETT - (Lakin Investigator, May 10, 1907) Garrett Gulick, an old and respected citizen of this county, died at his home, 15 miles north of Lakin Friday night. Mr. Gulick has resided in Western Kansas for 18 years, coming here from Illinois. He was born in West Virginia in 1828. Mr. Gulick leaves a wife and seven children, five boy and two girls.

HANSEN, HENRY - (Kearny County Advocate, Dec. 25, 1902) Henry Hansen, a German 78 yrs old, was found dead in his home, Monday, in North Kearny County. The Coroner's jury found a verdict that he came to his death by some explosive in the stove. He was found partly on the bed, with a cut in his head and one under the shoulder blade, which caused his death. Mr. Hansen was an old settler and a bachelor, a very eccentric man and did not mingle with his neighbors, or allow any of them to come to his house. It is not thought he was murdered.
     (He homesteaded the NE/4 of Sec. 17, Twp. 22, Range 38, July 20, 1892.)
     He was born April 1833 in Germany and came to U.S. in 1871.

MISCELLANEOUS KEARNY COUNTY BURIALS

HEBERN, MR. - Killed while digging a well on his homestead on the SW/4 35-21-36, by "damps". Buried in NE/4 3-22-35.

HEFNER, AGNES ANNABEL - Born Oct. 26, 1905, died Feb. 26, 1907, father, Luther Franklin Hefner, mother, Maude. (Buried SE/c SE/4 Sec. 4, Twp. 24, Range 37. This was the homestead of Luther Hefner.)
     (The Lakin Investigator, March 1, 1907) A little eighteen months old girl daughter of Mr. and Mrs. Luther Haffner, died at the home of her grand parents, a few miles north west of Lakin on Tuesday last, and was buried on Wednesday afternoon. The parents were visiting grandpa Haffner and family, when the child was suddenly taken ill and died in a short time. Rev. W. S. Prather conducted the funeral and neighbors and friends joined in the service of laying the remains of the little one in the bosom of mother earth.

HEFNER, HOY HYMERE - (The Lakin Investigator, Sept. 18, 1908) A little baby boy, about six months old, son of Mr. and Mrs. L. Hefner, died Wednesday morning.
     (The Lakin Investigator, Sept. 25, 1908) Again the icy hand of death has visited the home of Mr. and Mrs. Luther Hefner, claiming as its victim an infant son. It was born April 4, (birth records show born April 11) and died Sept. 16. It was sick but a few hours. The funeral was conducted by W. S. Prather and the little form was laid to rest in the family cemetery.
     (The Kearny County Advocate, Sept. 24, 1908) The infant son of Mr. and Mrs. Luther Hefner died Sept. 16, aged 5 months and 4 days. Funeral service conducted by Rev. W. S. Prather, was held at the Sunrise school house, and remains were buried in the family grave yard.
     (Burial on SE/c SE/4 Sec. 4, Twp. 24, Range 37.)

HILL, P.A. - (Kearny County Advocate, March 13, 1886) Died at his home in this place on Monday morning last, P. A. Hill, in the thirty-eighth year of his age.
     Mr. Hill came to this place from Iowa, sometime in May last, and after securing a claim, was engaged in running a hack from Lakin to Sunset City. He was a prompt and reliable man and pursued his avocation with remarkable zest, exposing himself in all kinds of weather in order to convey passengers or freight to their destination, and to this continued exposure is attributed the chief cause

of his death. He was sick for ten days or more, during which time a noble wife and medical attendance did all that they could to restore him to his wonted vigor and to alleviate his suffering, but to no purpose. The angel of death hovered near, and his spirit took its flight, not, however until he knew of his coming and assured his companion that he was prepared to go. Funeral services were conducted at the town hall by Rev. H. M. Carr, and largely attended by our sympathizing citizens. Two maiden sisters from Richfield, were here to attend his funeral, and his remains were buried near town.

In the '86 blizzard a man by name of P. A. Hill was driving stage between here and Sunset. Exposure during the blizzard of that year caused his death. His son, L. S. Hill, at that time only nine years old, now of Des Moines, Iowa, was here trying to locate the remains of his father, but could find no trace of them. They were buried in the grave yard west of town and probably were not marked, and when removed to the present cemetery were not identified, or else they still remain in the old grounds.

JOHNSON, FEMALE - (The Lakin Investigator, Dec. 29, 1905) A little three year old child, the youngest daughter of Mr. and Mrs. Frank Johnson, died on Monday night, and was buried Tuesday morning. Death was said to be due to tonsilitis.

KAYE, CHARLOTTE A.- Born Feb. 11, 1885, and died Feb. 9, 1887. Daughter of Omar and Dell Kaye. Buried in SE/c 20-21-35. Headstone still stands.

LANDER, JACK - (The Kearny County Advocate, Lookout Hill News, August 9, 1918) Little Jack Lander, the infant son of Mr. and Mrs. Herman Lander, died last Thursday morning at 7 a.m. He was a year old. The bright little fellow will be missed, for all who knew him loved him. Our sympathies are with the bereaved parents and relatives.

LINDSAY, LORENA - (Pioneer Democrat, January 28, 1888) Entered into rest early on the morning of January 22, 1888, Lorena Lindsay, infant daughter of Frank P. and Flora A. Lindsay, aged three months and twenty one days.

The exact cause of the little one's death is unknown, although the parents had had some misgiving about raising it at first, it seemed so frail, of late their doubts

MISCELLANEOUS KEARNY COUNTY BURIALS

were allayed by its rapid improvement, both in flesh and strength, until they were justly proud and happy in the possession of so bright and precious a treasure. The little one was put to bed on Saturday night, seemingly in good health, with the exception of a slight cold, which was considered of not much consequence, and slept as usual, as near as can be told. The next morning being the Sabbath, and having no cares burdening their minds, they slept later than usual, and on waking about half past six or seven, the mother turned down the covering to see how it fared with the child, and found that its spirit had returned to the God who gave it, and no sign whereby it was so. Who can realize the agonizing shock of that moment? Only those who like them have passed through the same trial. While we know in this life they can never again see that bright smiling little face, beautiful in death, because beaming with the light of heaven, still, that cheering presence which brought sunshine to gladen their hearts when dejected or sorrowful. On Monday at two o'clock sympathizing friends and neighbors met to perform the last sad rites. The short services were conducted by Rev. H. M. Carr, whose remarks were very impressive, especially did the oft repeated line "asleep in Jesus," seem singualarly appropriate as the beautiful little sleeper lay smiling as if ony "Asleep" in her narrow bed.

We extend to the sorrowing mother and bereaved father our heartfelt sympathy and condolence in this, their hour of deep sorrow. May the God of all comfort bestow upon them His heavenly benedictions.

"Ere sin could harm, or sorrow fade
Death came with friendly care;
The opening bud to heaven conveyed,
and bade it blossom there."

LYON, MARY E. - (Pioneer Democrat, August 28, 1886) Died, Mary E. Lyon, aged 19 years, 11 months and 10 days, August 25th, at the residence of her parents four miles north of Lakin. The deceased was born in New Jersey, and was converted and united with the M.E. Church at the age of 14, and remained an acceptable member until her death. Services held at the home, August 26 at 4 p.m.

"Christ leads us through no darker rooms
Then He went through before;
He that into God's kingdom comes,
May enter by this door,

MISCELLANEOUS KEARNY COUNTY BURIALS

Come Lord, when grace hath made me meet
Thy blessed face to see,
For if thy work on earth be sweet,
What will thy glory be!" Rev. W. V. Burns

MCLAUGHLIN, GIRL — (Kearny County Coyote, Omaha, Kansas, June 30, 1888) Died Wednesday, June 20, infant daughter of E. H. McLaughlin, of 22-35. The mother and father have the sympathy of many friends in the loss of their child. (N/2 17-22-35)

MCQUEEN, MYRTLE — (The Lakin Index, July 23, 1892) The first new made grave to be opened in the cemetery east of town, was dug on Friday last, and the remains of Myrtle, the thirteen year old daughter of Mr. and Mrs. Thomas McQueen, living north of Lakin, was laid to rest. She had been afflicted with a nervous disease for some time, but not until the first of the month was her complaint thought to be of a serious character. She was confined to her bed but six days previous to her death. A large concourse of friends and relatives followed her remains to the grave.

MICHEL, GEO. W. — (The Lakin Independent, Oct. 29, 1916) Geo. W. Michel, one of the oldest residents of North Kearny County, died Monday evening. The funeral was held Tuesday with interment in the family block near his late home. He had reached the ripe old age of 88 years. He was the father of Chris Michel.

MOFFIT, JOHN H. — (Kearny County Coyote, Omaha, Kansas, May 19, 1888) John H. Moffit died at his home in 21-35, March 12, 1888. He was 63 years old.
(The Kearney County Coyote, May 19, 1888) A coroner's jury was empaneled by Squire Logan on last Friday, May 11th, to inquire into the cause of the death of John H. Moffit. Mr. Moffit died at his home, in 21-35, on the 12th day of March, 1888, after being sick for about two hours. Mr. Moffit was about sixty three years old, and living with his second wife, who was much his junior. He had been in poor health for some time past. The evidence disclosed the fact that his sons, claim holders near by, were of the opinion that he had been poisoned; that he and his wife had not gotten along amicably together, that the symptoms just before his death were that he had taken strychinia, his muscular system being terribly agitated,

and having periodical spasms or paroxyms of great pain;
but the jury, after hearing all the evidence, and being
advised of the law in the premises, were of the opinion
that he came to his death from natural causes. Mrs.
Moffit has, since the death of her husband, John H.
Moffit, been married to a Mr. Washburn, and it is hoped
that the verdict of the jury will forever put a quietus
on the reports that were circulated to her annoyance, and
to the injury of her character. It is much better that
such serious charges against the good name of our fellow
citizens be examined by a legal tribunal, than that
gossip mongers should try and convict them without giving
them a chance at defense.

MOHR, INFANTS - Two children of John Mohr, not named, are
buried on the NE/c of the Baily quarter, NW/4 13-21-36.
One child died Jan. 7, 1892, and one died Feb. 16, 1898.

MORGAN, THOMAS - (The Lakin Index, Aug. 29, 1891) The
remains of Thomas Morgan, sr., were brought here from his
late home in the Bear Creek Valley, on Sunday last. and
interred in the cemetery west of town. Mr. Morgan was a
venerable old soldier of about 75 years of age, and was a
member of a Wisconsin regiment during the rebellion.
    (The Lakin Index, Sept. 19, 1891) Died, on the 22d day
of August 1891, at the old homestead Bear Creek bottom,
Thomas Morgan, his 75th year.
    Uncle "Tommy" as he was familiarily known, was one of
the pioneer settlers in western Kansas. He served in the
war, having enlisted at Pendeulac, in Co. C 17th
Wisconsin volunteers. His last years of life were passed
with his family on Bear Creek, this county, where some
eight years ago he started a stock ranch, and by good
management of all around him, had gathered a fair herd of
stock. Uncle Tommy was married in 1851, to his present
wife, and for forty years the old couple shared each
others pleasures and sorrows, until called to seperate.
His faithful companion and two grown children survive him
and mourn his loss. Peace to his ashes.

OSNER, INFANT - (The Kearny County Advocate, July 31,
1890) Died, near Kearny, on Sunday last, the infant
child of George Osner. The little one was buried Monday
in the cemetery at this place.

MISCELLANEOUS KEARNY COUNTY BURIALS

PALMER, ROBERT SCHUYLER - (The Lakin Index, July 16, 1897) The community was shocked last Saturday morning by the news that R. S. Palmer, a well known citizen of this county, had met death in a well at the home of J. M. Whinery, living 20 miles north, the afternoon before. They were cleaning the well and the sand bucket caught on the curbing as it was being let down. Fred Dye, who was running the windlass did not know this and continued to let down the rope, the weight of which loosened the bucket and sent it like a shot nearly two hundred feet to where Mr. Palmer stood on a temporary platform and struck on the back of his head. Death must have been instantaneous, as the back of his skull was chipped off as if done by an ax and the scalp was laid back on his neck. The sight was sickening. His brother, Asa Palmer arrived from Kingman County, Sunday night, to attend the funeral, Monday morning. The services were conducted by Revs. Carnine and Bonham. He was laid to rest in the Lakin cemetery by the side of his wife who died a couple of years ago.

Robert Schuyler Palmer was born in Clark County, Ky., and was 40 years, 1 month and 29 days old at the time of his death. He came to Kansas twelve years ago and located in Harper County, from which place he came to Kearny County, locating on a claim near where he was killed. He leaves three children, a daughter and two sons, the former 16 and the boys 14 and twelve years old, to battle with the world with out parental counsel. They will go to Kingman County to live with their grandparents, and with them goes the sympathy and well wishes of the entire community.

QUACKENBUSH, FRED - (Lakin Index, Jan. 8, 1897) Died in this city, Sunday night, at 10 o'clock, Fred Quackenbush, age nearly two years, the youngest son of Mrs. C. M. Quackenbush, and grandson of Rev. and Mrs. H. S. Booth. The body was laid away in the city cemetery, Monday. The death of Little Freddie falls with heavy weight upon the already over burdened heart of the mother, who but a few days since received the sad intelligence of the death of her husband, at Jacksonville, Florida. The death of Freddie was due to scarlet fever, and at the time of his death the three older children were sick of the same fever, which prevented the neighbors from rendering the kindly assistance due the family in their deep distress.

MISCELLANEOUS KEARNY COUNTY BURIALS

QUISSENBERRY, CHILD - (Kearny County Coyote, Omaha, Ks., Chantilly Chips, August 17, 1889) It becomes my sad duty this week to record the death of the infant child of Mr. and Mrs. J. R. Quissenberry, which occurred Thursday, August 8th. It was only five weeks old. They have the sympathy of the whole community in this their sad bereavement.

REAGAN, INFANT - (The Lakin Investigator, Man. 18, 1907) The infant child of Mr. and Mrs. Ned Reagan, died Tuesday night last. Just as a mother's love was being filled with joy and a young father's heart began to rejoice as he realized that a son had been born to his household, the little one was called, and his spirit took its flight to a better world. The many friends of Mr. and Mrs. Reagan will sympathize with them in their loss.

REYNOLDS, NELLIE - (The Lakin Investigator, August 14, 1908) The little two year old daughter of Mr. and Mrs. George Reynolds died Friday afternoon from a snake bite. The family had been visiting relatives in Kingman County, returning Wednesday. Mrs. Reynolds was cleaning the house and the two children were playing in the yard. They were attracted by the strange actions of the chickens that had found a large snake. The baby was bitten just above the ankle. Everything was done to keep the poison from spreading, but it was useless. The baby died in a few hours.

SEEGER, EARL DUANE - Earl Duane Seeger, 55, died April 10, 1994, at his home near Lakin.
He was born Sept 8, 1938, in Phillips County, the son of Harold J. and Violet Parket Seeger. He attended schools at Logan and Jetmore. He moved to Hutchinson in the late 1950s, living there for a number of years. He lived in various other places before moving to Kearny County in the late 1970s.
Since 1958, he had been owner/operator of the Tree Care Experts.
Mr. Seeger was a life member of the National Rifle Association, had organized the Jornada Trail Game Farm, Lakin, and was an avid sportsman. He was an Army veteran.
On Oct. 30, 1960, he married Louella B. Bartholomew at Hutchinson.

MISCELLANEOUS KEARNY COUNTY BURIALS

Survivors are a son, Earl Edward Seeger, Denver; four daughters, Debra Kiesel, Las Animas, Colo., Patricia Molina, Lakin, and Dona Seeger Altman and Ila Sue Cavender, both of Pueblo, Colo.; five brothers, Harold Manley Seeger, Denver, Cleo Seeger, Jacksonville, Ala., Jesse Seeger, Riverside, Calif., Delvin Seeger, Pueblo, and Larry Seeger, Leoti; four sisters, Alma Forqueran, Yuma, Ariz., Dorothy Michols, Sweethome, Oreg., Betty Pitts, Redlands, Calif., and Dona Gibbs, Jetmore; and five grandchildren.

He was preceded in death by his parents and two brothers, Virgil Seeger and Raymond Seeger.

Graveside service was held Thursday a mile and a half south, and a half-mile east of Lakin on KN Energy Road, the Rev. Pete Cousins officiating.

SEYDEL, FRANKIE EDWARD - (Lakin Pioneer Democrat, Lakin, Kearney County, Kansas, December 14, 1889) Died in South Side township, Kearney Co., Kansas, Dec. 6th, 1889, of croup, little Frankie Edward, only child of Mr. and Mrs. C. W. Seydel, aged 3 months and 4 days.

Little Frankie was a bright and beautiful child, and his sweet and winning ways endeared him to the parents' hearts, and made him the favorite of a large circle of relatives. May the father and mother be reminded by this sad event that now they have a treasure in Heaven, whom the Father's love will ever keep. May they ever strive to so live that they one day shall be again united to the little one now awaiting for them in the beautiful mansions above.

"Thou was't a bud too tender,
For this cold world of ours;
So God took thee to heaven
To bloom among its flowers.
Although we miss thee, darling,
And see thee here no more,
Yet thou art waiting for us,
Upon the golden shore.
Not lost; but gone before us,
Whilst we God's summons wait,
Hoping that our cherub, Frankie,
Will meet us at the gate.

The funeral services were conducted by Rev. W. B. Marsh, at the school house, Sunday afternoon at 3 o'clock, after which the remains were interred in the Lakin Cemetery.

MISCELLANEOUS KEARNY COUNTY BURIALS

SLAGER, HENRY - (Lakin Investigator, Dec. 6, 1899) Henry Slager, aged about 55 years, died at Mrs. Mary Currans's Friday evening, December 1st.
Mr. Slager was a stranger here and nothing could be learned of his home or family. He claimed to come from Missouri. He was first seen roaming around Deerfield, then next he came as far as Sam Corbetts and told them he was sick. Mr. Corbett cared for him as best he could under the circumstances and Friday brought him to Lakin and placed him in the care of M. J. Collins. Mr. Collins took him to Mrs. Curran's, where he was furnished with a comfortable room and bed. He lived only about an hour after being taken there. A subscription was taken and money enough raised by our citizens to purchase suitable clothing for burial. He was well cared for by Mr. Collins and others and was buried at the expense of the county. Other papers are requested to copy this item in hopes that it may reach his family.

SMITH, ALICE - (Pioneer Democrat, Lakin, Finney County, Kansas August 21, 1886) Died Alice Smith, August 12, aged 15 years, of typhoid fever, blood poisoning and congestion of the lungs. She was thrown from a horse and cut upon a barbwire fence July 5th, which caused blood poisoning, and a short time afterward was taken sick with typhoid fever. At the time of the wind storm she was taken out in the rain which brought on congestion of the lungs. The deceased was born in Rush Creek, Union County, Ohio. After a residence of five years at Kansas PO, Edgar County, Ill., she moved to this place two years ago with her mother and brothers. Rev. H. M. Carr delivered the funeral sermon at the residence of her brother, A. W. Smith, and a large concourse of friends followed her remains to the cemetery West of town. By her many estimable traits of character she won a large circle of friends who will long mourn her loss.

STAUGHTON, ROY - (The Lakin Index, Aug. 6, 1892) Another little mound was placed in the new cemetery on Wednesday afternoon last, caused by the death of Roy, the seven months old baby of Will D. and Nellie Staughton, living north of Lakin. The child had been sick some two weeks, and on Tuesday last the parents came down from their home to consult a physician, and his death occurred in a few hours after arriving here, at the residence of Dr. Lovin. Funeral services were held at the school house by Rev.

Nield, and sympathizing people of Lakin did all they could for the bereaved parents in the severe loss of their loved one.

STOCKING, LESTER E. - (The Lakin Index, Sept. 27, 1890) Our old friend, Lester E. Stocking, closed his eyes in death, at the residence of Mrs. J. E. Bennett, on Monday morning last, at the age of 71 years. He was born in Lake County, Ohio, and came to Lakin about one year ago. Although in feeble health since coming here, he lived beyond the allotted time of man, and no doubt welcomed the messenger when called to his rest. He was buried on Monday afternoon. Buried by the county.

TEDROW, HERBERT E. - (The Kearny County Coyote, November 19, 1897) The work of rescuing the body of the 16 year old son of Dr. Tedrow, who was buried in a well last week, by the caving in of the well, was abandoned, as hopeless. The rescuers got within 12 feet of the body but were compelled to quit their work, as the danger was too great for them to proceed further.
(The Kearny County Coyote, November 26, 1897) Young Tedrow, who met his death in a well, by the caving in of sand about two weeks ago, was rescued from his deep grave last Saturday. The work of rescuing the body was given up once, but again resumed with the above result. The remains were buried in the immediate neighborhood Saturday evening.
(Buried in NE/c 3-22-35. The Tedrow home was in NW/4 6-22-35.) Headstone is there broken in pieces.

VARBLE, INFANT - (The Lakin Index, Jan. 24, 1891) A new born infant of Mr. and Mrs. John Varble's was buried in the cemetery on Thursday. It died the following day after birth.

WAGONER, CHILD - (The Lakin Index, Nov. 12, 1892) A little child of farmer Wagoner died and was buried in the Kearny neighborhood, some days since.

WHITAKER, INFANT GIRL - (Kearny County Coyote, Omaha, Ks., February 15, 1890, Lakin Advocate of Feb. 8) Died in this city, Monday at 1 o'clock p.m., the infant girl of Mr. and Mrs. Whitaker. The little one was buried in the city cemetry, Tuesday afternoon. The sympathy of the community is extended to the parents.

MISCELLANEOUS KEARNY COUNTY BURIALS

WHITES, BOY - (Lakin Investigator, District No. 2 News,
May 20, 1910) The six year old son of Mr. and Mrs.
Phillip Whites, died from the effects of an operation
performed on his face at Great Bend. He lived two hours
after the operation.

WHORTON, BABY BOY - (Kearny County Coyote, Omaha, Ks.,
August 4, 1888) Again we are called upon to chronicle
the death of our other twin baby, which sad event took
place on last Monday morning, July 30, at 9 o'clock. Two
weeks prior we lost our little girl baby, and only to be
repeated by the sickness and death of the little boy, the
mate of the baby girl. His age was five months and 28
days. The little fellow suffered about three weeks with
cholera infantum, and what was supposed to be mountain
fever, until death rescued his pain. Such is life, as
autumn leaves fall before the winter wind, so life falls
at the touch of death. From the innocent babe to the
gray haired parent. While we grieve the loss of our
darling babies, we believe they are in the hands of an
Almighty being, who will guard and protect them with a
mother's love, and humbly submit to the inevitable
rulings of death, and give them up with sad hearts and
unwilling hands.
Thanks. We wish to return our sincere thanks to the many
friends for their kind assistance in our late sickness,
and hope, should they ever be so unfortunate as to meet
the sad afflictions we have met in the past three weeks,
in the death of our twin babies, that they may be
surrounded by kind friends in the hour of need. "A
friend in need is a friend indeed," and more especially
did the women of Omaha and vicinity come to our
assistance with their kindness and noble generosity, in a
manner that has won for them an everlasting appreciation
in our hearts, for which we again extend our warmest
thanks. Lon Whorton and Maggie Whorton.

WORDEN, MRS. POLLY - (Lakin Pioneer Democrat, March 8,
1890) Mrs. Polly Worden died at the residence of her
son, I. B. Worden, Saturday, March 1st, 1890, at 11 p.m.,
aged 79 years, 9 months and 18 days. Mrs. Worden was
born in Saratoga County, New York, May 11, 1810. For
years the flame of life could be seen growing fainter and
fainter, and the celestial fire growing brighter and
brighter, as day after day she repeated the same story
that she was only waiting for the Savior to call her from

this world to her sure reward. Although her death was not wholly unexpected, considering her advanced age and her long illness, yet her death coming so sudden and easy, almost without a motion, fell heavily upon the hearts of the little household that ministered to her hourly wants. She was converted and joined the Methodist Church when young and since which time she has been a faithful and exemplary Christian. Her remains were interred in the city cemetery, followed to the grave by a large concourse of sympathizing friends, March 3rd. Funeral services were held at the house by Rev. W. B. Marsh, who delivered a very appropriate and impressive discourse.

(The Advocate, March 8, 1890) "Grandmother" Worden, the venerable mother of J. R. Worden, died at her son's residence on Saturday night last and was buried Monday. She lived to a good old age and left a bright record of Christian grace and fortitude.

(John B. lived South of the River near Kendall.)

BIBLIOGRAPHY

Deerfield Cemetery Records, Deerfield, Ks.: 1903-1997.

Erwin, Don A. Garden City, Ks.: Letter of April 4, 1997.

Garden City Telegram. Garden City, Ks.: 1912-1997.

Garnand's Funeral Records. Garden City, Ks.: 1938-1997.

Hartland Herald. Hartland, Ks.: 1886-1891.

Hartland Standard. Hartland, Ks.: 1888-1889.

Hartland Times. Hartland, Ks.: 1886-1887.

Kearney County Advocate or The Advocate. Lakin, Ks.: 1885-1937.

Kearney County Coyote. Chantilly & Omaha, Ks.: 1887-1890.

Kearney Koyote. Kearney, Ks.: Jan-May 1887.

Kearny County Historical Society. _The Kearny County History Book, Vol. 1_. Dodge City, Ks.: Rollie Jack, Inc., 1964.

Kearny County Historical Society. _The Kearny County History Book, Vol. II_. North Newton, Ks.: Mennonite Press Inc., 1973.

Lakin Eagle. Lakin, Ks.: 1878-1879.

Lakin Herald. Lakin, Ks.: 1881-1884.

Lakin Independent. Lakin, Ks.: 1915-1996.

Lakin Index. Lakin, Ks.: 1890-1898.

Lakin Investigator. Lakin, Ks.: 1898-1911.

Lakin Pioneer Democrat. Lakin, Ks.: 1885-1890.

Lakin Union. Lakin, Ks.: 1895.

Nash and Davis Funeral Records. Lakin, Ks.: 1911-1988.

The Deerfield Farmer. Deerfield, Ks.: 1904-1905.

The Deerfield News. Deerfield, Ks.: 1909.

The Herington Times. Herington, Dickinson County, Ks.:
    Mch. 28, Apr. 4, 1918.

The Hutchinson News. Hutchinson, Ks.: 1965-1996.

Wadley, Ms. Rita. Hotchkiss, Co.: Letter of Sept. 22,
    1996.